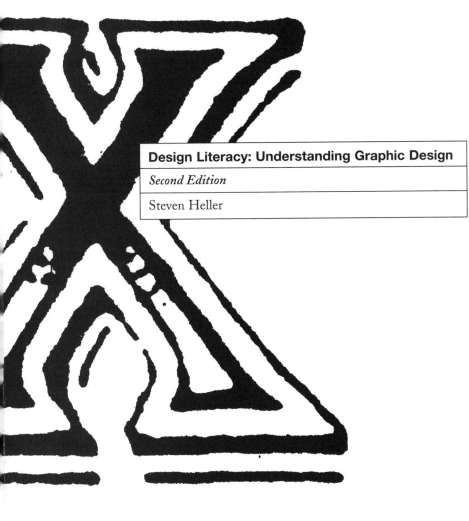

Design Literacy: Understanding Graphic Design

Second Edition

Steven Heller

ALLWORTH PRESS
NEW YORK

School of
VISUAL ARTS

08 07 06 05 04   5 4 3 2 1

Published by Allworth Press
An imprint of Allworth Communications, Inc.
10 East 23rd Street, New York, NY 10010

Cover design and page composition by James Victore
Typography by Sharp Des!gns, Inc.

LIBRARY OF CONGRESS CATALOGING-IN-PUBLICATION DATA
Heller, Steven.
Design literacy : understanding graphic design / Steve Heller. — 2nd ed.
p. cm.
Includes bibliographical references and index.
1. Graphic arts—History. 2. Commercial art—History. I. Title.
NC998.H45 2004
741.6—dc22
                                        2004009936

Printed in Canada

Dedicated to
Dr. James Fraser
for his Wisdom, Knowledge, and Generosity

Contents

TYPE

Acknowledgments

Design Literacy would be but a figment if not for the remarkable support and encouragement from Tad Crawford, the publisher of Allworth Press. Thanks also to Nicole Potter, senior editor, Monica Rodriguez, assistant editor, and to James Victore, designer of this and my other Allworth Press books.

Thanks again to Karen Pomeroy, who collaborated with me on the first *Design Literacy*, and who made invaluable contributions to a few of the essays retained for this revision.

Many of the essays in this book appeared in slightly different forms in design magazines. Much gratitude goes to the editors of these periodicals for their wisdom, expertise, and enthusiasm. Thanks to Martin Fox, former editor-in-chief, and Joyce Rutter Kaye, current editor-in-chief, at *Print* Magazine; Julie Lasky, editor at *I.D.*; Rick Poynor, former editor, and John Walters, current editor, at *Eye*; Hans Dieter Reichert, editor at *Baseline*, and Emily Potts, editor at *Step*. Also thanks to Caroline Hightower, former director, and Ric Grefe, current director, of the American Institute of Graphic Arts, for their counsel when I was editor of *AIGA Journal of Graphic Design*.

Finally, I also dedicate this book to all my past, present, and future students. —SH

In the first edition of *Design Literacy,* the introduction read:

> *There is now a realization that graphic design is not as ephemeral as
> the paper it is printed on. Certain advertisements, posters, packages,
> logos, books, and magazines endure as signposts of artistic, commercial,
> and technological achievement and speak more about particular epochs
> or milieus than fine art. Many objects of graphic design are preserved
> and studied as more than mere historical wallpaper. Curiously, though,
> the makers of these objects—graphic designers—have tended to
> undervalue the historical significance of artifacts found in their own
> backyards. Those who claim visual literacy are often ignorant when it
> comes to understanding and appreciating the objects that are imprinted
> with the language of their own practice.*

Despite the encouraging increase in design commentary and history in
classrooms, on blogs, and in magazines, the core presumption remains:
Those who claim visual literacy are often ignorant, etc. So, as I stated then,
and remain committed to now, this second edition of *Design Literacy:
Understanding Graphic Design* serves as an alternative to the omnibus
compilations that reduce graphic design to just so much visual noise, and
examines a variety of individual objects, focusing on their significance in
the broader histories of graphic design and popular culture.

Although graphic design can be defined as critical masses of
form and style that shift according to the dictates of the marketplace, an
understanding of a singular work or genre of works analyzed through
objective and subject criteria can be useful in determining how individual
designers have made graphic design function over time.

Rather than conventional case studies, which trace the process of
creation and production, the essays here address rationales, inspirations, and
histories of an eclectic collection of vintage and contemporary objects in all
media. Each essay represents a unique occurrence that is influenced by and
relates to other manifestations of the design culture. Here, objects are not
viewed as fetishes (at least, I try not to present them as such), but as
expressions of specific commercial or artistic needs, solutions to distinct
problems, and even demonstrations of unique personalities.

Moreover, these so-called object lessons are alternatives to such
pedagogical conventions as the "great master" principle, which addresses the

maker within a canon or pantheon; the "great movement" principle, which attributes certain characteristics to a school or ideology; or the "great style" principle, which categorizes design according to period, fashion, or trend (all of which I adhere to in other writings as the need demands). These methods are not invalid, but I contend that understanding the object in context removes graphic design from a purely formal arena and moves it to a cultural and political one.

In the first edition I selected work by many well-known designers, while for *Design Literacy (continued),* more anonymous work was recognized, in addition to those with clear provenance. In this revised edition there is a balance between known and unknown. Most of these essays examine single works or related multiples, though a few focus on larger genres when one piece alone does not tell a complete enough story. For instance, see the essays on cigarette advertisements for women (page 37), religious tracts (page 39), or modern paperback book covers (page 232).

Some objects have already been elevated to the design pantheon, such as A. M. Cassandre's Peignot typeface (page 161), Saul Bass's graphics for *Man with a Golden Arm* (page 221), or Milton Glaser's Dylan poster (page 286). Other inclusions are only marginally noticed, if noticed at all, in design history, such as Robbie Conal's *Men With No Lips* poster (page 29), Art Chantry's Propaganda poster (page 382), or the *East Village Other* (page 111). A few were selected because they are icons of their respective eras, like the peace symbol (page 14); others because they are curious designs that are barely footnotes in graphic design texts, like razor blade labels (page 391).

With artifacts that span the twentieth century—from Lucian Bernhard's 1906 *Priester Match* poster to Paula Scher's 1996 New York Public Theater posters—the essays in this book are best read as sidebars along a historical timeline. Nevertheless, the material is not organized chronologically, but thematically, according to the role the object has played in culture and commerce.

Sections include "Persuasion" (design in the service of control and influence); "Mass Media" (design as popular communication); "Language" (design as different idioms and vocabularies); "Identity" (design as signature); "Information" (design as guidepost and pathway); "Iconography" (design as symbol); "Style" (design as aesthetics and fashion); and "Commerce" (design as marketing tool). For this revision an additional section called "Type" bridges style, language, iconography, etc. Admittedly, some of the essays in one section overlap with another section, which is how design operates in the world anyway. Yet here, each object was selected for its respective category to provide a window on how these specific themes are served.

Wherever possible the designers are quoted, but *Design Literacy* is by no means a verbatim account of their respective processes. These essays combine analysis and critique, aided by the makers' descriptions but not solely based on their revelations. Moreover, this book includes commentary that sometimes echoes the canon, and at other times challenges it. The goal is to provide a viable foundation for understanding a process that will aid in developing literacy for design language(s).

I admit that reading this book will not provide a cure-all for design illiteracy. True design literacy requires a practical and theoretical understanding of how design is made and how it functions as a marketplace tool as well as a cultural signpost, which takes years of learning and experience to acquire. The title *Design Literacy* refers to sharing common knowledge—certain facts, impressions, and opinions—about graphic design and its broader cultural affiliations, but this is not a textbook about how or what to make. By way of confession, the title more precisely reflects a personal journey. Although I hope that the book will be used to increase knowledge, the essays collected here began as stepping stones in my own education—how I became design literate, not only regarding the language(s) of design but regarding the legacy, the individuals, and objects too.

This revision includes a majority of essays from *Design Literacy,* a lesser number from *Design Literacy (continued),* and a fair number of new pieces. The decision concerning what to write about is based entirely on my interest in (and passion for) objects that I have continuously researched over many years as part of larger histories or profiles I've written for magazines and books. The selection of what to include was based either on what I believe to be an important work by a significant practitioner (an archetype or paradigm of a particular genre), or simply on what sparks my curiosity.

Milton Glaser said of the first *Design Literacy,* "It is all meat and no potatoes," suggesting that my sidebar approach lacked the intellectual substance necessary to glue the essays together. According to Glaser, the first book was flawed because it did not make cohesive links between one object (or essay) and another. Rather than accept these stories as self-contained units, as they were intended, my esteemed critic wanted a more definitive overview that used the selected objects and themes as support for grand conclusions. My rationale for not doing that was simple: Conventional graphic design history has already been written as a linear narrative flowing from one movement, period, or style to another, and this is just one approach of many. The problem for me is that not all design fits snugly into well-organized categorical berths. Moreover, this book is a compliment to the late Philip B. Meggs's *A History of Graphic Design* and Richard Hollis's *Graphic Design: A Concise History,* rather than being a linear narrative.

I realize, however, that some themes covered in both *Design Literacy* and *Design Literacy (continued)* are not recognized as part of the graphic design canon, and that it is a stretch on my part to inject them into serious design discourse. Another designer whom I greatly admire said of the last volume that he strongly objected to seeing untutored or naïve design—such as anonymous shooting targets and raunchy 1960s underground newspapers—covered in the same venue, and with the same reverence, as highly professional work by (for example) Paul Rand, Will Burtin, or Saul Bass. Yet what better way to examine comparative merits of visual communication than to look seriously, and respectfully, at all forms on the design spectrum—high or low—if they reveal something important about the nature of what we do.

Since graphic designers draw inspiration from both professional and unprofessional sources, there is no reason to limit this only to haute design. I believe that common show cards (page 389), produced by job printers during the 1920s and 1930s, are as integral to the history of this field as the 1960s award-winning *West* magazine. Recognized and forgotten objects are equally valid in the course of discovery. Incidentally, the selections in this book are not driven by any specific ideology (e.g., Modern or Postmodern), which also accounts for the eclecticism of objects, ideas, and individuals presented here.

Design Literacy (Second Edition) is not merely my third (and final?) chance to correct flaws that certain critics found in the preceding volumes. Although I respect their viewpoints and accept the notion that a less eclectic, more thematically unified book has distinct virtues, I have elected not to shift my perspective this time around. Rather, as the title indicates, this continues my fascination for and inquiry into a variety of designed things and the ideas supporting them. Incidentally, this revision is not a hellbox (an arcane, hot, type term for a trash bin) of what was cut from the two previous books. In fact, many things from the first two books are nowhere to be found in this version.

To borrow Milton Glaser's descriptive and appetizing analogy, those readers who are looking for a full-course meal might still be hungry after reading *Design Literacy (Second Edition)*. Which is fine, because there is not one book or writer that will provide all the nourishment needed to achieve design literacy. For those who are happy with sizeable helpings of fresh insight, please feast on this revision.

Many of these essays are adapted from articles, essays, and reviews previously published in Print, EYE, U&lc, Baseline, Step, *and* I.D. *magazines and the* AIGA Journal of Graphic Design; *others were written expressly for this volume.*

PERSUASION

A red bulldog stares menacingly through stone-cold white eyes. A broken chain hangs from its neck. With sharp, spiky teeth it eagerly waits to attack unsuspecting fools, nitwits, and government buffoons.

Beware! This is not just some rabid canine, but the most unyielding watchdog ever conceived. Born not of flesh and blood, but of ink and brush, this bulldog was the embodiment of a nation's anger, the charged graphic emblem of *Simplicissimus*, one of the most biting, satirically critical magazines ever published. Its color was a flag, and its breed symbolized the snarling editorial policy of the weekly tabloid. Founded in 1896 in Munich, Germany, by a cadre of artists and writers that included Thomas Mann, *Simplicissimus* was fervently antibourgeois and unrepentantly *Volkish* (populist) in its rejection of materialism and modernization.

Simplicissimus, or *der Simpl*, as it was known, assailed German Kaiser Wilhelm II and his ministers, the Protestant clergy, military officers, government bureaucracy, urbanization, and industrialization while it lionized the peasant farmer and worker. The red bulldog symbolized the Volk, or common people, who were portrayed in the magazine's cartoons and caricatures as feisty opponents to the ruling class, even if in reality this was an exaggerated view.

The authorities used stern measures to muzzle the dog, but despite frequent censorship and periodic arrests, this illustrated tabloid rarely missed an appearance. When it was finally confiscated by the police, the black, red, and white poster on which the bulldog stood poised reminded friend and foe alike that *der Simpl* would not be chained up for long. Rows of these posters—designed in 1897 by Thomas Theodore Heine (1867–1948), a cartoonist and co-editor of *Simplicissimus*—were hung for months at a time and were replenished regularly with fresh ones. Bans, on the other hand, lasted only a week or two and usually attracted more new readers than they discouraged.

This was the power of *Simplicissimus*, the name borrowed from a fifteenth-century literary character, Simplicus Simplicissimus, who acted the fool around the aristocracy while tricking them into exposing their folly and corruption. This was Heine's reason for designing a somewhat comic bulldog mascot instead of a more frightening graphic icon.

The red bulldog was just one weapon in *der Simpl*'s graphic arsenal. There were other mascots, though none as versatile. Whether it was the angry version from Heine's poster or other, more comical iterations (including one of the bulldog urinating on the leg of an official), anyone looking for relief from Wilhelmian oppression could find an ally, at least once a week on paper, under the sign of the bulldog.

Der Simpl vehemently critiqued the status quo until the advent of World War I when it was conscripted as a tool of German propaganda. Even in its patriotic form it was biting, proving that humor could be effectively used for the wrong causes. After the war, during the 1920s and early 1930s, it resumed its critical stance attacking Italian fascism and the emergence of first German Freikorps (paramilitary right-wing militias) and later Nazism. During this era the *Volk* were no longer portrayed as heroes. Working and peasant class romanticism was replaced by foreboding and cynicism—a logical response to a devastating and horrific war. The Kaiser had abdicated prior to the war's end and was replaced by the Weimar Republic, the doomed democratic experiment that *der Simpl* reluctantly critiqued for its deficiencies and the incompetencies of its leadership. The red bulldog continued as the mascot, however, and *Simplicissimus* remained a social watchdog until 1933 when the Nazis came to power and made it into their lap dog.

Der Simpl is remembered for its golden age, from 1896 to 1914, when it published hundreds of strident political and social caricatures and cartoons attacking anything that suggested social and political folly. Few other journals had such a profound influence, not only on public opinion, but also on graphic style. The late 1890s was an era of artistic revolution, and *der Simpl*, together with its cousin the cultural journal *Jugend*, introduced to polemical graphics a variant of French art nouveau called Jugendstil. German Jugendstil was more rectilinear than curvilinear, rejecting the floreated decoration so popular in France. Emphasizing chiaroscuro values and bold economical brush strokes, *der Simpl*'s artists departed from common academic verities; in turn they practiced a proto-expressionistic art.

Simplicissimus was one of the unrecognized tribunes of early modernism. The red bulldog exemplifies modern simplicity. Drawing in the manner of a woodcut, Heine used white paint to cut away extraneous lines, leaving only the most descriptive features and penetrating expression behind. Heine's was the prototypical modern logo. In subsequent iterations the red bulldog was further geometricized, suggesting the roots of the late 1970s-era corporate logo.

In its day Heine's *Simplicissimus* poster was a radical departure from typically fussy placards layered with excessive ornamentation and multiple colors. The red bulldog set against black was the antecedent of the German Sachplakat (or object poster) introduced by designer Lucian Bernhard eight years later in Berlin. Bernhard's posters were characterized by a single object set against a flat color with only a bold headline to identify the brand being advertised.

Heine's red bulldog poster was arguably inelegant. The sans-serif logo of the magazine *der Simpl* was more refined than the poster lettering. Heine's lettering was crudely hand drawn (on those versions of the poster where the ten pfenning price was included, it was downright messy). Yet the poster was a totality. The lettering suggested immediacy and complemented the bulldog's tense, frozen stance. This is perhaps one of Heine's most brilliant, persuasive, and iconographic works; what followed were mere cartoons.

The Malik Verlag was established in March 1917 in the critical period before the fall of Imperial Germany and the birth of the Weimar Republic. This politically active German socialist publisher of periodicals, portfolios, broadsheets, and books of fiction and nonfiction—whose first periodical was entitled *Neue Jugend*, or New Youth—is the trunk of the historical tree of which American alternative publishing of the 1960s was only a branch and from which elements of contemporary graphic design have surely grown. Its leading graphistes, George Grosz and John Heartfield (1891–1968) are known, studied, and appreciated today; but the Malik Verlag as an entity is virtually unknown, though it played a major role in German left-wing politics, literature, and the graphic style of the Weimar period.

In 1915 before Malik Verlag was conceived, John Heartfield's brother, the poet Weiland Herzfeld, was introduced to George Grosz and "fell in love" with his drawings. "Grosz felt that was an inappropriate response," wrote Herzfeld in *The Malik Verlag 1916–1947* (Goethe House, New York). "He told me: '. . . Herzfeld, my works are worthless. Whatever you and I and any other incompetent people think of them is completely inconsequential. . . . If my drawings were of some value they would be paid for accordingly. . . .' His comments were the final impetus for the founding of the periodical *Neue Jugend* with Herzfeld as editor." The journal became an outlet for Grosz's political satires and "for all those who encountered opposition to their political ideas and lack of understanding by the public," continued Herzfeld. "We beg all European artists and intellectuals who are neither senile nor submissive to join us as contributors . . . ," states the call for contributors, which appealed to the cream of the German left. Many rose to the occasion with scabrous attacks against the ailing government.

Neue Jugend, then a quarto-sized monthly, was almost immediately banned in the autumn of 1916, and Weiland Herzfeld was coincidentally called to the Western Front. While he was away, in the spring of 1917, Heartfield resumed publishing *Neue Jugend* in its larger, newspaper format. Always the clever subversive, Heartfield had found a way to circumvent the ban by making the journal into a prospectus—an advertisement, essentially —for a portfolio of George Grosz drawings. Since this *Neue Jugend* was not strictly a publication the censors were befuddled.

During the war years all new journals and publishing houses needed a license, granted only when "pressing need" existed. While no such need existed for Heartfield and Herzfeld's left-wing publishing venture, they dreamed up a plan that would confuse the bureaucrats. Heartfield slyly stated in the application for the founding of the Malik Publishing House that German writer Else Lasker-Schüler's novella "Der Malik" (which translated from Turkish meant not only "prince," but also, fittingly, "robber chief,") had appeared in installments in *Neue Jugend*. "To complete its publication (keep in mind *Neue Jugend* had been banned), and for that reason only, a publishing house was needed," recalled Herzfeld. The authorities did not immediately catch on, granted the license, and the Malik Verlag proceeded instead to publish two George Grosz portfolios and two issues of a thinly disguised *Neue Jugend*.

The publication's design was an amalgam of variegated typefaces, elaborate surprints, and various geometric color blocks. Work on this journal marked an artistic turning point for Heartfield, who had destroyed all his more formal work and embraced anti-art as a means for social protest and propaganda. In 1915 Heartfield changed his name from Herzfeld to protest German militarism. He became a charter member of the Berlin dada group, whose members included George Grosz, Hannah Höch, Raoul Hausmann, Otto Dix, and Herzfeld. Heartfield originally adopted the title dada-monteur, eschewing the term *artist* in favor of *monteur*, which means "machinist," in an angry rejection of bourgeois art. He later changed to photomonteur because he believed that photography was the vanguard of a new art that would inevitably displace painting altogether.

The look of the new *Neue Jugend* was different, but the content continued in the style of the original monthly and, with its satire and pacifist stance, was just as outrageous in the eyes of the regime. Publication was summarily ceased in June 1917, but the journal existed just long enough for Heartfield to initiate the typographic revolution that would subsequently influence the New Typography. *Neue Jugend* was also a stepping stone for other German dada publications. The one-shot tabloid, *Jedermann sein eigner Fussball* ("everyman his own football," 1919), which included the first political photomontage created by Heartfield—a fan with the leaders of the new Weimar government superimposed—is a classic dada document. Two ongoing sister publications, *Die Pliete* (1919–1922) and *Der Gegner* (1919– 1922), designed by Heartfield with drawings by Grosz, were the agitational arm of the German communist party, which, like the members of the dada group and Spartakus Bund, fought against the emerging right wing, the Nazis.

Heartfield is remembered today for his strident anti-Nazi photomontages for the *Arbeiter Illustierte Zeitung* (AIZ), but as art director for the Malik Verlag he was an innovative jacket and cover designer. His graphic imprimatur formed the visual personality of the publishing house and, moreover, was the model for kindred publishers active during the 1920s.

Under Heartfield's direction the Malik Verlag was a wellspring of avant-garde graphic design. They were influenced by Russian and Italian futurism, yet introduced Germans to typographic experiments that were later brought to fruition by Russian constructivists, Dutch de Stijl, and German dadaists.

Tadeusz Trepkowski's (1914–1956) 1953 *Nie*
(Polish for "no") was the first Polish poster
to make an impact on American designers.
The ruins of a devastated city framed
within the silhouette of a falling bomb, in
its graphic way, was as expressive of the
horrors of World War II as the numbing
photographs of carnage published in *Life*
and other American magazines. Anyone
who saw multiples of this poster hanging
in rows on what remained of Warsaw's
streets understood that *Nie* was more than
an antiwar image, it was a testament to the
redemptive power of art.

   From the vantage point across
the Atlantic, Poland had resisted the
occupying Nazis only to be subsumed by
the Soviets. From here, Poland was a
prisoner behind the Iron Curtain, its arts
dictated by the constraints of socialist realism. *Nie*, the first glimpse that
many in the West had of powerful Polish poster graphics, was also the first
sign that Polish art was alive. Later, thanks to conspicuous exposure in
Graphis and the English-language *Poland* magazine, Americans learned
that the Polish poster was not only alive, but was flourishing in ways that
far exceeded their own graphic arts.

   It is ironic that a nation under the thumb of a repressive ideology
could produce a graphic style of such high quality and integrity. To
American designers, the Polish poster was the epitome of expressive
and stylistic freedom. In the United States, graphic artists and designers
had fundamental freedom, but even the most renowned were slaves to
client whim and prejudice. American business imposed fashions designed
to sell products in the competitive marketplace. Few deviated from these
conventions; experimentation was suspect. This isn't to say that American
design was uninspired, but the Polish poster was poetry, seemingly
unfettered by agendas of state.

Are artists inspired by the idea that visual language can subvert the tunnel vision of the state? The Polish posters that surfaced in the United States suggested that either the authorities were looking the other way, or artists, like Trepkowski, were brilliant subversives. The surreal images these artists created were the means to circumvent the strictures against free expression and, at the same time, invent new methods of discourse. Trepkowski's *Nie* poster was a humanist call to sanity, and most Polish posters were designed for cultural events that did not have to sell to consumer groups, please the chairmen of major corporations, or appeal to the special interests. They did, however, have to fool a regime that was suspicious of individual expression.

It is usual in modern warfare for aggressors to drop leaflets warning civilian and soldier alike to capitulate before the onset of massive destruction. At the beginning of the Gulf War, the Coalition Central Command in Qatar reported that it had saturated battle zones with literally millions of missives exhorting hostile troops to surrender at once. In the face of an overwhelming Air Force raining death from the sky, one might assume that a word from the wise would be sufficient. But these are not merely invitations to a survival party. Leaflets are the ordinance of psychological warfare, the purpose of which is to instill paralytic fear that will severely reduce an enemy's fighting capabilities.

Paper bombs are not as intelligent as smart bombs, nor as cagey as more sophisticated propaganda, but they are powerful in subtle ways. Leafleting is the art of artlessness, designed to convey a straightforward message without artifice or conceit—and the message contains two viable options: live or die. However, in addition to cautionary leaflets that offer the enemy safe haven from inescapable carnage, there is a genre of missive designed simply and specifically to undermine a battle-weary soldier's morale.

This variety is especially virulent when aimed at exhausted troops who, caught in quagmires during prolonged engagements, are more susceptible to doubt, despair, and free thought. Given the indescribable anxiety of battlefield encounters, after the initial adrenalin rush wears off, even the toughest veteran can be psychologically vulnerable, so the United States Army (and doubtless military forces everywhere) has long conducted training programs that teach soldiers to fight the crippling effects of emotional assault.

During the Cold War, when U.S. troops were always on the ready but experienced little direct combat, the Defense Department's Psychological Warfare Division produced simulated enemy leaflets that were routinely dropped during maneuvers in an effort to show troops what they might expect under real conditions. The leaflets on these pages were among those produced for extended maneuvers involving the 505th Airborne Division (c. 1955) and include four types of messages:

1. *Leaflets dropped by U.S. forces on the enemy.* One states, "You are facing the mightiest nation on earth. The United States Army has never been defeated. Behind us lies the enormous power of American production. This war can have only one outcome, your total defeat." Another proclaims, "We have gathered our strength. Massed American forces now begin to roll forward. You are retreating before the best-trained, best-equipped, most powerful military machine that the world has ever seen. We will drive you back into the sea. Your destruction is only a matter of time."

2. *Leaflets dropped by the simulated "Aggressor" on the U.S. Army.* In one that reproduces the self-assured U.S. leaflet quoted above, the enemy counters with defiant rhetoric: "CRUSHED: U.S. Forces, What Happened?" and on the flip side offers its own plan for capitulation. Among these leaflets is an ersatz dollar bill with the headline "Attention: This Is a Safe Conduct Pass" that guarantees that all "aggressor soldiers" treat surrendering troops "with courtesy and respect."

3. *Leaflets distributed by the Aggressor designed to demoralize U.S. troops by focusing on their daily deprivations.* One reads, "You could be in town TONIGHT. Yes, you could be enjoying yourself. . . instead of being holed up." Another leaflet showing a sexy devil of a girl reads, "Here's a Real Hot Offer. You Can Have It Made: Plenty of your buddies are in the Aggressor Rest Camp. There's no reason why you too cannot enjoy a hot meal without sand in your tray, a warm bed, and recreational activities . . ."

4. *Leaflets designed by the Aggressor to terrorize U.S. troops.* One reads, "The Aggressor Is Stalking YOU Day and Night . . ." and another states, "With every tick of the clock, with every passing minute, the Aggressor plunges deeper into your lines."

Crudely printed on cheap paper, usually in black and white, the typography and art is certainly competent but undistinguished. Nonetheless, the imagery is suitably menacing. Illustrated in a pulp comic book style, the Aggressor is not given any explicit national characteristics (i.e., Soviet or Chinese), but has a curiously alien demeanor. Perhaps it is the helmet, the most distinctive accessory of any combat uniform, with its protruding steel top-piece, or the European-styled collar patches (neither of which is used by the U.S. Army). Overall, the look is designed to scare on the one hand, yet offer a certain solace on the other. Drawings of U.S. troops on enemy leaflets are fairly sympathetic rather than demonic. But one ironically disturbing leaflet titled, "Everyone Has This Nightmare," shows a Lilliputian soldier drowning on a platter of (presumably appetizing) hot food, which is the Aggressor's reproach that U.S. soldiers in the field are victims of C-Rations (which really do taste like dog food) and would be better off in an Aggressor rest camp, safe from harm's way.

While ordinary military maneuvers are rarely a matter of life or death, they do test the mental and physical stamina of participating soldiers. These leaflets, and others like them, were purposefully designed to seduce the psychologically weakened troops during a dangerous juncture in warfare—the moment at which a decision is made to continue fighting or surrender. Even in a relatively safe war-game environment, there is a strong temptation to cave in to one's personal and collective hardships and ultimately shirk one's responsibility. As unconvincing as they may seem in retrospect, these plainly designed leaflets had a calculable psychological impact that military experts wanted to quantify through intense simulations. Surprisingly, the analysts found that the small number of those who actually used the safe conduct passes was larger than originally expected, leading to the conclusion that under severe battle conditions, a leaflet is just as formidable as a bullet or missile.

The Peace Symbol

There was probably no more galvanizing or polarizing emblem during the 1960s than the peace symbol—an upside-down, three-pronged, forklike mark in a circle, which symbolized the anxiety and anger of the Vietnam era. Although the basic form had roots in antiquity, it was popularized during the mid-1950s when H-bomb testing prevailed. The symbol was (re)designed in 1954 by an obscure English textile designer named Gerald Holtom for use by England's Campaign for Nuclear Disarmament (CND). Yet some sources claim that the sign, also known as the peace action symbol, was designed in 1958 for the British World Without War Council for use at the first annual Aldermaston Easter Peace Walk to promote world disarmament. It later debuted in the United States in 1962 in the cautionary science-fiction film about the tragic effects of nuclear testing, *The Day the Earth Caught Fire*, and within a few years was adopted for use as an antiwar insignia.

The symbol is supposed to be a composite semaphore signal for the letters *N* and *D* (nuclear disarmament), but its basic form also derives from an ancient runic symbol, a fact that casts some doubt on the *ND* theory. According to an article in a 1969 issue of *WIN* (Workshop in Nonviolence) magazine, sponsored by the War Resisters League (one of the 1960s foremost anti–Vietnam War activist groups), the peace sign derives from an initial iteration of a white circle on a black square. This was followed by various versions of Christian crosses drawn within the white sphere, which in turn evolved into the *ND* form. Referring to the Aldermaston march, *WIN* asserts that for subsequent demonstrations an *ND* badge was "devised and made by Eric Austen," whose research into the origins of symbolism underscored that the basic forklike symbol, or what he called the "gesture of despair" motif, was associated throughout ancient history with the "death of man," and the circle with the "unborn child." The reason for calling the upside-down fork a "gesture of despair" derives from the story of Saint Peter, who was crucified upside down in Rome in A.D. 67 on a cross designed by Emperor Nero, known thereafter as the "Nero Cross" or the "sign of the broken Jew."

Few who wear the peace symbol as jewelry today are probably aware of its legacy as a once-controversial emblem. Rather, it seems like a quaint artifact of the 1960s, not unlike psychedelic designs or bell-bottoms. Currently, it is used as a generic insignia for a variety of fashionable (if pseudo-) antiestablishment issues. In truth the symbol is anything but generic, and its origin is still controversial.

During the 1930s, decades prior to the nuclear disarmament and anti–Vietnam War movements but on the precipice of fascist dominance in Europe, the symbol was first devised by the English philosopher and socialist Bertrand Russell as an attempt "to depict the universal convergence of peoples in an upward movement of cooperation." During the late 1950s Russell was the chairman for the CND, present at numerous disarmament demonstrations and protests against English involvement in NATO at the very time the symbol was adopted as the CND emblem. It is therefore probable that Russell introduced to the organization the basic sign from which Holtom created his final design.

Russell was a former member of the Fabian Society (a fellowship of English socialists), which prompted the right-wing journal American Opinion to link the peace symbol, like the antiwar movement in general, to a broad communist conspiracy of world domination. "It is not at all surprising that the Communists would turn to Russell to design their 'peace sign,'" states a 1970 article in this journal, which continues: "A Marxist from his earliest youth, he greeted the Russian Revolution with the declaration: 'The world is damnable. Lenin and Trotsky are the only bright spots. . . .'" The journal further describes Russell as an active anti-Christian who was well aware that he had chosen an "anti-Christian design long associated with Satanism." In fact, the basic form, which appears both right-side up and upside down as a character in pre-Christian alphabets, was afforded mystical properties and is in evidence in some pagan rituals. Right-side up it represents "man," while upside down it is the fallen man. Referred to in Rudolf Koch's *Book of Signs* as "the Crow's foot" or "witch's foot," it was apparently adopted by satanists during the Middle Ages.

The Nazis routinely adopted runic forms for their official iconography, such as the SS runes (the insignia of Hitler's personal bodyguard). Indeed the Nazi iconography calls the crow's foot Todersune, or "death rune." Paradoxically, in a right-side-up position it was frequently used on death notices, gravestones of SS officers, and badges given to their widows. Not unlike the swastika itself, this runic symbol has positive and negative implications depending on its orientation. The downward version might be interpreted as death and infertility, while the upward version symbolizes growth and fertility.

Signs and symbols are easily transformed to mean good or evil depending on how they are sanctioned and applied over time—and who accepts said usage. Whatever satanic associations the crow's foot may have had (or still has), when Bertrand Russell "designed" this symbol he imbued it with more positive virtues of life and cooperation. Once adopted by the CND (and later by scores of other antiwar, ecology, civil rights, and peace and freedom groups), its meaning was forever changed to protest in the service of humanity.

Spectators described the first atomic bomb blast on July 16, 1945, at the Trinity Site in Jornada del Muerto, New Mexico, as "unprecedented," "terrifying," "magnificent," "brutal," "beautiful," and "stupendous." Yet such ordinary words failed to truly convey the spectacle because, as Thomas F. Farrell, an official of the Los Alamos Laboratory, later explained to the press, "It is that beauty the great poets dream about but describe most poorly and inadequately."

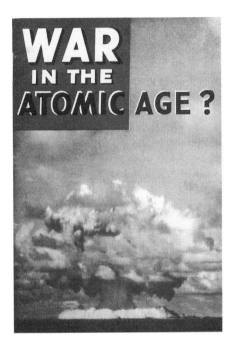

What the inarticulate scientists and military personnel in attendance had witnessed was an unparalleled event: a thermal flash of blinding light visible for more than 250 miles from ground zero; a blast wave of bone-melting heat; and the formation of a huge ball of swirling flame and mushrooming smoke majestically climbing toward the heavens. While the world had known staggering volcanic eruptions and devastating manmade explosions, and often throughout history similar menacing shapes have risen into the sky from catastrophes below, this mushroom cloud was a demonic plume that soon became civilization's most foul and awesome visual symbol—the logo of annihilation.

The mushroom cloud was nightmarishly ubiquitous, especially for children growing up during the late 1940s and throughout the 1950s, the relentless testing period of the nuclear age when the U.S. and the USSR ran their arms race on deserted atolls and in underground caverns. Newsreel accounts of Pacific ocean test sites and Cold War films warning of atomic attacks were not the only sources of trepidation. The U.S. government issued scores of official cautionary pamphlets, and the mass media published countless histrionic paperbacks, pulp magazines, comic books, and other periodicals that fanned the flames of thermonuclear anxiety. For this child of the atomic era, who was never totally accustomed to the frequent Conelrad (emergency network) warnings on TV and duck-and-cover drills at school, mushroom cloud patterns wallpapered my dreams for an excessive number of impressionable years.

Dreading the unthinkable was underscored by knowing the real. Everyone was taught about the historic shock-and-awe displays launched respectively on August 6 and 9, 1945, when two A-bombs destroyed the Japanese cities and incinerated citizens of Hiroshima and Nagasaki. This was not some H. G. Wellsian prediction or pulp science fiction apparition. The furies unleashed by these weapons left indelible scars on conscience and consciousness just as the blast's scorching heat literally etched dark shadows of vaporized humans onto the naked ground.

Paradoxically, though, the world's first atomic bomb, christened Little Boy, was as unprepossessing as its name was innocuous. It looked like an "elongated trash can with fins," said a crewmember of the *Enola Gay*, the B-29 that carried the Hiroshima bomb. To force Japan into accepting unconditional surrender, Little Boy and Fat Man (the plutonium implosion bomb dropped on Nagasaki) each deposited the power of over 12,500 tons of TNT and left a residue of radiation for years to follow.

The Hiroshima mushroom, small when compared to subsequent hydrogen blasts, looms large in the litany of terror because it was the first. "The city was hidden by that awful cloud, boiling up, mushrooming, terrible and incredibly tall," recalled Col. Paul Tibbets, pilot of the *Enola Gay*. "If you want to describe it as something you are familiar with, a pot of boiling black oil," related one of his crew. "The mushroom itself was a spectacular sight, a bubbling mass of purple-gray smoke, and you could see it had a red core in it and everything was burning inside," said the tail gunner, Robert Caron. "As we got farther away, we could see the base of the mushroom, and below we could see what looked like a few-hundred-foot layer of debris and smoke." And still another witness said the mushroom was "this turbulent mass. I saw fires springing up in different places like flames shooting up on a bed of coals. It looked like lava or molasses covering the whole city." Japanese accounts from the ground told of a blinding flash of light (*pika* in Japanese) and a deafening roar of sound (*pika-don,* or flash boom), yet outside the city limits, the sky was a beautiful golden yellow.

Americans greeted the bombings as a necessary means toward an inevitable end. Notwithstanding, when told of the bombing, Dr. J. Robert Oppenheimer, the scientist directly responsible for the Los Alamos A-bomb development teams, expressed guarded satisfaction, for he understood the power of what had been unleashed. A month earlier, after watching the triumphal first blast at the Trinity Site, he quoted from the *Bhagavad Gita: "I am become Death, the destroyer of worlds . . ."* He was plagued by guilt until his death in 1964. Nonetheless, the bombs were made, the atom was weaponized, and uranium and plutonium were stockpiled. Days after the first blasts, an additional Fat Man was being shipped to a U.S. airbase for its final Tokyo destination until President Harry S Truman, citing despair over the enormous number of casualties, decided to spare the city and its inhabitants.

After Hiroshima and Nagasaki, propagandists did not wait long to put a happy face on the ghastly new weapon and incorporate the mushroom cloud into popular iconography. The bomb itself (in its various unexceptional physical manifestations) was not iconic enough for widespread use as a modern emblem, but the mushroom cloud was monumentally omnipotent. Since the United States could smash and harness the atom (and with it, smash and harness Imperial Japan) the mushroom cloud initially represented superhuman accomplishment. It symbolized righteousness rather than wickedness.

But not everyone embraced this view. Only a few months after the end of war, one early opponent, former U.S. Navy Lieutenant Robert Osborn, an artist whose wartime assignment was drawing cartoons for training and safety brochures, published a cautionary manual of a different kind. This time, rather than teach sailors and pilots survival techniques under battle conditions, his book, titled *War is No Damn Good*, tried to save lives through condemnation of all armed conflict—especially the nuclear kind. While serving in the Navy, Osborn believed he had seen all the carnage imaginable, and supported the end result. But after viewing pictures from Hiroshima and its atomic aftermath, he realized the means were not beyond reproach, and as an artist he could not remain silent. Thus he created the first protest image of the nuclear age—a drawing of a smirking skull face on a mushroom cloud, which transformed this atomic marvel into a symbol of death. Although it was not the most profound statement, it was the most poignant of the few antinuclear images produced in the wake of World War II. For its prescience, it has earned a place in the pantheon of oppositional graphics.

But even Osborn's satirical apocalyptic vision pales before actual photographs and films of A-bomb and H-bomb blasts that were made of the many tests over land and under sea. One film is remarkable for the real-time eruption from a gigantic plasma bubble (like an enormous womb) into a gaseous fireball from which the mushroom cloud emerges. Others are incredible for the sheer enormity of the cloud compared to nearby buildings or ships. Detonations at sea routinely produced the best photo ops because the immense upward thrusting water column, the base of the mushroom, was so surreal. Seen from the air, the blast produced undulating surf that radiated for miles, churning up the otherwise calm sea. These images are horrific *and* hypnotic, and like cosmic fireworks, they were as fascinating as they were terrible.

Early in the atomic age the mushroom cloud also devolved into kitsch. Government and industry promoted "our friend, the atom" with a variety of molecular-looking trade characters and mascots. By 1947 there were forty-five businesses listed in the Manhattan phone book alone that used the word "atomic" in their name, and none had anything to do with making bombs. In 1946 the cereal maker General Mills published an ad in comic books that was illustrated with a mushroom cloud, offering children an "Atomic 'Bomb' Ring" if they sent in a Kix cereal box top. The ring featured a secret compartment and a concealed observation lens that allowed the holder to look at flashes "caused by the released energy of atoms splitting like crazy in the sealed warhead atom chamber." A savvy French bathing suit designer, Louis Reard, took the name "bikini" from the Marshall Islands—where two American atom bombs were tested in 1946—because he thought that the name signified the explosive effect that the suit would have on men. Another designer, Jacques Heim, created his own two-piece bathing suit, called "The Atome," which he described as "the world's smallest bathing suit." Designers of everything from alarm clocks to business logos soon adopted an "atomic style."

Comic book publishers made hay out of mushroom mania. Atomic blasts, like auto accidents, caught the eye of many comic readers and horror aficionados. Just as real photos and films of atomic tests seduced viewers, fantastic pictorial representations of doomsday bombs blowing up large chunks of earth tweaked the imagination. The sheer enormity of these fictional blasts, especially when seen on earth from space, raised the level of terror many notches. Similarly, B-movies in the nuke genre, with all those empty cities laid barren by radioactive poison, exploited the "what if" voyeurism that people still find so appealing. Books and magazine stories covered a wide nuclear swath. Novels like *Fail Safe* and *On the Beach* (both made into films) speculated on the aftermath of a nuclear attack and thus triggered fear (and perhaps secretly promoted disarmament too). But to sell these books, paintings of mushroom clouds were used in ridiculous ways. The cover for *On the Beach*, for example, is absurdly prosaic, showing a woman standing on a seaside cliff directly facing a mushroom cloud while waiting for her lover to return from his submarine voyage to no man's land. By current standards—even for mass-market paperback covers—this is dumb, yet effective.

An intelligent, though more frightening, mushroom cloud display is the montage of nuclear blasts at the end of the satiric film *Dr. Strangelove*, accompanied by the mournful lyrics, "We'll meet again/ Don't know where/Don't know when." In quick succession, a dozen or so detonations, taken from real test film footage, flash by to illustrate a fictional "doomsday machine" triggered when only one bomb falls to earth. Although this chain reaction is not real, it plays to fears that many lay people and some scientists had that the U.S. and the USSR each created such demonic devices. In that spirit, during the 1950s, the Atomic Scientists of Chicago and the Federation of American Scientists, in their magazine titled *The Bulletin of the Atomic Scientists*, adopted a "Doomsday Clock" that they intended to symbolize the world's proximity to self-destruction—a surreal but reasonable presumption.

Absurdity reigned during the nuclear age and afterward. In 1995, the fiftieth anniversary of the end of World War II, the United States Postal Service planned to issue a postage stamp showing the Hiroshima atomic mushroom cloud with the words: "Atomic bombs hasten war's end, August 1945." The Japanese government protested, and the stamp was canceled. For the mushroom to be so commemorated would be an affront to the memory of those killed, but would also serve to legitimize this endgame trademark rather than underscore that the mushroom cloud is and will remain the world's most wicked icon.

Black Power/White Power

Tomi Ungerer

From time to time circumstance fosters the climate for a radical cartoonist to emerge from the ranks—one who shocks the senses and at the same time redefines the form. When Alsatian-born Tomi Ungerer's (b. 1930) work premiered in the United States in the mid-1950s, it was a shock to complacency, not because his ragged line and farcical ideas showed a clear rejection of the sentimental and romantic realism published in most mainstream magazines and advertisements, but because his satire exposed folly that native-born cartoonists were afraid to touch, or even see. Writing in *Graphis*, Manuel Gasser said of Ungerer's audacity: "one cannot help noticing that he is a grown-up child. Children have a habit of coming out with the truth, even when it is least opportune."

Truth underscores Ungerer's 1967 poster on race relations in America entitled *Black Power/White Power*. First conceived in 1963 as the cover of *Monocle*, a short-lived satiric journal published in New York, this topsy-turvy image of a white man eating a black man's leg as the black man does the same to the white, was an acerbic, if unpopular, critique of the dangers within the burgeoning civil rights movement. Like a child void of propriety and manners, Ungerer naïvely, though harshly, looked at both sides of the color line and found that white and black militants were threats to a movement that most liberals of the day were unwilling to criticize. The cartoon was a pox on both their houses. By the time Ungerer published the cartoon as a poster (reportedly over a quarter of million were produced) tension between militant and nonviolent segments of the movement had become frighteningly evident.

Ungerer never felt restrained from making strong political commentary even if it offended those purportedly on his own side. Self-censorship was never an issue, and the absence of taboos in his work resulted in drawings that eschewed the clichés and universal symbols that neutralized most graphic commentaries. Being an outsider, an immigrant, and peripatetic wanderer allowed him to see through the artifice of American politics and society, and underscored his vision.

Born in Strasbourg, Alsace, Ungerer grew up under French rule and German occupation. "It gave me my first lesson in relativity and cynicism—prison camps, propaganda, bombings . . . all to culminate in an apotheosis of warfare. My taste for the macabre certainly finds its roots here," he explained. Ungerer lacked any formal art training but found solace in his art. Before embarking on a career, though, he joined the camel corps of the French Army in Africa, from which he was discharged for ill health. At the age of twenty-four, however, he came to the United States to be a freelance illustrator. He ultimately produced various children's books for Harper and Row. His most significant, *Crictor*, published in 1957, was the first children's book to feature a boa constrictor (then taboo) as its main character.

During the 1950s, Ungerer did not have outlets for his personal work, so he filled many sketchbooks with surreal cartoons. His *Underground Sketchbook*, which took him many years to get published, was a repository for biting comic commentaries about sex, war, death, and love. He eventually turned his attention from the general human condition to realpolitik. He rejected any semblance of idealism, especially in terms of war: "Some wars are necessary evils," he once wrote, "but Vietnam was stupid." His drawings and self-published posters were savage indictments of that war's brutality. There is the feeling in looking at sketches and posters showing soldiers brutally forcing Vietnamese to metaphorically swallow the American way of life, that everyone was had by the lies and duplicity of government and its leaders. "Because America is a gutless country," he argued. "I do a political drawing because of a need I have. Out of anger." But posters with the conceptual intensity of *Black Power/White Power*, born of pure emotion, ultimately became historical essays on the mechanisms of life. "I am not really an artist, I am a thinker. I just use my drawings as a tool to make my thoughts accessible."

An artist this mercurial might be expected to have a limited cult following, but to his surprise Ungerer became the wunderkind of American editorial and advertising art. He was given hundreds of commissions, notably a series of billboards for the New York State Lottery with the headline "Expect the Unexpected," showing absurd and ironic vignettes as only Ungerer could make them. This headline and Ungerer's ideas were eventually adopted by the *Village Voice*, New York's leading alternative newspaper, for its own advertising campaign. But the methods of the commercial world eventually soured Ungerer, and in 1970 he severed his relations. "My intention was to get away from Madison Avenue and its gold-medal-sucking bogeymen. After thirteen years of hard work I had developed an allergy to the media," he said about turning exclusively to graphic and written commentary—the activity he had been subsidizing through commercial fees. Taking on the occasional commission, during the 1970s and 1980s he remained a prolific visual essayist on the *comédie humaine.*

Seymour Chwast

The Vietnam War polarized the American people like no other conflict since the Civil War. Domestic battles between hawk and dove, right and left, and young and old were passionately waged in the media and on the streets, through words, music, and pictures. The nightly news barrage of film and video directly from Vietnam battlefields impressed the horrific image of this war on America's consciousness and inspired the prodigious amount of protest posters aimed at leaders and policies. Not since after World War I, when pacifist organizations on both sides of the Atlantic launched what was called a "war against war," have artists and designers produced as many testaments of conscience.

End Bad Breath.

The most ubiquitous icon of antiwar dissent, known simply as the peace symbol and designed by Gerald Holtom in 1954 as the logo of England's CND (Campaign for Nuclear Disarmament), appeared on countless Vietnam War–era flyers and posters and turned up in evening news footage emblazoned on some American soldiers' helmets. Other well-known poster images include the following: Lorraine Schneider's 1969 *War is Not Healthy for Children and Other Living Things*, originally used as an announcement for the California-based organization Another Mother for Peace; Tomi Ungerer's series of satiric posters, especially *Eat*, which showed a prostrate Vietnamese forced to lick the ass of an American soldier; *I Want Out*, by Steve Horn and Larry Dunst, a parody of the famous James Montgomery Flagg *I Want You* poster showing Uncle Sam dressed in bandages with his outstretched hand begging for peace; Edward Sorel's caustic *Pass the Lord and Praise the Ammunition*, showing New York's Cardinal Spellman, vicar of the U.S. Army, charging into battle with rifle and bayonet; *And Babies? Yes Babies!* the poster with a color photograph of the My Lai massacre (an American platoon's savage attack on civilian villagers); and *End Bad Breath* by Seymour Chwast, a comic woodcut portrait of Uncle Sam with his mouth wide open, revealing airplanes bombing Vietnam.

End Bad Breath, designed in 1968, was not as emotionally

wrenching as *War Is Not Healthy . . . or And Babies?* But through comic surrealism—the juxtaposition of a typical mass-market advertising slogan, the familiar characterization of American patriotism, and the childlike rendering of an air raid—the poster spoke eloquently of the criminal and banal that was American Southeast Asia policy. It suggested that behind the façade of Americanism, this nation was keeping the peace by engaging in an unjust war in a distant land.

Furious that President Lyndon Baines Johnson ordered American B-52s to bomb Hanoi in order to pound the North Vietnamese leader, Ho Chi Minh, into a humiliating submission, Chwast, like others within the growing antiwar movement, believed that the immorality of such increased U.S. intervention would have disastrous effects on both nations. This also forced Chwast to explore ways in which a solitary citizen might somehow influence government policy. A poster, a mere one-sided sheet of printed paper, could not have the same destructive power as even an infinitesimal fraction of the napalm used to defoliate the Vietnamese countryside, but it could have a curative effect. Short of acts of civil disobedience, which were increasingly frequent during the late 1960s, a poster was the best means for Chwast to express his own growing frustration. And just maybe, through its visibility and recognition, the poster might reinforce the antiwar stance of others.

End Bad Breath was not the first antiwar visual commentary that Chwast, who cofounded Push Pin Studios in 1956, had created for public consumption. Nor was it the first time he was involved in antigovernment protests. In the early 1950s Chwast was a member of SANE, a group that advocated and demonstrated for nuclear disarmament and included the support of artists and designers. SANE was the first well-organized postwar effort in the United States to build grassroots support against testing of the atomic and hydrogen bombs. In 1957, a few years before American advisers were deployed in Vietnam, Chwast wrote, illustrated, and self-published *The Book of Battles*, a collection of woodcuts that ironically represented historic battle scenes not as heroic but banal events. The small, limited-edition book was in the tradition of artists' commentaries that dated back to the seventeenth century and included Jacques Callot's collection of prints *The Miseries and Disasters of War* (1633–1635), depicting the horrors of the Thirty Years' War; Francisco Goya's prints *Disasters of War* (1810–1820), about the Napoleonic occupation of Spain; and Pablo Picasso's 1937 painting *Guernica*, memorializing the bombardment of a defenseless Spanish town.

But Chwast's effort was even more consistent with a genre of antiwar fables, exemplified in *The Last Flower* (1939) by James Thurber, with its childlike drawings and terse text that served as a cautionary parable on the nature of armed conflict, and *War is No Damn Good* (1946) by Robert Osborn, the first antiwar book of the nuclear age, the first time that the mushroom cloud is transformed into a death's head. In this same spirit Chwast used a simple visual lexicon to show centuries of warfare's futile recurrence.

In the early 1960s American military advisers were sent to Vietnam, followed by a limited number of ground troops. In 1964, just prior to the launch of massive U.S. buildups, Chwast designed his first protest poster, *War is Good Business, Invest Your Son*, the slogan based on a button that he had seen. During this early stage of the burgeoning "alternative youth culture," head shops as well as poster and button stores were popping up in so-called bohemian districts like the East and West Village of New York City and catering to a rebellious clientele. Wearing political and social statements on their clothing was fashionable, and buttons became one way of publicly expressing antiestablishment points of view. In addition to the ubiquitous peace sign and buttons with slogans like *I Am an Enemy of the People* and *Frodo Lives* (a reference to J. R. R. Tolkien's *The Hobbit*), *War is Good Business . . .* touched a very raw nerve among draft-age baby boomers.

Chwast borrowed the slogan for use on his darkly colored (blues, purples, and reds) poster, which included nineteenth-century decorative woodtypes and old engravings of a mother and a soldier. It looked akin to one of those vintage call-to-arms broadsheets that summoned civilians into battle in the days when war was a heroic exercise. Chwast sold the idea to Poster Prints, one of the leading commercial poster and button outlets, where it was retailed among an array of cheaply printed movie, rock-and-roll, and protest posters. Although it appeared decorative, *War is Good Business . . .* was by no means benign. Without employing such frightening images as dismembered bodies and napalmed children, the poster cautioned that war (and particularly the Vietnam conflict) exacted the most costly price.

By the time that the United States had committed total man- and firepower to the Vietnam quagmire, LBJ decided not to run for a second term as president (acknowledging public dissension). Nonetheless, he continued to aggressively pursue the war, which had gathered such momentum that it was not about to be concluded at that time. *End Bad Breath* acknowledged the frustration Chwast—and many Americans— felt over the inevitability of an out-of-control war.

End Bad Breath was distributed through Poster Prints, and— compared to the other inventory of celebrity and psychedelic posters—it was fairly strident. But Chwast admits it was by no means an innovation.

"This was the kind of illustration method that was being done in those days," he explains. "Little people on shoulders, things in mouths—So I didn't break any new ground." The woodcut, which Chwast chose to use because of its sudden-death immediacy, was not new, either. It was the medium of choice for German expressionist artists, many of whom were members of left-wing political parties during the early twentieth century. Anyway, novelty was less important to Chwast than effectiveness, and the poster did have an impact "if only as an icon for those of us who had already made up our minds about the war," Chwast comments. "But it certainly didn't change any minds."

Chwast does not harbor any false illusion that his, or any, poster made a difference in the eventual outcome of the Vietnam War. But when taken as one piece of ordinance in a larger arsenal, its impact is very significant. It may not have had the same widespread exposure as the nightly network news broadcasts (which arguably changed Americans' perceptions more than anything else); it may not have been as influential as rock songs like Country Joe and the Fish's "Fixin' to Die Rag." But it was a mnemonic representation of government folly that underscored deep-seated dissent and an effective component of the larger antiwar campaign. It was also ubiquitous in graphic design magazines and competition annuals, which presumably helped to raise the awareness, if not stimulate the activism, of those in the design profession.

Robbie Conal

The notice Post No Bills was coined in
mid-nineteenth-century England to
prevent the hangers of illegal placards from
littering London's otherwise dreary streets.
By law, the Post No Bills notice had to
appear approximately every four feet along
a wall or hoarding for it to be considered a
placard-free surface; but even the threat of
fine or arrest didn't daunt the erstwhile
posterist in the performance of his duty.
Since then, Post No Bills has become an
invitation to engage in the act of posting.
Once the only method of displaying
advertisements and proclamations for
those without access to mass media,
postering is still the cheapest and most
defiant means of reaching the public.

MEN **WITH**

NO **LIPS**

Few have challenged posting ordinances more than Venice,
California–based artist/activist Robbie Conal (b. 1944). As the leader of a
national band of agitators, he has flown coast to coast armed with rolls of
incendiary paper to supply an army of poster snipers. In reality, this army is
a loose network of urban poster guerrillas who in the wee hours of the
morning plaster their respective cities and towns with messages that
addressed a variety of social ills. Since the mid-1980s, Conal has produced,
at his own expense, an average of three posters a year on subjects he
believes mass media has failed to cover.

Conal's first foray into confrontational street art was an enigmatic
though provocative poster titled *Men With No Lips*, an attack on former
President Ronald Reagan's cabinet, whose tight-lipped responses to public
inquiry obfuscated the dismantling of social welfare programs at home and
the undermining of sovereign governments abroad. This poster, originally
designed to fit standard traffic light switching boxes—the most ubiquitous
unofficial poster surface in Los Angeles—was simultaneously hung on
building walls, hoardings, and lampposts in New York and Chicago. A
hybrid of fine art and agitprop, *Men With No Lips* was often mistaken for a

rock band advertisement. Yet after a few sightings the intent of the message to tweak Americans' hearts and minds out of complacency became clear.

Conal admitted his decision to become a postermaker was part of a "plot to escape from the friendly confines of the art establishment," which he joined as a painter after majoring in psychedelic drugs in college during the late 1960s. He called his brand of agitprop "infotainment," and admitted that the last thing he wanted to do as a nonsanctioned public artist on social issues was to be deadly serious. "I knew that people on the street would ignore the humorless message on their way to work in the morning, and besides, I had a sardonic twist to my sensibility. So taking a little lesson from advertising, I thought I would just pique people's interest. I wasn't interested in telling them what to think as much as getting them to think along with me, and giving them a little chuckle, too," he explained.

Conal's social activism stems from being a "red-diaper baby" raised on the "upper left side" of New York City by parents who were labor organizers. "The apple doesn't fall too far from the tree," he said. Although he spent a few years trying to reconcile the often rocky relationship between art and politics, Conal eventually discovered a process of painting and postermaking whereby he could publicly express his indignation on issues such as Iran-Contra, women's reproductive rights, and censorship.

His second poster titled *Women With Teeth* was the opposite of *Men With No Lips*. "Considering myself something of a feminist, I figured I should give [women] equal time and image," he said. The series included portraits of Nancy Reagan, Margaret Thatcher, Jeanne Kirkpatrick, and Joan Rivers (whom Conal felt had traded in her alternative culture birthright for an establishment pedigree); these also sprang up around the nation thanks to the increasing number of volunteer snipers he and his friends had recruited. The response was gratifying. "There was a lot of silent resentment on the streets," he reasoned, "so when stuff started showing up in this subversive way, I think it was like a voice for a lot of people who had been silent. This grass-roots little yelp had become a chorus."

The theme of accountability runs through Conal's work. And so his third poster titled *Speak*, which featured Conal's expressionistic rendering of Iran-gate principal Colonel Oliver North, was a mammoth wanted poster. Conal regretted that he did not have enough money to print two others in the series, *Hear* and *See*, featuring portraits of President Ronald Reagan and his security aide, John Poindexter, but he did succeed at getting *Speak* hung in some of the most visible locations around the country, including site-specific Washington, D.C.

The Paris student revolution of May 1968
was one of the most dramatic political
events in a decade noted for its tumult. In
a modern-day storming of the Bastille, a
coalition of more than ten million students
and workers mounted the barricades to
protest Charles de Gaulle's aging
conservative government. By the end of
the year the nation was paralyzed by
strikes and demonstrations. In contrast to
the social protest concurrently hitting
many nations, this whirlwind insurgency
actually shook the system, provoking
substantive though temporary concessions.

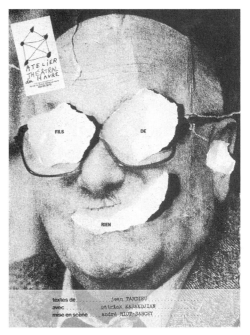

Intellectuals and workers were
brought to the battlements by their shared
interest in social reform and by their
indignation at the repression—most
aggressively represented by the
paramilitary National Police who were brought in to squelch the protests
through violence. Both groups were further induced by the daily barrage of
critical posters designed by the Atelier Populaire to inform and mobilize
the populace. This group of disparate painters, graphic artists, and art
students produced hundreds of iconic, one-color, brush-and-ink posters
that were pasted all over Paris and became an indelible symbol of the
popular uprising. In keeping with the character of collectivism, these paper
bullets were unsigned by any individual. Yet by the end of the brief
struggle, three of the most vociferous practitioners did become known, if
not individually at first, at least as the graphic arts collective called Grapus,
which later devoted itself to making graphic design for the communist
party, labor unions, and the public interest.

The original principals of Grapus were Pierre Bernard, Gérard
Paris-Clavel, and François Miehe. Each studied in Poland at a different
time under master poster artist Henryk Tomaszewski, where an
appreciation for anarchic design was nurtured. After leaving Poland,
Bernard worked for the magazine *Jeune Afrique* and Paris-Clavel at a

fashion studio. The trio came together in May 1968 at the École Nationale des Arts Decoratifs, where Miehe was a student and one of its political leaders. The revolution was just beginning. For three weeks they worked together in the Atelier Populaire No. 2, where each morning an assembly decided on the day's subjects. In the afternoon they designed the posters that by evening were printed and then sniped on the Paris walls.

By month's end the May Revolution was over for the Atelier Populaire. Hastily called national elections offered expedient solutions. "We were disappointed by the result of the elections," said Pierre Bernard, "but for ourselves this invitation to the political discussion was unforgettable." Such an electrifying month encouraged the trio to pursue the idea of influencing society through graphic arts. Despite France's venerable satiric arts tradition, French poster art was comprised of mundane product advertisements—even the best ones said nothing about society. Although nothing paralleled the Polish energy in the realms of politics or culture, Bernard was adamant. "We wanted to speak on the walls about cinema, theatre, poetry, history as had been done in Poland, and about politics as we had seen in the Cuban magazines," he said. "We needed a new type of client."

Among the most profound changes in government was the appointment of the author André Malraux as minister of culture. Malraux established a new school, the Institut de l'Environnement, to consolidate architects, urban planners, and industrial and graphic designers in common cause. Bernard and Gérard were awarded two-year scholarships by the institute to research and analyze the propaganda images of the Popular Front (1936) and the Coup d'État de Gaulle (1958). They studied linguistics and the arts of persuasion, and learned the importance of semiology in relation to form. They graduated, ironically, right before the school was closed for being, as the government ruled, a breeding ground for Marxist agitation. Realizing that scholarly pursuit was not going to affect society anyway, Grapus was founded to take an activist role in design. Based on the teachings of the institute and on the practice of collectivism as a means to render and disseminate ideas, they strove "to make the best image for the best politics in a materialist way," said Bernard.

The name Grapus is a nonsense word for graphics, but also refers to *crapules staliniennes,* "Stalinist scum," what the Grapus founders were at one time called by fellow leftists for being too rebellious. In its infancy the members of Grapus tried to work for the communist party and labor unions while they earned money working for advertising agencies. "After some months," recalled Bernard, "the two activities could not co-exist. You cannot simultaneously have two heads, two hearts, and two lunches with two different persons." Hence they dedicated themselves solely to social concerns. Yet convincing these normally suspicious groups to place both their trust and limited funds with this fledgling studio was difficult. Moreover, the Grapus style, a distinctive marriage of graffiti and collage made into colorful abstractions, was spurned by the communists as not being "strictly significant." Rather than a tired socialist realism, Grapus was interested in "making posters with strong metaphors to speak about human beings with blood, muscle, and smile," said Bernard. "We quoted Picasso, Léger, and Eluard as examples to follow. And we were proud of [this] new ideology." Calligraphy was used because handwriting was a symbolic means for the viewer to participate in the process. The reason for this was, as Bernard explained, "to find the tone of truth—you cannot lie when you write with your hand." Although the party did not say no to Grapus's efforts, they certainly resisted.

Grapus decided to remain independent, not tied to any party or group. Although they agreed with the goals of communist and labor organizations, they also keenly understood the lessons of history regarding ideology and the function of art. Without total independence it would be impossible to argue their own goals of quality, emotion, and aesthetics. Each time they proposed a design, they had to fight for this color or that typographic choice. Grapus's approach to polemical art was stern but not pedantic, strong but refreshingly and surprisingly festive. Because of Grapus's nonconformity, "Sometimes they [the party] considered us as terrorists," said Bernard.

Grapus's philosophy was based on an interpretation of Marxism that was flexible enough to conform to changes in political climate, and that often put them at odds with more doctrinaire groups. Ultimately, they split with the communist trade union over methodology and tactics. "Today each of us can say, 'I have not changed,'" Bernard admitted, "but we cannot say that together."

When Mikhail Gorbachev assumed power in 1985 the words *glasnost, perestroika,* and *demokratia* were not uttered. After a few years they became the most charged words of any language: glasnost, "new openness"; perestroika, "economic reform"; and demokratia, "popular rule." Ultimately, Premier Khruschev's admonition "We will bury you" was replaced by "Do you want fries with that?"

Glasnost posters were early manifestations of the flurry of social and political change that preceded the fall of the Soviet Union. Printed on flimsy paper, these posters expressed the frustrations and fears of a nation long under communist oppression. But the beginnings of change in Soviet graphics began much earlier than the Gorbachev years. The evolution in graphic design slowly gathered momentum towards the end of Khruschev's reign and continued through the early 1980s during the Brezhnev years.

When Gorbachev finally emerged as leader of the nation, Russia was still "the evil empire." Glasnost was not proclaimed overnight. But in terms of graphics the thaw had started. By 1985, when glasnost, perestroika, and demokratia were announced to the world, the initial evidence of this new graphic excitement emerged—or rather exploded—in the Baltic Republics of Latvia, Estonia, and Lithuania, where poster artists had already been exploring new methods of graphic presentation. Most of these new posters, which owe a debt to the Polish poster, were done for local cultural and performing arts events that had historically allowed artists more freedom.

In 1986 a new genre, the protest poster, was displayed at a Latvian political poster exhibition. Laimonis Chenberg of Riga had designed a poster called *Perestroika?* showing two saucepans with different colored covers. The symbolism, though seemingly obscure, was rather pointed. Chenberg challenged authority by visually suggesting that if the government could not achieve the simplest task, that of matching the right cover to the right saucepan, could perestroika really succeed? For the first time in decades an artist publicly questioned official policy. "For the first time in a long time, the artist had the right, and he took it immediately, to communicate his own view of the world and its problems," wrote a contemporary critic. It further signaled a "new orientation in political poster art," and triggered a chain reaction that was felt even in Moscow.

Glasnost posters were "called to life by a revolution from above and supported by the powerful mass movement from below," wrote historian Anna Suvorova. Unmentionable social ills were being addressed, including compassion for the handicapped, drug and alcohol addiction, prostitution, and AIDS. Governmental abuses were subject to criticism, including the bloated bureaucracy and remnants of Stalinism. "All the posters created by perestroika/demokratia in the setting of glasnost have the same distinction: a peculiar 'distrust' of the word," continued Dr. Suvorova. Slogans that defined the social realist posters of the past were rejected due to a "visual scheme and a plastic flow"—the very same artistic attributes that were once deemed bourgeois baggage. Compared to revolutionary posters of 1917 the perestroika posters lacked some of the spontaneity, drive, and mobilizing emotion, but, claims Suvorova, made up for it with logic and irony. With perestroika the poster became intellectual and therefore demanded that the viewer perceive unfamiliar images and codes, such as aphorism and grotesquery, to show the problems inherent in Soviet society. One Russian observer noted, "The poster nowadays is contradictory; it's not always precise and understandable for everybody."

This was a time of painful reappraisal of ingrained Soviet values and a shattering of old stereotypes. It was also a period of great peril. Immediately before the fall of the USSR glasnost was pronounced dead, perestroika was called a myth, and the term demokratia was considerably downplayed in official circles. Although the environment was more conducive to the publication of some sanctioned controversial posters, the union poster publishing house, Plakat, in Moscow, was still managed by old party functionaries who imposed constraints and limited production based on prejudice and fear.

There were still taboos. Glasnost and perestroika posters were tolerated as long as they did not criticize the Premier. Gorbachev shut down and fired the editor of Ogony, one of the leading publications in the country, for criticizing his effectiveness. Many poster artists, most of whom were under age forty, did not trust the system.

"There is freedom of speech. But what's more important, if glasnost holds up, the Russians will continue to have freedom after they speak," wrote the comedian Yakov Smirnoff in a 1989 *New York Times* op-ed article. In the end, what happened shook the world. The short period during which glasnost posters were designed marked a crack in the Iron Curtain that grew larger until it shattered. Today these glasnost poster images are a monument to the power of polemical art to change the course of history.

Women have come a long way from the presuffrage era when it was unladylike to smoke. Taken up as a *cause célèbre*, women's right to cigarettes was a smokescreen in the struggle for more fundamental rights. On the way to achieving first-class citizenship, women became first-class tobacco consumers. And if women were going to smoke, reasoned the tobacco industry, then why not encourage them to smoke a lot? By 1910 advertisements hinted that smoking was a right—by the 1920s it was a duty.

No expense was spared by Lucky Strike in recruiting female customers. To promote the image of sophistication a series of 1930s magazine ads featured stylized paintings of women decked out in evening finery. In "OK Miss America! We thank you for your patronage" a woman wearing a revealing, low-cut satin gown is so above the fray that she isn't even holding a Lucky, but the implication is that she had just finished a satisfying smoke. In the haughty "I do" advertisement a sultry bride pauses for a relaxed smoke and gives her vow to the cigarette of choice. Cigarettes were marketed as fashion accessories, but these ads, which ran during the Great Depression, were not targeted exclusively to women of means. Using smoke and mirrors, cigarette advertising suggested the promise of a better life.

Advertising wizards also made cigarettes seductive to women by invoking the ideal. High culture was used in one sales pitch that borrowed Henry Wadsworth Longfellow's "First a Shadow Then a Sorrow," to announce Lucky Strike's diet plan. "Avoid that future shadow," the copy suggested, "by refraining from over indulgence. If you would maintain the modern figure of fashion." Under an idealized color painting of a young woman haunted by the shadow of a double chin, the copy read: "We do not represent that smoking Lucky Strike Cigarettes will bring modern figures or cause the reduction of flesh. We do declare that when tempted to do yourself too well, if you will 'Reach for a Lucky' instead, you will thus avoid over indulgence in things that cause excess weight and, by avoiding over indulgence maintain a modern, graceful form."

Cigarettes were a staple for Depression-weary and later war-torn Americans. Yet despite the claim of weight control, they offered no viable health inducements. Even tobacco manufacturers acknowledged that frequent product usage resulted in coughing, throat irritation, and raspy sounding voices. The last was, however, promoted as sexy. To deflect public attention away from what the industry viewed as minor physical ailments, cigarette advertising exploited certain perceived health benefits, including increased vigor and stamina. Camels asserted that "Smokers everywhere are turning to Camels for their delightful 'energizing effect' . . . Camels never get on your nerves. . . ." Lucky Strike took the homeopathic route with their motto "It's toasted." A typical ad read "Everyone knows that sunshine mellows—that's why the 'TOASTING' process includes the use of Ultra Violet Rays . . . Everyone knows that heat purifies and so 'TOASTING'—that extra secret process—removes harmful irritants that cause throat irritation and coughing." By the late 1930s Lucky Strike had added the following tag line to its motto, "sunshine mellows—heat purifies."

Men played a role in cigarette advertising for women. They ran the agencies, produced the images, and wrote the copy that created the commercially correct woman. But in men's club fashion they also made fun of their own ludicrous stereotypes. In "Shanghaied by a Silly Salt? . . . Light an Old Gold" the *Esquire* magazine pinup artist Petty's voluptuous gal is hit upon by a licentious old gent, but the copy positions Old Gold as her saving grace: "When a retired skipper proves he is anything but retiring by dropping anchor alongside of you . . . don't let him scuttle your whole evening. Offer him an Old Gold . . . he'll welcome it like a breeze in the doldrums . . . while you breeze gracefully away."

Movie stars and starlets frequently appeared as spokespersons. In a 1943 advertisement, Betty Grable, star of the movie *Pinup Girl*, is shown in a soldier's barracks, reinforcing the idea that Chesterfield is overseas "With the boys. . . ." In the same spirit, Joan Bennett, dressed in her Women's Volunteer Army uniform, lit up "His cigarette and mine," another in a series of Chesterfield testimonials. To soldiers, cigarettes were as valuable as rations; to the tobacco industry the war was a boon. Ads invoked the image of American boys, exploited the image of American girls, and portrayed cigarettes to be as American as apple pie. After the war, men became active role models in ads targeted to women.

The cigarette ads created during the Great Depression and World War II targeted women with one purpose: to seduce by appealing to their patriotism and sense of fashion. While the stylistic manner of this seduction has changed since these ads were first printed, the method is still the same: appeal to weakness, bolster myth, and massage fantasy.

I knew a guy from work who stood in Times Square every lunch hour holding a large tattered sign that read: "Repent." Unlike the *New Yorker* caricatures of doomsayers in sackcloth and ashes, he wore regular street clothes and—rain or shine—preached through a bullhorn about the downside of eternal damnation. He also handed leaflets to passersby with such titles as, *Are You In Danger?*, *The Burning Hell*, and *The Consequences of Sin*. Returning to the office, he would leave a few leaflets *du jour* around the men's room. And while he was a likeable sort, there was something unsettling about his proselytizing, and even more unnerving were those crudely printed leaflets that accused everyone of a multitude of unpardonable sins.

I tried to ignore the leaflets on the grounds that they were pathetically designed, but actually, they were disturbing and compelling, precisely because they were so *under*designed (in fact, ugly as hell). As designers, we are so used to being bombarded with slick graphics and typography that when faced with crude missives like these, we automatically reject them as though they are laced with anthrax.

Sure, from a distance, designers have come to celebrate so-called vernacular design, but evangelical handouts have yet to be classified as such, because their graphic quality and content is more forbidding than a Chinese food menu or a Greek paper coffee cup. The rhetoric of persuasion in getting one to repent for one's sins is, arguably, more dour than menus that persuade you to buy the sweet and sour pork special. Moreover, if one does not believe in things like sin (original or otherwise), the Second Coming (or the First, for that matter), the Devil (or anything satanic), or the "vice of sexual immorality" (or any of the dozens of other prohibitions based on scripture), then these flyers are, at first glance, decidedly crackpot.

Of course, not all printed matter of a religious nature is designed as primitively as those—take Gutenberg's finest piece of printing, the

Mainz Bible, and the Celtic illuminated manuscript *The Book of Kells*, for instance. But the specimens that I've collected in the subway around Times Square and elsewhere in New York share a crudeness that can only be described as a common visual language—one that appeals to those who embrace the "Word." Meanwhile, those who produce these in large quantities truly believe that they will be read regardless of their physical attributes—indeed, the more austere, the more righteous.

Some leaflets are, however, better designed than others, and a few professional ones are clear exceptions to the rule. Chick Publications produces the most widely distributed and professional of all religious handouts. Hundreds of these small comic book–sized gospels and testimonies are drawn and written by Jack Chick, and follow a standardized format that has become so well known that the booklets have already been parodied. But despite the comic form, these publications are no joking matter. According to Chick's Web site (Mr. Chick refused to be interviewed for this article, and instead I was referred to *www.chick.com* for "all I needed to learn"), his career as "a publisher for Christ" began over forty years ago when a missionary broadcaster from the Voice of China and Asia told him that multitudes of Chinese people had been won to communism through mass distribution of cartoon booklets. Jack felt that "God was leading him to use the same technique to win multitudes to the Lord Jesus Christ." Thinking that what worked for communism would work for Christianity, he subsequently produced hundreds of comics, presumably for a young audience, of such parables as *The Loser* ("He was afraid of everything. But God changed Gideon from a loser to a great leader"), *Party Girl* ("A young woman's brush with death reveals Satan's plot for her destruction"), and *Sin Busters* ("Nobody can keep the Ten Commandments. Jesus is the only way to heaven"). Chick's conventional drawing style was at first considered sacrilegious in evangelical circles, but this master of dramatic narrative has managed to become ubiquitous in the gospel tract business over the years. The comics are issued on a frequent schedule and sold in bulk inexpensively through the Web site. Copies of each edition (often in various translations) are printed in the millions, and buyers are encouraged to distribute them on the streets for free.

Chick's pamphlets are the most ambitious, yet other exceptions to the usual fare include *The Bridge to Life*, produced by a company called "Navpress, A Ministry of Navigators," because it adeptly employs sophisticated typography as well as graphic smarts. This small booklet is comprised of step-by-step diagrams that effectively show man traversing the proverbial abyss of sin toward the precipice of salvation. Similarly, the full-color *High Alert: Security Risk* published by Preach the Word Ministries

Inc., which features photographs of the World Trade Center before and under attack, appears to be designed by a skilled Photoshop artist, as does *The Time Is Now* by the American Bible Society and *Is Jesus the Messiah?* by Chosen People Ministries (also known as Jews for Jesus). Each is replete with contemporary typefaces and Photoshop effects.

Given that the computer makes it so easy to produce proficient layouts, why are the majority of these grassroots missives so primitive?

"Simple," says "John," a clean-shaven, twenty-three-year-old proselytizer who recently handed me *There Is No Water in Hell* in the Times Square subway station. Published by Old Paths Tract Society, the handout was a blurrily printed four-page, two-color (red and blue) testimony that seemed like it had been set with hellboxed (no pun intended) discarded hot type. "My friends and I don't have computers, and if we did, I wouldn't know how to make a pamphlet look any better than this," he said. In fact, John buys his tracts in bulk from the publisher at $4 per thousand and distributes them on his own. Similarly, Agnes, a fortyish-year-old African-American woman, handed me a pamphlet titled *Now Is the Time to Act, Not Later On!,* an even coarser folded-over, four-page tract with a vintage line illustration that looked as if it werre photocopied from the early twentieth-century Bible. When I asked her, "Why does this look so faded?," her reply was: "This is what my pastor gives me and it's the best we can do." This tract was also published by Old Paths Tract Society, one of a handful of resources that supply congregations around the nation.

As these societies go, the one that produces what one might call the typical or "standard" design is the Fellowship Tract League (motto: "All tracts free as the Lord provides"). These are the pamphlets that my former workmate used to hand out and leave in the bathroom, of which my favorite was *The Burning Hell: Tortured Lost Souls Burning Forever.* It featured a rather expressive line drawing on the cover, printed in red and black, of Satan looming large, overseeing lost souls trapped in hell and engulfed by flames. Of all the four-pagers I received—including the intimidatingly titled *No Escape* and *It Is Finished* by Hope Tract Ministry, which basically said there is no hope for any of us—*The Burning Hell* is the most memorable. While definitely crude, it is decidedly honest. Satan is not some hokey horror-film apparition, but a convincing human form who embodies the banality of evil. The lost souls are not merely comic caricatures, but rather you and me (or maybe just me). And curiously, the abundance of red flame does not come off as kitsch, but rather as a startling graphic device with iconic impact.

While the Fellowship Tract League flyer touched a chord with this infidel, another tract supplier, Bible Helps, is the purveyor of most evangelical stereotypes. Its *Homosexuality, Is It Really—Natural? Sinful? Curable?* and *The Vice of Sexual Immorality* are the quintessential no-frills accusation leaflets. These pamphlets exude damnation simply through their 8-point, text-packed typesetting. They telegraph an attitude that, since you are going to hell anyway, you don't need legible text. Indeed, most of these flyers seem to begin with the same creepy theme (which is supported by the minimal graphics) that evil runs rampant in our lives, and we are all terrible people. Out of all the leaflets I was handed, only one showed any hope: "God loves to hear and answer our prayers!" Otherwise, the vast majority are relentless, perversely preoccupied with the personal and societal consequences of sin.

Although graphic design has long played a strategic role in the "corporate" branding of many organized religions, the grassroots print side of evangelical proselytizing is clearly stripped down to the bare bones. The graphic vocabulary is so void of substance and style that perhaps their designs are the sins in need of forgiveness.

A New York street poster has got to grab viewers by the throats and knock them on their asses. Otherwise it's as useless as yesterday's newspaper and as forgettable as most theater, movie, fashion, and cabaret posters hung daily. In the competition for city scaffolds, longevity is measured by days, sometimes hours. A memorable poster must stand out in the crowd and also leave the viewer with a mental "cookie" that prompts Pavlovian recognition—a tough order, given the multitude of stylish bills posted these days. Yet one of the most startling posters in recent memory did leave a potent after-burn. This violently rendered scrawl of the word "racism" not only eclipses trendy designs but is a strident commentary on an onerous theme. The poster is the word itself with a menacing metamorphosed *C* shaped like a mouth with fangs, outlined in red and poised to consume the other letters in the word. Created by New York designer James Victore (b. 1962), it is a symbol of racial hatred that forces the viewer to feel the violence that the word conjures.

During the summer of 1993, Victore, like millions of other New Yorkers, was disquieted by race riots that erupted between Hasidic Jews and their African-American neighbors in Crown Heights, Brooklyn. The intensity of this atavistic behavior was alarming, but so was the voyeurism of television news viewers. Victore believed that nightly press coverage had caused people to misconstrue the essence of racism. The physical spectacle was the main attraction, not the deep-seated issues leading up to the hostility. Victore felt that the only upside of such a tragedy should be the public's heightened awareness of what causes racism in the first place, but this was not the case. "I was troubled that the word was so overused that it no longer meant anything," he explains. "In the press, everybody was talking about racism-racism-racism. But nobody really knew what it meant. So I had this idea to show [the word] eating its young, and created a poster as simply as I could."

Rarely is a poster more effective than live TV coverage, but Victore's *Racism* added a critical dimension to the event. If Victore never created another polemic after this, he should be satisfied that he made a contribution to contemporary visual iconography. But this was not the first nor would it be the last of his visual commentaries. Although it is a standard against which his future work will be fairly or unfairly judged, it is one of many memorable images that he has created in a little over a decade since becoming a graphic designer.

In 1992, Victore designed and produced his first polemical poster, *Celebrate Columbus*—or what he calls the *Dead Indian*—to commemorate the five-hundredth anniversary of the "discovery" of America by Christopher Columbus. "My reason for doing the poster," he explains, "was because, at the time, everybody in media was saying that from one man's accidental discovery we are such a great nation." Victore suspected that the hoopla around the celebration, which was being criticized by Native American and other human rights groups, demanded further scrutiny, and he wanted to add his voice to revelation of, in his own words, "what I like to call the 'pox-infested blanket story,' the genocide of indigenous peoples by the American government. I wasn't trying to throw a stone through anybody's window. I just wanted to inject the notion that there's always another side, which at that time was getting lost. The whole revisionist, nationalistic view was getting stronger and stronger. I wanted to offer a small counterpoint."

Using his rent money Victore printed three thousand two-color posters, which showed a vintage photograph of a Native American warrior, whose noble face he drew over graffiti-style in black marker to look like a skull. With a couple of volunteers, he illegally pasted about two thousand copies on walls and scaffolds around New York. He also obtained the addresses of Native American groups in the United States and Canada and mailed them tubes containing twenty posters each. For all his effort, Victore's first stab at advocacy went mostly unappreciated. A request for an appointment with a Native American organization in Washington, D.C., was ignored. "I left the posters on their porch with a note and got no response at all." Meanwhile, back in New York, the police tore down as many posters as they could so as not to mar the celebration, yet enough remained intact on Columbus Day to have something of an impact. "I witnessed few people actually looking and reading," he acknowledges. Although it was a small return, he was encouraged.

At the time, Victore veered somewhat from commercial work toward an indy sensibility. It is axiomatic that new ideas rarely emerge from tried-and-true venues, so Victore hooked up with kindred renegades. He had met two bartender/actors who founded the Shakespeare Project, dedicated to performing Shakespeare in public spaces presumably as the Bard had originally intended. The payment involved was negligible, but Victore was given carte blanche with the posters, which he rendered without a hint of Shakespearean pastiche. Instead, as for Henryk Tomaszewski's theater posters, Victore rendered everything from image to type by hand to give a mood of immediacy and serendipity. At the same time that he did posters for *Macbeth*, *Twelfth Night*, *Taming of the Shrew*, and *Romeo and Juliet*, he produced *Racism* and had copies of them sniped around town together. *Racism* made an indelible impact on some, but Victore claims that the poster had much more recognition in professional competitions and design annuals (to which he submitted the work to give it added visibility) than on the street. Nevertheless, he was not deterred.

The first two posters were done on his own, but, accepting the adage about strength in numbers, Victore helped found a small alternative graphics collective along the lines of the Atelier Popular, the graphics arm of the 1968 French student uprising. Victore and five other young New York designers joined together to fund, conceive, and produce critical street graphics. *Traditional Family Values* was the first project done under the auspices of the group (although entirely his own concept) and his third poster. Designed to coincide with the 1994 Republican National Convention, it was an attack on right-wing U.S. Senator Jesse Helms's call for a return to so-called family values as a euphemism for his stands on antihomosexual and antiabortion rights. The image was an appropriated 1950s-era framed photograph of a real family of Ku Klux Klan members—Mom, Dad, the kids, and the Imperial Dragon—which, down South, when it was taken, was as natural as depriving "niggras" of their rights. But in the 1990s it served as a dark satiric commentary on these new objects of prejudice, not just in the South but all across America.

The second group project, *The Baby Bottle*, showed a typical bottle with measuring markings down the side that read "Whitey," "Towel Head," "Kike," "Gook," and other bigoted aspersions about race and ethnicity; it was not done for a special occasion but, rather, as a reminder in the tradition of cautionary and instructive schoolroom posters. As Victore notes, the message was "not to hand down to our children prejudice and hatred through casual remarks." Using a baby bottle was an apt symbol to suggest the matter-of-fact feeding of healthy and unhealthy ideas to children who accept any and all nourishment. The poster, however, did not have the splash the group had hoped for. Nor did it grab proverbial hearts and minds.

Victore admits that although the group was able to get more posters onto the street, "the collaborative didn't work as well as I had hoped. It was too easy to work together because somebody had an idea, and everybody else said 'Yes.'" Without more of an internal dialectic, the group dynamic was less about pushing and shoving each other to better solutions than about consensus. So it was disbanded.

By this time Victore realized that producing his own posters at his own expense was also counterproductive. He mailed hundreds out (and many of them were hanging in offices all over town), but he decided that the most effective way to achieve saturation was to convince an appropriate group to sponsor the work. Of course, balancing the artist's want with the sponsor's needs is tricky, even when the work is done for free, and Victore quickly learned that pro bono arrangements do not always result in the holiest of marriages. He complains, "Groups of this kind don't (for lack of a better term) understand the tool of the poster and the power that it could potentially have." But after a few failed relationships he found the perfect client for one of his sharpest posters in the venerated NAACP (National Association for the Advancement of Colored People), which was trying to shed its moderate civil-rights image and regain its activist aura.

The NAACP had produced a documentary film called *Double Justice*, about the racism inherent in the death penalty, and asked Victore to design its promotional mailer. Instead of using film stills he decided to do a large rendering of a child's stick-figure hangman game, where players guess letters that comprise a word, and for every wrong guess a body part is hung from a scaffold—simultaneously presenting both an innocent children's pastime and a terrifying symbol (when presented in the context of racism). The word that Victore used was "nigger;" the poster shows three letters: *g*, *g*, and *r*. "I got the idea for the hangman game when I was in the elevator leaving the meeting," Victore recalls. "I ran to my bartender, who was the guy from the Shakespeare Project, and said, 'What do you think?' He said, 'James, it's brilliant; they'll never take it.' But they took it." The elegantly simple poster was mailed to a list of the NAACP Legal Defense and Education Fund, Inc., lawyers who help people on death row. It was also sent to school teachers along with the video. "The last thing that I had heard from them (which was a while ago now) was that they got a call from [former U.S. Supreme Court] Justice Blackmun's office to obtain copies," says Victore. "So it was in Justice Blackmun's office just before he reversed his opinion on the death penalty."

The hangman poster (titled *Racism and the Death Penalty*) was the first of two posters for the NAACP that confront racially biased capital punishment. The second, *The Death Penalty Mocks Justice*, is a white-on-black drawing of a skull with a stuck-out tongue in the form of an American flag. Here Victore resorted to known clichés (something that he has managed to avoid in his other work), but he argues that in this instance it is the most effective means for getting the point across. "I could have come up with something more intellectual or some offbeat imagery, but the problem was that, for the people I was speaking to, I think it would have been too coy or too design-y. This was also for the NAACP, and it was going to go to lobbyists and lawyers and teachers, and without being trite or belittling, I want to speak in really simple forms and get an idea across in a gestalt manner, whether it's through your heart or your intellect or whatever."

Victore has a litany of peeves, many of which revolve around living in New York. Over the past few years the city has become inundated with "official" signs (dos and don'ts) bolted on lampposts, addressing the basic etiquette of living with millions of other people. Consistent with this trend, he did one titled *Use Mass Transit*, a bold gothic headline jammed together with childlike drawings of cars and trucks. Another poster, *Just Say No!* shows the severed head of Mickey Mouse with his eyes Xed out comic-style, which addresses Victore's assertion that New York is "being touristed to death. New Yorkers are becoming just like the great silverback gorillas who will now come down and will eat out of your hand." Victore believes that the Disneyfication of New York (the widespread colonization of Times Square and other city venues by Walt Disney Company hotels, theaters, and retail malls) is one of the city's root evils. In the vortex of New York's official celebration of Disney's civic improvements, this poster is a reminder that it is all a branding scheme.

Ashcroft . . . You're Next!

Micah Wright

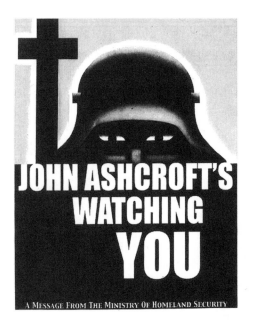

JOHN ASHCROFT'S WATCHING YOU

A MESSAGE FROM THE MINISTRY OF HOMELAND SECURITY

You may think you've seen Micah Wright's posters before, possibly in World War II history books or period movies, because he pilfers actual vintage posters and retrofits them with caustic new slogans. For example, there's one of a Statue of Liberty pointing her accusing finger (originally designed as an attack on Nazism), with the updated headline, "You, Stop Asking Questions! You're Either With Us or You Are With the Terrorists," while another shows a classic Uncle Sam in rolled-up shirtsleeves (originally anti-Japanese propaganda) with the headline, "Ashcroft . . . You're Next! Break Our Constitution, I Break Your Face," and yet another shows attacking GIs (originally a D-Day message) bearing the words "Attack Attack Iraq: Another War Will Surely Pull Us Out Of Recession!" Scores more featured on *http://homepage.mac.com/leperous/PhotoAlbum1.html* prompt a nostalgic twinge, yet hit a current nerve about homeland security and the second war in the Gulf.

Wright is a writer for television, film, animation, and comics, and recently has become an "amateur graphic designer." While he admits his limitations—"I usually work with a skilled artist on my mainstream media work because realizing on paper whatever image is in my head (via my own hands) is a skill I am sorely lacking"—thanks to user-friendly graphics programs, he is now the producer of a new kind of old-time agitprop.

Since Wright started his "propaganda project" on June 10, 2002, he has made about twenty digital posters per month. Drawing from a plethora of World War II propaganda posters and the occasional advertising image (e.g., by A. M. Cassandre), he writes new slogans (many under the auspices of the satiric "Ministry of Homeland Security") and slightly alters the images. "Sometimes I do this with real paint, other times with Photoshop, depending on the difficulty of the image retouching," he explains. "It's given me a sense of accomplishment that simply art-directing other artists never has." Although it may appear easy to parody a kitsch image, Wright states, "It's never enough to just start with a great poster . . . Sometimes I have to struggle with a striking image for weeks to find the perfect news story to attach to it, or it might take a while to wrangle the perfect turn of phrase to substitute on the poster."

It took him six months, for instance, to figure out what to do with the famous Rosie the Riveter *We Can Do It* poster. "I just knew I didn't want to waste that poster on a tag line that didn't make me laugh," he recalls, "and a conceptual breakthrough came one day when I was up late and it suddenly struck me that it looks like Rosie is not only rolling up her sleeve, but could also be giving someone the international 'up yours' move. From that realization, it was a short jump to 'Up Yours, Bush! I'm Keeping My Right to Choose!'"

Wright wants people to see the posters and laugh, but surprisingly (and unintentionally), they've started selling too. Wright claims over 150,000 people have visited the Web site since last August, and says he has sold 1,260 copies of different images, which are offered as prints, T-shirts, and coffee mugs. He further notes that two thousand people have sent him letters, and of that number, "probably 1,900 are extremely positive . . . people are genuinely pleased to see someone who believes in the 'verboten' —e.g., that Bush is a moron, that Ashcroft is pushing us all toward an East German–style snitchocracy, and that the current administration is using Osama as the boogeyman to scare people into voting for them." The other one hundred are, he says, "the most vituperative, hate-filled, ill-educated psychotics you'd never care to meet."

MASS MEDIA

In 1896 not one but two revolutionary periodicals were
introduced in Kaiser Wilhelm's Germany. *Jugend* codified
a distinctly modern graphic style, and *Simplicissimus*
translated it into graphic social commentary. Both
signaled a rebellion of youth against court-sanctioned
romanticism and dehumanizing industrialization. *Jugend*,
published by Dr. Georg Hirth, gave a voice and a name
to Jugendstil, or "youth style," and *Simplicissimus*, edited
by Albert Langen and Thomas Theodore Heine
(1867–1948), harnessed the graphic power of this new
movement as a polemical tool.

Jugend, a Munich weekly published from 1896 to
1926, was the principal outlet for the dissemination of
Jugendstil art and literature. Its fanciful cover illustrations
and changing logotypes defined a style that was built on
the rejection of the familiar and antiquated. Jugendstil
dismantled entrenched artistic conventions, including
classical approaches to rendering. It replaced realism with
abstraction and rococo embellishment with curvilinear
decoration. *Jugend* revealed a French influence (some of
its artists emulated Henri Toulouse-Lautrec), but was
nevertheless quite German in its adoption of gothic
lettering and imagery. Page layout was often dictated by
the complexity of the illustration, causing untold
headaches for the printer whose job it was to rag the type
to conform to the curvilinear designs.

Satire was the fuel that fired the profoundly influential
Simplicissimus, also a Munich weekly published from 1896 to 1944. Co-
edited by Th. Th. Heine, a poster artist and cartoonist, *Simplicissimus*, also
known as *der Simpl*, was at once the progenitor of a new graphic style and a
thorn in the side of the Kaiser (who saw to it that the artists were harassed
and imprisoned more than once). Although *der Simpl*'s covers were not as
adventuresome as those of *Jugend*, it nonetheless pioneered a graphic style
that influenced other pictorial journals throughout Europe. Most images
were given full-page display, accompanied only by a caption and headline.
Der Simpl's stable of contributors included modern cartoonist Bruno Paul

(1874–1968), whose woodcut-like brush-and-ink drawings were said to have influenced the German expressionists, and Eduard Thony (1866–1950), who lampooned the *Junker*—or military aristocracy—with such beguiling subtlety that even his victims admired the work. Issues such as political corruption, religious hypocrisy, and militarist stupidity were assailed, while the virtues of the *Volk*, or peasant class, were extolled in beautifully proportioned, stylized vignettes, and caricatures.

Jugendstil was a component of a short-lived but exuberant pan-European cultural episode that began in the late nineteenth century and ended before the outbreak of World War I. It was similarly practiced in Paris as art nouveau, in England as the arts and crafts movement, Scotland as the Glasgow school, Italy as Liberty, Austria as the secession, and Czechoslovakia as the Bohemian secession. Each nation imbued the style with its own social and political characteristics, but there was also a shared visual language rooted in a rejection of all things sentimental. Art nouveau inveighed against parochial nationalistic movements while promoting the international exchange of ideas. It refused to acknowledge any distinction between the "fine and lesser arts" and was both decorative and expressive.

Art nouveau was influenced by the simplicity of traditional Japanese design. Its practitioners swore allegiance to the natural object and cultivated an appreciation of symbolism. Theirs was a lexicon of sinuous, naturalistic, curvilinear forms. Jugendstil combined these organic impulses with a geometric edge. Pervasive in Jugendstil design was what one critic called "fantastical melancholy," communicated through Teutonic wit and folkloric symbology. Jugendstil took nourishment from William Morris's arts and crafts movement in England but did not reject all industrial things, which it instead sought to cover with decorative motifs. Jugendstil artists rejected traditional typography, choosing instead to render unique ornamental typefaces that worked harmoniously with an image. Brushed letterforms were used on posters and advertisements, while a few eccentric faces, notably those by Otto Eckmann, became emblems of the era.

Exponents of Jugendstil believed in the ideal that good design could change the world. While it had an impact, this was an unrealized goal that came to an abrupt end prior to World War I. Today Jugendstil is a stylistic reminder of rebellion against the status quo. The magazines *Jugend* and *Simplicissimus* were its clarions. Although it might seem tame in the postmodern epoch, Jugendstil possessed a quality that transcended the moment and continues to influence contemporary illustration and design.

The Composing Room of New York was no mere type shop. It was the vortex of progressive design activity from the late 1930s to the 1960s. No other type business promoted itself more aggressively, or so determinedly advanced the art and craft of type design, and in the process made such a significant contribution to practice and history. What began as a campaign to attract typesetting business from advertising agencies and book and magazine publishers evolved into one of the most ambitious educational programs that the field has ever known. It initiated type clinics, lecture series, single and group exhibitions, catalogs, and one of America's most influential graphic arts periodicals, *PM* (Production Manager), later called *AD* (Art Director), published bimonthly between 1934 and 1942.

The program, conceived and sustained for almost forty years by The Composing Room's cofounder, Dr. Robert Lincoln Leslie (1885–1986), was rooted in graphic arts traditions yet was motivated by his personal willingness to identify and promote significant new approaches even if they rejected tradition. What made The Composing Room so profoundly influential, in addition to being a recognized leader in quality hot-metal type and eventually photo-typesetting, was a commitment to explore design approaches with a blind eye toward style or ideology. Despite his own preference for classical practice, "Doc" Leslie (he was a licensed physician) or "Uncle Bob," as he was affectionately called, gave young designers a platform on which to strut their stuff.

Leslie assumed that a well-informed professional—indeed an enlightened one—would be a more discerning customer and so in a corner of his shop he created a graphic arts salon. Regularly frequented by Ladislav Sutnar, Alvin Lustig, and Herbert Bayer, this salon put his type shop at the center of what would now be called "design discourse," but then was practical design talk. The Composing Room's unparalleled efforts to elevate the level of graphic arts and typography may have been driven by commercial priorities but nonetheless formed a solid foundation for the celebration and documentation of graphic design.

In 1934 Leslie founded *PM: An Intimate Journal for Production Managers, Art Directors, and their Associates*, initially as a house organ. With its co-editor Percy Seitlin, a former newspaper man, this small-format (six-by-eight-inch) "journal" developed into the leading trade publication and outlet for traditional and progressive work, an American *Gebrauchsgrafik or Arts et Métiers Graphiques* (the latter published by the Deberny and Peignot Foundry in Paris, which also employed publications and exhibitions to further the French graphic arts). *PM* explored a variety of print media, covered industry news, and developed a strong slant towards modern typography and design. It was also the first journal to showcase the new European immigrants and included illustrated profiles on Herbert Bayer, Will Burtin, Joseph Binder, M. F. Agha, as well as native-grown moderns Lester Beall, Joseph Sinel, Gustav Jensen, and Paul Rand. In 1939 the name *PM* was sold to Ralph Ingersol, who started New York's only ad-less daily newspaper and called it *PM*, so the magazine changed its name to *AD*, which coincidentally reflected a creative realignment within the profession from production managers to art directors—marking a gradual shift from craft to art.

Each *AD* cover featured an original image and redesigned logo. E. McKnight Kauffer's was characteristically cubistic; Paul Rand's was playfully modern; Lucian Bernhard's was suitably gothic; and Matthew Leibowitz's prefigured new wave in its dada-inspired juxtaposition of discordant decorative old wood types. Although the articles were not critical analyses, they were nevertheless well-written trade pieces peppered with interesting facts and anecdotes. A news column, titled "Composing Room Notes by R. L. L." provided an account of commercial arts from a vendor's perspective. For sixty-six issues *PM* and *AD* documented a nascent profession as it grew out of a journeyman's craft.

Three years after starting *PM*, Doc Leslie took over a small room in The Composing Room shop that, with the addition of a display case and bright lights, was transformed into the *PM* Gallery, the first exhibition space in New York dedicated to graphic design and its affinities. Percy Seitlin described the premiere exhibition: "A young man by the name of Herbert Matter had just arrived in this country from Switzerland with a bagful of ski posters and photographs of snow-covered mountains. Also came camera portraits and varied specimens of his typographic work. We decided to let him hang some of his things on the walls and give him a party. . . . The result was a crowd of almost bargain-basement dimensions, and thirsty too. Everyone was excited by the audacity and skill of Matter's work." The magazine and gallery were symbiotic. Often a feature in one would lead to an exhibition in the other or vice versa. Doc Leslie believed "that there was an enthusiastic audience for a showcase featuring the work of artists-in-industry; and, furthermore, that the audience was larger than we had originally thought it ever could be."

In April–May 1942 the editors ran this note: "*AD* is such a small segment of this wartime world that it is almost with embarrassment, and certainly with humility, that we announce the suspension of its publication . . . for the duration," wrote editors Leslie and Seitlin. "The reasons are easy to understand: shortage of men and materials, shrinkage of the advertising business whose professional workers *AD* has served, and all-out digging in for Victory. . . ." The magazine did not resume publishing after the war but left a documentary record of an important period when American and European designers began to forge an international design language.

Photography records the gamut of feelings written on the human face, the beauty of the earth and skies that man has inherited, and the wealth and confusion man has created.

—Edward Steichen, *Time* magazine (1961)

Photography changed how the world was recorded. Likewise the "picture magazine" changed how the world was seen. The photojournalist Edward Steichen referred to this genre as a "major force in explaining man to man." But just as the invention of the photograph in the early nineteenth century made representational painting obsolete, during the past thirty years the spontaneity and immediacy of that other revolutionary medium, television, has made the picture magazine an anachronism.

Yet before television, picture magazines with rotogravure pages awash with halftones, printed with luminescent inks on velvety paper, were veritable eyes on the world. Photography may have been static, but, when edited like a motion picture and narratively paced to tell a story, the images of never-before-recorded sights offered audiences the same drama—and more detail—than any newsreel. Innovative editors at the leading magazines advanced revolutionary storytelling ideas that altered the way photography was used and perceived. With the advent of faster films and lightweight cameras, photography was freed from the confines of the studio; photographers were encouraged to capture realities that had been previously hidden in the shadows.

As photography evolved from single documentary images into visual essays, the forms and formats of presentation changed as well. From the mid-nineteenth to the early twentieth century, the picture magazine evolved from a repository of drawn and engraved facsimiles of daguerreotypes into albums of real photographs. With new technology in place, innovation was inevitable. Soon sequences of integrated texts and images, designed to capture and guide the eye, were common methods of presenting current events of social, cultural, and political import.

While photojournalism (though not officially referred to as such) had been practiced since 1855, when Roger Fenton made history photographing the Crimean War, the ability to reproduce photographs was really possible only after 1880, when Stephen H. Horgan's invention of the halftone was tested at the *New York Daily Graphic* and ultimately improved upon by the *New York Times*. Moreover, prior to 1880, cameras were so large and heavy that they impeded candid or spot news coverage. That is, until the Eastman Kodak Company reduced the camera to a little box, which launched a huge amateur photography fad in Europe and America (and encouraged publication of amateur photography magazines). These pictures were often informal; they were the turn-of-the-century equivalent of Polaroid's instant pictures in the 1960s and of digital snaps today— immediate photographic gratification.

Professionally speaking, the most important technological advance occurred in Germany after World War I. In 1925, two compact cameras, the Ermanox and the Leica, were marketed to professional shooters. These cameras made unobtrusive photography possible while providing an excellent negative for crisp reproduction. The Leica was the first small camera to use a "roll" of film (actually, standard motion-picture film) and was fitted with interchangeable lenses and a range finder. The Ermanox was equally efficient, although it used small glass plates, which were soon superseded by film. The small camera became merely an extra appendage, freeing the shooter to make quick judgments.

One of the chief beneficiaries of this new technology was the weekly *Berliner Illustrierte Zeitung*, then the most progressive of the early picture magazines, whose photographers elevated candid photography to high art and viable journalism. *BIZ* captured the artistic tumult and political turmoil of the 1920s and bore witness to extraordinary global events in a way unlike any other picture magazine. Its photographers— precursors of the now-pesky paparazzi—reveled in shooting candid poses of the famous and infamous. And in concert with a new breed of "photo" editor they set standards for the picture magazine built on what photographer Erich Salomon called *Bildjournalismus*, or photojournalism. In the decades that followed, *BIZ* was a model for imitators and a point of departure for innovators.

Erich Salomon fathered the candid news picture for *BIZ* and dubbed himself "photojournalist." Although a lawyer by profession, once he was bitten by the camera bug, he devoted his life to photography. By force of will, tempered by an acute understanding of the social graces, he secured entrance to the halls of government, homes of the powerful, and hideaways of the well-to-do. He devised intricate ways to capture the rich and famous unawares on film, and he published these photographs with impunity. He busted the formal traditions that the high-and-mighty found acceptable and brought mythic figures down to size. Today these images, collected in books, are vivid documents of his times.

When Salomon began shooting in the late 1920s, Kurt Szafranski was appointed editor-in-chief of *BIZ* and its sister publication, the monthly *Die Dame*. Both magazines were part of the House of Ullstein, Germany's largest periodical publisher. Salomon was already working in Ullstein's promotion department when photography became his obsession. He showed Szafranski his now-famous candid pictures of exhausted delegates to the League of Nations and was immediately awarded a contract to work for *BIZ*. Szafranski also employed other pioneers of photojournalism—Martin Munkacsi, the action photographer, and André Kertész, then a travel photographer.

Szafranski and his colleague, Kurt Korff (both of whom eventually moved to *Life* magazine in New York), were early experimenters with the essay approach—a form that required a variety of pictures and concise captions linked together to build impact and drama. According to the principle of the "Third Effect," when two pictures are brought together and positioned side by side, each picture's individual effect is enhanced by the reader's interpretative powers. This juxtaposition was sometimes possible with disparate images but usually required thematic pictures reproduced in radically different scales. Sometimes, it would be accomplished with serious conceptual photographs; at other times, novelty pictures—such as a stark close-up of a horse's head next to, say, a close crop of a similarly featured human's head—made a comic statement. Yet for all their innovation, *BIZ*'s photographic essays were usually strained juxtapositions of pictures, not stories in the truest sense. The key to success—the integration of image, idea, and words—was frequently lost amid poor and ineffectual layouts.

Münchener Illustrierte Presse, a popular Bavarian picture magazine, however, took the photograph and ran with it. Its editor and art director was a young Hungarian émigré named Stefan Lorant, who, before leaving his native Budapest in his early twenties, was already an accomplished photographer and film director. He decided to settle in Munich rather than America or England because he was fluent in German. Fortuitously, he fell into the job as assistant to the editor of *MIP* and, owing to his remarkable energy and ambition, was very soon afterward named its photo editor.

Lorant was inspired by *Berliner Illustrierte Zeitung*, yet he also understood that it had failed to use photographs as effective narrative components.

Over the course of a few years, he guided *MIP* into a realm of unique photographic endeavor. Partly through intuition, partly through basic inquisitiveness, he discerned exactly what was wanted of a picture journal and directed photographers to follow his vision. Lorant convinced Erich Salomon to contribute to *MIP* and also sought out new talents who, as he said, "not only took beautiful pictures but who had similar curiosity and journalistic savvy." An elite corps was assembled, including Felix H. Man, Georg and Tim Gidal, Umbo, Kurt Hubschmann, and Alfred Eisenstaedt (who was later hired by Henry Luce to shoot for *Life* magazine).

Lorant said that he encouraged photographers "to travel and shoot as many pictures as possible" so that he could mold an essay. Editorial space was no object; a good feature story would run for as many pages as warranted. Lorant, who was an admitted autocrat, designed the layouts himself. Although the basic layout conventions already existed, Lorant introduced certain design tropes, including what might be criticized today as excessive use of geometric borders, overlapping photographs, and silhouettes. But despite a tendency to fiddle, he acknowledged that his most successful layouts were those where he left pictures alone. He believed that when astutely edited and dramatically cropped, one striking picture reinforced the next and so furthered the narrative. He was partial to photographs that emphasized pure human expression. And one of his most famous assignments was sending Felix H. Man to spend a day with Mussolini in Rome. The photos—an exclusive—were extraordinary exposés of a day in the life of the duce in the course of his mundane acts of power. Lorant's layout focused on two key, though contrasting, features: Mussolini's rarely seen, relaxed body in the context of his charged imperial surroundings.

Although *MIP* was not devotedly partisan, total objectivity in a Weimar Germany fraught with dissonant ideologies and political violence was difficult. *MIP*'s picture exposés often focused on the darker side of Nazi rallies and leaders. It wasn't surprising, therefore, that Lorant was summarily imprisoned when Adolf Hitler assumed power in 1933. Had it not been for the persistence of his wife, a well-known German actress at the time, in obtaining his release (and the fact that he was still a Hungarian citizen), Lorant's future would have been bleak. After being released, he emigrated to England, wrote a bestselling book entitled *I Was Hitler's Prisoner*, and launched two new picture magazines: the *Weekly Illustrated* in 1934 and *Picture Post* in 1938. Between these two publishing milestones, Lorant also founded *Lilliput*, a humor magazine to rival the venerable

Punch. After the war he emigrated to the United States, where he edited documentary picture books.

During the late 1920s and 1930s, the impact of German *Bildjournalismus* had spread to many of the world's capitals, but none more so than Paris. *Paris Match* was arguably the most popular picture magazine, but the newsweekly *VU*, founded in 1928 and edited by Lucien Vogel, a photographer and publisher of *La Gazette du Bon Ton* and *Jardin des Modes*, was the most innovative in terms of the picture essay. Vogel had always been interested more in politics than in fashion and was fascinated by the power of photography to document (indeed, comment upon) current events. The early issues of the magazine had an erratic mix of politics, sports, culture, and spot news as well as carrying book excerpts about the adventures of Babar the Elephant by Vogel's brother-in-law, Jean de Brunhoff. But in later years photographers like André Kertész, Robert Capa, and Brassaï provided memorable reportage. Capa's most famous photograph, which depicted a Spanish loyalist soldier in midfall who had been hit by a fascist's bullet, was originally published in *VU*.

Vogel believed that graphic design was critical to the success of his magazine. *VU*'s logo was designed by French poster artist A. M. Cassandre while Charles Peignot, proprietor of the Deberny and Peignot Foundry, consulted on interior typography. A Russian émigré, Irene Lidova, was the first art director; beginning in 1933, her layout assistant was another Russian, Alexander Liberman. He assumed her position a few years later (and subsequently became the art director of *Vogue* and the creative director of all Condé Nast publications until his retirement in 1995).

Vogel knew the trick of how to make pictures tell a story. One of his pioneering efforts was the double-truck spread, for which a strong photograph was greatly enlarged to mammoth proportions. Pacing photos from large to small to huge to small again provided impact and surprise. Vogel had a profound influence on Liberman, who later finely tuned the journalistic photo essays in *VU*. He ascribed his ability to freely manipulate pictures to the fact that "there was no cult of photography at that time." He could edit photographs and design layouts without the kind of interference from egotistic photographers that is often tolerated today. He further spent long periods ensconced in the darkroom, projecting photos onto layout sheets, cropping and juxtaposing images. He also played with photomontage. Eventually, he took responsibility for *VU*'s covers. Vogel would often make rough sketches that Liberman would execute via photomontage (signing them "Alexandre").

By 1936, Vogel's left-wing leanings had a profound effect on *VU*'s overall content (essays excoriating the fascists became more frequent), and the magazine's bias was alienating advertisers as France was turning more vociferously toward the right. Owing to diminishing capital, Vogel was forced to sell the magazine to a right-wing businessman who kept Liberman on as managing editor for a year. Ultimately Liberman could not tolerate *VU*'s new political orientation. After his departure, the quality of *VU*'s photographic essays declined.

Photography as both information and propaganda medium did not go unnoticed by manipulators of thought and mind. Throughout Europe, and especially in Germany, the picture magazine was used to win the hearts and minds of certain constituencies. Among the most influential of these was the socialist/communist-inspired *Arbeiter-Illustrierte Zeitung* (Worker's Illustrated News), which began in 1921 as an offshoot of *Sowjet Russland im Bild* (Soviet Russia in Pictures), designed to propagate a positive image of the Bolshevik workers' paradise. *AIZ* was edited by Willi Münzenberg, who was a fervent supporter of the Russian Revolution and saw the picture magazine as a vehicle for aiding German workers in their struggle against capitalism.

When *AIZ* began, obtaining photographs that addressed workers' concerns from the leading picture agencies was difficult. Münzenberg developed a strategy to encourage societies of amateur photographers who would, in turn, become photo correspondents. In Hamburg, in 1926, he established the first Worker Photographer group, which grew into a network of viable shooters throughout Germany and the Soviet Union. He further founded a magazine called *Der Arbeiter Fotograf* (The Worker Photographer), which offered technical and ideological assistance.

Bertolt Brecht once wrote Münzenberg that "the camera can lie just like the typesetting machine. The task of *AIZ* to serve truth and reproduce real facts is of immense importance, and, it seems to me, has been achieved splendidly." Actually, while the photographs in *AIZ* were objective accounts of workers' triumphs, the layouts often served to heroicize (and therefore politicize) the activities covered. Except for its ideological orientation, *AIZ* was really no different than the Nazi counterpart, the *Illustrierte Beobachter* (founded in 1926), which employed similar photojournalistic conventions. But when the Nazis assumed power in 1933, *AIZ* was deemed contraband.

Three years earlier (1930), John Heartfield, who was then art director and copublisher of the *Malik Verlag*, had begun doing satiric photomontages (a marriage of dada and caricature) that graphically ripped the façade off Nazi leaders and functionaries. Montage was key to *AIZ* in the years of the Nazi ascendancy because, with the Worker Photographer Movement in Germany officially crushed, obtaining usable (socialist) imagery was impossible. Only through photomontage—the ironic juxtapositions of realities in the service of polemics—could the magazine continue to convey strong messages.

The last issue of *AIZ* to be published in Berlin was dated March 5, 1933; Münzenberg then moved the operation to Prague. But *AIZ* went from a circulation of 500,000 copies in Germany to around 12,000 in Prague. Attempts to circulate a smuggled miniature version into Germany were unsuccessful. In 1936 *AIZ* was renamed *Volks Illustriete*; two years later, when German occupation of Czechoslovakia was imminent, the magazine was moved to France, where it published only one issue. Until *AIZ* ceased publication in 1938, it was a satiric thorn in the side of the Nazi régime. Most of the picture stories are now forgotten, but Heartfield's photomontages are celebrated today as prime documents of agitation and protest.

AIZ influenced *USSR in Construction*, which published monthly between 1930 and 1940. Founded by Maxim Gorky, its declared editorial mission was to "reflect in photography the whole scope and variety of the construction work now going on in the USSR." Toward this aim *USSR in Construction* was published in editions of five different languages— German, English, French, Spanish, and Russian. As rotogravure magazines go, with its multiple die-cuts, inserts, and gatefolds, it was exceedingly more lush and inventive than others of its genre. The magazine employed the leading Soviet documentary photographers, including Max Alpert and Georgy Petrusive, and the most prominent graphic designers, notably Lazar El Lissitzky and Alexander Rodchenko (with Varvara Stepanova). Constructivist typographer Solomon Telingater was also brought in on occasion to design the type.

Early issues contained unremarkable pictorial sequences with expanded captions. But by 1931, when John Heartfield arrived in Moscow for an extended visit, he was invited to design an issue on the Soviet petroleum industry. His photographic cover showing oil derricks cropped on a dynamic incline was a stunning departure from the previous, somewhat bland, typographic treatments. The magazine's nameplate (or title) was composed in a dynamic manner using sans serif letters thrusting, like a gusher of oil itself, toward the sky. Heartfield showed that a graphic designer was capable of transforming the most common photographs into dramatic tableaux. Nevertheless, another two years passed before the editors allowed Lissitzky the freedom to make radical changes in layout and typography.

Both Heartfield and Lissitzky contributed something that had been missing: a sense of narrative. Lissitzky, who had been practicing book design, seamlessly integrated pictures and text and allowed generous space for mammoth blowups of documentary photos and heroic photomontages across spreads and gatefolds. Juxtaposing unaltered and manipulated images told the story of Stalin's "glorious" régime and the progress that technology and industry brought to the post-revolutionary Soviet Union. Gradually, *USSR in Construction* evolved a style of visual rhetoric characteristic of socialist realism. Maxim Gorky introduced *USSR in Construction*, pushed the boundaries of this genre, and became a paradigm of pictorial propaganda later used in magazines published in fascist Italy and Nazi Germany. Indeed many of his tropes—overlapping pictures, multiple duotones on a spread, mortised inserts—have ultimately been used in commercial catalogs and corporate annual reports. Maxim Gorky introduced the concept of "romantic realism," which addressed the idyllic future of the state. But the magazine folded during the war years and returned afterward in a smaller size and with more mundane layouts.

Photography is a uniquely viable medium (and inexhaustible art form); as practiced in these pioneer picture magazines, the journalistic photo essay is all but extinct (except in coffee-table art books). Despite the attempts of such contemporary magazines as *Double Take* and *Blind Spot*, the photography magazine, that weekly window of news and views, is an anomaly today.

| **Direction** |
| Paul Rand |
| |

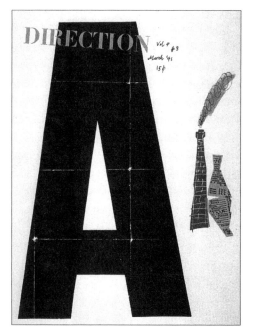

"He favors Le Corbusier's underlying philosophy . . . his avoidance of ornament, his dependence upon masses, proportions, and inherencies for success in the solution of a problem," exclaimed the October–November 1938 issue of *PM* magazine of Paul Rand (1914–1996), at twenty-four years old the leading American proponent of functional design. "Artistic tricks divert from the effect that an artist endeavors to produce, and even excellent elements, such as bullets, arrows, brackets, ornate initials, are, at best, superficial ornamentation unless logically and reasonably employed," Rand explained. But at that time these graphic accoutrements were considered soothing to most clients. So how did Rand succeed in expressing himself, and otherwise change conventional practice? The answer can be found in a series of covers designed for *Direction* magazine between 1939 and 1943.

Rand was reared in the commercial art bullpens of New York and understood the needs of American commerce. He never intended to be a radical, but from the outset of his career he had an instinctive understanding of modern painting, a passion for popular art, and a flair for wedding the two. He was harshly critical of the lack of quality in American design practice, and believed that even the most common aspects of everyday life could be enriched by an artist's touch.

Although he was enthused by the new currents in art and design, he refused to mimic or follow them blindly. Rand insisted that it was not only wrong but also "uneconomical from the aesthetic point of view" merely to borrow or separate from context without understanding the factors that brought an original into being. He further gave credence to Le Corbusier's dictum that it is necessary to understand history, "and he who understands history knows how to find continuity between that which was, that which is, and that which will be." *PM* concurred: "Rand is unhampered by traditions. . . . He has no stereotyped style because every task is something new and demands its own solution. Consequently, there is nothing labored or forced about his work."

Rand's artistic awakening came in the late 1920s at the New York Public Library where he explored the stacks and pored through volumes of *Commercial Art*, the British trade journal that published articles on the European avant-garde practitioners, including expatriate E. McKnight Kauffer. He had a second epiphany at a little magazine store adjacent to the Brooklyn Academy of Music, where in 1929 he bought his first issue of *Gebrauchsgrafik*, the most influential German advertising arts magazine ever published. It was in this periodical that Rand learned about the practice of, and the term, graphic design.

By 1938 Rand had produced enough noteworthy design that he caught the eye of Marguerite Tjader Harris, the daughter of a wealthy Connecticut munitions manufacturer. She was intent on having Rand design covers for *Direction*, an arts and culture magazine that she published on a shoestring, which featured articles by Le Corbusier, Jean Cocteau, and other avant-gardists. She offered Rand no recompense, but plenty of freedom and, ultimately, a couple of original Le Corbusier drawings. But Rand had another motive, "In a country that was used to decorative work, the common sense way to have what I was doing accepted was to do it for free," he explained.

More than any other project, the *Direction* covers exemplified the timelessness that Rand attributed to the most significant art and design. "When I designed a cover of *Direction*, I was really trying to compete with the Bauhaus. Not with Norman Rockwell," clarified Rand. "I was working in the spirit of Van Doesburg, Léger, and Picasso. It was not old fashioned. To be old fashioned is, in a way, a sin."

Each *Direction* cover illustrated a particular theme or point of view; the first, and his most politically astute, showed a map of Czechoslovakia torn in half, representing the nation's evisceration by the Nazis. Contrasted with an E. McKnight Kauffer *Direction* cover showing a realistic hand impaled by a Nazi dagger, Rand's abstract depiction was both subtle and eloquent. Rand avoided conventional propagandistic tools in favor of imagery he believed would serve as both art and message. His 1940 "Merry Christmas" cover was a visual pun that substituted barbed wire for gift wrap ribbon. Rand photographed real barbed wire against a white background lit to pick up the shadows. Little red circles made by a hole punch represented spilled blood. The barbed wire was a striking mnemonic symbol for oppression. "It pinpoints the distinction between abstract design without and abstract design with content," he insisted.

"You can be a great manipulator of form, but if the solution is not apt, it's for the birds."

The surprising juxtaposition of visual elements and universal symbols was born of necessity. Messages had to be conveyed quickly and efficiently. Since there was no budget for materials he often used handwriting instead of type for many of the covers. He even pieced together the stenciled masthead (a precursor of the stenciled IBM logo, perhaps) from letters in type catalogs. His images were often assembled from various elements. "Collages don't imitate reality," he stated. "The machine aesthetic dictated that you don't do things by hand anymore." Nevertheless, the *Direction* covers did not slavishly conform to such modern principles, and hand drawing was used on occasion.

Rand was the first to confess that these breakthrough covers were not entirely unique. "I never claimed that this was great original stuff," he confided. "Other guys in Europe were doing this kind of thing." But even though he admitted to paying homage both to Picasso and the surrealist art magazines *Verve* and *Minotaur*, Rand created a unique visual vocabulary—and a collection of memorable magazine covers—that was unlike anything being done in the United States at that time, or for a long time after.

Paperback cover art was at its high—or low, depending on your point of view—from the 1940s to early 1950s when a dozen or so New York–based reprint publishers were in fierce competition. Of all of them the Dell Book "look" was the most distinctive. Dell's innovation was the colorful locator maps that positioned each book in the city, street, house, even room in which the plot developed. The series was referred to as Mapbacks, and for little less than a decade, before the maps were replaced with conventional blurbs, they were among the most popular line of mysteries, thrillers, and romances on the market.

The Dell Publishing Company was founded as a pulp house in 1922 by George Delacorte, Jr., a twenty-eight-year-old who built an amazingly profitable business by publishing pulps, mass market magazines, and comic books. Delacorte was an astute observer of popular trends. Noting the success of Pocket Books he decided to start Dell Books around 1941. By 1943 the first editions were released. To limit his liability and ensure efficient production, he entered into a partnership with Western Printing and Lithographing Company of Racine, Illinois, one of America's largest commercial printers, whose staff selected titles, created art, and printed Dell Books while Delacorte distributed them.

Dell Books competed successfully because their covers—initially promoting crime stories by Ellery Queen, Rex Stout, Michael Shyne, and Brett Halliday, among others—had sexual allure. Although many of the wartime paperbacks used romantic realism to present seductive scenes, Dell used surrealism to suggest racy content. Sex was used, disavowed, and then used again as a marketing tool. The ebb and flow of sexual imagery was nevertheless arbitrary. Rather than using market surveys, the publishers decided on their own about how much was too much. To transcend the saucy and hard-boiled pulp aesthetic perpetuated in Delacorte's magazine division, Dell's Racine-based art director, William Strohmer, and his assistant, George Frederiksen (who also painted a number of the covers), turned to expressionistic art that used dramatic symbolism to suggest the theme or plot. The leading staff artist, Gerald Gregg, had adopted various Dali-esque conceits—fragmented body parts and floating objects—which he rendered in airbrush. His distinctive symbolic style was enhanced by the airbrush's smooth, continuous tones and the artist's preference for bright colors.

A lot of the lettering in the 1940s paperbacks resembled splash panels of comic books. Dell's lettering, exclusively hand drawn by Bernie Salbreiter, owes more to movie titles. *In Paperbacks, U.S.A.: A Graphic History, 1939–1959* (Blue Dolphin Enterprises, 1981), Piet Schreuders writes that in popular culture paperbacks fit somewhere between the comics and B-movies: "American paperbacks have had a close relationship with the Hollywood film . . . the film noir and the psychological thriller." Gregg's cover art for *Crime for a Lady*, a back view of a tiny trench-coated man whispering into an oversized woman's ear, is a comic book cliché reminiscent of B-movie posters from the 1930s and 1940s.

Dell's covers were sometimes crude and often simple. The simplicity of their imagery may have had something to do with the fact that most Dell artists never read the manuscripts. They were given titles and an oral summary of the contents, a process that was bound to result in a reliance on clichés. Although the cover concepts were based on summaries, the back covers, Dell's exclusive "cartographic fantasies" required a close reading to determine what part of the plot would be depicted and then rendered (almost exclusively) by Dell's in-house map-maker, Ruth Belew. Dell used maps as a standard feature from 1943 to 1951. They were based on the scene-of-the-crime diagrams found in tabloid newspapers.

The style that distinguished Dell Books for less than a decade ended around 1951 when the art department moved from Racine to New York. Romantic realism was prevailing in illustration, especially for magazines, and Dell's New York art director, Walter Brooks, championed the sexy realism of Robert Stanley, one of Dell's leading realist artists. He modernized the overall look by adopting sans-serif lettering and replacing maps with blurbs. These changes did not hinder sales, but they ended a special era in posterlike paperback art.

The public knows him for his animated titles for the PBS television series *Mystery!* and the sets and costumes for the Broadway productions Edward Gorey's *Dracula* and *The Mikado*. Through his numerous books and theatrical productions, Edward Gorey (1925–2000)—illustrator, author, playwright, theater and ballet set designer—has carved out a unique place in the world of arts and letters. The imaginary tableaux in his books and stage plays are replete with turn-of-the-century appointments (lace curtains in windows, marble mantelpieces, four-poster beds, vases of aspidistras, and ornate funeral urns) and peopled by a cast of eccentric and sinister gents, dames, and tykes as well as a menagerie of autochthonous hippos, birds, alligators, bats, and cats. Through his macabre crosshatched drawings and staccato linguistic rhythms, Gorey (the name is certainly appropriate) has created a world that transcends all sense of time and place. His surreal black humor is literally a study in light and dark in which the unspeakable is spoken, the unthinkable is thought, and the horrific—murder, mayhem, and unexplained disappearances—is comic.

In 1953, he published his first book, *The Unstrung Harp*, an odd thirty-page tale illustrated in a satiric Edwardian manner, about the trials and tribulations of the mythical author Clavius Frederick Earbrass, a pathetic figure in a fur coat who lives alone in a stately house full of portraits and statuettes that look exactly like him. That same year, he accepted a position in the art department of Anchor/Doubleday, where he did pasteups and lettering. He also designed about fifty book covers before leaving in 1960. These illustrated covers comprise a small but significant chapter in the history of paperback cover design and in the legacy of the white-bearded, fur-coated man who made them.

All but forgotten today, these covers established a visual personality for a company that was founded to reprint many of the world's classic texts, some of which were previously published in paperback versions during the late 1930s and 1940s, when virtually all mass-market books were adorned with prurient covers designed to pander to the voyeuristic reader. Then the style was to cover such literary classics as Tolstoy's *War and Peace* or Dostoyevsky's *Crime and Punishment* with bosomy damsels in distress, but by the late 1940s, cooler, more rational heads prevailed. In the 1950s, certain paperbacks aimed at serious readers were given more sophisticated cover art by such modern designers as Alvin Lustig, Paul Rand, Rudolph de Harak, and Leo Lionni. Gorey's covers for Anchor/Doubleday were not orthodox modern design but they were astute interpretations of the texts, handsomely designed, and smartly composed.

Gorey's involvement began inauspiciously. He had known Doubleday editors Barbara Zimmerman and Jason Epstein from his days at Harvard. He visited New York just before Christmas of 1952, when they were starting Anchor Books, and did a few freelance covers for them. In turn they offered him a job in their small art department. "At first I turned it down," Gorey recalls, "because I didn't want to live in New York. . . . So much for that. I realized that I was starving to death in Boston and took the job the next year."

Gorey was born in Chicago, where he graduated from high school in 1942. He applied to the University of Chicago, Carnegie Tech (as it was known as in those days), and Harvard. "I went to this kind of fancy, intellectually (so to speak) reputable private school in Chicago, so in those days it was fairly easy to be admitted to Harvard," he explains. "I couldn't get in now if I crawled on my hands and knees from here to Cambridge." After he was discharged from the army in January of 1946, he received his acceptance to Harvard and attended on the GI Bill. "So I trotted off to major in French, without bothering to discover whether they had a particularly good French department or not."

At that time Gorey was drawing pictures, "if that's what you want to call it," he quips about his seeming lack of motivations, "with the intent of nothing at all, I assure you. I've never had any intentions about anything. That's why I am where I am today, which is neither here nor there, in a literal sense." So he took the job in the publishing-house art department, which, he admits, wasn't too taxing. "In fact, when I saw some of the pasteups that other people did, I thought that these well-known artists [like Ben Shahn and others who did covers] really were all thumbs. I never had much patience with having to redo other people's pasteups, which looked like they'd just flung the lettering on the page."

In addition to this menial work, he designed covers. His first, *Lafcadio's Adventures* by André Gide, revealed Gorey's aptitude for classical drawing with an idiosyncratic twist. The style was rooted in nineteenth-century representationalism but was not so easily pigeonholed into a specific time frame. His second cover was what he describes as "a kind of tacky little drawing of the Globe Theater from the air, which I found someplace and copied for a book on Shakespeare by Mark van Doren." In addition to the linear drawing style, Gorey's finished lettering looked as though it were a comp or a sketch of hand lettering that approximated real type. At that time, paperbacks either had calligraphic or typeset covers, but Gorey's style was betwixt and between: "I was stuck with hand lettering, which I did very poorly, I always felt—but everybody seemed to like it," he says. In fact, when he published his own books, all except the first were hand-lettered in the manner of his earlier book jackets.

Gorey was not the first to employ hand-drawn letters. Paul Rand initiated the practice because typesetting was too expensive and deducted from his overall fee; hand lettering ultimately became a defining characteristic of his book-cover design. Gorey was not concerned with the costs; rather, "I didn't really know too much about type in those days, and it was simply easier to hand-letter the whole thing than to spec type. Eventually, though, I did a lot of things that weren't hand-lettered, as far as book jackets were concerned." But lettering became a trademark of his own work, and he also rendered it for other designers who, he says jokingly, "were even less competent in lettering than I was."

In addition to his regular diet of French literature, he also enjoyed reading British novels and had an admiration for British book-jacket illustration, which influenced his overall style. A voracious reader his entire life—"I was much better-read than most of the people who were doing artwork"—Gorey did not, however, do a lot of preparation for his covers. "I was usually handed the assignment, and there would be some little paragraph summarizing the plot," he explains. It rarely mattered anyway, since his style was so individual that the covers themselves did not illustrate the respective plots as much as they evoked moods.

Gorey developed stylistic and compositional conceits that recur throughout this work. "There were certain kinds of books where I followed a routine," he admits, "such as my famous landscape, which was mostly sky so I could fit in a title. Things like *A Hero of Our Time* by Mikhail Lermontov, *Victory* by Joseph Conrad, and *The Wanderer* by Henri Alain-Fournier tend to have low-lying landscapes, a lot of sky, sort of odd colors, and tiny figures that I didn't have to draw very hard." He also maintained a muted and earthy color palette—rather surprising, given that paperback convention demanded covers that were miniposters, able to grab a reader's eye in an instant. Explaining his palette, he says, "It was partly because you had to keep it to three [flat] colors, plus black. I guess I could have picked bright reds or blues, but I've never been much for that. My palette seems to be sort of lavender, lemon yellow, olive green, and then a whole series of absolutely no colors at all." One of these so-called no-color covers was

Gorey's interpretation for Kafka's *Amerika*, which shows a Goreyesque character—an almost-skeletal silhouette standing on the closely cropped deck of a ship entering New York harbor. With only a hint of pink in the clouds, this otherwise-dark, lugubrious image is not the typical prequel for Kafka's critical vision of America but rather a snapshot of every new immigrant's fears upon entering a strange land.

For someone who professed not to know where he was going professionally, Gorey's covers reveal a skillful and unique sense of composition. He created not only a strong identity for Anchor but also memorable icons for the books themselves, regardless of his opinion about their contents. Notable is his work for the Henry James novels published by Anchor, which Gorey insists was "all a mistake" because this is one author "whom I hate more than anybody else in the world except for Picasso. I've read everything of Henry James, some of it twice, and every time I do it I think, 'Why am I doing this again? Why am I torturing myself?' Everybody thought how sensitive I was to Henry James, and I thought, 'Oh sure, kids.' If it's because I hate him so much, that's probably true."

Most of Gorey's work was illustrative, but for a few books he designed only lettered covers (what he insists on calling "tacky hand-lettering"). One such was Kierkegaard's *Either/Or*. The reason, he admitted, was fairly simple. "Was I planning to sit down and read Kierkegaard at that point? No, I wasn't! And it wouldn't have helped if I had, I'm sure. I probably would have been completely paralyzed."

Gorey left Anchor in 1960 when Jason Epstein started the Looking-Glass Library with Celia Carroll. "The idea was that it was going to do for children's books what Anchor had done for the parents," he explains. "The books were not paperbacks but rather paper-over-boards, and it was really quite a good series. Well, the paper was perfectly dreadful, but, then, the paper for everything in those days was perfectly terrible." Gorey illustrated a few books, including *War of the Worlds* ("the less said about those, the better"); he was both art director and an editor. The books conformed to Gorey's taste in nineteenth-century British literature, including *Spider's Palace* by Richard Hughes and *Countess Kade* by Charlotte M. Young. After two years the imprint folded and Gorey moved more into his own realms.

The drawings for his stories and books (many of which are anthologized in his three *Amphigorey* collections or archived at the Gotham Book Mart in New York City) are rooted in the visual language that developed while designing covers for Anchor/Doubleday. These covers are, therefore, artifacts from both a transitional period in paperback history and the formative years of Gorey's unique career.

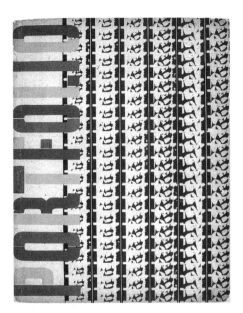

Portfolio, published between 1949 and 1951, was the model of a twentieth-century graphic and industrial arts magazine. It elevated design and set the standard of magazine layout that few publications then or now could equal. "The format itself should be a graphic experience," editor Frank Zachary explained. The hefty nine-by-twelve-inch periodical designed by Alexey Brodovitch (1898–1971) incorporated special inserts, including shopping bags, wallpaper, and three-dimensional glasses. And publisher George Rosenthal, Jr., spared no expense in buying the best paper and the best of everything else.

"Then we decided to sell advertising," recalled Zachary. "Well, we hated the ads we got. So we said, 'Hell, we're not going to mar our beautiful magazine with crummy ads.' We were terribly idealistic." Void of such visual encumbrances, *Portfolio* was a hybrid, part book and part magazine. A subscription cost twelve dollars a year for four issues and a few thousand people subscribed. Rosenthal handled the finances, while Zachary developed the writers. He also collected all the photographs and illustrations for the stories.

Convention dictated that magazine covers be pictorial. But the first issue of *Portfolio* was like no other; it was type design, transparent process-color squares printed over the *Portfolio* logo which was dropped out of black. Like a main title for a motion picture, the cover introduced the cinematic interior. Brodovitch, the acclaimed art director for *Harper's Bazaar*, who introduced the new photography to fashion magazines, paced his layouts as though they were storyboards for films. The key to success was dynamic juxtapositions: big and small, bold and quiet, type and pictorial. Brodovitch splayed comps out on the floor, mixing and matching, moving pages and entire stories around as needed.

Zachary planned the issues with Brodovitch at his office at *Harper's Bazaar*. "We got along very well because I let him have his head,"

Zachary recalled. "But he was no prima donna. He worked in the most fantastic way. For example, I would come in, say, at seven o'clock in the evening with the idea of how many pages we had for an issue, and how many would be devoted to each story. I would come back [the next day], and Holy Christ, there was this magnificent layout. He used the photostat machine like a note pad. He would get stats of every photo, often different sizes of the same piece, in tiny increments that might vary from a quarter inch to an inch, or from an inch to two inches, and so on. You would see him surrounded by all these stats. But as he put them down, my God, all of a sudden a spread materialized beautifully proportioned, everything in scale, with just the right amount of white space, type and picture mass. I learned so many nuances of art directing just from watching him."

Portfolio premiered in late 1949 and lasted for only three issues. During this time, Zachary was also editor of *Jazzways*, a one-shot magazine on the folkways of jazz. The cover was designed by Paul Rand and among the interior photographers was Berenice Abbott. In addition Zachary and Rosenthal published paperback photo albums under the Zebra Books imprint. These were the first of their kind to present good photojournalistic portfolios for just twenty-five cents. The titles included *Murder Incorporated*, the first book on the Mafia; *Life and Death in Hollywood*, a pre–Kenneth Anger look at the foibles of the glitter capital; and *Naked City*, the first collection of pictures by famed New York street photographer Weegee. Each sold between 150,000 and 250,000 copies with all profits poured back into *Portfolio*.

The third and last issue of *Portfolio* was its most beautiful. To underscore Brodovitch's concept of this magazine as analog to film, the cover for #3 was the image of a film strip. But the dream of an ad-less magazine had turned into a nightmare. Financial problems did not weaken Zachary's resolve to publish (he even approached Henry Luce, publisher of *Time* and *Life*, to buy the magazine). But in 1951 the prime financial backer, George Rosenthal, Sr., decided to summarily kill *Portfolio* rather than incur further losses. Had it continued who knows what impact *Portfolio* would have had on magazines of the era. More than fifty years have passed and this special magazine is a landmark of design history.

A design icon doesn't come along every day. To be so considered it must not only transcend its function and stand the test of time, but also must represent the time in which it was produced. The cover of *Industrial Design*, Vol. 1, No. 1, February 1954, was not just the emblem of a new publishing venture, but a testament to one man's modernism; one of the last works created by Alvin Lustig (1915–1955), who suffered an untimely death from diabetes in 1955 at the age of forty.

Despite failing vision, Lustig was deeply involved in the design of the first two and nominally with the third issues of the magazine as art editor, art director, and art consultant, respectively. He saw his role as the framer of ideas that were visual in nature. Although he never had the chance to develop his basic design concepts further, he left behind a modern design icon, the cover, and a format that continued to define the magazine for years after.

Industrial Design was the brainchild of publisher Charles Whitney, who also published the successful *Interiors*. In 1953 he was convinced by his friend and advisor George Nelson that the time was right to introduce a specialized periodical devoted to practitioners of this burgeoning field. *Interiors* already featured its own industrial design column that had evolved into a discrete section, which Whitney realized had commercial potential as a spin-off. *Interiors* was also so beautifully designed that *Industrial Design* could have no less than the visual panache of a coffee table book/magazine, replete with foldouts and slipsheets, not unlike the legendary design magazine *Portfolio*, published between 1949 and 1951. To accomplish this an eminent art director was sought. This was the age of great magazine art directors—including Alexey Brodovitch, Alexander Liberman, Otto Storch, Cipe Pineles, and Alan Hurlburt—and Whitney fervently believed that a magazine's design would be the deciding factor in its success. Hence Lustig was entrusted with considerable authority to design the magazine as he saw fit.

On the editorial side, however, Whitney decided to take a calculated risk by promoting two young *Interiors* associate editors to co-editors of *Industrial Design*. Jane Fisk (now Jane Thompson of the architectural firm Thompson and Wood in Cambridge) and Deborah Allen may have been inexperienced in the field of industrial design but nevertheless had a clear plan to introduce a distinctly journalistic sensibility into professional publishing that emphasized criticism and analysis rather than the puff pieces common to the genre. As it turned out, this became a point of philosophical contention between the designer and editors.

If they had a choice the editors would have preferred an art director who, as Thompson explained, "would have been in the trenches with us," a team player with journalistic instincts rather than a distant presence with a formalist sensibility. Because Lustig designed the initial dummy and subsequent two issues in his own studio and returned with the completed layouts to the editorial offices, he had made certain assumptions about the presentation of content that were often inconsistent with the editors' vision. "We did not want the words to be gray space, we wanted them to have meaning," recalled Thompson about wanting more spontaneous design responses to the material. But instead of being journalistically intuitive, Lustig imposed his formal preconceptions and designed the magazine as he would a book.

Blocks of text type were indeed used as gray matter to frame an abundance of precisely silhouetted photographs. But if there was a problem it was more in the editors' minds than Lustig's design. While it was not as journalistically paced as say, *Life* magazine, *Industrial Design* was respectfully, indeed elegantly neutral, allowing for a wide range of material to be presented without interference. Moreover, it was what Whitney wanted, so the editors reconciled themselves to building the magazine's editorial reputation through informative features written by authors not previously associated with trade publishing.

Thompson nevertheless hated the first cover with its tight grid and silhouetted photographs. Instead she wanted to disrupt the design purity with a few well-composed coverlines. She further favored a conceptual method of intersecting photography and text, resulting in an editorial idea, not a pure design. Lustig thought coverlines would sully the design and intersecting ideas would be too contrived. Years later, Thompson grudgingly admitted that maybe Lustig's judgment was wiser: "He wanted to make a strong simple statement, which he believed (perhaps erroneously since *Industrial Design* did not have to compete on the newsstand) had to stand up against the covers of the elegant fashion magazines." Lustig's design set the standard for future covers, and his successor, Martin Rosensweig, continued to produce covers for a few years afterward that more rigidly adhered to the same formal practices.

Despite these creative tensions, the early issues of *Industrial Design* reveal a shift in the nature of professional publishing from a trade to cultural orientation that was in no small way underscored by Lustig's classically modern design.

Holiday
Frank Zachary

When it began in the 1930s, *Holiday* magazine was clean and orderly, but its layout was made with a cookie cutter. In 1955 Frank Zachary (b. 1919), former editor of *Portfolio*, who had learned art direction from Alexey Brodovitch, changed all that. Zachary began as photo editor, but when he worked with pictures he made layouts that were not just picture spreads in the conventional sense, but cinematic presentations in the Brodovitch tradition. Noting a dramatic difference, *Holiday*'s editor, Ted Patrick, offered Zachary the job of art director. "Jesus, Ted," responded Zachary to the offer, "I'm okay, but why don't you try to get Brodovitch? He's the real master." Zachary introduced Patrick to Brodovitch, but the two did not hit it off.

Zachary knew little about typography, but he did have experience laying out the pictures in Zebra Books—small thematic pictorial mass-market paperbacks—that taught him the importance of scale. He saw himself as a journalist, not a designer per se, more interested in using the photograph to tell the story than to prettify a page. "I learned the picture is the layout. If you have a great picture, you don't embellish it with big type. You make it tight and sweet," he said. Soon he developed a cadre of talented photographers who brought life to the magazine through thematic picture essays. Among them were Arnold Newman, Tom Hollyman, John Lewis Stage, Robert Phillips, Fred Maroon, and Slim Aarons, many of whom followed Zachary years later when he became editor-in-chief of *Town and Country*.

Photography was the heart of *Holiday*, illustration was its soul. Zachary rejected the prevailing sentimental illustrative approaches used in most American magazines; he eyed European artists, specifically from England and France, for their surrealistic comic vision. "Frank brought sophisticated illustration to American magazines," recalled a colleague. "Other art directors brought powerful or clever images, but Frank brought an unprecedented sophistication. Of course it came from Europe since in the early 1950s there weren't too many Americans practicing sophisticated pen work."

Through *Holiday*, the artists Ronald Searle, Andre François, Roland Topor, Domenico Gnoli, George Guisti, and Edward Gorey (one of the few native Americans) were given latitude to develop their own picture essays and portfolios. Zachary avoided the reigning stars—"that would be too easy," he argued—but rather discovered his own galaxy. In most cases the artists transformed themselves in this environment. "Frank gave me a lot of firsts," recalled Ronald Searle. "From around 1959 to 1969 he gave me all the space one could dream of, the chance to fill it with color, the freedom to travel, and what proved to be the last of the great venues for reportage. Off to Alaska! Cover all of Canada! Bring me ten pages on the dirty bits of Hamburg! No expense spared. The years of travel for Frank gave me experience that cannot be bought. There was only one problem, he always called me 'Arnold' instead of Ronald. Then he probably always called [photographer] Arnold Newman 'Ronald,' so it balanced out."

Zachary developed what he called "environmental portraiture," common in contemporary magazines but unique in the early 1950s. "I would say to a photographer, 'If a guy is a multimillionaire painter, I want to see a whole lot of his paintings in the background and on top of that I want to see his castle in the background, too.' A photographer just couldn't walk in and take a picture of a subject; he had to assemble the components of the subject's life," explains Zachary. An example of environmental portraiture is a photograph for a special issue of *Holiday* on New York City showing highways and parks czar and power-broker Robert Moses standing omnipotently on a red girder over the East River. The shot illustrates Zachary's willingness to expend a tremendous amount of effort to photograph one perfect image. That is what defined his remarkable art direction.

Alexander Liberman

For Alexander Liberman (1912–1999), the Russian-born art director of *Vogue* and later editorial director of Condé Nast from 1942 to 1995, design was a means. Making elegant layouts was never an end. Nor was it his métier. "Elegance was [Alexey] Brodovitch's strong point," Liberman exclaimed in the authorized biography *Alex: The Life of Alexander Liberman* (Alfred A. Knopf, 1995), "The page looked very attractive. But in a way, it seemed to me that Brodovitch was serving the same purpose that [M. F.] Agha [art director of *Vogue*] had served, which was to make the magazine attractive to women—not interesting to women." Liberman wanted to break the design obsession, "so I defended a more journalistic approach—rougher lettering, no white space, crowded pages, messier layouts." Some of the more elegant layouts in *Vogue* throughout the 1950s (the ones that are celebrated in the Art Directors Club annuals) were either designed by his associate Pricilla Peck or produced in spite of himself because *Vogue*'s editor-in-chief, Edna Chase, was not interested in messy layouts. "He was tilting at windmills," argued biographers Dodie Kazanjian and Calvin Tompkins about his preference for tabloid-styled typography.

Liberman became a layout man in 1933 for *VU*, the illustrated French weekly, where he worked with photojournalists such as André Kertész, Robert Capa, and Brassaï. They had not yet become the great photographers or as Liberman said: "There was no cult of photography at that time." But with them he learned how to effectively lay out tension-packed visual essays. In 1940 Lucien Vogel, the creator of *VU*, had come to America to work with Condé Nast and urged the publisher to bring Liberman to America as well. Upon arriving he did layouts for *Vogue* (at fifty dollars a week), until one day Agha unceremoniously fired him. "That was on Friday," Liberman recalled. "On Monday Condé Nast asked to see me, not knowing I had been fired. I brought my gold medal [which he received for an exhibition design in the Paris World's Fair of 1937], and we talked." At the time Nast was fighting against the clichés of fashion presentation, such as obscure typography and strange handwritten titles. Nast admired the newly started *Life* magazine and wanted *Vogue* to be more modern, in fact, more like a newsmagazine. "So when he learned from Vogel that I had been involved with a newsmagazine he was very excited . . ." continued Liberman. "He said 'a man like you must be on *Vogue*.' He asked Agha to come in and said 'I want Liberman on *Vogue*.' Since Condé was an absolute monarch, Agha never told him he had fired me."

Liberman's success was further guaranteed not just because Nast valued the young Liberman's judgment, but also because he was taken under the wing of the former editor of *Vanity Fair*, Frank Crowninshield, who, since the demise of his own magazine had been the fine arts consultant editor of *Vogue*. One day during Liberman's first month on the job he was playing with a Horst photograph of a girl in a bathing suit lying on her back balancing a beach ball on her feet. He substituted the O in *Vogue* for the ball, which had no fixed logo in those days. "Crowninshield happened to be walking through the art department . . . he stopped to look at Alex's design, which impressed him enormously," wrote Kazanjian and Tompkins. "'There's a genius in the art department,' he told Nast."

In those days fashion plates were photographed in their hats and "royal robes." The main *Vogue* pages were created in Paris and arrived in New York entirely laid out. When Liberman was appointed *Vogue*'s art director in 1942 he rebelled against Parisian dominance. "I had always resented the fussy, feminine, condescending approach to women by women's magazines," he asserted. "I thought it was important to shake up this rather somnolent society. If we had to show hats, I tried to mix hats with contemporary life." He also introduced art into fashion photography, and had Cecil Beaton photograph a model in front of some Jackson Pollock paintings. He admired the lack of artifice in photographs by portraitists Nadar, Atget, and August Sander. "Fortunately, Irving Penn came into my life," Liberman boasted. "He worked as an assistant with me in the art department on design and layout until one day I said, 'Why don't you go and take the picture.'"

Clarity and strength of communication are what interested Liberman. He admitted that graphic design for its own sake was meaningless, and was never so "sensitized to type" that a sixteenth of a millimeter spacing mattered. He rejected fancy typefaces and in 1947 changed the logo of *Vogue* from an elegant Bodoni to Franklin Gothic, which he claims until then was only used in newspapers. "I thought it had strength and looked modern. All the captions and the titles were set in Franklin Gothic, which was then revolutionary in women's publications."

"[I]mperfection was the essence of what Liberman was looking for—the breakthrough from fantasy and artifice into the here-and-now," wrote Kazanjian and Tompkins. "It was the antidote to the 'visions of loveliness' that Mrs. Chase and generations of *Vogue* readers cherished—visions that Alex wanted to banish forever from the pages of *Vogue*, in part because he felt that they were demeaning to women. *Vogue* was not really about fashion, he always said; it was about women."

Like Brodovitch, Liberman focused his creative energy on photography; he encouraged many women photographers to enter a field largely dominated by men. Liberman urged *Vogue*'s editors to publish photographs of Dachau concentration camp by Lee Miller, a former model who learned photography from Man Ray. "Nobody realizes that *Vogue* published them," he related. "But for me this was practically a justification for being on *Vogue*." For Liberman the lessons of Lee Miller's and Cecil Beaton's war photography changed the style of fashion photography. News photography in general and the emergence of a daring paparazzi forced a rethinking at *Vogue* that exceeded the boundaries of visual presentation. "I've always felt that *Vogue* was one of the strong pioneers for democratization, for women's rights, and for breaking down false cultural values," asserted Liberman.

Like Brodovitch, Liberman shared the belief that cinematic pacing was the visual backbone of a magazine. However, Brodovitch saw photography as an art form while Liberman believed that "photographs . . . were documents—momentary glimpses of something that could be printed in ink on a magazine page and eventually discarded. That was their function and their fate," wrote Kazanjian and Tompkins. Liberman made layout sequences the way a film is cut, trying to communicate moods through narrative imagery. "I hate white space because white space is an old album tradition," he charged. "I need to be immersed in the subject matter."

Liberman's approach has been subjected to harsh criticism from other designers who argue that his contempt for design has lowered the standards of magazine layout. But his anti-design fervor was sincere, and his disgust for anything that was visually flabby and antediluvian influenced all the magazines he touched. The most significant change in *Vogue* from the 1960s to the 1980s was its shift from bold elegance to striking sensationalism. Reversed type and other strong typographic devices (such as torn edges and screaming headlines) borrowed from the sensationalist press were used to accentuate motion, catch the eye, and communicate the message. "Much bolder type is intended for faster communication," explained Liberman. "White space does not exist, but a certain power, a daring has emerged that wasn't there even when I first used Franklin Gothic. In retrospect it seems dainty."

Scope
Will Burtin

Bacteriology is about as interesting to graphic designers as typography is to bacteriologists. But for graphic designer Will Burtin (1908–1972), German-born son of a French chemist, learning to understand molecular biology, endocrinology, and bacteriology was like working with a classic cut of Didot or Bodoni. Making such complex data accessible to himself and others was as pleasurable as designing an elegant page of text. The role of the graphic designer, he wrote in *Print* (May 1955), was to increase the average man's understanding "between what the reading public knows and what it should know."

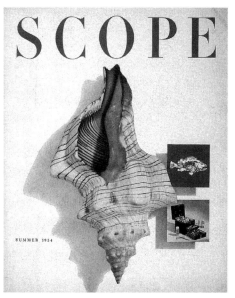

His professional life was, therefore, devoted to designing the kind of information that decorative designers reject as humdrum. Indeed such technical material might have remained forever ignored by aesthetics, relegated to dry textbooks, if Burtin had not become the champion of beautiful functionality. As design consultant for the Upjohn Company— one of America's largest producers of pharmaceuticals—from 1948 to 1971, he made functional design as attractive as any book or poster. Burtin refused to shy away from complexity, rather he interpreted it and then cast it in an accessible light. This was evident in the layouts and covers he designed while art editor for *Scope*, Upjohn's scientific house organ.

Burtin, who left Hitler's Germany in 1939 after being ordered to design posters for the Nazis, adopted Thomas Jefferson's dictum, "To learn how to keep learning is the mark of civilized man." He believed that designers had to know about more fields than just design, and among the ones he embraced, science was integral to every area of human activity. Science, the exploration and prediction of phenomena, is the holy grail of civilization, and for the sake of clarity scientists reduce time, space, and thought into abstract symbols. "The designer stands between these concepts, at the center, because of his unique role as communicator . . . interpreter, and inspirer," Burtin wrote in *Graphis* #4 (1949).

In this sense Burtin and Upjohn were the perfect match. His graphics for their advertisements, catalogs, and *Scope* were rooted in simplicity and directness with emphasis on the message. But Burtin imbued each piece with unique attributes that identified the work as his own. "Integration" was his mantra. It was also the defining trait of his graphic signature. "In designing booklets, posters, ads, exhibits, and displays, I noticed that the integration of job components towards a dramatic end-product asked for a measure of discipline difficult to define," he wrote. But he defined it as the marriage of order and instinct—learning everything there is about a particular subject and then allowing instinct to drive the design. In 1948 he designed an exhibition for the AD Gallery, entitled "Integration: New Discipline in Art," which demonstrated how he, and by extension others, clarify scientific information for general consumption. "Understanding of space and time relations is a main requirement in visual organization. In printed design images are superimposed on paper surfaces. The spaces inside and between letters, between lines of type, their relationship to illustration, are vital factors, which determine the eye's access to the basic information," he explained in terms that added a scientific dimension to graphic design.

Preoccupation with the graphic communication of scientific phenomenon and theory dominated Burtin's practice. As art director of *Fortune* from 1945 to 1949 he developed a vocabulary for conveying information through the design of charts, maps, graphs, and diagrams that made complex data discernible and understandable. Ladislav Sutnar noted in *Visual Design in Action* (Hastings House, 1961) that Burtin developed two basic approaches: The purist, where charts and diagrams were compressed into a two-dimensional projection, with color used to facilitate understanding; and the dramatized approach, the grouping of visual data with poster-like impact as in a chart describing how cosmic ray trajectories bombarded the earth. For this Burtin used airbrush to transform a photograph of the globe into a scientific diagram so concise and beautiful that it functioned both as art and information. This was the foundation on which he built even more intricate, yet no less accessible, graphics for *Scope*.

"Who said that science cannot achieve beauty," Burtin argued in *Print*. "What nonsense, that art cannot contain scientific truth! It is human limitation, deficiency of understanding, that make one or the other not do what they can do." Much like Leonardo da Vinci, Burtin asserted that art was the queen of sciences, a means of obtaining knowledge and communicating it to all generations. Being a designer was being a scientist. Design was about clarity, not sterility, and *Scope* was the embodiment of this goal. Originally designed by Lester Beall, *Scope* already had a modern format; its type was elegant and the graphics were sprinkled with signposts that guided the viewer through a hierarchy of information. Burtin took this to an even greater level of virtuosity. Edited for physicians, *Scope* was intended to improve the understanding of modern therapeutics, establish goodwill, and help sell Upjohn's products, yet Burtin gave it entry points that allowed access to the average reader, as well. It is no wonder that Burtin's mastery at translating tough scientific concepts—the ability to transform technical language into visual symbols—afforded readers a clear grasp of the material.

For the professional reader, arcane medical articles were not cluttered with dreary text boxes and drab flow charts. "The choice of format was . . . of great importance, not only to give the new journal the distinction we wished it to have but to appeal appropriately to the physician," explained Burtin in *Print*. The house organs already in existence ran the gamut in design from the most conservative to the most modern, and from those that used design sparingly to those that were highly and almost flamboyantly ornamental. Since conservatism was inappropriate for a journal devoted to a rapidly progressing science, contemporaneousness of design seemed mandatory but frivolousness seemed out of place. Burtin's designs were conceptually acute and couched in an idiom that was scientific in its clarity. His use of photographs of microscopic imagery gave the work an abstract quality that suggested modern art. And in the modern spirit, design was not used for its decorative effect but as an integral part of the scientific presentations. Even the covers of *Scope* were designed not only to be attractive, but also to suggest the content. Inspired by contemporary art, the visually poetic collages and montages echoed formal elements of modern plastic art. In so doing Burtin developed a visual method that influenced how the pharmaceutical industry approached advertising and promotion for years to follow.

Herald Tribune

Peter Palazzo

Good newspaper design was rare in 1963. Most dailies were composed by a makeup desk, not an art director or designer. At the end of the day or night after the "lockup," as it was called, a more or less logically ordered newspaper was printed and delivered. The *New York Herald Tribune* was the exception to that rule.

Founded in 1924, the *Trib* was as drab as the "Old Gray Lady," the *New York Times*. Then, in 1963 it was miraculously transformed into something modern. It sported a livelier front page—not a typical presentation of news stories set in monotonous straight vertical columns, but a menu of appetizing world, national, and local events. It ran a unique summary of the paper's contents on the front page: a column of flush left/ ragged right type with Bodoni subheads that introduced as many as eight separate items stretching down the left side of the page. Slightly wider columns and gutters throughout the paper made it more legible when contrasted to the tightly packed, eight-column *New York Times*. The headline typefaces were more consistent than in other newspapers. The photographs were noticeably larger, too. And most importantly, there were many clearer entry points into stories.

The *Trib*'s makeover gave it a visual cohesiveness that allowed smooth navigation through the mass of information. It was a counterpoint to the screaming headlines and seemingly arbitrary layouts of the tabloids. The design was actually so "friendly," that readers initially complained that they couldn't take it seriously. But that didn't last long.

The new *Trib* was the work of Peter Palazzo (b. 1932), an advertising and publications designer who shoved American newspapers into the late twentieth century by enhancing news presentation through journalistic design. Not a single design element was superfluous, each was a signpost that guided the reader through the traffic of a daily newspaper. Prefiguring today's information glut, the *Trib* announced that design would have to play a meaningful role in the communication of ideas.

The daily *Herald Tribune* was revolutionary, but the rebirth of the Sunday paper was even more remarkable. The *Trib's Book World* and *New York* magazine were the prototypes of the modern newspaper supplement. Although the Sunday *New York Times* was stuffed with various sections and supplements, its makeup lacked a defining character. Conversely, Palazzo's *Book World* was typographically elegant—even to the untutored eye. He rejected the *Times*'s bland visual diet of famous works of art and stock author's photographs in favor of imaginative illustrations by contemporary illustrators. These portraits, caricatures, and conceptual spots were entry points providing access to the sometimes dense literary criticism. They also synthesized, galvanized, and made accessible complex ideas. Although the black-and-white line made them reminiscent of nineteenth-century book illustrations (e.g., Tenniel's for *Alice in Wonderland*), they were not nostalgic interpretations of bygone themes.

The original *New York* magazine published as the Sunday supplement of the *Trib* was another milestone. There had been magazine supplements in most Sunday newspapers dating back to the early 1900s. But *New York*'s seamless marriage of editorial and visual ideas was unprecedented. It gave birth to both the "new journalism" (first-person reportage) and a new graphic journalism (smartly packaged information and visual essays). Typified by generous white space (unusual in newspapers), elegantly unobtrusive Caslon typography, gritty photography, and conceptual illustration, *New York* was a "slick" magazine on newsprint. Its covers defined a new fashion: many of the images were ordinary yet felt extraordinary through cropping and scale. The covers were single images often of a typical New York scene, rather than illustrating a story inside. A typical cover, a close-up of an everyday parking meter, was simple, memorable, and so New York. The celebration of the mundane object was consistent with trends in pop art.

Palazzo also transformed the "fronts" of all the other Sunday news sections so that they were designed like magazines. Photographs and illustrations were large, but rooted in good news judgment. Each section had a distinct look, while conforming to the whole. Palazzo orchestrated a presentation that neither fought with nor trivialized the news.

Unfortunately the new *Trib* did not last long. In 1963 a crippling newspaper strike forced an unhappy merger between three papers, the *Trib*, the *New York World*, and the *Journal American*, resulting in the *World Journal Tribune*. Although rooted in the design principles of the *Trib*, the trifurcated daily failed to garner a sizable audience and did not survive for long. In its wake, the *New York Times* began its makeover, and other newspapers followed suit. Yet in the beginning the *New York Herald Tribune* stood alone but influenced many.

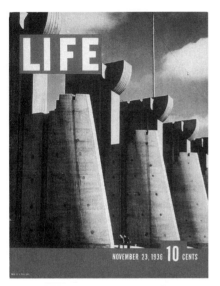

Life magazine was born during a period of sweeping social and political change, and quickly became the eyes and conscience of its continually expanding readership. Few magazines captured the world through such a powerful lens. No other picture magazine—certainly neither *Look* nor *Colliers*—could guide (or mold) the average American's perceptions of the world, nation, and neighborhood. *Life*'s photo essays alternately celebrated individual courage, attacked tyranny, praised technology and science, and focused on the trivial, superficial, and ephemeral sides of life. Publisher Henry R. Luce described photography as "a new language, difficult, as yet unmastered, but incredibly powerful"—the most important machine age communications medium because it offered an objective window on the world. Yet *Life*'s pictures were mastered and managed by photo editors who saw the importance of manipulating gesture and nuance. Before television no other medium reached as many individuals at once; and for decades no magazine stamped the collective consciousness with as many indelible images.

For all its influence, however, *Life* was not an original idea. Even its title belonged to a fifty-seven-year-old New York humor magazine whose publisher greedily held on to it until declining sales forced him to sell its name for $92,000 in 1936. The buyer was thirty-eight-year-old Henry R. Luce, cofounder of *Time* and *Fortune*. By the early thirties the idea of starting an American picture magazine was definitely in the air. Publishers like Condé Nast and the Cowles Brothers (who published the first issue of *Look* a month after *Life*'s premiere) were contemplating their own. Luce aspired to develop a suitable theater for photographs long before he founded *Life*. *Fortune* was the inadvertent rehearsal. With *Fortune* Luce wanted to make the "most beautiful magazine in the world," but not a photography magazine per se. Nevertheless a key component of *Fortune*'s visual personality was striking still-life and journalistic photographs by Margaret Bourke White, Erich Salomon, and Edward Steichen.

The first complete, though unprinted, total dummy of what would become *Life* was produced in February 1936; it was designed to be a sixteen-page picture supplement for *Time*. The contents included features on skating champion Sonja Henie, Mexican politics, Czech president Eduard Benes, young Katharine Hepburn, the queen of England, and a variety of other views. This was the first clear definition of what would become *Life*.

The dummy was not greeted with praise. Paul Hollister, a top advertising executive at Macy's and self-described graphics expert, was disappointed with the design of the dummy. When he received a copy he had the temerity to write Luce a harsh critique: "It is inconceivable that even an avowed dress-rehearsal just for 'fun' should have turned out so far short . . . Great God—that a magazine should make even a tentative peek looking like this. . . . The dangerous thing is you have good raw material; it must not be butchered." Instead of earning Luce's rancor, Hollister's candor earned him the job of revamping the dummy. "My task," he later related "was to make a better pattern of each page, conforming to a total 'basic format' character: to 'sell' each page for itself, each picture within that pattern; to suggest changes of pace; to clean up margins and gutters; to eliminate sloppy disturbances and tricks from the page." After spending the ten days of his vacation cutting and pasting, he delivered an accordion-folded dummy that when spread out revealed the entire format at a glance. Luce did not respond for two weeks, but when he did he invited Hollister to lunch and reportedly said in front of his executives: "Good! Now we have an editorial prospectus! Now we have a basic format. . . . Now what do we do?" Hollister's reply was a profoundly condescending characterization of art directors:

What you do is get an art director and put him at a drawing board. Put tire tape over his mouth, because whatever he has to state should drain off through his fingers onto paper. Never let an art director talk.

On a table at his left put your basic format dummy for reference. On a table at his right feed him batches of photographs, with a note saying you want one, two, four, eight—any number of pictures you need, for each batch, and any suggestions you have for playing up any particular angles of the picture story.

So he makes layouts from the pictures.

If they are right, you pat him on the head. If they have strayed from the mood of the basic format, you take a small hammer, which you have chained to the wall for the purpose, rap him smartly over the skull, point severely to the basic format dummy—cry "No, no, no! Naughty!" He then repents and makes the layout right, or you get yourself a new art director.

At Hollister's urging Howard Richmond, Macy's chief designer, became the first art director of *Life*. With Richmond on the layout board, the second dummy was published for the week ending September 25, 1936. The content and design were closer to what would become *Life*'s trademark design until the 1960s: a loose grid noted for varied and often unattractive gothic typography. There appeared to be a conscious rejection of design nuances in favor of a jumbled tabloid look. And yet the layout seemed to be appropriate for the stark black-and-white photography on disturbing subjects, such as: "Hitler Speaks," about the pageantry of a Nuremberg Rally; "Cotton Pickin'," about the squalid conditions of Southern black laborers; and "Seen in Catalonia," about the horrors of the Spanish Civil War. Reviews came in quickly, and many were harsh even within the *Time* ranks. One executive wrote a memo to Luce saying that if the potential for a picture magazine existed this dummy was not it. "I found that I knew no further facts nor had I added to my visualized sense of the scene. . . . I think any reader would finish the dummy in half an hour or less." Another critique came from commentator Dorothy Thompson who called the magazine "unmodern," and said that she expected something that would burst upon the eye "with the sort of inevitableness which has always been your [Luce's] genius."

Luce was not deterred. Richmond was given the job to design in a matter of days what became one of the most emblematic magazine covers in the world. Yet it was a freelance artist/illustrator, Edward Wilson, who suggested that the cover always be a black-and-white photo, a full bleed on all sides. Richmond added the sans serif logo dropped out of a red rectangle positioned in the upper left corner of the cover. After much discussion among *Time*'s executives it was decided that a stationary logo was better than a movable one and it became the most identifiable design element of *Life*. Richmond also recalled taking a photostat and putting it on red paper with the paper extending over the picture. Luce liked it. The red was agreed to because Luce believed that if it worked for *Time*, it would be lucky for *Life*.

The first issue of *Life*, not unlike the rehearsal dummy, was a photo album rather than a well-paced collection of sophisticated photo essays in the tradition of the Berlin or Munich illustrated weeklies. This changed within the next two years as *Life*'s picture editors and photographers became more confident about their missions. But although the stories and editing became tighter, the quality of the design betrayed a conscious effort not to rise above basic functionalism. It could be argued that the matter-of-fact format allowed the photographs the room to breathe. That the no-style design style was actually consistent with *Life*'s style of photography, which rejected artifice (i.e., photographers like Edward Weston or André Kertész were never to be found in *Life*). But it could also be argued that *Life*'s graphic neutrality was an impediment to its being a truly superb magazine.

   Life's influence on America was greater than anyone, even Luce, ever imagined. *Life*'s mix of truly remarkable photo essays (particularly leading up to and during World War II) by masters of photojournalism and terse writing style proved to be a winning combination. *Life*'s editors understood the importance of packaging a picture story with the right balance of words. *Life*'s caption and headline style—with its emphasis on clear, simple facts—guided the reader's interpretations of the evidence supplied in the photographs so that there was scant ambiguity. *Life* was not merely a window, but a clearinghouse for information that only pictures could convey.

In revoking *Esquire*'s second-class mailing privileges the Postmaster General of the United States charged that the magazine was obscene and that its content was not "information of a public character." Although this sounds like the kind of detour around the First Amendment that Senator Jesse Helms might try, this action was actually taken in 1943 against a ten-year-old magazine whose reputation for taboo breaking was at that time more accidental than deliberate. Publisher David Smart never intended for *Esquire* to be revolutionary when he founded it in 1933, but rather to serve as a deluxe men's companion of literature, fashion, art, and women. It was the latter, specifically the sultry "pinups" painted by Alberto Vargas, creator of the Vargas Girl, that prompted the official action. *Esquire* immediately appealed its case to the Supreme Court, which in 1946 ruled that the Postmaster General had no discretion to withhold any privileges simply because it failed to live up to some vague standards of public morality. Justice William O. Douglas wrote that such an act would be "a power of censorship abhorrent to our traditions."

This wasn't the last time *Esquire* ignited public controversy or challenged public taste. Indeed for many of its almost six decades *Esquire* has been an American publishing institution without equal in the realms of art and literature, and sometimes politics. It has been alternately a trendsetter and bellwether. It has at times rocked the foundations of propriety, challenged cultural traditions, and has itself been shaken under the pressures of public opinion.

Henry Wolf (b. 1925) was hired as graphics editor of *Esquire* in 1952, five months after he joined the promotion art department as a junior designer. He was twenty-six, one of the youngest design stewards at any national magazine. Not only his age but also his elevation from the chorus line, or art bullpen, to a leading role on the masthead was the stuff of publishing industry legend. Arnold Gingrich, *Esquire*'s founding editor—who set the tone of the magazine in the 1930s with an entertaining mixture of high literature and a touch of salaciousness—had returned to the company after resolving a major disagreement with publisher David Smart that had forced the former's temporary retirement. Since Gingrich left in the early 1940s, *Esquire* had taken a nose-dive, becoming ostensibly a girlie magazine with some mediocre fiction and fashion sections. When he returned, Esquire's layout was tawdry, replete with crass novelty lettering and sentimental cosmopolitan-styled illustration. He sought to cure its most superficial ills with a bright new talent.

Wolf took a year or two to get the magazine the way he liked it. The first big changeovers included conceptual photographic covers (shot by Dan Wynn and Ben Somoroff), streamlining of the rather horsy *Esquire* masthead (by Ed Benguait, who was in the art bullpen) into a distinctive logotype, introduction of simple interior typography, and development of a stable of expressive illustrators (including Tom Allen, Robert Weaver, Tomi Ungerer, Rudy de Harak, R. O. Blechman, and others). "Still," he lamented, "I couldn't get rid of the girlie gatefold for some time because Gingrich didn't want to lose that part of his audience."

Gingrich's tastes molded *Esquire* and influenced the young Wolf. "I do a magazine I'd like to get in the mail," stated the dapper man-about-town in an interview with Edward R. Murrow. "I like fishing, I like cars, I like some girls." He also appreciated what his editors and art director liked, and so gave Wolf as many as eight pages in each issue to present whatever he wanted. In the late 1950s *Esquire* was not just a collection of random stories and features, but an entity with a massive "editorial sandwich" as well. While some vestiges of the past remained, such as the girlie pics and gag cartoons, during Wolf's tenure the editorial mix changed considerably. Wolf's interests in high and low culture was manifest in exciting photo shoots by some of America's most promising image makers. Indeed all writers and artists wanted to be showcased in *Esquire*. Ben Shahn and Richard Lindner did illustrations for one-hundred-and-fifty and seventy-five dollars.

Wolf left in 1958 and was replaced by his assistant, a young cartoonist and writer, Robert Benton (b. 1932), who later became an Academy Award–winning director (*Kramer vs. Kramer*). Benton was art director during a period of "fun anarchy." Gingrich was loosening control, and two editors, Harold Hayes and Clay Felker, were in a face-off for the editorship. For most of Benton's tenure no one was really in charge, allowing him freedoms that otherwise might have been impossible. Benton is credited by many of those with whom he worked for evolving editorial illustration to its next conceptual stage. Robert Andrew Parker, for instance, walked in from off the street with a series of "Imaginary War" paintings that Benton rushed into print. Milton Glaser recalls that "Benton was inventive and funny, and gave a very special stamp to the magazine during his period. It differed from Henry's *Esquire* not in terms of design but on the literary side. He had great ideas for stories that he and [writer] David Newman [later his movie collaborator] were always generating. To a large extent they formed the backbone of *Esquire*'s character at that time." Benton and Newman's most lasting contribution was *Esquire*'s "Dubious Achievement Awards." Each year the "Dubies" laid waste pompous, hypercritical, and scandalous public figures with biting wit and needle-sharp truth, sometimes just bordering on libel.

Around 1963 Harold Hayes won the hard fought editorship of *Esquire*. About the same time Benton left to begin his movie career. David November was brought in as graphics editor to, as one observer puts it, "do the mechanicals for Harold." In practice, Hayes, a rather astute editor, was doing the art direction—and doing it poorly. The magazine was beginning one of its slides when Sam Antupit (b. 1932) was introduced to Hayes. Antupit had previously been Wolf's assistant at *Harper's Bazaar* and *Show*, and was working at Push Pin Studios when outgoing editor Clay Felker, whom he knew casually, asked if he would like to be art director of *Esquire*. Antupit took the job with the proviso that he have full control of the visual content of *Esquire*. The only caveat to which Antupit did not object was that George Lois (b. 1931)—whose agency Papert Koenig Lois was doing innovative advertising at the time—would conceive and design the covers. "It didn't bother me," admitted Antupit "because there was so much to do anyway. And Harold made a really good political point: . . . every editor felt that his or her articles were the best in the magazine and that they should be featured on the cover. Hayes said that it was up to him to decide which was the most important and not anybody else. But he couldn't do that without alienating his editors. So here was the perfect thing. An outsider read all the manuscripts and picked the one he wanted to illustrate on the cover. Sometimes he didn't pick Harold's lead. The Andy Warhol soup can thing was not the main featured article, but it was one of the best covers George ever did."

George Lois's *Esquire* covers produced from 1962 to 1971 are icons of graphic art, publishing, and American history. Many collaborations with photographer Carl Fischer took an average of three days to produce and are considered among the most memorable propaganda imagery in any medium. Harnessing the technique of photo manipulation, Lois and Fischer's covers equal the acerbity and acuity of pioneer German photomontagist John Heartfield. The trenchant coverlines were written by

Hayes and Lois together. "Half the sentence would be said by one, and then the other would interrupt and finish it," recalled Antupit.

But Antupit did not sit on the sidelines. His first act was to reformat *Esquire*. He standardized all the column widths and made room for illustration. His goal was to let a reader open the magazine anywhere and know that it was *Esquire*. The type was understated by today's standards, but playful. He consistently used many new illustrators (including one student per issue) because, he said, "the same few old hands were used to excess by most national magazines, thus creating a visual sameness." But there was a fine line between the *Esquire* look and that of other magazines. One of Antupit's proudest accomplishments was a story on the building of the Verrazano Narrows Bridge (linking Brooklyn to Staten Island) with dramatic photographs by Bruce Davidson. The photo essay was so strong that Gay Talese was assigned to write an accompanying text. Despite their power, Antupit said, "It started out being twelve pages, but that was too much. To have all photography without text was no longer *Esquire*. It was *Life* or *Look*."

During the late 1960s *Esquire* covered the social and political revolutions of the era. While many of its covers announced stories about political folly and changing mores, its sardonic parodies, Dubious Achievement Awards, campus supplements, and other features underscored a commitment to a generation of "New Left" constituents. For a while, under Harold Hayes, *Esquire* even seemed to shed its male focus for a more ecumenical stance. But contrary to appearances Hayes was no radical. As Antupit said, "Harold would get a lot of his ideas from *Time* magazine. Here we're all going to openings and talking with writers and getting cut by the leading edge, and Harold's reading *Time*. . . . He was never a flaming activist." But he had an "absolute genius" for putting the wrong writer with the right idea. "Sending Genet and Beckett to the Democratic Convention was brilliant. I think Harold just wanted us to keep everybody off balance," said Antupit.

| **Seventeen** |
| Cipe Pineles |
| |

The announcement for "An Evening with One of the Best," a lecture series in the late 1980s sponsored by the Art Directors Club of New York, promised to be an illuminating conversation with six veteran advertising art directors and graphic designers. The title of the evening was not false advertising, but the event was more than a little tainted. The participants were all men. Once upon a time, few would have raised an eyebrow at this, but when these evenings were held in the late 1980s, women had already become the majority gender, if not in advertising, then in graphic design. One woman who should have definitely been invited to participate was Cipe Pineles (1910–1995). As art director of *Glamour*, *Overseas Woman*, *Seventeen*, and *Charm*, the Viennese-born Pineles had as much, if not more, influence on publication design and illustration in America as any member of the Art Directors Club.

In 1948 Pineles became the first female member of the New York Art Directors Club (founded in 1921) and was eventually the first woman inducted into the Art Directors Hall of Fame. That she broke the sex barrier was indeed the reason for receiving a two-column obituary (with a photograph) in the *New York Times*, an honor usually reserved for individuals who have made lasting lifetime achievements. Although Pineles would have vehemently denied that this was an accomplishment on which to hang a legacy, it certainly was significant at a time when men—young and old—jealously guarded the gates to the exclusive sanctum. Pineles was proposed for membership in the late 1930s but was repeatedly turned down until, the story goes, her first husband, William Golden (she was also married to Will Burtin) refused to join, saying that he wanted no part of a men's club. Pineles was admitted the next day.

As a Pratt graduate, Pineles started looking for work in the early 1930s, landing a job with Contempora, a consortium of internationally renowned designers, artists, and architects, where she designed modish fabric designs and displays. In 1933 she was hired as an assistant to Dr. M.

F. Agha, art director of *Vanity Fair* and *Vogue*, where, as a novice at publication design, she received an invaluable education from this brilliant taskmaster. "We used to make many versions of the same feature. If we did, let's say, twenty pages on beauty with twenty different photographers we made scores of different layouts in order to extract every bit of drama or humor we could out of that material. Agha drove us to that because he was never happy with just one solution. And he was right too. We learned that magazine design should never play second fiddle to advertising," Pineles explained. Five years later she was appointed art director at *Glamour*, a poor relation to *Vogue*, targeted at women who couldn't afford the high cost of dress-up. Pineles was told that while money was no object at *Vogue*, at *Glamour* she'd have to do whatever she could on a meager budget. She made the proverbial silk purse, but was so indignant over Condé Nast's demeaning posture over this magazine that she left *Glamour* in 1944 to become art director of *Overseas Woman*, an army magazine for American servicewomen stationed abroad. From there she moved to *Seventeen*, a magazine that defined the teenage market for girls.

"That was the best job I had because the editor was attuned to the audience, and no matter what anybody else did, she and I knew that for seventeen-year-olds the subjects had to be done in a special way," Pineles recalled. She personalized her art direction in the sense that if she showed a cape, she chose the model, the accessories, and the atmosphere in which the garment was presented. Often, she also conceived the issue's theme. "Subject to the collaborative process with editors, art assistants, and artists, my personality was pervasive but not obtrusive."

As art director she transformed American illustration from a saccharine service to an expressive art. "I avoided illustration that was weighed down by cliché or convention, and encouraged that which was unique to the editorial context," Pineles said. She launched the illustration careers of the likes of Seymour Chwast and Robert Andrew Parker (whose work was then showing in art galleries) and commissioned illustration from painters Ben Shahn, Jacob Lawrence, Kuniyoshi, Raphael Soyer, and Robert Gwathmey. She was convinced that the magazine's audience of teenage girls was intelligent enough to appreciate sophisticated art and so she gave her artists unprecedented freedom. The convention in the late 1940s and 1950s was for art directors to give the illustrator rather detailed instructions of what passage or sentence to illustrate. Rather than force her artists to mimic the text, Pineles allowed them to paint what they felt. "If it was good enough for their gallery then it was good enough for me," she explained. The artists also made her design differently. "My sense of magazine pacing was altered because I had to separate one artist from another by distinctly different stories. And I was forced to use different typography than I had been used to so as not to compete with the illustration."

Her photographic sense was equally unconventional. Pineles found fashion to be a fascinating subject, and was interested in the effect it had on the way people felt about themselves. But she despised the haughtiness of *Vogue*'s fashion photography and urged *Seventeen*'s photographers to focus on real life situations. "Make the models look normal," she charged.

Type was as important as image. Pineles developed sound typographic principals on which *Seventeen* was based. "Changing the typeface for the headlines or the body type were outside manifestations. Although they would make the reader think that the magazine had changed, but actually, in order to make substantial alterations the contents had to be tackled from the outset," she explained. Nothing was formulaic. Type was designed according to the same expressive mandates as illustration, and her layouts had a timeless quality.

As an art director, Pineles described herself as personally responsible for interpreting in visual terms the contents of a publication, from appointing photographers and artists to certain features, to deciding to use many typefaces or just one. "But most important is the talent to harness it and create momentum so that the reader will keep turning the pages."

Eros and Avant Garde

Herb Lubalin

Few graphic designers embody the aesthetics of their times as totally as Herb Lubalin (1918–1981). From the late 1950s to the early 1970s he was American typography. He built a bridge between modernism and eclecticism, joining rational and emotional methodologies in the service of commerce. His conceptual typography made letters speak and words emote. He was a pioneer of photo-typography and promoted the practice of smashing and overlapping letters. He liberated white space from the orthodox moderns by refusing to follow the edict that "less is more." He experimented in the marketplace, not the academy, and once his radical approaches to type and page design surfaced in design annuals and shows they were thoroughly accepted and ultimately turned into fashion.

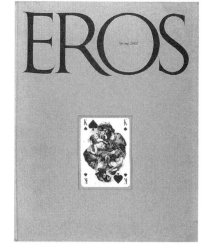

"We've been conditioned to read the way Gutenberg set his type, and for five hundred years people have been reading widely-spaced words on horizontal lines Gutenberg spaced far apart. . . . We read words, not characters, and pushing letters closer or tightening space between lines doesn't destroy legibility; it merely changes reading habits," Lubalin once wrote. He based his own approach upon the ideas of earlier twentieth-century type/image-makers, such as Kurt Schwitters and Lazar El Lissitzky, and

then further married type and image into a single composition. Lubalin's work was very much of his time, and his understanding of the impact of the new technologies on contemporary perception was visionary. In 1959 he argued before an assembly of typographers that television had begun to have an influence on the way that type was read, and likened this kinetic quality to the speed with which type shoots by on advertising on the sides of buses. He reasoned that in this environment smashing letter forms together and including images in a rebus-like manner made type easier to decipher.

Lubalin had a tremendous impact on the practice of American and European graphic design for a generation. His hothouses were *Eros* and *Avant Garde*, which he art directed and designed. The former was America's first unexpurgated celebration of erotica, the quintessence of magazine pacing and composition at the time (despite its high design merits, its publisher, Ralph Ginzburg, was convicted and imprisoned for pandering through the U.S. Mail). The latter was a slightly more acceptable expression of the social and cultural flux within American society as influenced by the antiwar movement, civil rights, and the alternative New Left and youth cultures. A hybrid that crossed a magazine with a literary journal, *Avant Garde* lived up to its name. It was square (the size of a record album) in shape not in content, and featured illustration and photographs that busted the verities of 1950s sentimental and romantic commercial art. Both publications were alternatives to mainstream design conventions, but not in the raucous and anarchic sense, like the underground and psychedelic graphics of the same era.

Although Lubalin was soft-spoken, almost painfully shy when addressing people, he spoke loudly through design. His headlines for articles and advertisements were signs that forced the reader to halt, read, and experience. Story titles were tweaked and manipulated to give Lubalin just the right amount of words or letters to make an effective composition. The graphic strength of "No More War" (originally an advertisement for *Avant Garde*'s antiwar poster competition), which featured block letters forming the pattern of an American flag with a bold black exclamation point at the end, became an icon of the Vietnam war epoch. Lubalin rarely missed the opportunity to make his own variant of concrete poetry. Making words into sculptural forms was one of his typical mannerisms.

Some of the smashing and overlapping was contrived, and the conceit ultimately became self-conscious. But since Lubalin was its inventor, even the excesses must be viewed in the light of one who was testing the limits of form. For example, the Avant Garde typeface has been misused by a generation of designers who could not master Lubalin's distinctive ligatures. Lubalin played with and modernized these historic letter forms, but releasing the family of ligatures to the public as the key characteristic of the font was a mistake. In most other hands, Avant Garde became a silly novelty face; in Lubalin's, it was a signature.

Lubalin pushed design sometimes beyond the ken of his contemporaries. With few exceptions his experiments were conducted under marketplace conditions, which at once provided certain safeguards and made taking liberties all the more difficult. Lubalin's was not design for design, but design for communication.

In 1953 when the first *Push Pin Almanack* was
published it would have been impossible to
predict that its four principle contributors,
Seymour Chwast (b. 1931), Milton Glaser (b.
1929), Reynold Ruffins (b. 1930), and Edward
Sorel (b. 1929), would develop a graphic style
that challenged the prevailing ethic of
functionalism imported from Europe (during the
Bauhaus immigration), practiced by some
leading American corporate and advertising
designers, and manifest in work by exponents of
the Swiss International Style. Yet when that first
four-inch-by-nine-inch compilation of facts,
ephemera, and trivia illustrated with woodcuts
and pen-and-ink drawings was mailed out as a
promotion for these freelancers, other New York
designers and art directors began to take serious notice. Indeed the *Push
Pin Almanack* brought in so much work from book, advertising, and film-
strip clients that the four Cooper Union classmates decided to leave their
day jobs and start Push Pin Studios, the major proponent of illustrative
design in America.

The *Almanack*, originally conceived by Chwast and Sorel as a
bimonthly promotional piece, was consistent with emerging historicist
design trends. Victorian, fat letter type had previously been revived for use
in advertising during the 1930s, fell out of favor in the 1940s, and was
revived again in the 1950s when Otto Storch, art director of *McCall's* began
using Victorian woodtype and ornament for editorial layouts. Indeed a taste
for things old fashioned was returning, apparently as a reaction to what was
perceived as cold, humorless modernism. "It was called the *Push Pin
Almanack*," Chwast said in a 1990 interview, "because it was a quaint
name—and quaintness was popular in those days."

The contents were usually tidbits excerpted from books and
periodicals and illustrated in styles that evoked the past. Each issue related
to seasonal themes and included a few articles written especially for the
Almanack on graphic design topics. Although it might be compared to Will
Bradley's early 1900s *Chap Book* and other printer's keepsakes, the *Push Pin*

Almanack was a special publication in the early 1950s, since most commercial artists who advertised their services to the trade were doing it in very straightforward, unimaginative ways. The *Push Pin Almanack* was a paradigm of conceptual acuity.

Six issues of the *Almanack* were published before the studio was started and two after. The printing of three thousand copies and the typesetting were basically done for free (or at cost) in exchange for designing and publishing the supplier's ad in the *Almanack*. Other operating expenses were paid for through the sale of small ads sold after the first issue.

The narrow *Almanack* format was, however, creatively limiting. Wanting more freedom to explore different themes and graphic approaches, the *Almanack* was transformed into the *Push Pin Monthly Graphic*, which began as a broadside, printed in black and white on one sheet (usually newsprint). While the elegant and emblematic logo was designed by Glaser in a variant of German Fraktur, each studio member conceived at least one of his own issues, as well as combining their talents when the theme called for it. Themes were not exclusively design oriented. There were issues on railroading, dada, and *War and Peace*. The subjects reflected the variegated interests of their makers. Chwast remembers conceiving an issue chronicling his first trip to Italy, which included photographs and drawings, and Glaser developed an issue on Italian sculpture. In these issues the Push Pin members further developed their interest in historical styles in a contemporary context.

The response to the *Graphic* went beyond immediate commercial success. It was historically significant in that it exerted an extraordinary influence on individual designers, and so the entire field. To this day, designers who were beginning their careers in the late 1950s and early 1960s recall how excited they were when a new issue arrived in the mail. For Push Pin included designers with varying talents sharing a distinctive methodology—a passion for what today would be called mass popular culture—who had an ability to translate their particular vocabulary of forms into mass communication (and selling) tools. They did so through a marriage—long rejected by the modernists—of drawing and typography. The *Push Pin Monthly Graphic* (and the subsequent *Push Pin Graphic*, renamed because they could never keep to the monthly publishing schedule) proved that designer/illustrators were not simply pairs of hands doing the bidding of a client divorced from the total context, but were creatives capable of developing ideas in totality. And Push Pin's work was not simply derivatively decorative, but originally witty.

Beginning as a newsprint tabloid, the *Push Pin Graphic* eventually came in a variety of sizes and shapes, evolving into discrete books and booklets on a variety of subjects, usually six times per year. The most memorable issues were on art deco automobiles (what Chwast referred to as "Roxy" style), "The Kings and Queens of Europe," "Rhymes by Edward Lear," "The Push Pin Book of Dreams," "Good and Bad," "The Kiss," "Rock and Roll," a collection of wooden targets (Paul Davis's first significant work as a junior member of Push Pin), and Chwast's tour de force, "The South," a series of classic (and often racist) Southern stereotypes as backdrops for photographs of slain civil rights leaders. To heighten the polemic, a die-cut bullet hole pierces through the heads of the civil rights workers until in the last picture,. The bullet hole shatters the calm of an image representing the Old South, which is inset against a backdrop of the civil rights march on Washington. This poignant and caustic commentary was one of the few *Push Pin Graphic*'s with such an overt political message.

By the mid-1970s, the contributions made by Push Pin Studios had become part of the mainstream and the *Push Pin Graphic* had lost some of its innovative spark. To rejuvenate himself and expand into different realms of design, Glaser left Push Pin in 1975 and founded his own design firm. Chwast kept the Push Pin name and in 1976 decided to revamp the *Graphic* into a standard, nine-by-twelve-inch magazine format printed in full color. Chwast's goal was to make it commercially viable by rigorously selling advertising and subscriptions. He printed eleven thousand copies of each issue and eventually garnered around three thousand subscribers at the rate of fifteen dollars yearly (mostly designers in the United States and abroad who were not on the complimentary mailing list). Interest was high, but as a commercial property, the *Graphic* was losing money at a prodigious rate. Nevertheless, as a magazine it continued for four years and twenty-two issues.

Despite a seeming abundance of advertisements from graphic arts suppliers (mostly designed by Chwast and given in return for their services), financial pressures ultimately took their toll. "The All New Crime Favorites" issue was the last *Push Pin Graphic*, and perhaps not coincidentally it was the least interesting of all the issues. In all, eighty-six issues were published from 1953 to 1980, and ran the gamut from silly to profound. In its early incarnation the *Push Pin Graphic* had an incalculable influence on the conceptualization of graphic design and provided other firms and studios a model, and indeed a medium, to show their conceptual skills. But taken as a whole, the eighty-six issues show the evolution of a significant graphic style (and its makers) that not only eclecticized American graphic design, but also changed the style and content of American illustration.

Few American magazines can claim to be agents of change. Most, even the once ubiquitous *Life* magazine, are reporters or chroniclers of their time and place. Others like *Vogue*, *Bazaar*, and even *Rolling Stone* have supported, cultivated, and propagated fashions, styles, and trends, but did not invent them. Most magazines are lightning rods, not lightning.

Among a generation weaned on World War II and raised on the sour milk of McCarthyism, the late 1950s and early 1960s was a period of intense cultural and political reevaluation. In the 1960s the new bohemians began to push the boundaries of propriety through sexual and cultural expression in two magazines. *Ramparts* on the West Coast and *Evergreen* on the East were the clarions of new aesthetics, politics, and morality. *Ramparts* was the voice of the political left and *Evergreen* was the voice of the cultural left. The former re-introduced muckraking to American journalism, the latter introduced banned authors' controversial texts. The former exposed CIA involvement in American colleges and universities, the latter revealed the erotic side of the American subculture.

In terms of design these were not 1960s versions of 1920s constructivist, futurist, or dada manifestoes—the more raucous underground newspapers of the late 1960s are a more accurate visual analog. Yet in content these magazines were no less radical than the political and cultural progressive journals of the 1920s. *Ramparts* and *Evergreen* conformed to appropriate design verities, with legibility the most important. "I never wanted a magazine where the design overpowered the content," asserted Fred Jordan, *Evergreen*'s managing editor from 1957 to 1971. Similarly, Dugald Stermer (b. 1936), *Ramparts*'s art director from 1964 to 1970, explained that a classical design format, rather than an anarchic approach, "lent more credibility to what must have seemed then like the hysterical paranoid ravings of loonies." The significance of *Ramparts* and *Evergreen* to the history of design is not as form givers but as conduits for various graphic forms in the service of politics and culture.

Evergreen Review was founded in 1957 as a quarterly literary magazine that published writers and poets whom its parent company, Grove Press, was already publishing in books. In 1952 Grove Press was a small, insignificant New York publishing house which was bought by Barney Rossett, a sympathizer of alternative politics and aficionado of radical literature whose tastes were influenced by progressive European writers. Grove was the first to publish Henry Miller's *Tropic of Cancer*, William Burroughs's *Naked Lunch*, and Samuel Beckett's *Waiting for Godot* in America. Each book challenged America's puritanical values and intellectual standards; for in those days descriptions of the sexual act were veiled, and four-letter words were forbidden by the major publishing institutions. Rossett busted taboos and thwarted convention.

Evergreen began in a quarto format, at first publishing Grove's authors and expanding outward. Fred Jordan administered to the unillustrated layout of the quarterly and a few years later the bimonthly. In the late 1950s he used art photographs, including pictures by Robert Frank, as the primary illustration, and eventually he introduced ribald cartoons by one of Grove's author/artists, Tomi Ungerer, the black humorist from Alsace-Lorraine who became the golden boy of American illustration in the 1960s. In 1964, with issue #32, Rossett relaunched the magazine as a monthly, called it simply *Evergreen* (from a tree that grows in the grove), and filled it with stories and art designed to provoke the establishment. *Evergreen* was the vortex of cultural flux. "We printed subway and wall posters showing covers of the magazine with the tagline, 'Join the Underground,'" recalled Jordan.

That same year, 1964, Dugald Stermer was hired as art director for *Ramparts*. Founded in 1962, *Ramparts* was published by Edward Keating, a lawyer who had sunk a private fortune into a magazine that he described as having an anticlerical, liberal Catholic bias. Those early issues of *Ramparts*, which Stermer says was named for the "Ramparts We Watched," looked like a college literary magazine, with its unrelated typefaces, amateurish illustrations, and unsophisticated layouts. *Ramparts* was not a threat to the body politic. Keating was not an America basher, but rather a concerned citizen who saw aspects of America turning sour.

Ramparts was the "soft wing" of the left. This began to change in 1964 when Warren Hinckle III, then *Ramparts*'s brash promotion director, and Howard Gossage, a veteran San Francisco advertising man (who was also on the *Ramparts* advisory board), gradually took control away from Keating.

Hinckle was named editor and Bob Scheer, a budding young investigative journalist, was hired as foreign editor. The former, who was not allied with any political movement or ideology, was a muckraker in the Hearst tradition and viewed sacred cows as moving targets; the latter, who maintained a healthy skepticism of all "isms," uncovered and sourced the earliest stories about CIA involvement in the Vietnam War and on American college campuses just prior to the emergence of a national antiwar movement. With Hinckle's taste for muck and Scheer's remarkable news instinct, *Ramparts* began to publish hot national stories ignored by most national media.

One of *Ramparts*'s most inflammatory stories was the confessions of a Green Beret who quit over the secret war in Vietnam. In fact, *Ramparts* drew stories from other disaffected government and military personnel whose consciences were bothering them, but who at that time—a few years before the Pentagon Papers story broke in the *New York Times*— could not sell their stories to the newspapers. The mainstream press was skeptical of such antigovernment attacks and more or less followed an "America Right or Wrong" stance. Stermer recalls that the goal of *Ramparts* was to "just raise hell."

Evergreen and *Ramparts* were two sides of the same coin. They were competitors only in that they appealed to the same audience, but enjoyed a rather a large crossover of readers and subscribers. Both magazines were sold on newsstands in the largest metropolitan areas, and given such visibility there was a mandate to look inviting.

Ramparts's design was based on classical, central axis book design. Stermer used Times Roman, with dingbats and Oxford rules to accent pages. At the time using book design for a magazine format was unique, and subsequently influenced the formats of *Rolling Stone* (which in fact copied Stermer's grid for its first issues) and *New York* magazine. Being an illustrator, Stermer had a healthy respect for conceptual illustration and commissioned quality work by known artists despite the magazine's pauper-like fees. He lured Edward Sorel into *Ramparts* by offering him a monthly visual column—Sorel's Bestiary, where the likenesses of famous people were portrayed as satiric animals in acute attacks on sacred cows. He commissioned Push Pin Studios, including founders Seymour Chwast and Milton Glaser. Robert Grossman did one of his best Johnson caricatures for *Ramparts*. Paul Davis did a number of covers, including one of South Vietnamese doyenne Madame Nhu as a cheerleader for Michigan State, where it was asserted in a *Ramparts* investigative report that the CIA was recruiting operatives for clandestine work in Vietnam. Stermer also hired Ben Shahn out of virtual retirement to do a portrait of the early antiwar senator William Fulbright. In the 1960s Shahn was under attack by the art establishment for being a propagandist. Stermer also commissioned Norman Rockwell to paint a portrait of Bertrand Russell. As art director Stermer also had a say in the editorial direction, which allowed him leeway in developing stories and features, including a memorable photo essay on the American town that endured the most Vietnam casualties.

Likewise, Ken Deardorf (b. 1935), *Evergreen*'s art director of longest duration from 1967 to 1972, designed an airy, economical format that relied on art and photography to define the magazine's visual personality. Deardorf did not have the same editorial power as did Stermer to assign articles and graphic features, but given a commodious working relationship with his editors, he was master of *Evergreen*'s visual persona. While it did not overtly resemble *Ramparts*, Deardorf admits he owes a debt to *Ramparts*'s elegance and simplicity.

Deardorf was not an illustrator, but like Stermer, he had a healthy respect for conceptual illustration. *Evergreen* used many of the same artists, including Robert Grossman, Edward Sorel, Seymour Chwast, and Paul Davis, who created one of the most highly charged visual icons of the 1960s—the Che Guevara cover. Deardorf had a policy of trying out at least one new artist per issue. One such newcomer was Brad Holland who did some of his earliest editorial work for *Evergreen*, including an illustration for the premiere publication of "Viva Vargas" by Woody Allen, the story on which the film *Bananas* was based.

Ramparts's investigative stance required strong political covers, such as the John Heartfield-like photomontages by Carl Fischer, who at the same time was collaborating with George Lois on *Esquire* covers. *Evergreen* did more erotic than political covers. Rossett, the sole arbiter of covers, was convinced that the cover, not the content, sold the magazine. Given that much of Rossett's groundbreaking legal precedents were through the publication and litigation of sexually sensitive material, and that he believed that sex was a key political issue, it is logical that much of the visual material in *Evergreen* was indeed sexual. Fred Jordan added that the left in the mid- to late-1960s was not yet in tune with the nascent women's movement or above sexual exploitation. It wasn't until the end of the 1960s that the feminist movement began to exercise some control over left-wing publishing. At *Evergreen* Jordan cited the resignation in the late 1960s of two important male contributors over sexploitation; and Stermer admitted, even though *Ramparts* was not overtly exploitive and ran some stories about the feminist movement, they had a blind spot, too. "The feminists had no reason to trust us," he admitted.

Rossett was no stranger to government censorship and litigation, and *Evergreen* was enjoined and seized, more than once, owing to its sexual content. One case involved the Nassau County district attorney's injunction against a 1964 issue citing pornographic content. According to the complaint, a confidential informant employed at the bindery "observed black and white photographs in the magazine which showed the nude human form, possibly male and female, but reputed by fellow workers to be two females; and that the forms portrayed various poses and positions indicating sexual relations. My informant further stated having read portions of the printed material . . . [that it consisted] of four-lettered obscene language." In fact, the pictures were shot through a can of Vaseline and were barely visible to the reader much less the informant, who was a part-time employee of the bindery and whose husband was a retired police officer.

Ramparts was no stranger to legal hassles, either. The most threatening was the time Dugald Stermer arranged a 1967 cover shoot with Carl Fischer that showed his and three other *Ramparts* staffers' hands holding their burning draft cards—a symbolic gesture of nonviolent resistance against the war that broke at least two federal laws. The statute that was broken was known as the Disrespect Law, referred also to the burning of money or the flag. Since the disrespect was towards the symbol itself, Stermer determined that it didn't matter whether the cards were real or facsimiles, and so decided to burn the real thing. Not surprisingly an act of such defiance, commonly perpetrated in street demonstrations and now codified on the cover of a national magazine, forced the government to impanel a federal grand jury to investigate a possible indictment. While Stermer and Scheer initially wanted to fight the case as a freedom of the press issue, their counsel, Washington lawyer and football team owner Edward Bennett Williams refused to let his clients risk imprisonment and persuaded them to plead not guilty should an indictment be handed down. In the end, however, Williams pulled strings with his friend Lyndon Johnson, one of the bitterest of *Ramparts*'s enemies, to squash the investigation. In the end, the cover was a powerful emblem of Vietnam protest.

Ramparts and *Evergreen* have not published for almost three decades, but to look back at them now is not an exercise in nostalgia. They should not be seen merely as documents of the 1960s, but as monuments of activist publishing, where the writing, art, and design were brought together to make a revolution.

Robert Hughes once described the weekly pasteup night at the *East Village Other* (*EVO*) as "a dada experience." The year was 1970, and none of those who were toiling into the wee hours of the morning at one of America's first 1960s-era underground papers (founded in 1965) knew what he was talking about. "Dada was the German anti-art, political-art movement of the 1920s," he explained in a nasal Australian accent. "And this is the closest thing I've come to seeing it recreated today."

Hughes, the new art critic for *Time* magazine, was as welcome as any other weekly observer. Pasteup night at *EVO* was open to anybody who came up to the dimly lit second floor loft above Bill Graham's Fillmore East, a former Loews Theater on Second Avenue and Sixth Street just next door to Ratner's famous dairy restaurant. In the 1920s and 1930s the Lower East Side neighborhood was the heart of New York's Yiddish Theater. Since 1967 (the Summer of Love) it was referred to in the press as the "East Village," the hippie capital of the East Coast.

Starting at 8:00 P.M. and lasting until dawn, the volunteer layout staff, under the watchful eye of *EVO*'s seventeen-year-old, self-appointed art director Stephen Cohen took the jumble of counterculture journalism and anti-establishment diatribe that was the paper's editorial meat and threw it helter-skelter onto layouts that bore a curious resemblance to the digital typography done in *Ray Gun* during the 1990s. Anyone could join in whether they had graphic design experience or not, yet many of the gadfly layout artists were usually too stoned to finish. Corrections for their pages were often waxed at the office and cut-in during the long subway ride to the printer in Brooklyn.

The pasteup night was a 1960s tribal ritual. The plentiful joints and acid tabs were advance payments for a good night's work. The art director routinely emerged from the editor's office around 8:30 P.M. with a shoebox full of the stuff, as well as with the night's layout assignments, which included at least three pages of "intimate" classifieds. The layout crew would help themselves to the grass and manuscripts, find their tables, select their decorative ruling tapes, benday and transfer-type sheets, and settle down to design pages.

The *East Village Other* premiered in 1965 and quickly evolved from a neo-beat community organ into an alternative culture clarion. It was among the first to publish the masters of underground comix, including R. Crumb, Spain, Kim Deitch, and others. Intentionally or not, it borrowed graphic techniques from dada and surrealism. The cover of one early issue was a photomontage (in the manner of German satirist John Heartfield) of a serpent emerging from the battle fatigues of America's commanding general in Vietnam, William Westmoreland. For irrepressible irreverence, for dogged antiestablishmentarianism nothing could match the *East Village Other*. As a testament, it was declared contraband by the United States armed forces.

As for its graphic design, *EVO* was resolutely formless. While it had an anchored editorial page, the features and regular columns were unfettered by aesthetic or functional rules. The layout staff of between five and ten people on any given Thursday were all erstwhile amateurs without a clue how to create consistent design even if they wanted to. This had been true since its inception, but occasionally a professional would wander in, someone who knew the ways of the grid and central axis composition, who would attempt to insert a "correct" page into the anarchic mélange. But rather than bring order to the chaos, in the end, all approaches were thrown into the stew that was *EVO*.

In the final years of *EVO* during the early 1970s, the biggest influence on the layout sessions was the work of a veteran animator, Fred Mogubgub who drew obsessively intricate designs for the covers (including the masthead) and some inside pages. He usually indicated that they be printed as a split fountain (the gradual mixing of two colors from top and bottom of the page) going from unreadable yellow to garish orange to bright red. Mogubgub's quirky, detailed, comic style for Seven-Up and Bit-O-Honey television spots had changed the look of animated commercials in the early 1960s, but he left Madison Avenue to pursue an unrealized film career. Along the way he had altered the style of *EVO*.

By 1972 the *East Village Other*'s circulation, which in its heyday hovered around seventy-five thousand, had plummeted to five or six thousand. It was kept afloat only by the sex advertisements and classifieds. Indeed this was consistent with the general demise of the underground press. The issues of *EVO* printed on cheap newsprint are difficult to find these days—they were either discarded or have turned to dust. The few that remain, however, represent a remarkable period of counterculture publishing, naïve design, and youthful exuberance that marked a truly democratic period (prefiguring zines and the World Wide Web) when cheap communications were available to many.

When he was thirty years old Mick Jagger predicted that nothing could be more embarrassing than singing "Satisfaction" at age fifty. Today the elder rocker eats those words. "Satisfaction" has become such a classic that it remains in the Stones's concert repertoire. Likewise, in the 1960s few would have imagined that *Rolling Stone* magazine would still be publishing after all the other counterculture rock magazines had folded. But having endured rock music's various fads, *Rolling Stone* is editorially vigorous and smartly designed. Like the Rolling Stones, *Rolling Stone* is an institution that sets standards.

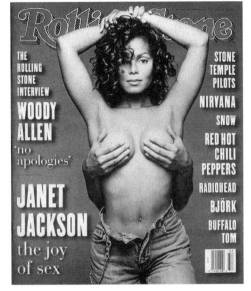

 Rolling Stone has changed through the years, though not as a slave to fashion. In each of its incarnations, during the tenures of art directors John Williams (1967–1968), Robert Kingsbury (1968–1974), Mike Salisbury (1973–1974), Tony Lane (1974–1976), Roger Black (1976–1978), Mary Shanahan (1978– 1982), Derek Unglass (1982–1987), and Fred Woodward (1987–present), the magazine has steered its own course through design fashions and trends. When it premiered in 1967, psychedelia prevailed in *Rolling Stone*'s home town of San Francisco, but the only concession to this popular style was the hand-drawn logo designed by psychedelic poster artist Rick Griffin (which was replaced in 1976). The rest of the magazine appeared in classical dress, down to the Oxford rules framing each page. When compared to the anarchic layout of most other underground newspapers *Rolling Stone* was not alternative, it was progressive.

 When the magazine approached middle age in the late 1980s, Fred Woodward (b. 1953) decided to reprise many of the classic design characteristics that had been allowed to atrophy over time, such as Nicolas Cochin type, Oxford rules, and woodtypes. This was not nostalgia. *Rolling Stone*'s design direction does not retreat into the past for safe and easy answers, but rather builds upon imaginative typography and iconic photography. What distinguishes *Rolling Stone* from most other magazines is that its layouts are based on ideas—playful, historical, and unconventional—not knee-jerk responses to the latest computer font or trick.

Wit and play are hallmarks of *Rolling Stone*'s pages, especially in a layout like "Big Shot." While it helps to have a great photograph, not every designer would have taken advantage of the opportunity to use the big inner tube as a mnemonic element. The type is not particularly elegant—it's kind of horsy, but in the right proportions to all the other elements on the page. Moreover, the dot on the *i* is just silly enough to be brilliant—by echoing the tube it anchors the type. This is not serendipity, but planned play.

Two decades ago *Rolling Stone*'s key competitors were *Circus*, *Creem*, and *Rock*; they more or less covered the same subjects from different perspectives. The others approached rock and roll as fashion. So did *Rolling Stone*, to a degree, but it was also a forum for news, reviews, and commentary. *Rolling Stone*'s format underscored the writing. The others emphasized pictures. As the others died, *Rolling Stone* matured into middle age, though it would be erroneous to say that its format is aimed only at a late thirty- or forty-something audience. In the argot of today, it is age-unspecified.

Nevertheless, not every rock and roll aficionado wants news and analysis when squibs and gossip will do. Not every music fan cares about design elegance, in fact some say it's an anachronism. Some anachronism. *Rolling Stone* remains true to Alexey Brodovitch's vision of magazine design and his "astonish me!" principle that layouts should be well modulated for maximum impact and readability. *Rolling Stone*'s graphic persona at once rebelled against and defined a late 1960s design aesthetic, and, over time, evolved into something classic. *Rolling Stone* has aged well because its editors appear to understand what its readers want, and its designers realize that serving them needn't be about flagrantly busting convention. Unlike most magazines, *Rolling Stone* has known when to reinvent itself, and while representing a field that is mired in fashion, it has avoided its traps.

Parody is a form of derision that ridicules a
work or its style by adapting and
deliberately distorting its features.
"Certainly parodies have been committed
since the dawn of man's existence (7:38
A.M., daylight savings time)," Richard R.
Lingeman explained in the *New York Times*.
"According to one scholar . . . the earliest
identifiable parody was by a Sumerian
named Aktuk, who parodied the famed
Epic of Gilgamesh." Visual parody has roots
in antiquity as well, notably in Greek
pottery by anonymous artisans. It was also
common in major artworks during the
Italian Renaissance. Pellegrino Tibaldi's
frescoes on the Palazzo Poggi in Bologna,
for example, are playfully mocking of
Michelangelo's style. Today, Tibaldi's
frescoes are intact and highly respected not

as jibes at the Renaissance master, but as artworks on their own terms.
Countless other commentators and jesters have, however, not been as revered
for their parodies. History tells of many who suffered dearly for satirizing a
monarch, dictator, or prelate. Lingeman reports that the rebellious Aktuk
"was sentenced to twenty years as a galley slave—a cruel punishment at the
time since there was very little water in that part of the world."

The job title "Lawsuits," listed in *MAD* magazine's masthead, is
no joke. In the late 1950s and early 1960s, when *MAD* was publishing
acerbic parodies of American consumer culture, many corporations and
products were pilloried in mock ads that were not merely harmless or silly
jests, but focused attention on such hot issues as rising medical costs,
alcohol and tobacco dependency, homelessness, and environmental crime.
Parodies of popular advertisements so realistic as to fool the casual reader
might have been secretly enjoyed by Madison Avenue's bad boys, but many
of their high-billing clients did not find anything funny about parodies that
overshadowed their original ads. "Madison Avenue was savvy enough to
know it would result in bad publicity," reported Maria Reidelbach, author

of a history of *MAD*. The magazine was, however, never sued for its parodies of print ads, but it was sued for its song parodies that paired famous tunes to ridiculous lyrics. "The suit charged that the parodies were 'counterparts' to the originals since they could be sung to the tunes of the original," continued Reidelbach. Although two New York State courts agreed with *MAD* that the spoofs were indeed parody, and that "parody and satire are deserving of substantial freedom—both as entertainment and as a form of social and literary criticism," *MAD*'s publisher, William Gaines, realized it was prudent to have a lawyer on permanent retainer to block and tackle any potential litigants.

Such are the vagaries of parody, that *MAD* took precautions to prevent charges of trademark infringement by routinely altering the names of products (i.e., Crest toothpaste became Crust) while keeping the identifiable characteristics of a product or institution through mimicry of a package, logo, or ad format. One of *MAD*'s classics is a 1961 parody of the drug company Parke Davis's once ubiquitous Great Moments in Medicine campaign. Each ad featured a detailed painting of a warm-hearted healer tending to the sick and infirm. *MAD* lampooned the campaign by showing a doctor (holding back a smirk) presenting his inflated bill to the horrified patient and family members around the sick bed. The caption read "Presenting the Bill, reproduced here, is one of a series of original oil paintings, Practicing Medicine for Fun and Profit . . ." The tag line read: "Park-David . . . pioneers in bigger medical bills."

MAD's spirit was later adopted by Topps Bubble Gum for their extraordinarily successful, yet decidedly sophomoric Wacky Packs, a send-up (aimed at preteens) of well-known supermarket products, featuring pernicious puns on famous brand names. "Rather than a negative parody," argued Wayne Small, a marketing analyst, "Wacky Packs actually reinforced brand names in the minds of children." Nevertheless, under the threat of legal actions Topps made a number of out-of-court settlements with offended corporations. Indeed, consistent with the Reagan administration's support of big business, during the 1980s the courts enforced stricter rules against defaming corporate (as opposed to individual) reputations.

Parody is a tricky and dangerous art for two primary reasons. First, because it involves fidelity to the original work. Second, because as an instrument of criticism and entertainment parody can infringe on intellectual property. Since parody is "a form of derision," even benign parodies are bound to get somebody's head out of joint. Moreover, the law is somewhat vague in its definition of what constitutes a violation of intellectual property rights, and what action is taken depends on the perception and inclination of the victim. Serious parody, no matter how biting, is more acceptable than that which is irresponsible or libelous. Parodying well-known images or icons not to satirize the host form directly, but to make additional commentary is common among graphic designers. As a graphic design tool parody makes sense only when the relationship, or visual pun, between the original and the new work is comprehensible. A successful parody is one that exploits the original style and character of a work for the purpose of making humorous and insightful commentary. A good parody makes sense; a bad one, none.

Back in 1968, underground comix attacked the peremptory values of a conservative society that less than a decade earlier had imposed strict rules of conduct on its youth. During the early to mid-1950s, at the height of the social and political purges known as McCarthyism, Congress was engaged in an investigative frenzy to root out Communists in government and adverse influences on the culture at large. They believed that American kids—the offspring of a victorious postwar nation—were susceptible to forces of evil filtered into the collective unconscious through such inflammatory media as comic books. Threatened with government regulations and fearing diminished profits, the comics industry agreed to police itself through the Comics Code Authority, which, like the film industry's Hays Office, applied strict watchdog standards to any and all content prior to bestowing its seal of approval. Any deviation from its list of standards (which prohibited gratuitous violence, sex, and disrespect toward authority) was met with swift punitive measures, notably banning distribution to all stores in which the majority of comic books were sold.

Pressure on the creators, manufacturers, distributors, and retailers of comic books resulted in products that upheld prescribed American values. Neutering comics did not hinder sales; instead, restrictions fomented rebellion over time. After almost a decade of a predictable *Superman*, puerile *Archie*, and tiresome *Sgt. Rock*, a generation of American kids became teenagers, with pent-up inhibitions that demanded venting. During the late 1960s, the busting of strictures emerged in youth movements that were expressed through political radicalism, civil disobedience, hallucinogenic experimentation, free love, and raucous rock and roll. Virtually overnight (after fermenting for a decade), American culture was transformed by a youth culture that reclaimed art, writing, music, and, ultimately, comic books from the guardians of propriety.

Thirty years ago, *Zap #1* was the spearhead of the comic book revolution. The 1998 release of *Zap #15* marked the comic's extraordinary longevity; it is still published, once every two years. Before *Zap*, early underground comics appeared in such underground newspapers as New York's *East Village Other* and its sister publication, the *Gothic Blimp Works*, where R. Crumb, Kim Deitch, Gilbert Shelton, S. Clay Wilson, and Spain Rodriguez launched assaults on convention. To describe the effect of this work as inspirational would understate the incredible power of such fervent taboo busting on a generation weary of trite comic superheroes and superboobs. While these undergrounds looked like comics and read like comics, in fact they were "com-mix," a combination of a conventional visual language (that is, the panel and balloon motif that dates back to the late nineteenth century) and scabrous story- and gag-lines heretofore banned from mainstream comic books.

Zap began as a co-mix of artists bound together by their collective contempt for conventional mores, yet their various individual perspectives allowed them to showcase a number of themes through different forms and distinct characters. Among *Zap*'s earliest contributors, founder R. Crumb was known in the counterculture for his string of bizarre, ribald, and racy characters, including Fritz the Cat, Mr. Natural, Angelfood McSpade, Dirty Dog, and Schuman the Human; Victor Moscoso and Rick Griffin were progenitors of the vibrating, psychedelic rock-concert posters that took San Francisco and the world by storm; and S. Clay Wilson was known for living out his perverse fantasies through dark comic figures.

Zap #1 featured Crumb's work exclusively as a vehicle for the artist to pay homage to pre-code comics and to communicate his admittedly deranged view of conventional life. Under the caustic advisory "Fair Warning: For Adult Intellectuals Only," Crumb introduced a selection of tales that had spiritual roots in *MAD* magazine's irreverent satire. But while *MAD* eschewed sex and politics, Crumb reveled in it. Among his earliest stories, we find "Whiteman," a tale of "civilization in crisis;" "Mr. Natural Encounters Flakey Foont," a jab at spirituality; "Ultra Super Modernistic Comics," a tweak at high art; and his now classic "Keep on Truckin'," an absurdly funny slapstick. In retrospect, these comics seem tame when compared to later underground raunchiness. But, at the time, even comical gibes at frontal nudity, recreational drug use, and racial stereotyping (for example, Angelfood McSpade, a bug-eyed African cannibal, sold a product called "Pure Nigger Hearts") tested the tolerance of accepted standards.

When *Zap #1* premiered, Victor Moscoso and Rick Griffin were among the most prominent graphic artists of the San Francisco rock-and-roll ballroom scene. A year earlier, Wes Wilson, Stanley Mouse, Griffin, and Moscoso launched a graphic style that undermined prevailing modernist notions of formal rightness by introducing vibrating color, illegible lettering, and vintage graphics to posters that were complex assemblies of type and image, designed to be read while high. Always the experimenter, Moscoso, who had been interested in serial imagery when he was a painter studying at Yale in the early 1960s, was beginning to play with skewed sequential photographs for use as a Christmas card for an old high school friend, the animator and film title designer Pablo Ferro. Also in an experimental mode, Griffin had done a poster send-up on the *San Francisco Chronicle*'s comics section. After seeing this poster, which was "like Disney on LSD," Moscoso recalls, "it turned me in the direction of cartoons as opposed to photos."

At first, Moscoso was hesitant to devote himself to comic strips. He was already spending the better part of a week designing two and sometimes three rock posters, which were printed on good paper and therefore more tangible than the underground tabloids printed on cheap newsprint and destined for landfill. "Why should I do something that's going to be thrown away?" he asks rhetorically. Instead Moscoso and Griffin together created a series of posters for Pinnacle Productions in LA, promoting Janis Joplin and Big Brother, B. B. King, and PG&E.

"At the bottom [of the strip] were three comic panels, which Rick drew," Moscoso says about the inspiration that gave them the idea to do a comic magazine combining their talents through alternating panels. "I did a template for each of us on eight-by-five-inch cards," he says about the format. "We were using a Rapidograph at the time, and, since we each had the same template, we'd start drawing anything that came into our mind in a box and alternately put one next to the other in a nonlinear fashion so that the development would be purely visual."

Originally, the comic was just going to include Moscoso and Griffin's collaborative artwork. "We were already doing our respective drawings when we saw *Zap #1* [after] Crumb had started selling it on Haight Street," Moscoso recalls. "Crumb asked us to join because he admired Griffin's cartoon poster. In fact, Crumb did a comic strip in *Zap #1*, which was a direct bounce off that poster. So he asked Rick, and Rick said, 'Moscoso and I are already working on this stuff.' So he invited both of us to join in." Crumb also asked S. Clay Wilson, who offered up a ribald comic-strip drug fantasy titled "Checkered Demon." With this, Moscoso and Griffin decided to shelve their collaboration, and each did their own strips.

Given the quartet's respective popularity on the two coasts (Moscoso and Griffin on the West, and Crumb and Wilson on the East), *Zap #2* was an immediate success. However, despite their hippie ("mine is yours") roots, Moscoso wanted to ensure equitable distribution of profits and copyright. "After having been burned so much in the poster business," he says about his intellectual property travails, wherein he was denied the rights to many of his images, "I set up a publishing deal with Print Mint, which was a distributor of my and Rick's posters already. When *Zap #2* came out, here's Moscoso and Griffin and these two new guys, Crumb and Wilson, in the same stores where Rick and I were selling very well." The poster and head shops that had sprung up in hippie strongholds of big cities and college towns allowed independent distributors a network that bypassed the Marvels, DCs, and all the other Comics Code Authority publishers. By the time *Zap #3* and *#4* were published, sales were as high as 50,000 copies each for the first printing. (Subsequent printings increased that number into the six-figure range.) Originally, half of the profits after expenses were earmarked for the distributor, and half for the artists. In the meantime, however, the Print Mint changed ownership; after some unfair dealings on their part, Moscoso renegotiated with Last Gasp (the distributor of Zap today).

The first two issues of *Zap* were fairly innocuous compared to *Zap #3*, the special 69 issue ("because it was 1969," explains Moscoso). Rocking the boat with its risqué content that lived up to its "Adults Only" advisory, *#3* was spiritually akin to Tijuana bibles (the cheaply produced, sexually explicit eight-page comics imported to the United States from Mexico during the 1930s and 1940s). This issue was sandwiched between two separate front covers designed by Wilson and Griffin, respectively; it could be read front to back and back to front. The hinge was in the middle, a Moscoso-designed turnaround center spread that featured drawings of Daisy and Donald Duck engaged in comic-book hanky-panky.

At the same time that *Zap #3* was in the works, Crumb revealed a set of photocopied pages that he had originally prepared for what was to be the first *Zap*. Unfortunately, he had given the artwork to a publisher who disappeared with the originals before publication. "Fortunately, Crumb had xeroxed the pages, including the covers," recalls Moscoso. He continues: "In those days, the xeroxes picked up the line, but not the solid black. So Crumb had to fill in all the solids." Moscoso and Griffin agreed that, since Crumb had this entire comic book together, he should publish it just as it was, without the other contributors, and they would call it *Zap #0*. The only thing he changed from the original was the cover. "We didn't very often ask each other for advice," says Moscoso about the time that Crumb asked for him for his thoughts about a drawing showing a man floating in a fetal position with an electric wall cord plugged into his derriere. "I looked at it and I said, 'It don't look right, Robert. The guy is in a fetal position with electricity surrounding him, so to have the cord go into his ass doesn't make as much sense as if it went into his umbilical cord.' And he actually took my advice."

Not to diminish Crumb's major contributions to *Zap* or underground comix in general, Moscoso credits S. Clay Wilson with inspiring the contributors to feistily bust taboos. "First Wilson comes out with the 'Checkered Demon,' then 'Captain Piss Gums and his Perverted Pirates,' in which he is drawing my worst fantasies! Frankly, we didn't really understand what we were doing until Wilson started publishing in *Zap*. I mean, he's not a homosexual, yet he's drawing all these homosexual things. He's not a murderer, yet he was murdering all these people. All the things that he wasn't, he was putting down in his strips. So that showed us that we were, without being aware of it, censoring ourselves."

Once the self-imposed constraints were lifted, the *Zap* artists, who now included Spain Rodriguez and Robert Williams, began to explore their own addled fantasies. "Each one of us started looking at our own work asking, 'How far out can we go along the model that Wilson had set up?' The only thing was it had to be our individual stories. I, for one, was not going to do 'Captain Piss Gums.' Instead, I had Donald and Daisy eating each other in the '69 issue because I was getting back at Walt Disney! I mean, I love Walt Disney. But here Mickey and Minnie have nephews, but nobody fucked. So this was my chance."

In this sense, *Zap* quickly became an arena to test the Supreme Court's "community standards" doctrine, which allowed each community to define pornography in relation to the local consensus. As on the edge as it was, *Zap #3* was unscathed. *Zap #4*, on the other hand, stretched those standards beyond the limit and was, therefore, enjoined by the San Francisco police. The seeds of discontent were born in features including the explicitly titled "A Ball in the Bung Hole," by Wilson, "Wonder Wart-Hog Breaks Up the Muthalode Smut Ring" by Shelton, and "Sparky Sperm" by Crumb, which was placed between front and back covers of a dancing penis. But the strip that forced the police's hand was Crumb's "Joe Blow," featuring Dad, Mom, Junior, and Sis in a satire of the incestuous all-American family. Or, as Moscoso explains: "You can cut off a guy's penis and devour it (as in 'Heads-Up' by Wilson), you can even chop people up into little pieces, but you can't have sex with your children." The *Zap* artists thought they "could knock down every taboo that there was." Instead, the police busted City Lights bookstore in San Francisco, and, in New York, *Zap #4* was prohibited from being sold over the counter.

Nevertheless, after paying a fine, City Lights proprietor and poet Lawrence Ferlinghetti continued to sell the contraband and subsequent issues without incident. Predictably, the attention caused *Zap*'s reputation and sales to rise. As for the artists, "I never did an incest story," says Moscoso, "and Crumb never did an incest story again, as far as I know . . . not for *Zap*. However, we did not self-censor. . . . It was just after a while we got it out of our systems."

Although subsequent issues were spared legal harassment, they were no less explicit than the offending issue. By the 1970s the raunch factor in underground comics was commonplace, and, with the liberal court's First Amendment rulings, it was fruitless to expend legal energy in cracking down on them. Moreover, *Zap* seemed to serve a purpose in venting the urges of a generation that needed to push boundaries. In fact, *Zap* is today a textbook study of how fringe ideas are no longer mysterious or threatening when they are unleashed. In *Zap #7*, for example, Spain introduced "Sangrella," which serves as a paean to sadomasochistic lesbian eroticism with a sci-fi twist, addressing the extremes of such weird fetishism. In retrospect it is little more than a ribald jab at the sexlessness of superheroes. In *Zap #8* Robert Williams's "Innocence Squandered" is less prurient than it is a satiric commentary on how pornography is adjudicated in the courts. Actually, by *Zap #11*, although sexual references proliferate, the strips became more experimental in terms of form and content. In this issue Crumb's "Patton," about the great blues performer Charley Patton, is a masterpiece of comic strip as documentary. In the same issue Spain's "Lily Litvak: The Rose of Stalingrad" transforms a little-known historical fact into a comic strip that is kindred to the heroic comic books of the World War II era. And in *Zap #13* even Gilbert Shelton turned his attention from fantasy to real life in "Graveyard Ghosts," a brief tour of Père Lachaise Cemetery in Paris.

Thirty years, fifteen issues, and (according to distribution figures) millions of copies later, *Zap* has not changed all that much. The same contributors, minus Griffin (who died in 1995), are still pumping out an issue every two years. During a period in American history when political ultraconservatives are blaming the 1960s for all social ills, it is interesting to note that even in maintaining its consistency, *Zap* is not the wellspring of radical raunch that it once was. American tolerance for the abhorrent was long ago stretched beyond *Zap*'s boundaries. "The fact that we're even still selling these things actually is remarkable," Moscoso admits. "These things should have gone by the wayside a long time ago, by all logical standards. But there are people who still read this crap! Not bad for a piece of trash. Really."

SPY

Stephen Doyle

I am not a maniac about knowing who cut what face or if it's true to the original drawing," said Stephen Doyle (b. 1956), the cofounder of Drenttel Doyle Partners in New York, who in 1986 also designed the format of the original *SPY* magazine and supervised its first four issues. "I am a maniac about legibility and whether something is interesting enough to be set into type in the first place. With all the expense involved in typesetting one better be damn sure that a manuscript is worthwhile." Doyle described himself as a "translator" who believes in the power of typography to induce readers to read.

This may seem disingenuous coming from the designer who has promoted typographic anarchy in *SPY*, the New York–based satiric journal of culture and politics that defined the 1980s while it pilloried its leading players. But if Doyle encouraged the use of four-point text type and bled copy blocks off the page, it was consistent with a faithfulness to content. When articles in *SPY* were composed in multiple text faces of varying weights—some on excruciatingly tight column widths—Doyle was simply responding to the demands of the magazine. "*SPY* had many different voices," Doyle explained, "so we kept flipping type styles to reflect that. The editors liked sidebars so we used them everywhere and even gave the sidebars their own sidebars. We let the type be the messenger for the manuscript. So the type misbehaved because the manuscripts misbehaved. It was as though we let the writers design the magazine."

Doyle's design respected the content and rejected decoration for its own sake. In *SPY* every visual element had a purpose. "*SPY* was like a magazine in therapy," Doyle continued. "It was so much about the process of making magazines that we let it all show." *SPY*'s frenetic pace was a reflection of media-blitzed America, but Doyle based its visual persona on a variety of personal precepts, too. "I have a theory," he said, explaining why much of the type is set small enough to require a microscope. "People will read what they want to no matter how big or small the type. And while I don't believe in obscuring a message, through scale changes, one can nevertheless have a little fun with it." Doyle took a lot of heat for his Lilliputian preferences, but never repudiated himself. For *SPY*'s first anniversary party Doyle even designed an invitation with the necessary information set in two-point Granjon italic in the form of an exclamation point—he included a magnifying glass. "I wouldn't have done that with a lot of copy," he admitted, "But some things just call out for it."

A few years after it premiered, the *SPY* style was mimicked by other magazines, usually in instances where the subjects didn't merit it. Doyle reacted by turning down the volume. Doyle's typography is not really about misbehaving. As he has pointed out, the inspiration for the original *SPY* was not the urban environment or deconstructionist architecture, but a 1540 polyglot Bible where each language is set in a different typeface.

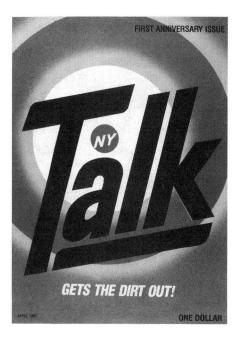

Tabloids developed their malodorous reputation because of the gutter journalism practiced by their earliest proponents in Britain and the United States. It wasn't until after 1900 that the term tabloid, which originally connoted a newspaper half the size of a standard broadsheet (about the size of today's *New York Times*), became synonymous with the lurid and scandalous. In 1919 two cousins, Joseph Medill Patterson and Robert Rutherford McCormick, began publishing the *New York Daily News*. Its reduced, tabloid size was immediately successful, being easier to hold and read on New York's sardine-packed subways. The *Daily News* was assured even greater circulation by its unbridled preoccupation with sex and violence, conveyed by screaming headlines and full front-page halftones. It became the largest-selling tabloid in America and spawned many competitors. One of these was Bernarr Macfadden's *Daily Graphic*, which entered into an unprecedented circulation war, giving its readers the most reprehensible displays of gutter publishing ever practiced. Despite, or because of this, tabloid mania flourished in the 1920s until loud outcries from the protectors of the public's morals tempered, somewhat, the rumor, sex, and gore.

Recently, there has been a more benign reason for publishing a tabloid: economy. Printers could offer publishers twice the product for half the price. For this reason a tabloid explosion began in the mid-1960s, coinciding with the free-speech movement and subsequent rise of youth culture. Low-budget underground or counterculture papers appeared around the country and abroad. Anarchic drug, sex, and political weeklies, like the San Francisco *Oracle*, the Los Angeles *Free Press*, and the *East Village Other*, were in the vanguard of this movement. They were cheaply produced, inexpensively sold (average twenty-five cents), and widely read. They were records and totems of their times.

The tabloids' design was governed by a marked lack of money and technology, and administered by naïfs, who, armed with press-type, benday and patterned Letraset screens, ruling tapes, Addressograph phototype, freebie photographs, and raunchy comix, produced raw but expressive nongraphic design. Despite the differences in approach, the instinctive underground layout practiced then and the mannered culture tabloid design of today are remarkably similar.

Underground papers began declining in the late 1960s. A new genre of alternative "sex-culture" papers (many published by the underground papers themselves to make money) stole a fickle audience that preferred nudity to profundity. The underground tabloids finally died in the mid-1970s with the end of Vietnam War, the resignation of Richard Nixon, and as the "me" decade was taking hold. At the same time, a national paper shortage resulted in the decrease of the standard tabloid size and an increase in production costs. Moreover, many of those involved in underground publishing either were irrevocably burned out, or simply grew up and became interested in more conventional lives and livelihoods.

Those designers who used the underground press as a kind of graduate school—including Roger Black of *Rolling Stone* and Ronn Campisi of *Fusion*—wed the street-smart design and exuberance they learned with conventional design practices while working for more establishment journals. Hence, during the mid-1970s a second wave of counter-culture tabloids emerged, such as the *Real Paper*, *Boston Phoenix*, and *Chicago Reader*, among others, which were neither raw nor anarchic, but rather found solace in convention. Indeed, the only editorial difference from regional consumer magazines like *New York*, was that the tabloids appealed to a slightly younger, but nevertheless upwardly mobile readership. In terms of their design and editorial bent, these publications were upbeat, yet somewhat staid blends of New York's *Village Voice*, the *New York Review of Books*, and *Rolling Stone*. Their purpose was to educate, inform, and otherwise provide readers with reviews and calendar features.

Slightly before the second wave crested, the granddaddy of new tabloids, Andy Warhol's *Interview*, appeared. In the early 1970s a few avant-garde artists gave vent to their ego needs by publishing artsy, gossip-filled magazines. That Warhol's was the only one to survive was a tribute to a basically sound idea: interviews with movie stars, glitterati, and eccentric personalities otherwise ignored by the establishment press, and a forum for fashion-conscious writers. The first issues were quarterfold formats, with lackluster design and no exceptional visual personality. But *Interview* quickly developed a constituency and, during the late 1970s, a distinctive look when Richard Bernstein was commissioned to do regular full-color cover portraits. *Interview* developed into an odd but enjoyable amalgam of

W, *Vogue*, and *Harper's Bazaar*, spiced with a dash of *People*. Its gossipy tone appealed to culture vultures, those maturated groupies who thrived on avant-gardism. *Interview* became a safe haven for the Jekylls and Hydes of society called Yuppies, who were squeaky clean by day and down and dirty at night. *Interview*'s interior is minimally designed, like a hip *New York Review of Books*, to allow for maximum photographic impact, and so as not to compete with its advertising. Nevertheless, it has influenced the appearance of many subsequent culture tabs.

By the late 1970s, boomers born in the late 1950s and early 1960s were clamoring for their own cultural voices. On the West Coast, punk was the predominant attitude and style. Its proponents in Los Angeles spawned a neo-underground tabloid called *Slash*, a raucous blend of type, image, and neo-underground comix (cartoonist Gary Panter was the leading practitioner), and perfected what has been called the "ransom note" style of cut-and-paste design (somewhat related to futurist experiments in the teens). In San Francisco, a bizarre publishing diversion, *Wet: The Magazine of Gourmet Bathing*, ingeniously wed the 1970s sexual preoccupation with fashion-conscious nihilism cut, of course, with tongue-in-cheek, ribald wit. *Wet*'s art director practiced an ad hoc, gridless approach to layout (at least for the first year, after which *Wet* changed design and editorial format and dropped bathing from its title). *Wet* signaled a post-underground obsession with esoterica.

On the East Coast, *Fetish*, a similarly arcane culture tab, was published and designed by David Sterling and Jane Kosstrin. But *Fetish* was a linchpin of sorts. Its content was not sex or drug oriented, but was a somewhat rarefied exploration of "the man/object matrix in contemporary culture" (translation: articles on art, architecture, and design against an avant-garde backdrop). Although its design was once described as a marriage of underground and Condé Nast fashion-magazine sensibilities, it made a purposeful departure from ad hoc gridless design, to a controlled, yet playful, anarchy (or "new wave" design). Also on the East Coast, new wave/ punk music and its offshoots gave rise to tabloids like the *New York Rocker* and the *East Village Eye* (apparently a reference to the *East Village Other*'s eye logo). Both had a random and skewed approach to layout that resembled their underground forerunners, but without the naïve integrity.

Although it seemed that the underground aesthetic was not entirely dead and the torch had only changed hands, the truth was that alternative culture had changed. Politics was no longer operative, rather interest in material culture was dominant. The antiestablishmentism, so naively practiced by the underground, was codified by a new group of design-literate practitioners. Outrageousness became an end in itself, manifest in the design clichés of the period—a Mad Max, Road Warrior, post-Holocaust vision of life wed to a skewed 1930s modernism. It quickly emerged as a distinctly identifiable style, easy prey for style merchants, the entrepreneurs who learned from the 1960s that even the most sincere youth culture can be a profitable commodity. Punk was co-opted and commercially packaged as new wave. A domino effect began, in which a plethora of new wave products—from clothes to watches to records— created a need for eye-catching advertising, which in turn created demand upon publishers for outlets.

In Los Angeles, the surge in chic, trendy, and not altogether uninspired new wave–styled publicity for boutiques, restaurants, and galleries fostered the tabloid *Stuff*, ostensibly an elegant supermarket handout whose only editorial content (save for a few insignificant text pages) was its paid advertising. Indeed, some of the ads were designed with more zest, imagination, and panache than a lot of conventional graphic design. On the East Coast, similarly focused "square" tabloid/ magazines, including *Details*, *Paper*, and the full-sized tabloid, *New York Talk*, were merely editorial environments for advertising. As a rule these East Coast periodicals ran "soft" feature stories, picture spreads, and random items covering their cultural milieu. Although each masthead listed a considerable number of contributing writers, it is fair to say that the writing would not overtax the average reader. At best it would entertain and at worst, separate one page of ads from the next. Still, these publications should not be totally dismissed as fluff.

A famous photograph taken by Berenice Abbott in the early 1930s shows a packed newsstand in midtown Manhattan with more than one hundred different magazines for sale (most for about a nickel, as compared to today's average three-dollar cover price). Despite the varied photographs, illustrations, and titles on their covers, many of the publications look alike. Graphic style is a visual indication of a cultural period. Many of the magazines in Abbott's photograph are in the deco mold—then the dominant style. Although style represents a period, it does not always state content. In every period there are manifestations that define the dominant attitude and those that copy it. That many of today's culture tabs look the same is simply a signpost of a design-conscious and technologically advanced period. Some of the publications discussed here will be forgotten, like the hundreds of me-too undergrounds published during the late 1960s and early 1970s. Others will make a lasting contribution to (rather than merely being a reflection of) the visual culture and the culture as a whole.

The Face

Neville Brody

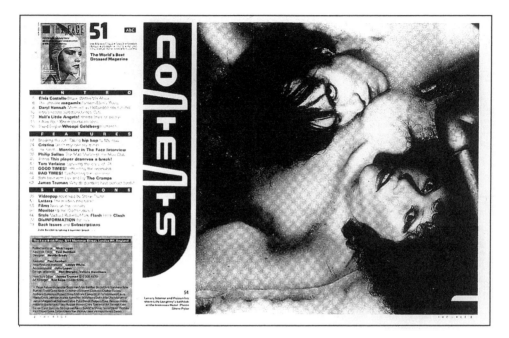

Neville Brody (b. 1957) was weaned on the dada-inspired nihilism of British punk in the 1970s. But *The Face*, his first important magazine design, was no neo-punk tabloid, but a slick, youth culture magazine that combined a 1920s avant-garde sensibility with contemporary style. The magazine focused on music, film, nightlife, art, dance, and the lifestyle of Britain's hip culture. Brody was twenty-four when he joined *The Face*, bringing his rebellious punk sensibility to a larger, consumer-oriented venue. In Nick Logan, editor and publisher, Brody found a sympathetic collaborator. Logan never undertook any market research, preferring to trust his instincts. He gave Brody great freedom to invent the visual structure of the magazine, even to the extent of moving the masthead logo all over the cover (including sideways). Budget limitations and tight deadlines (Brody would design forty pages in as many hours) were offset by on-the-spot, risk-taking decisions on design and editorial content that would be impossible in a larger publishing house.

In 1976 Brody entered the Royal College of Printing expressly to learn enough about visual communication to use it for his own ends.

Although he rejected fine art as elitist, his early work centered on images, and when he used typography it was in a similar, illustrative way. A decided contrarian (if a teacher approved of his work, he redid it), Brody found a catalyst and a philosophical home in the anticommercialism of the punk movement. Just out of school, he joined designers like Barney Bubbles, Malcolm Garrett, and Peter Saville in designing record sleeves. He first worked for the design studio Rocking Russian, then for Stiff and Fetish Records, two of the most popular independent record labels in Britain. Set up by Jake Riviera, a friend of Bubbles, Stiff Records was a freewheeling environment where outrageousness not only applied to sleeve design, but also to marketing schemes. Stiff once printed a sleeve with the wrong band on the cover hoping fans would then buy the corrected version. Brody relished the creative freedom but became disenchanted with the commercial manipulation.

Brody's first few issues of *The Face* were image oriented. "I hated type," he once confessed. In fact, in school he dismissed type as incredibly boring. This admission belies the fact that under Brody's art direction, *The Face* was a wellspring of typographic quirkiness. Brody presented text in a straightforward manner but surrounded it with compelling imagery, headlines, lead decks, and subheads. He soon realized he could extract as much emotive energy from the typography as from the imagery. Inspired by the work of Russian constructivist Alexander Rodchenko, Brody began to use heavy rules and hand-drawn, sans-serif typefaces, and to craft letterforms that functioned like emblems and crests. Typefaces were custom designed for headlines; letters were truncated, squashed, lopped off and blurred; fonts were mixed within a word; icons replaced letters within words, and headlines combined with symbols and functioned like corporate logos. "I had no respect for the traditions of typography, because I had no understanding of them," Brody explained.

As his confidence grew, Brody used the magazine as a virtual stage allowing himself more freedom to question the very core of visual expression. He reframed the magazine as an ongoing dialogue with the readership where idiosyncratic graphic signposts and icons, which may have initially appeared incomprehensible to the reader, gained meaning through consistent application over a series of issues. Brody, uninhibited by the edge of the page, treated the magazine as a continuum where what happened on page five connected to what happened on page fifty-five. He re-examined the use of page numbers, considering symbols instead. Regarding the contents page of a magazine he said, "You decide to have a contents page to act as a key—it's an advert for the magazine, a second cover, equivalent to the back of a book jacket where you read the blurb."

In 1984 the contents page logo in issue #50 was a banner-like emblem with mixed-font typographic forms. The letterforms were sideways, but were drawn in such a way that when looking at them straightforwardly the *T*'s became pluses, the *E* became an *M* and *C* doubled as a lower case *N*, introducing multiple interpretation. From issue #51 through #55 Brody incrementally deconstructed the graphic elements within the logoform as well as the exterior shape itself, until only abstract glyphs in a strong rectangular shape were left. In deconstructing the contents page logo over several issues he tested the limits of readability and the strength of continuity.

The Face was unorthodox, but not anarchic. "Everything in *The Face* was reasoned; every single mark on the page was either an emotive response or a logical extension of the ideas," said Brody. It was the interweaving of two narratives, one visual and one textual on a gridded plane. Brody's headlines became objects, like in the February 1985 issue a custom-designed *M* for the opening spread of an article on Madonna becomes in the March issue the *W* to lead into an article on Andy Warhol. It was not a joke, or a response to a budget cutback, but a visual analog of the way Warhol appropriated imagery. The grid was a simple system to complement the complexity and innovation Brody brought to it, yet definitive enough to convey unity.

Brody envisioned a magazine that would inspire other designers to ask more questions, not provide a crib sheet for quick graphic solutions. "Essentially, I think I failed. My ideas were weakened into style. The very thing I used in order to get the ideas across—a strong personal style—was the thing that defeated reception of the ideas," Brody lamented in 1990, years after leaving the magazine. *The Face* ultimately did become a style guide. In 1986 he moved on to *Arena*, also edited by Logan, who, disregarding market failures of larger publishing houses, like *Cosmo Man* for Condé Nast, decided it was time for a magazine that targeted a male audience. *Arena* was a more sophisticated version of *The Face*, a consumer-oriented quarterly publication featuring upscale people-watching fashion, sports, and travel in addition to the mainstay lifestyle articles that had worked for *The Face*.

Frustrated with the appropriation of his work, Brody decided to stop designing "the new thing." After the first two issues of *Arena*, which resembled *The Face*, he returned to classic modernist methods. He used Helvetica and chose typefaces like Garamond Light Condensed and Kabel Bold for headlines and cover lines. Photographic quality was paramount. This was a postmodern homage to the Swiss school, yet it was not Swiss, but rather "Swiss Tech," the marriage of Swiss-influenced typography and futurist composition. But critics and imitators were not far behind, and graphic style in Britain edged toward this neo-modernism.

By 1988 Brody's career reached a turning point. The publication of *The Graphic Language of Neville Brody,* written by Brody and his collaborator Jon Wozencroft, coincided with an exhibition of his work at London's Victoria and Albert Museum. Both were misinterpreted as self-congratulatory hoopla. Almost immediately afterwards, Brody, suffering from a severe case of overexposure, stopped getting British work, which triggered a financial crisis. At the age of thirty, the man who had been called the first graphic design superstar needed to regroup. He found new clients in Japan and Europe. He immersed himself in digital technology. Testing entrepreneurship, he became a partner in FontWorks, the British arm of FontShop, the international font-distributor started by Erik Spiekermann. In 1991 he launched the experimental type magazine *Fuse* with Wozencroft as editor. A quasipromotional tool for FontShop, each issue of *Fuse* presented a set of typefaces in a digital format organized around a theme, background material on the fonts and their designers, printed style sheets, and an editorial essay.

In *Fuse* #10, Brody introduced Freeform, a collection of abstract shapes. It was designed with the articulation of a typeface, it had a certain rhythm, coloring, and repetition, but it abandoned the consensual meaning of the alphabet in favor of pure emotional impact. Freeform was criticized for its illegibility and dependence on a personal visual language. Brody explained, "It's moving from representational to expressive typography. I think the parallel with what happened in painting is absolutely precise. . . . Putting desktop technology in the hands of the nondesigner liberates the designer from the necessity of representation in the same way that the camera liberated the artist."

From *The Face,* whose typographic idiosyncrasies prefigured the modern digital revolution, to *Fuse,* which attempts to describe the intersection of the linguistic and the pictorial, Brody has been unwavering in his quest for a new visual sensibility based on ideas. Always more comfortable with questions than answers he asked, "In the West, the Roman and Greek alphabets provide the basis of the consciously designed letterform, but you can carry this further back to the ancient Egyptians' use of hieroglyphs or even to ritualistic markings in caves. At what point does true typography begin?"

| Emigre |
| Rudy VanderLans and Zuzana Licko |
| |

Deconstructivist typography, an idea more or less inspired by linguistic theory, had a complicated birth and many midwives. During the 1970s Basel designer Wolfgang Weingart developed a system of typographic reordering as an alternative to the dominant *Neue Grafik* or international style. On the surface his radical approach was chaotic, yet underneath it was built on a structure of hierarchical logic. Many of Weingart's exponents were schooled in academic modernism and found that this new method released them from old strictures. The modern method was becoming unresponsive as shifts in technology, economy, and politics began to unhinge the canonical absolutes.

The spread of electronic media and computer technology began to suggest, if not define, new ways to present information. With new interactive media, graphic design could no longer be one dimensional. As traditional methods of designing books and magazines were challenged, visionary American designers like April Greiman and Dan Friedman found new ways of busting the grid. Harnessing the primitive characteristics of electronic media and making strengths out of technological weakness resulted in new methods that, over time, evolved into a language. The use of multiple layers of discordant typefaces integrated with imagery became, on the one hand, a commentary on the information deluge, and, on the other, a signpost that underscored new perceptual pathways. A similar discordant eruption in typography took place in the late 1890s, the Victorian era—the chaotic, nascent period of commercial design when job printers purposely mixed different typefaces together in the service of fashion and function.

In 1983, a year before the introduction of the Macintosh computer, Rudy VanderLans (b. 1955) and Zuzana Licko (b. 1961), the former Dutch and the latter Czech, founded an alternative culture magazine they called *Emigre*. What started as a cousin of the 1960s underground newspaper developed into the clarion of digital typography and design. The first Macintosh and its primitive default faces inspired *Emigre*'s founders to focus on design. VanderLans called it "a cultural force," rather than a passive observer. Emigre Graphics (later Emigre Fonts), the type business, became a pioneer in typeface design, and *Emigre*, the magazine, propagated the faith. Emigre Fonts introduced some of the earliest and quirkiest dot-matrix and, as the technology improved, high-resolution digital typefaces. *Emigre* magazine showcased the leading proponents and exponents of a new typography that wed youthful rebellion, evolutionary imperatives, and intellectual curiosity into type and page designs that challenged the canonical rules. These designers sought to reach audiences that were either disinterested in, or turned off by orthodox modern approaches, and they developed visual codes that forced reevaluation of conventional type design.

As *Emigre* challenged the status quo it earned the ire of certain proponents of classic modernism. Massimo Vignelli referred to the new typography as "garbage," and in "The Cult of the Ugly" (*Eye,* No. 3, Vol. 9) I (Steven Heller) called it a "blip in the continuum of graphic design history." This antipathy was not entirely a knee-jerk reaction to the new, but it did reveal an inevitable generational schism. On the surface trends and fashions were being scrutinized, while underneath lurked discomfort with change.

Once released from the safe haven of the laboratory the tension between young and old ignited. Progress in art and design is certain, but the baton is rarely passed smoothly. Action and reaction in design are as natural as the changing tides, and just as necessary. Arguments force practitioners of all ages to assess and defend. Stasis, the hobgoblin of creativity, is invariably disrupted. The approaches promoted by *Emigre* encouraged a reevaluation of old methods and aesthetics in the light of a new technological era. They became touchstones for progress but, paradoxically, also provided templates for mimicry.

It is axiomatic that when a progressive method becomes popular its edges are smoothed. By the time the avant-garde enters the mass consciousness many of its successful experiments have already been diluted, reduced to little more than style. In fine art the acceptance of radical approaches into the mainstream may mean victory for their proponents, but ultimately the most progressive forms are neutered to appeal to a larger audience. The outsider in graphic design is even more of a contradiction. The commercial nature of design necessitates that what's outside be brought inside or become irrelevant. Regardless of how determined *Emigre* was to forge new directions, they were incapable of preventing appropriation.

The cultural feeding frenzy that overtook the *Emigre* "style" was predictable. What *Emigre* initiated was co-opted by scores of mainstream, cultish manifestations—from magazines to MTV. The ethos further outgrew its experimental stage and became the "cool" or "hip" way to communicate. But this should not diminish *Emigre's* impact or significance.

VanderLans and Licko, while launching a business, took the necessary, courageous leaps that pioneers must take. *Emigre* was not just the standard-bearer of the new design style, but was, and continues to be, the bearer of standards for experimental digital typography. Through the shift from hot metal to phototype and even to computer type, although the mechanics of type had changed frequently, the fundamental nature of type had remained constant. While other serious type designers initially adapted traditional methods to the digital medium, *Emigre* pushed the boundaries. VanderLans and Licko were not satisfied to follow tradition, and ultimately they created a tradition of their own.

Françoise Mouly (b. 1955) and Art
Spiegelman (b. 1948) were married in 1982.
Within a few months they gave birth to a
publishing business which they named
Raw Books and Graphics. It was
consigned to a corner of their loft in Manhattan's SoHo district, where it quickly
grew into a healthy concern. Mouly, a
native of Paris, had been an architecture
student at the Ecole des Beaux-Arts and
worked as a colorist for Marvel Comics in
New York; Spiegelman, a native New
Yorker, was an underground comic strip
editor and artist with a unique analytical
approach to comic page construction. The
comics brought them together; and
because they agreed that viable outlets did
not exist in America for the kind of
experimental work that interested them,

they decided to fill the void left by the demise of underground comix in the
mid-1970s by starting a publishing venture that would somehow provide a
forum for new and radical forms. This entrepreneurial commitment thrust
them into the roles of publisher and editor, and more reluctantly into being
the virtual foster parents to a group of artists whose unconventional styles
and approaches were given little encouragement in mainstream publishing
circles. Within a few years *RAW* magazine, the flagship of Raw Books and
Graphics, had enlivened a moribund field.

The reasons for starting Raw Books and Graphics were compelling. "There was no place worth appearing in," Spiegelman said. "There
were magazines interested in me, but they wanted me to bend myself out of
shape to do comics that would be fitting for them." Mouly had already single-
handedly published *The SoHo Map and Guide,* an ambitious first project
that sold advertising space to SoHo merchants. Now she wanted to learn
printing, so they bought a used multilith press and rebuilt it in their loft.

"The real genesis of *RAW*," admitted Spiegelman, "was Françoise's
goading it into existence, because it had a certain logic after she began

getting involved in publishing. That meant setting up a makeshift distribution system so that things she printed could get around, which she did. And then her being ready to take on something more ambitious. For a while it seemed that might be books rather than the magazine, but the advantage after we did the first issue of *RAW* (which we swore we would never do again) was that we'd already set up something we could build on. A book is always another book and requires a whole new constituency to be gathered each time. The magazine gave us a core of readers." *The SoHo Map and Guide* provided enough capital to publish a first issue, and the makeshift distribution Mouly had set up eventually paid them enough to keep going without further infusions of outside capital.

In a way, *RAW* evolved from Spiegelman's anthology *Breakdowns*, at least in adapting the book's expansive dimensions (eleven by fourteen inches), which enabled him to print his strips at almost their original size. There were other reasons for the new magazine's format, too. "*RAW* started at a time when there were a number of large-size cultural tabloids, such as *Wet*, *Fetish*, *Skyline*, and *Interview*," recalled Spiegelman. "The only thing they had in common was the fact that they were 'new wave,' with a large size and a new sensibility. So whether it was fashion, architecture, art, or politics, they sat next to each other on the newsstand. Whatever vestigial marketing sense I had said that if we did comics as a large-size thing, they could sit next to the architecture magazines and nobody would say 'where should the comic book go?'"

From the outset, Spiegelman and Mouly wanted a three-letter title in the tradition of *MAD*. They went through many ideas before settling on *RAW*, which for them meant "having vital juices intact" rather than untamed or aggressive. To this they added a new, enigmatic subtitle with each issue, among them, "The Graphix Magazine for Damned Intellectuals," "The Graphix Magazine of Abstract Depressionism," "The Graphic Aspirin for War Fever," and "The Graphix Magazine that Over-estimates the Taste of the American Public." By comic book standards, *RAW*'s premiere issue was tame: every element was purposefully designed. But in the beginning *RAW*'s design was a disquieting mix of what seemed like trendy new wave detailing, and, by modernist graphic design standards, a comic book heavy-handedness. Every page had an obtrusive running head, an inelegant rule with a panel in which the artist's name appeared, and a page number dropped out of a circle. Although this became *RAW*'s signature design element, when it was first introduced it appeared a distracting conceit. Each contents page was an artwork in its own right, with overprints, drop-outs, and other design details that echoed the punk graphic aesthetic of the time.

RAW #1 was printed on heavy white paper and included a small comic book by Spiegelman called "Two-Fisted Painters" (one of his many strips devoted to exploring and satirizing the comic form). The front cover had a color panel pasted on it to give Spiegelman's stark black-and-white illustration another dimension and to compensate for the lack of full-color printing. "A lot of attention was paid to its objectness," said Spiegelman, who was creative consultant for Topps Bubble Gum Company during that period, and has always harbored a fetish for novelty that he translated into the magazine. Though many of the strips were visually raw compared to those of slick mainstream comics, their surreal and heady unpredictability forced the reader to take notice. By *RAW* #5, which Spiegelman and Mouly agree was the most challenging issue, the various mixtures of typography, art, and novelty were so well integrated that *RAW*'s style was decidedly its own. *RAW* had become a genre.

"It was never meant to be a long-lived project," sighed Spiegelman, revealing his characteristic angst. "It was meant to be a demonstration of how something could be in a better world, and ended up having its own logic and momentum; it began, more or less, steering us rather than us steering it. And I think that's still true." That momentum was generated in part by the *RAW* artists, who were being given a venue in which to grow and were not eager to give it up. "Once everything was set up," continued Spiegelman, "it was just as easy to feed it as to kill it."

RAW certainly did fulfill a need. It became a veritable mecca for quirky and visionary artists and storytellers from all over the world. From the initial five thousand print run, subsequent runs increased incrementally to almost twenty thousand by *RAW* #8, the last of the large-format issues. Among the relative newcomers were Gary Panter, who already had a cult following for his *Jimbo* strip, which appeared in a West Coast punk magazine called *Slash*; Charles Burns, who had only ever published spot illustrations before sending his meticulously drawn translations of 1950s horror and love clichés to *RAW* for consideration; Jerry Moriarty, who was teaching at the School of Visual Arts in New York and barely getting published before *RAW* picked up his "Jack Survives," a surrealistic view of the banal; and Mark Beyer, with his *art brut* tales about depression and death. Other homegrown discoveries included Drew Friedman, Ben Katchor, and Mark Newgarden.

Spiegelman and Mouly also published the cream of the European comic strip artists, including the brilliantly designed strips of Joost Swarte from Holland and Ever Meulen from Belgium; the explosive graphic fantasies of Pascal Doury and the *noir* storytelling of Jacques Tardi, both from France; and the seductive comicalities of the Spaniard Javier Mariscal.

In his effort to separate *RAW* from underground comix, Spiegelman featured the masters of the genre and published new stories by Robert Crumb, Kim Deitch, Justin Green, and Bill Griffith. He wanted to provide a forum for illustrators, too, but most of those he invited failed to produce. The notable exception was Sue Coe, who provided some of the most strident polemical visual commentary in *RAW*, as well as two *RAW* One-Shot books, *How to Commit Suicide in South Africa*, a visual indictment of the effects of apartheid, and *X*, a paean to Malcolm X.

In the time since Raw Books and Graphics was conceived, more *RAW*-inspired magazines were published. *RAW* itself has been seriously analyzed for pushing the limits of the form, and for reviving the nascent intelligence of the American comic strip. This cottage publishing entity that Spiegelman and Mouly invested their hearts into has, arguably, done more to awaken Americans to the integrity of the comic strip than all the efforts of comics writers, artists, and producers since comic strips began in the American newspapers almost one hundred years ago.

Good magazine design is not simply a process of imposing tried and true formulas, but one of creating formats that complement an editorial viewpoint. Yet much magazine design is tried and true because publishers want to be safe. Advertisers prefer it that way.

On rare occasions magazine designers rise above the design clichés imposed by marketing experts, and when an intrepid designer does take the plunge notice must be taken. Every so often a magazine captures the Zeitgeist. In the mid-1970s *Wet: The Magazine of Gourmet Bathing*, with its premiere cover showing two photographs, taken ten years apart, of a mother

and her daughters sitting naked in a bathtub, marked a shift from "underground press" politics to cult fetishism. In the early 1980s *Emigre*, with its alternative cross-cultural coverage and raucous type design, suggested a new wave was about to crest. In 1990 *Beach Culture*, a journal of West Coast watersports, became the cult magazine of the moment when it surfaced in design competitions and annuals nationwide. Its primary audience was surfers, but it became the benchmark of 1990s design. Its sole designer, David Carson (b. 1956), transformed the magazine into a showcase for radical typography and design tomfoolery.

Beach Culture was full of design indulgences and technological trickery, but it also included striking photography and illustration by talented artists, such as Geof Kern, Marshall Arisman, Milton Glaser, Matt Mahurin, and Henrik Drescher. As a chaotic pastiche of typographic excess it was often unreadable, but conventional readability was not necessarily a virtue given its context. *Beach Culture* catered to an audience that was able to navigate the visuals and text. No one ever said a surfing magazine should look mainstream. But neither was there a demand that it be cutting edge.

Certainly most other surfing magazines were void of distinguished design. Since surfing is such a specialized activity and writing about it is arcane, one would hardly have expected a surf magazine to be typographically innovative or risqué.

Beach Culture was born out of a two-hundred-page annual advertorial called *Surf Style* that included puff pieces about the products advertised therein. Carson embraced the publisher's idea to make *Surf Style* into a real magazine. This former design intern at Surfer publications, former art director of *Skateboard* magazine and *Musician*, had studied typography with designer Jean Robert in Switzerland and learned about the power of vernacular forms and how type could be made expressive through abstraction. After the premiere issue of *Beach Culture* many advertisers dropped out, confused by its odd mix of beach and culture, yet enough of them remained to continue publishing. Carson seized the opportunity; following in the footsteps of contemporary design progressives, such as Wolfgang Weingart, Rudy VanderLans, Rick Valicenti, and Neville Brody, he began his own expedition into new—and often illegible—realms of visual presentation. Carson's spin on typographic anarchy was different than his predecessors. He not only infused his pages with wit and irony, but also accepted that a magazine page is ephemera.

In one issue he ran a story in three conventional columns of type, but rather than reading the traditional way, vertically down, it read horizontally across with each sentence jumping from one column to the next. "Usually, I take my design cue from the story or art," said Carson, "but this time I just did it to have fun. Once the reader caught on I'm sure they had fun too." On another page Carson designed the page numbers to be larger than the main headline, a joke in itself, but when the editor changed the order of the pages, he kept the original number on the page because, he explained, "I just happened to like it there." In the final issue (of a total of six) the page numbers were eliminated and jump-lines simply said "continued." These hijinks forced the reader to find his or her own way.

Initially, Carson used the newest Emigre typefaces. "I wanted to use whatever was totally new and untried," he explained. However, he became more dependent on existing typefaces and published a "Special No Emigre Font Issue" (a reference that went over the heads of most surfers). "Emigre faces were becoming like clip art, too identifiable, too dated," he explained. "*Beach Culture* was trying to be fresh, and I was using typefaces that were appearing everywhere because they were hip and cool; it was just too easy."

Carson went further to make design that was difficult for his readers *and* writers. "In the beginning there were some writers who were real upset that their stories were too hard to read, but I found after a few issues that the very same writers who complained about crazy design were also upset if their article was not given that kind of treatment." Giving an article his special attention signaled that it was important. By the final issue, Carson had taken this premise to the extreme by obliterating most headlines. Letterforms were overlapped, overprinted, smashed, and otherwise covered by black, mortised, random bands abstracted to the point of incomprehensibility. Carson was designing for the code-busters to make sense of it all.

| **Colors** |
| Tibor Kalman |
| |

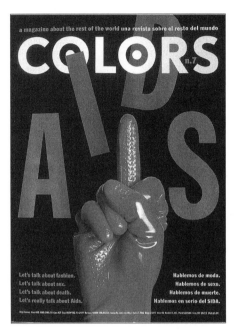

Critics argue that Benetton's highly visible, captionless double-truck ads and billboards featuring, among other images, a dying AIDS patient, war-weary refugees, and an Angolan rebel soldier nonchalantly holding a human bone, are sensationalist ploys to manipulate public perception. And for what? To sell sweaters? Yet Benetton claims that its motive in publishing such imagery is not just to garner the most publicity for the least possible PR dollar (although this certainly has been the effect), but to use their position as a successful business to communicate strong, if unpopular, messages about society and the world.

Productless advertisements are not new. During World War II, American corporations showed support for the war effort through institutional advertising that wed patriotism to corporate identity. Since the 1960s, Mobil Oil has propagated corporate citizenship through editorial ads on op-ed pages. In the 1980s Esprit, Kenneth Cole, and Ben and Jerry's devoted advertising and packaging space to promote social and environmental causes. But in the 1990s Benetton went a step further with a compelling campaign created by advertising director Olivero Toscani that attached the Benetton logo to a series of sensitive issues. What began as "The United Colors of Benetton," a product-based series of ads showing multicultural kids and promoting ethnic and racial harmony, evolved into captionless double-truck journalistic photographs of the kind mentioned above, which ultimately begot Benetton's own magazine, *Colors*.

Colors is not a fashion or style magazine in the "downtown," experimental, post-punk tradition; nor is it an institutional or corporate house organ. Rather its editorial focus is dedicated to presenting a harshly realistic, though often humorous, world view. Tibor Kalman (1949–1999), editor-in-chief of *Colors* from 1990 to 1995, characterized the magazine as a cross between *National Geographic*, *Life*, and *The Face*.

The primary reason for starting *Colors*, noted Kalman, was that Toscani was unhappy with the magazines in which he advertised; "He would get insane when *Vogue* and *Vanity Fair* had the audacity to turn down Benetton ads because they crossed the line from being safely elegant to strongly editorial." Toscani wanted a magazine that would build upon what he was already attempting to do through advertisements, and Kalman, who had been working with him on researching the photographs, wanted a magazine that would do nothing less than "change the world." Hence the bilingual (English and Italian) *Colors* was "The first magazine for the global village," said Kalman, "aimed at an audience of flexible minds, young people between fourteen and twenty, or curious people of any age."

Colors is ostensibly a visual magazine because no matter how good a translation of text is, some meaning or nuance is always lost. An image needs no translation. The magazine further intended to be "nomadic and focus on subcultures and tribes," and its design has been just as "nomadic." Under Kalman's tutelage *Colors* did not adhere to a single format. Each issue had a different graphic configuration (although the same gothic typefaces were repeated); the first three had radically different sizes and shapes. "It was not tied to any one environment." Kalman explained. And since he believed that most magazines trade on despair, he wanted *Colors* to be naïve enough to look at the world in an optimistic way. That proved to be a real challenge.

In its often disturbingly vivid coverage of such themes as deadly weapons, street violence, and hate groups, *Colors* offered a disquieting contrast to the publisher's own fashion products. Even the way it was printed, on calendered pulp paper, which soaked up ink and muted the color reproductions, went counter to the brightly lit Benetton shops with happy clothes in vibrant colors. *Colors* was not Benetton's darker alter ego, but it did serve to "contextualize," as Kalman defined it, Toscani's advertising imagery. Indeed the basis for much of the criticism leveled at Benetton's advertising campaign had been the absence of context. Without a caption or explanatory text the images appeared gratuitous—shocking yes, but uninformative. The campaign signaled that Benetton had some kind of a social conscience, but the ads themselves failed to explain what it was. With *Colors* the advertisements appear as teasers for a magazine that took stands on issues of war and peace, love and hate, power and sex.

Colors explored themes routinely ignored by the mainstream press, such as "How Much?" a story about how much money entrepreneurs pay for human body parts throughout the world, and "What's Sexy?" a compendium of what turns people on around the world. *Colors'* fourth, and most charged, issue was devoted to racism and expressed the need for tolerance and coexistence in the world. By avoiding sappy clichés and timeworn stereotypes, Kalman's brief editorial set the stage for a conflicting catalog of bitterness and hope: "We don't usually dwell on the bad news. And racial violence is definitely bad news. But this issue of *Colors* is about how race affects our lives and how racism can take many forms, not all as obvious as those we've presented here. These pictures are our way of showing the problem quickly and bluntly. It will take us longer to show you the solutions."

Like a serum that employs disease to immunize the body, *Colors* turned racist to fight racism. A feature titled "Who Are You?" spoke through a racist's voice to spew hundreds of slurs, epithets, and obscenities used by different ethnic and racial groups to describe their neighbors and enemies. In "So, What's the Difference?" the racist ploy of comparing and distinguishing physical characteristics was co-opted by using photographs of various kinds of ears, noses, and hair to show that physical differences are, in fact, endemic to humanity. In a stark photograph of two bleeding fingers, one black and the other white, the message that there is no fundamental difference is made vivid. In the same feature people from around the world were asked to describe difference within their various native and adopted cultures: "For the time being, I'm the only Ibo boy in Hungary. The people I work for love me for being an Ibo," replied a young boy; "I do not belong to a race. I am Egyptian. In my country it makes no difference what color you are or where you come from. The main difference here is rich and poor," said another. A disturbing feature, "How to Change Your Race," examined various cosmetic means of altering hair, lips, noses, eyes, and, of course, skin color to achieve some kind of platonic ideal. "What if . . ." was a collection of full-page manipulated photographs showing famous people racially transformed: Queen Elizabeth and Arnold Schwarzenegger as black; Pope John Paul as Asian; Spike Lee as white; and Michael Jackson's already altered features are further given a Nordic caste. "Race is not the real issue here," Kalman noted. "Power and sex are the dominant forces in the world."

But not everyone was pleased. A man in a Rolls Royce was arrested in London after smearing black paint over Benetton's store windows. He told the police that it was in retaliation for Benetton's irreverence towards the Queen. In Japan, twenty-five thousand copies of *Colors* were burned because authorities were afraid that the feature on epithets would seriously offend Japanese people, and they feared reprisals against Benetton's Japanese employees.

The racism issue of *Colors* touched raw nerves. It also proved that design in the service of a strong message could influence people. The problem was, people do not always want to be influenced in such ways. Numerous Benetton store owners were reluctant to offer the magazine; some adamantly refused. *Colors* was volatile and unpredictable. It was the first official organ of a mainstream corporation not to be dictated by demographic surveys or bottom-line policy. The magazine mirrored the passions of its editors and contributors rather than the marketplace and offered readers challenging ideas rather than safe clichés.

"Lettering is an active and vitally needful civilizing factor and must from henceforth play a much greater part in our life. . . . It will help to vitalize individual capacities and hence further the development of the whole of our future civilization," proclaimed a 1936 editorial titled "Writing and Lettering in the Service of the New State" in *Die Zeitgemässe Schrift*, a magazine devoted to students of lettering and calligraphy. The state was the Third Reich and the lettering was Fraktur, the traditional German blackletter that had lost favor during the Weimar Republic years when the New Typography challenged its dominance. Yet by 1933 the Nazis, who assailed modern sans serif type as "Judenlettern," brought Fraktur back

Der Kampfbund für Deutsche Kultur, Ortsgruppe Frankfurt-M u. der Deutsche Buchdrucker-Verein Frankfurt-M laden zum Besuch der Ausstellung

Die schöne Deutsche + + Schrift

im Kunstgewerbemuseum, Neue Mainzerstr. 49, ergebenst ein. Von Montag, den 6. Oktober bis Freitag, den 19. Oktober, von 10-2 Uhr geöffnet

with a vengeance. Such was the influence of Adolf Hitler over every aspect of German life that lettering and typography were harshly scrutinized by party ideologues.

Joseph Goebbels, Nazi minister for propaganda and enlightenment, initially decreed that blackletter be returned to its rightful place representing German *Kultur*. So in the early years of the Reich, blackletter became the official *Volksschrift* (lettering of the German people). However, they who decreeth also taketh away. After registering complaints about Fraktur's illegibility (purportedly from Luftwaffe pilots who could not read tail markings), Martin Bormann, Hitler's secretary, forbade the use of Fraktur in 1941 and ordered all official documents and schoolbooks to be reprinted. Overnight, blackletter became "Judenlettern," and roman type made a triumphant return. Although blackletter continues to evoke the spirit of Nazi authoritarianism, this summary fall from grace only adds to the historical confusion.

Blackletter, as Paul Shaw and Peter Bain state in the introduction to their catalog for the exhibition *Blackletter: Type and National Identity* (the Cooper Union, April 1998), is shrouded in mystery, mystique, and nationalism. The polar opposite of the geometrically based roman, blackletter, they explain, "is often misleadingly referred to as Old English or gothic [and] is an all-encompassing term used to describe the scripts of the Middle Ages in which the darkness of the characters overpowers the whiteness of the page." It is based on the liturgical scripts found in Gutenberg's 1455 Mainz Bible and precedes Nicolas Jenson's earliest roman alphabet by fifteen years. Blackletter developed throughout German-speaking Europe during the fifteenth century in four basic styles: textura (*gotisch*), rotunda (*rundgotisch*), schwabacher, and Fraktur. It has been reinterpreted in various manifestations and styles. The essays and time lines that comprise Shaw and Bain's catalog trace the dialectic between blackletter and roman and set the stage for the even more fascinating ideological issues inherent in the history of the type form.

Blackletter was always much more than an alphabetic system. The most illuminating essay in *Blackletter*, Hans Peter Willberg's "Fraktur and Nationalism" offers a vivid narrative of blackletter's ideological development. Prior to the Napoleonic wars, for example, tensions between the German states and France inflamed virulent nationalism, which encouraged official recognition of Fraktur as *the* German type, bestowing upon it the same passionate allegiance as a national flag. Throughout the nineteenth and twentieth centuries, blackletter symbolized the best and worst attributes of the German states and nation. In the 1920s Jan Tschichold (a leftist who briefly changed his name to Ivan in solidarity with the Bolsheviks) denounced "broken type" as nationalistic, while Rudolf Koch, who also designed the sans serif Kabel as well as his own version of Fraktur, supported, to quote Willberg, "the 'German Way of Being,' which manifested itself in the 'German Way of Writing.'" Other considerations, such as rationalism versus romanticism, later entered the debate for and against blackletter. The German left used Fraktur almost as much as the right, yet the type has been criticized most for being "Nazi-letters."

Given the negative perception of blackletter, one might presume that, after the Nazis' defeat in 1945, the type would have forever fallen into disrepute. But, as Yvonne Schemer-Scheddin explains in her essay, "Broken Images: Blackletter between Faith and Mysticism," an astute analysis of past *and* present usage, the type was retained by those businesses for whom conservative or traditional values could best be symbolized through Fraktur (including those in the fields of gastronomy and beer production as well as newspapers, for their mastheads) and as a fetish for those loyal to neo-Nazi ideologies. Since German federal law forbids any display of the swastika, blackletter continues to serve a ritualistic and symbolic role for extremists. At the same time, not all blackletter revivals are the property of skins or neo-fascists. Contemporary typographers from Jonathan Barnbrook, to Zuzana Licko, to Michael Worthington have reinterpreted blackletter in a variety of ways, and their quirky alphabets adorn gothic novels, heavy-metal CDs, and countless magazine and television advertisements for hip products. Probably most young designers have not even considered the ramifications of blackletter. Despite its ancient history, does blackletter's short stint as the face of evil shroud or inhibit its continued application? Indeed, this type, and type in general, is not just a vessel but a catalyst of meaning, message, and ideology, and as such, it poses questions still unanswered.

Walter Gropius, founder of the Staatliches Bauhaus—the state-funded school of arts and crafts—in Weimar, Germany, began his revolutionary school "not to propagate any style, system, dogma, formula, or vogue, but simply to exert a revitalizing influence on design." The Bauhaus was born in 1919. Germany had just lost a devastating world war. A fragile new republic had been established with its constituent assembly in Weimar, but despite the hopes of the Weimar Republic, the nation was in economic turmoil. The Bauhaus derived its strength from the social ferment, but ultimately suffered from the relentlessly belligerent political environment. For the Bauhaus to have been closed down only months after the Nazis came to power in 1933 suggests that it was a radical political institution at odds not only with German tradition, but also with Adolf Hitler's nationalist ideology. In fact, though the Bauhaus was built as a "Cathedral of Socialism" on a foundation that included Marxist theories about art and industry, politics per se was not primary.

The Bauhaus was established to help save the German economy by preparing a new generation of artists and artisans to deal effectively with the increasing demands of industrialization and its profound impact on society and culture. Gropius and his Bauhaus faculty sought to end the designer/craftsman's "alienation" from labor, and were dedicated to the concept of the "unified work of art—the great structure, bringing together the artist, producer, and consumer in holy union."

At the outset the Bauhaus resolved to reform society through education. It would democratize art by removing the distinction between "fine" and "applied" art, and by making art responsive to people's needs. The earliest Bauhaus manifesto offered a program that was, however, difficult to maintain given the complexities of German life. Plagued by outside critics and internal dissent, this so-called spiritual stage of the Bauhaus lasted only until 1923, replaced during its second phase (1923–1925) by new teaching methods based on quasi-scientific ideas and a machine age ethic. The third phase began when, in 1925 (continuing roughly until 1928), the Weimar government withdrew financial support, forcing the school to relocate to Dessau. It was there that Gropius built his Bauhaus school building—a monument to functionalism in which outward visual form is organically related to its internal function. It was in Dessau, too, that the workshop was transformed into a kind of laboratory program, and where, during a short spurt of economic growth, the school, having tailored its teachings to the demands of industry, developed products that rightfully represented a Bauhaus style. In 1928 Gropius retired leaving the Bauhaus to Hannes Meyer (a devout socialist) who was removed in 1931. The directorship next went to Mies Van der Rohe, who moved the school one more time before its permanent closing to an old telephone factory in Berlin.

Before its demise the Bauhaus was one of the most influential design institutions in the world in the fields of architecture, furniture, fixtures, textiles, scenic design, typography, and advertising. Its students were taught to think of themselves not as divorced from society, but as integral to it. Typographers, for example, were not aesthetic specialists nor service-oriented craftspersons, but practitioners of communications open to all possibilities—from abstract to conventional materials.

The Bauhaus typography workshop contributed ideas collected under the banner of the New Typography, the movement of progressive typographers and advertising artists who rebelled against antiquated tenets of design. This was a philosophy, not a style, based on the dictum that "form follows function," in which typography became a virtual machine for communication. The modern movement of the 1920s, though a rebellious one, reconciled contemporary and classical values by rejecting timeworn verities in favor of timeless utility. Functionalism was the hallmark of Bauhaus typography.

For decades, a tension has existed in typography between rationalism and expressionism, or rather objective versus subjective aesthetics. Jan Tschichold, who helped codify the New Typography in 1925 and eventually returned to traditional methods, wrote in his decidedly conservative *The Form of the Book*: "The aim of typography must not be expression, least of all self-expression. . . . In a masterpiece of typography, the artist's signature has been eliminated. What some may praise as personal styles are in reality small and empty peculiarities, frequently damaging, that masquerade as innovations." Yet despite this admonition, Tschichold was the chief proselytizer for a movement that attacked visual redundancy that was the byproduct of traditionalism. His doctrine of asymmetry literally stood type on its ear in an effort to garner greater attention. His predilection for sans-serif over serif faces was based on what he and other modernists believed were objective truths. Yet critics accused them of perpetrating myths to support their assertions of legibility. Perhaps the Dutch typographer Gerard Unger is correct, writing in *Emigre* #23, "Tschichold's preference for sans-serifs . . . was based upon emotional considerations."

The Bauhaus and the New Typography busted the conventions of placement and layout and eliminated ornament and symmetrical composition. In place of the classical page appeared "constructed" sans-serif typefaces and bold black and red rules designed to fragment the page and control the eye. During the 1920s the New Typography was viewed as an extraordinary departure from commonplace design. Ultimately, though, even it became yet another set of rules against which to rebel.

When Lewis Carroll painstakingly curled lines of hot metal type into the shape of a mouse's tail in *Alice's Adventures in Wonderland* (1865), he engaged in typeplay that would seldom be repeated in children's books for another fifty years, and would take another sixty to become the trend it is today. Since children's books offer many possibilities for creative play it is curious that for so long children's typography remained comparatively tame. Certainly in the post–World War II period artists under the spell of modern art liberated both style and content. Following the postwar baby boom mainstream book publishers, particularly in the United States, reconsidered their audiences and took risks with subjects, styles, and, to a lesser extent, layouts. Ignoring librarians' warnings against overstepping the strict conventions that they had persistently maintained through choosing what books to buy for their libraries, publishers allowed artists and writers to push the limits of children's book art by challenging taboos—like allowing a snake to appear as a book's main character for the first time in Tomi Ungerer's 1959 *Crictor*.

As for design, in the nineteenth century a page of text was routinely set as a tightly leaded block, sometimes relieved by an initial cap or spot illumination. Picture and alphabet books, though graphically more exciting, were nonetheless typographically subdued to avoid distracting the child. For a brief period during the 1920s children's books were transformed by the modern revolution. Lazar El Lissitzky's suprematist classic, *Of Two Squares* (designed in Vitebsk in 1920 but first published in Berlin in 1922), which was based on his famous political poster, *Beat the Whites with the Red Wedge,* was the first break from traditional children's layout and content. According to N. Khadzhiev in a 1962 essay "El Lissitzky Book Designer" (reprinted in *El Lissitzky*, Thames and Hudson, 1968), it was the first time that the artist applied the revolutionary typographic language that he would later use in adult-oriented ads and brochures. *Of Two Squares* used only symbolic abstract forms, or what Lissitzky called "elementary means," rather than representational narrative devices. Lissitzky wrote that he intended to engage all children in a thrilling game: "Don't read the story, take paper sticks, your building bricks, and put it together, paint it, build it." The book flows like a comic strip or film. "All the frames are linked by the uninterrupted movement of simple related figures in a sequence which ends in the final chord of the red square," explained N. Khadzhiev. "The words move within the fields of force of the figures as they act: these are squares, universal and specifically plastic forces are brought forth typographically."

Of Two Squares inspired Kurt Schwitters, Käte Steinitz, and Theo Van Doesburg's *The Scarecrow* (Aposs-Verlag, 1925), in which the letters *B*, *O*, and *X* are characters of the comic story about a pitiful scarecrow who is unable to scare anything and runs afoul of a farmer. These witty typecase anthropomorphisms, a shift from naturalism to symbolism in children's iconography, tested the limits of visual and textual comprehension. Like *Of Two Squares*, *The Scarecrow* was originally derived from adult typographic experiments, in this case Schwitters's own Merz nonsense poems. *The Scarecrow* was certainly in Lissitzky's mind when in 1929 he designed his second children's book, *Addition, Subtraction, Multiplication, Division*, in which capital letters were transformed into bodies and limbs of a factory worker, farmer, and Red Army soldier, each a symbolic component of Soviet society used as mnemonic tools to teach arithmetic. "This is how to use letters to put together every kind of arithmetical method—try it yourself!" Lissitzky commanded his readers. This book, however, was never published and only the dummy remains. Following Lissitzky's inspirational path, Piet Zwart created *Het Boek Van PTT* in 1938 to inform children about the Dutch postal, telephone, and telegraphic company (PTT). Full-color photomontages, three-dimensional objects, and necklaces of typographic material were combined in an anarchic but decidedly transparent step-by-step instructional guide that was as playful as it was sophisticated.

This typographic revolution did not, however, make an impact on the conventions of children's book publishing because the books were not printed in large enough quantities and generally landed on the shelves of collectors rather than children. James Fraser, editor of *Phaedrus: An Annual of Children's Literature Research*, said there was also a lack of interest in these avant-garde experiments among average readers: "I used to find ex-library copies of the avant-garde experiments in surprisingly very good condition, while copies of the standard text and picture books were tattered and worn." Indeed for substantive change to have occurred a radical shift in adult design conventions would have been necessary, which even during the 1920s when experimental design was at is zenith did not affect the children's book genre. Educators maintained rigid standards over how children were to be taught, and children's librarians generally decided which books were suitable to that task. Adults determined the conventions that governed the content and design of picture books for prereaders, picture/story books for young readers, and illustrated novels for older readers. Illustration was either realistic or fanciful, typography was straightforward and legible—any deviation from these norms was termed inappropriate. Neil Postman writes in *The Disappearance of Childhood* (Delacorte Press, New York, 1982) that "a particular form of information, controlled by adults, was made available in stages to children in what was judged to be psychologically assimilable ways." Until the advent of television (and now, increasingly, digital media) the printed book was the vessel in which this information was stored and distributed; its presentation has, therefore, always been controlled by adult assumptions about what best suited children. Left unchallenged, many assumptions were further adopted as marketing truths.

By the late 1930s children's book design was in a few instances influenced by the New Typography in the form of sans-serif typefaces in asymmetrical compositions. In *The Noisy Book* (Harper Brothers, 1939) by Margaret Wise Brown, machine-inspired Futura set with skewed line breaks approximated the sounds of household appliances and larger machines. Yet during the 1940s and 1950s forums of the American Institute of Graphic Arts codified standards of legibility for children's books to which most publishers adhered. Readability was vigilantly preserved, and change in children's book typography during the early postwar era was marked by little more than the occasional switch from typefaces like Janson or Garamond to Futura or Akzidenz or Grotesque rather than adoption of constructivist, dadaist, and futurist experimental typography. Picture books were usually composed of classical book types that were rarely integrated into the art. Even an avant-garde masterpiece like Bruno Munari's *Alfabeteire* (Giulio Einaudi, editor, 1960), with illustrations that are dada-like collages of "found" letters, the sans-serif body text is discretely set apart from the images.

Yet certain anomalies did influence the field: *Funny Folks from Gardentown* (Whitman, 1938) by Tony Fraioli sidestepped typographic convention with quirky hand-drawn letterforms that complemented his witty anthropomorphic drawings of fruits and vegetables set against black backgrounds (which, incidentally, librarians considered lugubrious). Hand-drawn letterforms subsequently became more common (although black backgrounds have not). Cursive lettering for *The Story of Babar, the Little Elephant* (1933) was once criticized for being inaccessible to young readers who were unable to decipher script. Yet referring to this and even earlier cursive books dating back to the late nineteenth century, James Fraser suggested that "brighter children tried to puzzle it out or asked adults to help with difficult words until they got it." Over time, handwriting became a common means to teach script. Typewriter type, another un-childlike letterform, was associated with the adult world until *Typewriter Town* (E. F. Dutton, 1960) by William Jay Smith, a playful experiment using the typewriter characters to create images. Influenced by Lewis Carroll's mouse's tail, it was also consistent with contemporary typewritten concrete poetry for adults. In *Little 1* (Harcourt Brace, 1962) by Paul and Ann Rand, typewriter type was boldly used to complement the improvisational collages and rhythmic text. As an integral part of the book's visual personality it also made typewriter type more acceptable.

From the 1950s to the 1980s children's book design was largely overshadowed by developments in children's book art. Even books by progressive artists Maurice Sendak, Tomi Ungerer, and Leo Lionni did not unhinge typographic convention. "Typography should be seen and not heard, because reading is functional and should not be tampered with," said Lionni, whose more than forty books are set only in Century Schoolbook. He insisted that the defining element of a picture book is the *picture*, not the type. "The picture is the story, the type conveys the narrative." Yet this began to change in the late 1980s when type design became more integral to the entire children's book as the author/illustrator became more of an active participant in the design process and the computer forced the widespread reevaluation of typographic principles in all print media. In the late 1970s, experimental typography gave adult-oriented print communications more playful veneers; constructivist, futurist, and dadaist

Once upon a time Paul Rand used three stylish lowercase letters on a poster promoting winter sports. This solitary word, *ski,* was the first time that the typeface Peignot was used in the United States. It was 1938 and it was the last time Rand would ever use it, but Peignot became one of the most popular letterforms of the 1930s and 1940s. It was an emblem of the age, a reflection of the Parisian *moderne* style.

Peignot, designed by poster artist A. M. Cassandre (1901–1968), still has currency as a display letter and is sometimes used to evoke the art deco period of the late 1920s to mid-1930s. Peignot was a quirky sans-serif face notable for its thick and thin body and the use of upper-case letters in its lowercase form. The typeface is famous for both its style and versatility, and its designer is well known for his significant contributions to the history of the poster, but little is known about the man for whom the face was named, Charles Peignot, or his influential Parisian type foundry, Deberny & Peignot. This is a case where the typeface is more than a mere letterform, it is a monument.

The history of graphic design usually focuses on the artists who produced the most visible and viable work, not the so-called vendors. While Cassandre's designs are celebrated, the catalyst or patron who encouraged, published, and paid for the work goes largely unheralded. This is the fate of Charles Peignot, who at one time employed Cassandre and other leading European designers including Herbert Matter, Alexey Brodovitch, and Charles Loupot. Peignot was to modern graphic design what Ambroise Vollard was to modern printmaking. He was not simply the manager of a successful type business, he was the embodiment of French typography for more than five decades. An arbiter of taste, a courageous experimenter, an adventuresome publisher, Peignot brought what one of his collaborators, the type designer Maximillen Vox, calls a "Gallic-Roman" design attitude (rooted in constant change) to the Anglo-Saxon world.

Hence, Peignot's legacy is a virtual timeline of typography, technology, and modern graphic design.

In the 1920s the future of an international typography rested in German experiments. Paul Renner had designed his seminal Futura, the geometric sans-serif that became the emblem of modernity. Understanding this, Cassandre and Peignot began investigations that led step by step to the Peignot typeface (named by Cassandre). The face was the offspring of two spiritual parents: the Bauhaus and the Renaissance. After many false births, Cassandre and Peignot concluded that it would be pretentious to think of creating a completely new face and decided to work along traditional lines, while at the same time avoiding copies of what had been done. "Copying the past does not create a tradition," wrote Peignot. Cassandre had the idea of going back to the origins of letterforms. "Was there not something to be learnt from the semi-uncials of the Middle Ages?" queried Cassandre. "The idea of mixing the letterforms of capitals and lowercase seemed to us to contain the seed of new developments within traditional lines." The result was a mixture of letters, which Peignot knew would take the public some time to adjust to.

In 1937 Peignot was launched in a spectacular way as the "official" typeface of the World Exhibition in Paris. It had been chosen by Paul Valéry for inscriptions on the two towers of the Palais de Chaillot. A fabricator produced cardboard stencils for making complete alphabets, and these were used for many mural inscriptions on the exhibition stands. The response to the type was overwhelming. And like a proud father, Peignot kept tabs on its use to such an extent that weeks after Paul Rand's *Ski* poster was issued, Rand received a telegram of thanks, signed Charles Peignot.

Every designer has used the typeface Cooper
Black at least once in his or her professional
life. It is as indelibly part of design as ritual is
of religion. Once one of the world's most
ubiquitous metal typefaces—and the heaviest,
owing to its great mass—Cooper Black is a
truly twentieth-century type, as emblematic
as Futura or Univers. While it was not the
first type to have rounded serifs, it is the most
authoritative of the so-called fat faces. Used
for advertising and editorial display, Cooper
Black is as eye-catching as a charging bull
and as loud as a carnival barker. If there had
never been a Cooper Black, the world might
never have known Ultra Bodoni, one of the
many behemoths designed to compete in the
ever-widening fat face market during the
mid-1920s.

The man who designed Cooper Black
is Oswald Cooper (1879–1940), Oz or Ozzie
to his friends. Cooper was a native of Coffeyville, Kansas. In his teens he
settled in Chicago to pursue illustration. He eventually became one of the
leading practitioners of what became known as the Chicago style. In the
early 1920s and 1930s American design was a mélange of regional dialects,
each emanating from a big city under the influence of a single person's
mannerism or the confluence of a few. Lettering, typography, and
illustration were the defining media, and advertising was the primary
outlet. The Boston style was attributable to W. A. Dwiggins and the New
York style to Frederic W. Goudy (both of whom spent time in Chicago),
but the Chicago (sometimes called the Midwestern) style was founded by
Cooper. He combined calligraphic skill with typographic expertise to create
advertisements that were modern in character and classic in form. While
respecting tradition, he understood the needs of an expanding mass
commercial market.

Cooper stumbled into his lifelong vocation by accident. He left the
comforts of his Kansas home at eighteen, bound for Chicago to study at

the Frank Holme School of Illustration. There he was inspired by his lettering teacher, Frederic W. Goudy, to pursue a broader practice. Goudy, the most prolific of all American type designers and director of Holme's typographic department, befriended Oz and helped him earn his tuition by assigning him jobs setting type for correspondence course booklets. This was a happy career move since Cooper had realized that he wasn't very good at drawing pictures but had a real knack for the lettering arts. Soon he was appointed as a lettering teacher.

While teaching at Holme, Cooper met a young man, Fred Bertsch, who ran an art-service agency next door to the school. Bertsch loved Cooper's work and in 1904 they entered into the perfect partnership; Bertsch, a consummate salesman, and Cooper, the gifted artist, formed Bertsch & Cooper with the goal of establishing a full-service typeshop, including typesetting, layout, copywriting, and design. But opening a typeshop was expensive even then; and while they had plenty of ambition, money was in short supply. As a small studio Bertsch & Cooper based its initial reputation on hand lettering for small local jobs and later large national campaigns. Eventually, their financial success allowed them to open the full-service shop they had dreamed of, which gave Cooper the opportunity to test his other talents. "Cooper, of course, had brilliant capacities as a craftsman in the field of printing and of advertising layout," wrote typographer Paul Standard in *The Book of Oz Cooper* (The Society of Typographic Arts, Chicago, 1949). "But in his endowment was also a gift for language, and through its discipline a power of clear and forthright expression . . . his text sought to persuade, not stampede."

The quality of Cooper's lettering was equal to the strength of his writing. Cooper's letterforms were not simply novelties, but "lessons in structural form, in free and friendly balance," wrote Standard. Cooper created as many new designs as he could, yet he had an instinctual distrust of things superficially modish and conceptually strained. "Types too dexterous, like tunes too luscious," he once waxed, "are predestined [sic] to short careers. If William Caslon had improved his types as much as they have since been improved by others they would not have endured, for sleek perfection palls on the imperfect persons who buy and use type."

Actually, Cooper stumbled into type design almost as accidentally as he did lettering. His first type was drawn and cut, unbeknownst to Cooper and without his permission, in 1913 by one of Morris Fuller Benton's staff artists at American Type Foundry (ATF). Cooper had routinely created customized lettering in advertisements for one of Bertsch & Cooper's largest clients, the Packard Motor Car Company. The ads were so widely seen that the lettering caught Benton's eye. Type pirating was a fact of life and ads were neither signed nor attributed to any artist. Benton immediately ordered the type redrawn and founded in metal, and called it Packard. But Benton was also a man of integrity; when he learned that the original was designed by Cooper he paid a fee and attributed the design to him.

Shortly afterward, Barnhart Brothers & Spindler Type Foundry (BB&S), America's second largest, approached Cooper to design a complete family based on his lettering. Cooper did not immediately accept the offer, reasoning that he was first a lettering artist, not a type designer, and he was very busy with his own business. Bertsch, however, was not only Cooper's partner but his biggest promoter and worked feverishly to get Cooper into the limelight. Bertsch called Cooper the "Michelangelo of lettering," and urged him to accept BB&S's offer. In 1918 Cooper's first typeface was released, named Cooper, and later renamed Cooper Old Style.

In the early 1900s typefaces were vigorously marketed to printers and type shops, often through ambitious type specimen sheets designed with the same artistic flourish as period sheet music. BB&S was particularly aggressive and succeeded in popularizing Cooper's first normal-weight roman (Cooper). They further made it the basis for a continuing family. The second in the series was the famous Cooper Black, the most novel of early-twentieth-century super-bolds. BB&S declared that Cooper Black was "the selling type supreme, the multibillionaire sales type, it made big advertisements out of little ones." Cooper responded that his invention was "for far-sighted printers with near-sighted customers." Owing to its novelty, it caused commotion in certain conservative circles. "The slug-machine makers thundered against the black 'menace.' But the trend was on—the advertising world accepted the black in a thoroughgoing way and the orders rolled up in a volume never before known for any type face," wrote a type seller of the day.

Other related type designs followed in quick succession in what became known as "the black blitz." Cooper Italic was described by Cooper as "much closer to its parent pen form than the roman." Cooper Hilite was made by the simple expedient of painting a white highlight on a black proof of Cooper Black, with patterns cut and matrices engraved accordingly. "It's good for sparkling headlines; it cannot be crowded like the black, but must have plenty of 'air,'" wrote Cooper. Cooper Black Italic was completed in 1926 to cash in on the swell in sales of Cooper Black. Cooper Black Condensed was designed shortly afterward to have twenty percent less heft and be generally more useful. A complete metal font of Cooper Black weighed almost eighty-three pounds (thank heavens for transfer type) and strained the back of many a typesetter, so the condensed version was thought to save on costly chiropractor bills.

Cooper's designs initiated trends, but he refused to take part in "the itch of the times." Nor was he a fan of what in 1928 he called "the balmy wing of modernism." However, his last face, designed in 1929 for BB&S, originally called Cooper Fullface and later changed in ATF catalogs to Cooper Modern, was, in fact, consistent with the dominant styles. Of this face Cooper wrote, "This style, lately revived by the practitioners of the 'modernistic' typography, has created a demand for display letters that comport well with it—letters that reflect the sparkling contrasts of Bodoni, and that carry weight to meet the needs of advertisers, Cooper Fullface is such a letter."

In the 1930s Cooper curtailed his type design, and before his death in 1940 he turned his attention to protecting what he had created. Fighting for copyright protections for himself and all designers, he tried to convince the government that patents should be awarded for typefaces. He chided his colleagues about copying, too. Copying is shameful, he argued: "To work in the style of current trends or past periods is all right, but do it in your own way. Study the work of the leaders, but never have another's work before you when you are trying to create. There was never a great imitator—not even in vaudeville. The way to become a master is by cultivating your own talent."

Typography, like the hemline, changes as fashion dictates. So, in the 1960s, a growing trend in universal typography began to outstrip the utopian ideal that had provoked missionaries of the modern to establish rules governing the use of limited type families and compositions. While the masters of this form, Paul Rand, Rudolph de Harak, and George Tscherny, expertly practiced the art of typographic neutrality to frame strong visual ideas, others, who designed with blind adherence to those tenets, produced bland compositions that typified the mediocre in corporate communications.

In the 1950s, the distinction between quotidian commercial art and sophisticated graphic design was defined by a high standard of typographic craftsmanship. In the period before the widespread application of phototype, hot-metal typesetting required considerable refinements to avoid horrendous results. Skilled typographers rejected faces that led to disaster, like the novelty and poster faces common in print advertising. The remnants of bygone eras were summarily dismissed. Systematic type composition was the key to design purity. But, by the 1960s, a reaction to what had become the rigidity of the overarching international style—in addition to a distinctly natural, creative urge to move ahead of the curve—prompted designers to push the boundaries of type.

Push Pin Studios revived Victorian, art nouveau, and art deco letterforms for display and body copy in reaction to the rational Swiss approach of the late 1950s and 1960s. Returning typography to a period of exuberance before Jan Tschichold's *The New Typography* (published in 1928) imposed its revolutionary strictures on modern design, Push Pin Studios advanced the notion that graphic design ran the gamut from serious to playful while solving a wide range of problems. Type did not have to be a neutral element on a pristine page but, rather, could be an expressive voice—a means of giving the written word character and nuance. This was made possible by the shift toward phototypesetting, which, in turn, encouraged typographic revivals. So by reintroducing passé commercial art styles and reviving forgotten letterforms, Push Pin introduced an individualistic typographic language rooted more in graphic ornament than precisionist grids.

Late modern typography, distinguished by the clean and simple compositions of both classical and modern typefaces, was changing the look of advertising from chaotic to eloquent and at the same time was more expressive too. Through Westvaco's *Inspirations,* Bradbury Thompson promoted "talking type." By tweaking traditional letterforms into visual puns, typeset words became both verbal and visual. This concept was further pursued by Robert Brownjohn, who imbued letters with sound and motion, making them visual components of a word or phrase. Ivan Chermayeff made otherwise static type appear kinetic in a print prefiguration of today's on-screen typography. The letterform as pun was further tested in advertising layout by Gene Federico, Lou Dorfsman, and Herb Lubalin. With precision, Federico made type and image into total compositions. Dorfsman used type not only to convey a message but also to be part of rebuslike compositions. Lubalin exploited the type-as-sound idea and further explored the sculptural eccentricities of letterforms to their communicative advantage. He demonstrated that the shape of letters signified as much as their content; he would set excruciatingly tight lines of text, smashing bodies together as if to animate the forms. For these designers, typography was, in fact, illustration, sometimes complementing and often substituting for pure imagery.

As type directors and graphic designers were convinced to switch to phototype, typography became more stylistically and compositionally eclectic. The large variety of typefaces available on Typositor made typographic experimentation more commonplace. Although the grid was still a sacrosanct element of modern design, the liberties that designers were taking was beginning to affect the dominant ways of working. And, with the advent of psychedelic typography in the late 1960s, characterized by radical optical exaggerations in historical faces from the Victorian and secessionist periods, it appeared that the language of typography was in for a reevaluation.

Typography in the 1960s was transitional, a word that connotes flux but not necessarily instability. The classical or orthodox moderns established a true standard for "good typography," but standards ultimately beg to be challenged. The critical response of the revivalists and eclecticists was an alternative that became yet another style. Bridging these groups were those individuals who took from both extremes to create a design language that became the quintessential expression of the times.

Style is not a four-letter word, yet it does imply superficiality, conformity, and a foolish enslavement to fashion. The moderns condemned these attributes as detrimental to clear and efficient communication. And although the postmoderns reveled in stylisms, they insisted that theirs were not merely fads or fancies but rather necessary stimulants to ensure more engaging communications. The pendulum swings, and today the naysayers warn that obvious style must be avoided because it relegates the designer to a prison of the ancient or recent past. Hence, style is condemned as a tool of obsolescence.

TONEELSCHUUR
SMEDESTRAAT 23, 2011 RG HAARLEM

TONEELSCHUUR
SMEDESTRAAT 23, 2011 RG HAARLEM

TONEELSCHUUR

However, style is also a signature that need not be insincere or bankrupt. It can also be a cue for an underlying visual persona born of complex aesthetic and conceptual issues. Remember, graphic design is as much about signaling a message to a receiver in a unique, sometimes idiosyncratic, way as it is about neutrally conveying ideas and information. When style is efficiently used, it serves as an identifier and entry point. At its most successful, style modifies language as an accent indicating from where and perhaps from whom the message derives.

As style goes, the graphic narratives and distinctive hand-lettered typography by Dutch designer, illustrator, and cartoonist Joost Swarte (b. 1947) is a tapestry of twentieth-century influences as viewed through a visionary's lens. Swarte's style draws directly from one of the century's most ornamental epochs, between the 1920s and 1930s, when art moderne (or art deco) reigned supreme as a commercial alternative to utopian modernism. But Swarte's interpretation of these fundamental modernistic attributes, among them rectilinear letterforms and ziggurat/sunburst printers' ornaments, are adapted as elements of a personal vocabulary. Swarte's routine references to the past are so consistent that his ownership is undeniable. Despite déjà vu among those who know the origin of his most common hand-lettered faces, over the course of his development they have become inextricably wed to his own hand. Letters that were used over half a century ago are revived not simply for the sake of pastiche but rather to express his own aesthetically playful urges.

Swarte's is a seamless weave of both *moderne* and comic influences. His work is multidimensional and relies on letterforms to complement his narrative drawings. Regarding the latter, the influence of the simple linearity of the cartoon character Tintin by the Belgian artist Hergé is most apparent. "In the beginning I drew in Hergé's style to study how he did it and I found it suited me well because I could draw so many details in architecture and objects," explains Swarte, with a nod to his passion for buildings and ephemeral design objects. Swarte coined the term "clear line" to describe Hergé's approach and his own. Yet he is quick to affirm that the line alone is only a means to achieve an end.

Swarte uses lettering and line drawing like personal speech. His singular vision emerges through a combination of dramatic, witty, and absurd comic images within a total narrative. As a designer, he enjoys artifacts of the past, but as storyteller he starts from zero. And where he diverges from his main influence is clear in this statement: "Hergé tries to take the reader to the real world, I take the reader into *my* world."

The galaxies for Swarte's world are comic strips, children's books, record covers, posters, wine labels, shopping bags, ex libris, magazine covers, postage stamps for the PTT (the Dutch postal service), and architectural interiors. He has published his own comics magazines including *Tante Leny* (Aunt Leny), and *Vrij Nederland* (Free Netherlands); in addition, he served as a contributor to *Submarine* (a Belgian counterculture journal), *Charlie* (a French humor paper), *Humo* (the Belgian TV and radio guide), the Dutch comics magazine *Jippo,* and *RAW,* through which he was introduced to the American public. Whether a publication contains an exclusive collection of his work or the occasional contribution, there is no mistaking a "Swarte" for the work of any other artist. Style combined with conceptual mastery are his virtues.

Swarte's style is ultimately secondary to the tales he tells. Six stories originally published in *Charlie,* for example, are collected in the 1979 book *Modern Art,* of which the title story is a satire on the nature of style and art. It stars Anton Makassar, one of Swarte's cartoon alter egos about whom Swarte says: "As always with comics, you invent your character out of your character so that parts of yourself come out of a character *in extremo.*" Another Swarte stand-in is the character Jopo de Pojo (he chose the name because it sounded so pleasing), who reflects Swarte's shy and isolated side, while Makassar (named after the city in Indonesia) suggests the artist's self-proclaimed professorial side. "He is a bit of an inventor. He always comes up with crazy ideas, and is proud of himself. That's me, too." The third part of the personality puzzle is Pierre Van Ganderen (which, translated, means "of simple mind"). "He is a working man who does what he has to do, who is a bit childish and sometimes naïve."

Swarte is not wed to conventional cartoon situation comedies but, rather, varies his story lines as much as he pushes the technical boundaries to transcend any hint of nostalgia. For example, although the adventures of Makassar resemble 1920s comic artist George McManus's "Bringing Up Father," it is clearly synthesis not revival. "A young artist must grow out of the past to build up a solid background," he says. "But one must find one's own way out of nostalgia and stop looking too much over the shoulder." When 1930s type design and early-twentieth-century cartooning converge, a certain timelessness is evoked. Of Swarte's mastery, Art Spiegelman, former *RAW* editor/publisher, explains that he "has a refined visual intelligence wed to a sense of humor and history. He experiments within a tradition, and is always trying things that are so daring yet made so simple that by the time they are accomplished it looks so easy that it betrays the courage involved."

Every part of Swarte's lettering and drawing is meticulously rendered. His clear line may be reduced to the necessary strokes, but his images are flooded with ideas. Ironically, in an era when coarse, expressionistic *art brut* is in vogue, Swarte's circumspect precisionism is often called retro. Yet attention to detail is not stylistic conceit, it is timeless.

Zuzana Licko

For those who experienced firsthand the digital-type revolution that began in the mid-1980s, it was nothing short of liberating. For the first time since Gutenberg, the means of creating complete alphabets for repeated text and display application was not limited to rarefied specialists but was available to anyone possessing a little beige box called a Macintosh—anyone, that is, inclined toward letter design. At first the characters made for the computer screen were blocky and bitmapped, as if they were boxes inked on graph paper, which indeed they were in the digital sense. The constraints imposed by nascent computer software, seventy-two-dot-per-inch computer screens, and dot matrix printers gave rise to letterforms that were both functional and aesthetically limited. Nonetheless, the very idea that designers could compose *and* create their own type spurred an initial frenzy for custom alphabets that ranged from sublime to ridiculous.

One of the pioneers of the new fontography is Zuzana Licko (b. 1961), who started designing typefaces in 1985 for use in *Emigre,* the homespun culture tabloid founded in 1983 by her husband Rudy Vander-Lans (b. 1955), a former page designer for the *San Francisco Chronicle.* Designing on the early Macintosh before the advent of sophisticated page-layout programs, WYSIWYG, and Hypercard was itself a feat of ingenuity, but seeing beyond computer limitations required a vision born of that proverbial mother—necessity. Licko's plunge into the design of coarse-resolution type was prompted by a need to overcome the conformity of Mac default faces and to create a distinct identity for the fledgling magazine (not, at that time, recast as the clarion of postmodern graphic design, which is its legacy today). What *Emigre* became for graphic design culture is underscored by Licko's contribution to the history of digital-type founding; the *Emigre* venture proved trailblazing on two fronts. Licko's early designs—including her initial typefaces (c. 1985) called Emperor, Universal, Oakland, and Emigre—further helped launch the unique type business Emigre Graphics (later Emigre Fonts), which spawned today's indy digital-type industry.

Licko's education in graphic design and typography (she received a B.A. from the University of California at Berkeley) included one course in calligraphy, which, as she recalls, "was nightmarish" because the instructor insisted that calligraphy could be done properly only with the right hand. Licko has what she calls "the gift of being left-handed," and so she did her homework assignments with her left hand while pretending to use her right during class time. She admits that "the results were awful!" and, ultimately, she rejected calligraphy entirely. Nevertheless, Licko recalls that she marveled at the functional beauty of typefaces while studying graphic design. "I was blown away when I realized the power that typeface designs have on a typographic piece of design. Without touching the layout, [just] change the typeface design, and voilà! you have a completely different design."

However, the process of designing typefaces remained a mystery until Licko laid hands on her first Macintosh. "As it turns out, bitmap fonts were the perfect place for me to start learning about type design because I love the building-block approach," she says, referring to the puzzlelike way in which letterforms were constructed by linking squares (or bits) together. From that moment on, her experience and skill with more sophisticated typeface designs evolved at a pace commensurate with the Macintosh's ability to produce more complex font programs. However, when she began using her new Macintosh for *Emigre,* mastering the new tool, not sophistication, was the primary issue. She continues: "As graphic designers, we enjoyed the newfound ability to test and implement the faces directly within our design work." Of course, the results were primitive and decidedly of the moment. Yet, *at* the moment, few could predict whether or not Mac-generated bitmap type would slowly wear thin. Eventually, a new standard emerged.

Within what then seemed like the blink of an eye, the introduction of high-resolution PostScript outline technology enabled Licko to develop several high-resolution designs based upon her earlier bitmaps, including faces called Matrix, Citizen, and Lunatix. Although these were based fundamentally on classical forms, given the computer's limited memory, Licko had to compensate by limiting the characteristics of each face to the bare essentials. Thus even the most traditional-looking face, such as Matrix, retained sharp edges that gave it the appearance of a stone inscription on the one hand and a novelty form on the other.

For Licko, overall appearance was less important than how a face functioned within technological constraints. Her mission at the time was to work within limitations, which meant that her faces took on certain characteristics endemic to the computer, which, in turn, caused an alternate appearance in layouts that used the faces. Incidentally, in 1999, she revisited and successfully reworked some of her early bitmap ideas through new fonts called Base 9 and Base 12, which offer compatible screen and printer fonts to solve the current dual need of low-resolution screen display and high-resolution printing with an integrated typeface design.

Licko's inspiration usually comes from the particular medium that she's involved with at any given time (and the needs posed by that medium). "I search out a problem that needs to be addressed or a unique result that a production method can yield, such as my early experiments with bitmaps, and later purely geometric forms." The results were faces that have become emblematic of the digital epoch. "My latest interest in creating somewhat more traditional text faces," she continues, "is a result of *Emigre* magazine's increased publishing of in-depth articles, which require fonts appropriate for lengthy text setting."

Having one's own magazine to design typefaces for offers untold advantages. Most type designers create faces on commission for a publication or an institution, with little opportunity to make certain that they are truly seaworthy; some produce speculative faces for others to sample, thus ceding control of the typography. But with the opportunity to actually flow new type into a vessel such as *Emigre* for testing in layouts by a sympathetic designer (in this case, VanderLans), Licko has been allowed to check the tolerance of her work under the stress of real-world conditions. In turn, *Emigre* has been the ultimate proving ground and specimen sheet.

For the first decade, when *Emigre* was a hothouse, Licko (and other designers) showcased often quirky work. But when the size of *Emigre* decreased with the thirty-third issue (winter 1995) from a luxurious tabloid to a standard magazine format, and when the content switched from highly visual to heavily text, a changed occurred for Licko and *Emigre*. Licko relays: "We needed a typeface appropriate for lengthy text setting; this presented the opportunity to take on the challenge of doing a revival." For Licko, this was uncharted territory.

Revivals are common fare for most type designers, and the classics are fair game for update, renovation, or rehabilitation. Type designers—a critical lot to say the least—are always finding flaws in original designs that "drive them crazy." In Licko's case, she became fascinated with Baskerville, the popular alphabet by the English founder John Baskerville (1706–1775), who influenced the "modern" designs of Didot and Bodoni but had his work severely criticized during and after his lifetime for being what type historian D. B. Updike referred to in *Printing Types* (Harvard, 1922) as "sterile." "From personal experience, I could sympathize," Licko wrote in her 1996 introduction to her own revival of Baskerville, the typeface Mrs Eaves (named after Sarah Eaves, the live-in housekeeper who became Baskerville's wife and later ran his printing business).

Originally revived in 1917 (owing to an interest by Bruce Rogers) and later reissued by Monotype and Deberny & Peignot, Baskerville often plays second fiddle to Caslon. But Licko selected it for its familiarity as well as for its formal features. "Since Baskerville is a neutral and well-known design," she explains, "it allowed me significant leeway in the interpretation, while retaining the familiarity of a classic." Baskerville was also chosen because it is the ultimate transitional typeface, the category between old-style and modern types. Licko states: "I ruled out old-style models for the idiosyncratic reason that I'm personally not attracted to typefaces which are reminiscent of calligraphic influences (probably for the opposite reason why calligraphers tend to dislike bitmap or geometric designs)." She adds that "an old style would not have been a natural choice, given my experience and sensibilities." Her subsequent revival was Bodoni, but for *Emigre*'s first-ever text revival, Licko wanted to avoid the austerity of the thick and thin strokes of early modern design.

Revivals are curious beasts. A designer is usually faced with the dilemma of either making minor adjustments or radical renovation. Arguably, the former is what the originator might have done if technology or other factors were different; the latter challenges the dotted line between fealty and reinvention. Licko says that there are no conventional limitations because every type designer brings his or her own perceptions to a particular face. And, about her own effort, she admits: "Perhaps some would say that Mrs Eaves is far removed from Baskerville's basic model and may question it being a true revival. The fact that Mrs Eaves is not a slavish replica is one of the reasons why we chose an original name, rather than calling it Emigre Baskerville."

Revivals are, of course, about critical reevaluation and then change—in perception, typographic needs, or technology. Licko notes that "the idea of fixing, or improving, a classic is relative to usage. Some typefaces are more appropriate for certain uses than others and some may have a wider use than others, but there is no absolute measurement for typeface designs that calculates good versus bad." The fixing done to a classic typeface that makes it suitable for one use may make it less suitable for another. Moreover, adds Licko, "A revival also exemplifies the idiosyncrasies of the type designer doing the revival. If two designers do a revival of the same typeface, each designer's interpretation will be unique, based upon . . . relative sensibilities, vision, and skill."

With Mrs Eaves, Licko's point of departure was one of the most critiqued characteristics of Baskerville's original—the sharp contrast between stems and hairlines, which naysayers in his day believed was a hindrance to legibility. Licko wanted to understand the criticism, if not as well disprove it, so she opted to "explore the path not taken. After all, the sharp contrast evidenced in Baskerville was new at the time of its creation due to recent developments in printing and papermaking technologies. In his pursuit of 'perfect' printing, John Baskerville developed ultrasmooth and brilliant white papers, as well as intensely black printing ink." Ultimately, Licko's analysis forced her to conclude that she should retain the overall openness and lightness of the face. So she reduced the x-height, relative to the cap-height, which gives Mrs Eaves the appearance when set of being one point-size smaller than it really is. In roman, bold, italic, small, and petite caps, Mrs Eaves is a very readable face that is also quite elegant, not unlike a hot-metal impression. It turned out to be one of Emigre's best-selling font packages ever.

Crossing over from "original" to revival, Licko learned an unexpected lesson. "I've found that doing a revival is in many ways easier than designing a typeface from scratch. Because the fine details, which can be very time-consuming, are prescribed by the model, there are fewer stumbling blocks in the development." Of course, she continues to pursue new designs as a means of exploring the unexplored. But her subsequent revivals have given her the opportunity to study and better understand the details that she would never fully appreciate by merely observing, studying, or using the typeface. In light of Mrs Eaves, Licko asserts: "In subtle ways, a revival forces me to accept certain design decisions that I would not have made myself, to integrate a different way of thinking."

Teal Triggs, Liz McQuiston, and Sian Cook

During the late 1960s, when the feminist movement was in full tilt, two women writers known for their satiric essays in *Bitch,* a New York–based underground newspaper that they edited, decided that the English language was the principal tool of male oppression against women. Therefore, their publication would not include any word that had a gender-specific prefix or suffix, such as "man" or "son." Instead, the neutral word "one" was substituted so that the word "person" became "perone," and the word "woman" (which they deemed was most subjugated of all words) became "woperone." They applied the new spelling to common nongendered words as well, like "many" (peroney), "season" (seapone), and "manifold" (peronefold), which forced readers to examine the so-called masculine dominance in the English language. However, the editors ultimately admitted that these linguistic alterations were unwieldy in their own writing, and after an issue or two they reverted back to standard spellings.

The point, however, was clear. Woperones were afforded second-class citizenship in ways that were matter-of-factly ingrained from birth in the minds of both genders. And although certain habits, such as written language, were not going to change overnight—or as easily as the popular acceptance of the alternative Ms. instead of Miss or Mrs. (which, in fact, did not happen overnight)—it was important to expose cultural and societal absolutes that were prejudicial and detrimental toward women. Even if the spelling experiment was just a satiric exercise that reached a small number of readers of an arcane alternative newspaper, it was a good lesson in how archetypes and stereotypes are retained through inertia. It was also an indication that other confrontations were in the offing.

Gender issues have not been ignored by the graphic design profession—which prior to the 1980s was predominantly a men's club and today is weighted more toward women in designer and design management roles. Yet, although female graphic designers have increased their overall presence and individual prestige within the field, few have used their design and communications skills to redefine or restructure visual language. The editors of *Bitch* realized that while it was not easy to alter basic lexicons, it was important to raise fundamental issues about gender inequities that had been simmering below the surface for ages.

Toward this end, yet with greater determination to make a substantive (and educational) impact, members of a design collective in England called the Women's Design and Research Unit (WD+RU)— founded in 1994 and including Teal Triggs (b. 1957), Liz McQuiston (b. 1952), and Sian Cook (b. 1962)—sought means of addressing continuing inequities within the design field. They targeted the once-arcane yet newly democratized digital realm of font design as both a forum and medium for altering values and perceptions. They decided to create a font comprised of symbolic pictographs and word-bites that were engaged by using conventional keyboard strokes. This, they hoped, would be an effective way to both enter and engage the consciousness of users.

The resulting font, Pussy Galore, named after the bombshell heroine of James Bond's *Goldfinger* film and memorably played by the actress Honour Blackman, was begun in 1994 and completed in early 1995 (although it continues to be somewhat open-ended in terms of final form). It was commissioned by Jon Wozencroft, the editor of *Fuse* (the experimental-type magazine published by FontShop International), for publication in *Fuse 12: Propaganda* (winter 1994), but only a portion of the entire typeface was published at that time due to a variety of technical reasons.

Pussy Galore, the fictional character, was what McQuiston and Triggs call a "femme fatale with a mission," who maximized her sensual endowment as a tool of power rather than subservience. "She was wonderfully sexy and at the same time strong and in control," says Triggs. "We hope by appropriating Pussy Galore as a term and typeface title that it will get people to think twice not only about its use but also about other words that usually denote [the] negative. . . concerning women. We also wanted to use language which celebrated women—hence the ambiguity of the term."

So, whatever contemporary or nostalgic images or ideas that Pussy Galore evokes in the minds of beholders—cocksmanship or Blackman's sexual omnipotence—the font offers unique independent frames of reference that reveal numerous myths about women. In this way, Pussy

Galore is a "conceptual typeface" designed to help explore the roots of misconceptions about women propagated through contemporary vocabularies of Western culture. As Triggs explains in *Baseline: Issue 20* (1995), "Pussy Galore is an 'interactive tool' which invites response and urges you to talk back, challenge, and reassess, not only [about] how women have been constituted by language, but also the structure of language itself."

Pussy Galore is not, however, a typical typeface—in fact, "typeface" may be the preferred description because it functions in relation to a keyboard but an inaccurate one because Pussy Galore bares no relation to a conventional alphabet. Rather, it is a clever commingling of Otto Neurath's Isotype system of the 1930s and a sampling of printer's cuts and dingbats. The pictographs and word pictures that comprise the Pussy Galore font are fragments of narrative that individually serve as stop signs and, when fashioned together, as vehicles for various archetypes and stereotypes.

The keyboard is employed to create pathways in order for the user to make references and associations with the characters of the font. It acknowledges the conventions of language (e.g., vowels, consonants, upper and lower case) and uses shift, option, and normal keys to launch functions that allow for additional layers of exploration. For example, conventional "level one" keyboarding of any word will render a string of ideological statements (graphic picture boxes that frame such words or sayings as "sisters," "rights," "grrrls," "mother," "power," "Thelma & Louise"). Progression through each additional keyboard level takes the user through a journey into what Triggs describes as a multilayered web of associations and representational sets of ideas about women, such as the following:

Level 1 *normal* = empowerment of women
Level 2 *shift* = ugly stereotypes
Level 3 *option* = personal choices
Level 4 *shift+option* = vulgar and sexual language

The complex layering of messages embedded in this font, including fragmented line drawings of the female anatomy, gives users the chance to make serendipitous juxtapositions through random access or specific polemical statements by deliberate applications. Asterisks appear on selected icons/words indicating additional strata of information, such as textual quotes or images-sequences, which are accessed through other operating programs contained in the disc's suitcase. Accessing these alternative strata, the user is allowed to highlight, among other things, a selection of "Hidden Heroines" who have made important contributions to art, design, and film. In addition, other elements are likely to appear throughout, including a witty animated sequence of women's hands ranging from a revolutionary raised fist to a diamond-clad glove. Humor is an effective mediator in the communication of Pussy Galore's decidedly ideological messages.

Although Pussy Galore was created for an experimental design venue, it is not intended for a visual elite of sophisticated graphic designers alone. The digital nature of the font is accessible to anyone with a minimum of computer savvy. It serves both as a graphics tool for those who choose to integrate some or all of its forms into layouts or as a game of digital hide-and-seek for those who choose to uncover all the hidden messages. "Through the user's 'personalization' of the typeface," Triggs adds, "Pussy Galore's aim of embracing democratization is underscored, removing any reliance upon 'artistic' sophistication which might render it alien to popular use." The "letterforms" have indeed been created as simple shapes or pictograms for the user to reconstruct or redesign, and the possibilities are numerous: Through certain keyboard configurations a picture of Eve's snake might be juxtaposed to a floppy "dumb blonde" hairdo. Likewise, strings of characters or words develop accidentally depending on the user, "but each connection is heavily charged with meaning and value," says Triggs. "In this way technology is used to help users assemble their own visual languages, bringing to the typeface unique experiences, individual prejudices, and interpretations."

It is not likely that Pussy Galore will be bundled with the iMac or any other personal computer, at least not in the near future. But there is no reason why it should not be. Although conventional wisdom might argue that an essay in the *World Book Encyclopedia* (which is bundled on many computers) on feminism is a more straightforward method of conveying factual information, Pussy Galore's interactivity ultimately invites more questions and presumably greater engagement in the issues it raises. What began as an attempt to challenge typographic principles in an experimental context has become a model of how new media encourages novel methods of communication. "The old gal has fared really well!" Triggs concludes. "We are really surprised that Pussy Galore has taken on a life of its own. What is really satisfying is when we get correspondence from students in New Zealand, Brazil, Mexico, and the United States who want to explore further the ideas we propose in research essays and in their own use of the typeface. We always said if we reached just one student/designer, the whole project was worthwhile!"

Chris Ware is a scribe's scribe and the producer of such contemporary illuminated manuscripts as *Jimmy Corrigan: The Smartest Kid on Earth, Rocket Sam, Big Tex,* and the *Rusty Brown* comic strips, as well as the ACME Novelty Library comic books. Cloistered away in his Chicago studio, Brother Ware spends untold hours meticulously lettering countless covers, splash panels, and dialog boxes with such panache that even simple conjunctions like "and,"

"thus," "later," and "meanwhile" are imbued with the import reserved for more expressive bon mots. Like most comic artists, Ware is a compulsive letterer, but unlike most, he is also an artful typographer who, for over a decade, has refined a unique typographic language that bridges comic art and graphic design.

During the 1990s, when a surfeit of stylishly distressed and often foolishly stylish digital fonts were routinely issued, Ware crafted some of the most artful alphabets and colorful letterforms seen in print, most of them for his own comic books, but occasionally for less obvious venues too. One of these was the 2001 "Summer Reading" special issue of the *New York Times Book Review* (under my humble art direction), for which he redesigned the otherwise immutable masthead, rejecting all traces of the standard Bookman typeface to conform to the visual character of the comic strip that began on the cover and continued inside. The only residue on the cover of official "Times style" was the Old English *Times* logo anchored to the masthead, which Ware re-lettered to match a much older version of the logo rather than the contemporary one.

This was not, however, arrogance or hubris on his part. In fact, Ware is one of the most sincerely unassuming artists I have ever known. Instead, he is so devoted to the most arcane details of vintage commercial art that he actually knew that the earlier Old English version (long obsolete) had an iota more calligraphic flourish than the newer, ever-so-slightly streamlined version. Yet more importantly, he put in the extra effort (which is considerable when one is on a tight deadline) to render these intricate letters by hand. And that's not all. Throughout the interior of the *Book Review*, Ware used an original, quirkily curvilinear abstract display lettering style that transformed the publication from its usual literary look into a typographic carnival that transported the unaware readers some-WARE-else.

Indeed, Ware's comics are so conceptually astute and compositionally engaging that they cannot fail but connect with their audience. Among the key attributes of this connection, his sympathetically melancholy characters (Jimmy, Rusty, and Quinby the Mouse among them), his nostalgically futuristic worldscapes, and his genius for conveying subtle time shifts in two-dimensional space are all components of compelling narrative. But it does not take a design critic to realize that his ingenious typography is equally (perhaps more) essential in enabling access to an eccentric comic world that could otherwise be opaque. Ware's various lettering and typographic compositions, though they will never be mistaken for the neutrality of Helvetica or Univers, exude a curiously universal allure and a timely timelessness, like that of a personal signature. Yet one will be hard-pressed to find any of his custom (and nameless) faces in digital type foundry specimen books.

Although Ware's comics are receiving wide exposure these days (his critically praised 2000 book *Jimmy Corrigan: Smartest Kid on Earth* remained a bestseller two years after its release, and he was featured as the only comics artist in the 2002 Whitney Museum Biennial in New York), his lettering is not for sale. Rather than being commercial property, his type is a personal signature and each typographic confection stems from a private obsession. "A type company asked me to do some fonts a while back," Ware explains, "but I realized that seeing my lettering appear on billboards and annual reports would be about the most horrifying thing imaginable. Besides, I don't really think of my lettering as 'fonts'; it's more or less circumstantial to the page on which it appears, and I try to let my instincts shape how it looks."

In addition to instincts, however, Ware is inspired by Victorian, art nouveau, and a multitude of nineteenth- and early twentieth-century commercial display styles, specifically from old sheet music, magazines, advertisements, record labels, and fruit and cigar labels. "I steal constantly from all sorts of things," he admits, "especially when something emotionally affects me, either for reasons of color, composition, letter style; sometimes it's even something as simple as the ascender and descender width relative to each other. I'm sure that if I'd taken a class about this stuff, I'd know much better why it all works the way it does, and I wouldn't have to fumble around in the dark so much." Yet fumble, fiddle, or fidget, Ware has raised his lettering beyond mere pastiche into realms of reincarnation. Ware is a veritable born-again "show card" letterer who, back before computers and photostats, effortlessly rendered one-of-a-kind lettering for signs, windows, and displays.

Of course, all comic strip artists worthy of the art must be skilled letterers. But Ware acquired his skill long after he had been doing a regular strip for the student newspaper in Austin. "Up to that point, I'd sort of considered type and lettering secondary to storytelling, some kind of additive decoration, at best a sort of 'mood setter,' at worst, simply titles and logos," he explains. But once he began studying early twentieth-century newspaper strips (as well as later R. Crumb comix) Ware realized that the older-style lettering radiated what he calls "a warmth and a humanity that contemporary lettering didn't, and that it had a potential as a primary 'expressive element,' if I can say that without sounding too academic."

He was smitten by the hand-done quality of the old methods, and he decided to learn the craft (or what he calls "the disposition, or whatever it was that made this old lettering so great") himself. Since he had self-consciously eliminated all words from his own comics for a number of years ("to try and communicate everything through gesture and rhythm," he explains), Ware was now ready to bring words back into them. "I wanted to get to the point where my lettering was as or more important than the pictures were, as second nature as drawing—that a font or a type style would come to me as naturally as a word would come to a writer; that I would 'feel' the type the same way I did the pictures and the words; i.e., that the cartooning would be of a whole, like a writer's 'voice.'"

Ware allows that it was a tall order. "But I started to realize that comics were really more of a visual language rather than simply rows of pictures with words tacked on top of them," he says. "And I had an inkling that perhaps by taking more of a typographic approach to the entire medium rather than a purely artistic—or even worse, illustrative—one, I might arrive at something formally that made a more direct emotional hit than I had up to then."

Ware lacked formal lettering training, so for many years he'd teach himself by copying examples from old Speedball manuals, the bibles of commercial show card writing from the 1920s through the 1950s. Yet the desired effect was elusive. "I always gave up in disgust, sensing that somehow there was something missing in the instructions," he says, "I just couldn't get the hang of it from those stupid pen-stroke diagrams." So

Ware devoted increasingly more attention to display lettering, trying to learn how to use a ruler and a ruling pen. By his own account he struggled on hopelessly, until one day, shortly after moving to Chicago, he found a box of original advertising lettering art for a small novelty concern, the Val-Mor Company, in an old novelty store named Uncle Fun.

The store's owner, Ted Frankel, had briefly worked for Val-Mor before it went out of business, and had retained a stack of original sign drawings that he one day presented to Ware. "I don't think there was a greater single effect on me than this one benevolent gift of dusty old Bristol board," Ware happily sighs. Meanwhile, from this Holy Grail he instantly understood exactly how the lettering process worked, what materials were used—ruling pens and brushes—and how letterers evened out the bottom of their letters with white ink. The problems he had been wrestling with in his own strips suddenly "clicked" in his mind. "There was a clarity, as well as a humanity, to this old type—I thought it was unbelievably beautiful; it glowed with a care and respect for the reader. Most importantly, though, it suggested to me how I might approach my 'drawing,' or more specifically, cartooning, and I began to refine my methods to reflect a more typographic approach."

To this day, Ware equivocates that his cartooning is not drawing per se: "It's more like typography, a mechanical sort of 'picture lettering,' which is why I guess some people hate it and say that my stuff is unemotional. I think it's probably the same sort of approach that Dan Clowes and Charles Burns have taken—their stuff was a real inspiration, obviously, along with Ernie Bushmiller—though I doubt they were anywhere near as ridiculously self-conscious about it." Self-conscious or not, describing his drawings as typography underscores the essence of his unique comic characters. While they do not necessarily have the overt emotionality of a Clowes (*Ghost World*) or the satirically goofy personas of a Crumb, they are imbued with graphic power that makes them mnemonic. His characters Jimmy and Rusty, for example, are akin to early twentieth-century trade characters, logos that adhere to the memory and evoke emotion and recognition. The characters are typographic not simply because they are geometrically rooted, but because they are vessels for meaning. Hey, but that's enough ethereal analysis for now. Technically speaking, Ware's typography relies on an incredible facility for achieving perfection.

What separates Ware's lettering from that of so many of today's typographers and some type designers, too, is fealty to the hand. Everything is hand-drawn on Bristol board with pen, brush, and ink—excepting, of course, the blocks of typeset text he occasionally uses, which are pasted on the originals, or assembled in Quark (like the introductory pages for the comics, etc.). Regarding the claim in the first paragraph of this article that he spends untold hours lettering, Ware quantifies that, saying, "On an average strip, the actual balloon lettering usually takes an hour or two, the 'logo,' an hour or two. The whole strip takes about forty hours. The cover of the last issue [of ACME Novelty Comics] took about three weeks." And that is because he rendered what he refers to as "super-fancy engraving lettering" that "I've pathetically tried to imitate in the comic books sometimes, that's more of just a personal challenge to see if I can do it, to see if I can get that sense of delicacy and care into my stuff—which I never do."

The sheer virtuosity of Ware's lettering should belie his effacing modesty. But when asked to explain why he is so painstakingly perfect while Crumb's work, for instance, is so rough-hewn, the answer suggests his motivating force: "He's a good artist and I'm not." But he quickly adds, "I don't know—I used to cartoon much more loosely, with a crow quill, and still do in my sketchbook, though I want the fictional stories I do, at least, to have a distance to them—a sort of mechanical clarity—that I can't get from just a pen."

Over the years Ware has focused on expanding his lettering repertoire. His self-published journal *The Rag-Time Ephemeralist*, devoted to a passion for arcane turn-of-the-century American music, is exquisitely lettered and accurately typeset (with lots of Cooperplate and Latin Condensed) to suggest late nineteenth-century magazines like *Phrenology* or *Frank Leslie's Monthly*. It is a masterpiece of typographic history. And it is this love of history that keeps Ware interested in pursuing type. But when pressed as to why exactly he renders a new logo for his weekly Rusty Brown comic strip, he doesn't extol the virtues of art or history. He's got a more practical motive: "I do a different one every week, just to keep things lively, and to keep in practice."

| Template Gothic |
| Barry Deck |

If period typefaces such as Broadway from the 1920s, Helvetica from the 1960s, or Avant Garde from the 1970s had been designed at any other time in history, would they have been as symbolic of their times? Or were they such total products of their eras that the question is moot? When William Caslon designed his only sans-serif typeface back in the early 1800s, it was considered an aesthetic monstrosity. Had it been created in the 1920s, however, when geometric sans-serif faces stood for progressive ideals, it would have been accepted without question. Typefaces, like automobile and clothing design, contribute to the Zeitgeist. But what makes the character of a

particular type so endemic? "The process by which particular typefaces come to embody the look, mood, and aspirations of a period is mysterious and fascinating," wrote Rick Poynor in *Eye* (No. 6, Vol. 2, 1992).

Timing may not be *everything*, but it does have a lot to do with why typefaces appeal to the public's taste at any given moment. It certainly explains why CalArts graduate Barry Deck's (b. 1962) Template Gothic (1990), a vernacular-inspired yet futuristic-looking typeface, became the most emblematic font in an epoch replete with emblems. At the time of Template Gothic's inception graphic design was experiencing technological shifts that altered methods and mind sets. Modernism was being challenged by a growing number of heretics opposed to its dogma; universality had become the hobgoblin of cultural diversity; and Swiss-influenced typography had become cold and trite. Template Gothic was one designer's attempt to explore alternative influences that were more or less deemed taboo. "The design of these fonts came out of my desire to move beyond the traditional concerns of type designers," Deck explained in *Eye* (No. 6, Vol. 2, 1992), "such as elegance and legibility, and to produce typographical forms which bring to language additional levels of meaning."

Some designers hold the traditional approach as sacrosanct as any religious doctrine. "Type is rigid and implacable," wrote Frederic W. Goudy in *Typologia* (1921). But others see the past as a foundation upon which to build new traditions. "We've had five hundred years of movable type now we have mutable type," conceded Matthew Carter in *Fine Print on Type* (1990). This mutable type requires mutable typographic rules. As Katherine McCoy wrote in *Design Quarterly* (No. 148, 1993), "Gone are the commercial artist's servant role and the Swiss designer's transparent neutrality. . . . Forms are appropriated with a critical awareness of their original meaning and contexts. This new work challenges its audience to slow down and read carefully in a world of fast forward and instant replay. . . ."

After twenty years of grid-locked design, reappraisal was inevitable. Rudy VanderLans and Zuzana Licko of Emigre had already opened up the laboratory doors, while academic hothouses, such as Cranbrook and CalArts, were encouraging students to push the boundaries. Conventional typeface design reprised or adapted historical models while strictly adhering to the tenets of balance and proportion. Conversely, the "new" typography started from zero. Without the benefit of precedent to guide them, type designers sought more eccentric influences both from exotic and mundane sources. Template Gothic was literally taken off the wall. "There was a sign in the laundromat where I do my laundry," Deck said. "The sign was done with lettering templates and it was exquisite. It had obviously been done by someone who was totally naïve." Although the stencil was itself professionally designed, manufactured, and commonly sold in stationery stores, the untutored rendering of the ad hoc laundry sign exemplified a colloquial graphic idiom that many designers viewed as a foreign language.

Designers have for a long time dug up and collected visual detritus from the street as a kind of deep background. Even the moderns appreciated old hand-painted signs as quaint artifacts from an era before sophisticated design methods brought light and order to the world. Given the postmodern ethos for revaluation, many of these same artifacts were elevated to monuments of visual culture. In much the same way that the Trajan Column in Rome provided the ancient inscriptions for the subsequent design of roman letters, the template inscriptions that influenced Deck were the basis for a distinct alphabet. Deck did not simply mimic the original, he built an aesthetic principle that challenged the prevailing concerns about legibility and accessibility.

Perhaps the best reason for Template Gothic's success was that it evoked the present *and* the future. A composite of low- and high-tech, it combined the vernacular traits of the mass-produced stencil and the futuristic character of early computer lettering. At the time it was released it captured the conscious and unconscious needs of designers to break from the recent past. In addition, Template Gothic is a curiously workable—user-friendly—mélange of irregular, tapering strokes, thick and thin bodies, and inconsistent weights, or what Deck called the "distortive ravages of photomechanical reproduction." Conceptually playful and experimentally serious—purposefully imperfect—Template Gothic is a postmodern discourse on the standards and values of typographic form. It is also a distinguished display and text face with tremendous versatility.

Manson/Mason

Jonathan Barnbrook

On the surface, the spiky roman typeface Manson, reminiscent of medieval inscriptions and replete with crucifixated *T*s and *O*s, exudes a kind of mysterious Gregorian atmosphere. But Jonathan Barnbrook's typeface is more than a family of quirky letterforms, it is a case study of how and why typefaces are named, and the relationship that a user has to both the name and face. Christened after mass-murderer Charles Manson, according to Barnbrook in *Emigre* (No. 23, 1992), this is merely a "different way of looking at the naming of a typeface." Shortly after it was introduced, Manson was criticized not for its form, but its name. One of the letters to *Emigre* read: "In a time of random violence, individual, organized, and institutionalized, why are you naming a typeface after Charles Manson? As part of our media culture, in fact a well-respected one, what kind of humor are you projecting? What kind of responsibility are you neglecting? This is no subtle joke. We are shocked at your inhumanity and callousness."

Although Barnbrook's description of Manson in *Emigre* did not sufficiently address the reason for celebrating this particular criminal, he did offer this: "While reading the word *Manson*, associations with other words such as *mason* and *mansion* might be evoked, names that do not relate somewhat to the elegant look of the typeface. The surname Charles also sounds quite sophisticated. But then you realize that it's the name of a mass murderer and you re-assess your attitude to the typeface." Barnbrook's doublespeak may not do justice to his seductive medievalized Roman derived from his 1991 design of Exocet, based on a primitive Greek stone carving. Nevertheless, taken at his word, this is not merely a novel or gratuitously named typeface, but rather a test of what motivates someone to choose a particular type.

The name Manson forces the user to address a fundamental

relationship. What, for instance, does the face signify? Aesthetics aside, why would someone buy a font with such a namesake? Apparently the name is more experimental than the typeface design itself, for it tests the limits of signification and association. While most typeface names are comparatively benign, something called Manson cannot avoid conjuring up images of violence and criminality, in the same way that *Nixon* conjures deception and deceit. Given this name, the quirky letters are no longer just the distant relations of ancient Greek inscriptions, but are kissing cousins of the swastika tattoo carved into Manson's forehead or the words *Helter Skelter* that were drawn in blood on the walls of Sharon Tate's home.

Bowing to criticism, however, and thereby eschewing the issues that Barnbrook initially sought to raise, the 1995 Emigre Fonts catalog included a specimen of Manson renamed Mason; perhaps suggesting the Order of Masons, which itself has a cultist underpinning, or the ethnocentric comedian Jackie Mason, who has a large cult following, or more likely it refers to a stone mason, from whence the inscriptions derived. But despite revisionist nomenclature, the name Manson not only sticks, but also gives the face an aura, if not a meaning, that it would not have had if it were originally called Mason. As proof, two recent book jackets for *The Death of Hitler* and *The Violence of Our Lives: Interviews with American Murderers* used Manson/Mason for what critics of this nomenclature would assert were the wrong reasons: to signify and/or dignify violence. Although only designers who know the name, not the average reader, will actually get the reference, the impetus to use this face was its name, which when linked to these specific titles reinforces the idea that this typeface represents violence.

Typefaces are given names either to define otherwise abstract letterforms according to purpose (e.g., News Gothic), or to celebrate the face's maker or inspiration (e.g., Benguiat), or to sell a particular fashion (e.g., Cubist Bold). In the 1930s, A. M. Cassandre named his transitional sans-serif Peignot after Charles Peignot, the design impresario who helped launch his career; Frederic Goudy called one of his numerous type designs Deepdeen after his rural New York State retreat. And Milton Glaser called his popular display face, originally used on his *Dylan* poster, Baby Teeth because of the physical relationship to a baby's pearly whites (yet it could easily have been called Stairstep for the same reason). The majority of classical text faces are named after their designers: Garamond, Bodoni, Firmin Didot, Baskerville, Caslon, Gill, Cooper, and Bernhard are the major street signs of typography. Naming a face after its creator is one way to ensure immortality, or at least notoriety.

LANGUAGE

S lodí jež dováží čaj kávu	*195*
(With the Ship that Carries Tea and Coffee)	
Karel Teige	

The modern design movement was born in Western Europe and Russia, but didn't stay there for long. During the period of creative ferment between the world wars, Poland, Hungary, and Czechoslovakia also became capitals of the new design and New Typography. Even with the rise of totalitarianism, which brought the engines of progressive expression in

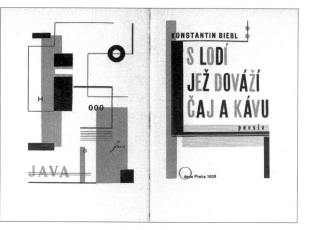

Germany and the Soviet Union to a grinding halt—squelching Russian constructivism and productivism in the early 1930s and closing the Bauhaus in Germany in 1933—avant-gardists continued to work freely in Warsaw, Budapest, and Prague. Hitler and Stalin had not begun their respective occupations of these autonomous states until the late 1930s, allowing a brief respite for avant-garde art and design to develop before the war and postwar repression.

After World War I, Prague, Czechoslovakia's capital, was the crossroads for exponents of the new cultural "isms." The progressive movement of longest duration was a group called Devetsil, a confederation of left-wing writers, artists, sculptors, photographers, filmmakers, and typographers. They were known unofficially as the Czech Bauhaus, even though they were more diverse philosophically and methodologically than their German counterparts.

No one can trace where the name *Devetsil* actually came from. (In Czech the word is a pun on two roots: a botanical term meaning "spiky butterbur" and a mathematical term meaning "nine forces.") Nor is it known how many people were active members. Like other twentieth-century design "isms," Devetsil wed art to technology in an effort to unite form and function. In this respect, it was informed by the sociopolitical ideology manifest in the USSR that spread throughout Europe during the 1920s. Devetsil's leader, Karel Teige (1900–1951) was a prolific writer, poet, critic, painter, designer, and typographer whose visual models included constructivism and surrealism. An ardent socialist, he developed a concept called *ars una*, a modernist reprise of the nineteenth-century movement to integrate art into every aspect of life. In the 1920s he devoted himself to typography and "pictorial poetry," producing, editing, and designing books first in a constructivist and later in a surrealist spirit.

Teige promoted strict typographic standards consistent with those of the European avant garde. Elementary, unadorned geometric forms devoid of any bourgeois decorative vestiges made communications more functional. In his early work, from around 1922, Teige used one basic device, a black circle, which was both eye-catching and a "word symbol" representing the avant-garde's larger rejection of archaic and contemporary superficial design trends. "The relationship between Teige's theoretical work and his typographic rules can be demonstrated by the circle," wrote Karel Srp ("Karel Teige and the New Typography," *Rassenga,* 1965). It represented a variety of things, a sun, a ball, a human head. "According to Teige the neutral geometric forms did not lose their identification with man. . . . Teige's functionalism was strongly anthropocentric." Therefore, the circle was not merely an abstract image on a page. Teige believed that abstract paintings were decorative, and therefore circles should never be used in painting because it was form without sense. The circle used in a book or journal cover, however, was endemic to the structure and meaning of text. Teige concurred with El Lissitzky's notion that the modern book should be looked at before it is read, but reading was the ultimate functional goal.

Of his many book and book jacket designs the title pages and "illustrations" for *S lodí jež dováží čaj a kávu* (*With the Ship that Carries Tea and Coffee,* 1927) by Konstantin Biebl is a unique application of constructivist form for its combination of elementary graphic devices and pastel palette, an example of how kindred designers in different parts of the world reinterpreted the language of modern design based on their own requisites.

Devetsil members longed to travel to exotic lands, and as spokesman for the movement, Teige announced, "The most wonderful thing would be to live in a fast train coach." Since Bohemia does not border on an ocean the members were ostensibly landlocked. Only Biebl dared make a long journey over land and sea to Ceylon, Sumatra, and Java. His book, a wanderer's travelogue in poetic verse, was not, however, illustrated with conventionally nostalgic or romantic pictures of distant places, but rather abstractly, in dynamic compositions using typecase materials, similar to El Lissitzky's typecase illustrations in *For the Voice,* Mayakovsky's book of socialist poems.

In Teige's 1927 essay, "Modern Type" (which echoed similar manifestoes by Lazar El Lissitzky and Lásló Moholy-Nagy), he argued for a radical shift in general standards, rejecting tedious layout techniques for dynamic typographic forms. He brought Bauhaus sobriety to Czechoslovakia, and though he would later be inspired by the raucous typographic and collage antics of German dada, his constructivist vocabulary inspired many young designers to leave tradition behind.

Depero: Futurista

Fortunato Depero

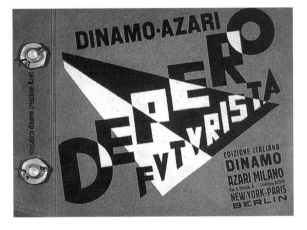

Redefining the spiritual and material world fell to visionaries, "men of talent and memorable fools," who led the shock troops of modernism. Inspired to action, the Italian Fortunato Depero (1892–1960) cosigned the "Futurist Reconstruction of the Universe," a manifesto aimed at world renewal by "cheering it up" through the overhaul of everyday objects—interior decoration, clothing, publicity, mass communications, postal art. Depero was a significant part of the late first and second stages of Italian futurism, an early and exceedingly influential European avant-garde movement that altered the process of artistic production and the role of the artist in society. Futurism's founder, poet F. T. Marinetti, proclaimed in the 1909 *Futurist Manifesto* (published in the Parisian newspaper, *Le Figaro*): "United, we must attack! We must create with absolute faith in the imperishable richness of the earth! There can be no nostalgia! No pessimism! There's no turning back! Boldly, let us advance! Forward! Faster! Farther! Higher! Let us lyrically renew our joy in being alive!"

Marinetti espoused a permanent artistic and political revolution. He rejected traditionalism in favor of "the new religion of speed," mythologizing the machine—the automobile and later the airplane—as a totem of the modern spirit. Technology, though somewhat primitive in Italy, was the savior of mankind, and futurism was the avant-garde of the masses.

At age twenty-four, Fortunato (meaning good luck) Depero was already artistically formed, with a distinct stylistic personality. While he shared Marinetti's belief in "art action," Depero was engaged in considerably more playful pursuits. And, although he followed the movement's political dictates, his personal politics were based on aesthetics. "In Depero one rediscovers applied art, the happening, kinetic art, dadaist provocation, abstract painting: to sum up, a heritage of so many new directions of art," wrote Italian art historian Giorgio Ruggeri.

Much of Depero's design prefigures today's postmodern and new wave eclecticism in its form and color.

Depero was an indefatigable proponent of futurism. He wrote for newspapers, promoted the futurist book, founded and directed the machine art magazine *Dinamo*, organized personal exhibitions, and worked in the theater as a set and costume designer. He was commissioned by Diaghilev to make a set and costumes for *Le Chant du Rossignol*. He invented an "onomalanguage," a free word, free sounding, expressive verbal rigamarole. He represented the futurists at the 1925 Paris exposition of modern decorative and industrial art, exhibiting his life-sized mechanical men. He produced futurist radio programs. He decorated cabarets, bars, restaurants, and dance halls. With his wife Rossetta, he opened the *Casa d'Arte Futurist* in Rovereto, Italy, where he made wooden constructions, furniture, and costumes for a mass clientele. He designed futurist clothing, vests, and jackets. And in 1923 he moved to New York for three years where on West Twenty-third Street he opened Depero's Futurist House, selling everything from paintings to advertising graphics, and propagating the futurist "style" to a culture that thought of all European modernism as "futurist."

Depero triumphed with book design and production. During the 1920s the "book-object" was seriously practiced as a futurist art form— the marriage of futurist layout and typographical experimentation. For the 1927 *Biennale Internazionale delle Arti Decorative* in Monza, Italy, Depero designed a book pavilion built entirely out of giant block letters. It was a grand architectural achievement, but not as historically important as his bolted art catalog, which, along with Tulio D'Albisola's famous tin book *Futurist Words Set Free: Tactile Thermal Olfactory*, is emblematic of futurist applied arts. *Depero: Futurista,* as it was called, is a lavish compendium of his own design work (including many advertisements he had designed for Campari) covering the years 1913 through 1927. Depero was predisposed to an "Aztec deco" sensibility that was influenced by set-back skyscrapers. Depero's use of bright colors and collaged colored papers was a startling contrast to the rather conservative realism that then held sway. Reproduced in letterpress, it was bound, in machine age fashion, by two stainless steel bolts.

By 1927 Depero was recognized as an innovator. His synthesis of dynamic and expressionistic graphic forms was undeniably original. He reconciled craft, fine, and applied arts; and, believing that product advertising was the means to stimulate a dialogue with the public, he took on commissions in Italy, including a highly visible series for Campari. In the 1932 manifesto, "The Art of Advertising," Depero announced, "The art of the future will be powerfully advertising art." And he continued that "All last centuries [*sic*] art was advertising oriented." The suggestion being that the paintings of the past, exalting war, religion, and even love, were instruments of sales. Depero believed that the artist's individuality expressed as a selling tool was the best means to stimulate artistic dialogue with the public. Therefore, he would only work for clients (such as Campari) who gave him license. With such assignments he deliberately used the product as the source of his own iconography, inspiring, he believed, "a new pictorial taste for the image."

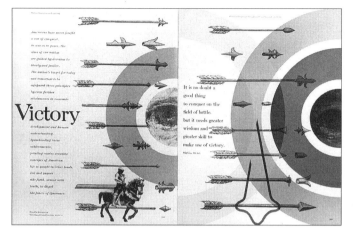

A graphic designer's influence is not measured by how many acolytes mimic his style or by how many awards he has won, but rather by what he alone has contributed to the visual language. Since such judgments are subjective, the criteria used to determine influence might be an answer to the question: If the particular designer had never existed, would the field be worse off? To be more specific, if a young man from Topeka, Kansas, by the name of Bradbury Thompson (1911–1995), had not left his job designing high school yearbooks, and had not come to New York City in the late 1930s, would a significant chapter of American graphic design history have been written?

If not for Thompson, Westvaco *Inspirations*, which in the 1930s was a paper company's spiritless promotional brochure, might never have become the bible of graphic design and textbook for a generation. If Thompson was never a magazine art director (*Mademoiselle*, *Art News*, and others), book, postage stamp, or advertising designer; if all he ever accomplished during his fifty-year career was to design and edit sixty issues of a periodical that he transformed into a journal of modern layout and typography—including special issues devoted to such themes as "Type as a Toy," "Primitive Art as Modern Design," and the phonetic "Monalphabet" (which eliminated the need for separate upper- and lowercase letters)—his place as a pioneer of American graphic design would still be locked in for the ages.

In 1938 Thompson left the American heartland without a clue that he would eventually become the art director and designer for some very influential magazines, or a teacher at Yale University, or one of the chief designers for the United States Postal Service. He just came East to work for one of those fabled art directors in the big city that he had read about in design magazines he found in the Topeka library. From the outset he had a curiously modernist bent (curious because conservative middle America was not a conducive environment for modern thinking).

Westvaco *Inspirations* was a compendium of what Thompson believed to be the best of contemporary practice. *Inspirations* reported on the prevailing ethos, aesthetic, and philosophy of graphic design. But it was more. Thompson promoted his vision, which wed the European modern spirit to a respect for classical heritage. "My early interest in type came from the humanist typographers," explained Thompson, "the classic types of Europe from the fifteenth, sixteenth, and seventeenth centuries. Later, *Vanity Fair* [art directed by M. F. Agha] influenced me in the use of sans-serif type—especially Futura." His appreciation for unadorned layout further evolved from studying the behemoth fashion magazines of the 1930s, while his graphic adventurism came from an intimate knowledge of printing and its potential. Thompson was never inhibited by low-budget constraints nor primitive technologies. His belief in the rightness of form was less about ideological purity than an interest in the most effective means to communicate information.

Thompson liberally borrowed from all arts—painting and sculpture, photography and drawing, realistic and abstract—to prove the limitless possibilities of the design process. One of his most well-known designs, an *Inspirations* spread titled "Kerr-choo-oo," presents type that is not read as a word but as sound. Although inspired by Apollinaire's *Calligrammes* and F. T. Marinetti's *Parole in Liberta*, it was decidedly American in its wit.

Inspirations brought classical, modern, and eclectic sensibilities together in the form of a manifesto, not the rabble-rousing kind that emanated from futurism or dada, but a soft-spoken kind—which characterized Thompson to a T—that sought to teach rather than preach. Thompson was not radical, but modern in the catholic sense: anything was possible within his aesthetic parameters; anything was doable as long as quality was the goal. Thompson's experiments were, moreover, rooted in terra firma—the real world. *Inspirations* was a progressive's introduction to new ideas about graphic forms and their applications in the marketplace, not the clouds. Everything presented in the publication (including his convention-busting Monalphabet) was appropriate within the convention of visual communications.

The qualities that made *Inspirations* unique were rooted in its conventional production. The constraints of letterpress printing and hot metal composition stymied creative activity, but Thompson maximized the limitations, pushed the boundaries, and tested the resilience of design. One of the single most important lessons he taught through the example of *Inspirations* was that type could be made expressive, emotive, personal, and still be part of a tasteful composition. "There is no creative aspect of graphic design more enjoyable or rewarding than the indulgence in play," he once wrote.

Thompson was also smitten by French and German poster art of the 1930s, which integrated type and image as one entity. He saw these word and picture compositions as the signpost to future design possibilities. "In working on Westvaco *Inspirations* I just naturally applied all these forms," he explained. Yet he did not merely mimic existing forms.

Thompson never possessed a style per se, rather an attitude. His magazine layouts were void of artifice, but decidedly modern. His book design was based on classical models. How did he reconcile the two sensibilities? "Appropriateness," he explained. "You can't get away from tradition, if you want to bridge past, present, and future."

Lorca: Three Tragedies

Alvin Lustig

The 1953 paperback cover for *Lorca: Three Tragedies* designed by Alvin Lustig (1915–1955) is a masterpiece of symbolic acuity, compositional strength, and typographic ingenuity. It is also the basis for a great many contemporary book jackets and paperback covers. The American book jacket designers' preference, in the late 1980s and 1990s, for fragmented images, minimal typography, and rebus-like compositions can be traced directly to the stark black-and-white cover for *Three Tragedies*. This and other distinctive jackets and covers designed by Lustig for New Directions transformed the photograph into a tool for abstraction through the use of reticulated negatives, photograms, and setups.

Lustig's approach developed from an interest in photomontage originally practiced by the European moderns, and particularly the American expatriate E. McKnight Kauffer. When Lustig introduced this technique to American book publishing in the late 1940s, book covers and jackets were predominantly illustrative and rather decorative, with an abundance of hand-lettered novelty faces. The Lorca cover was a grid of five symbolic photographs tied together in poetic disharmony. Before this type of cover was introduced, European art-based approaches were not even considered by American publishers. Perhaps they were thought foolhardy in a marketplace where hard-sell marketing conventions were rigorously adhered to. Or, just as likely, the leading book jacket designers of the day were ignorant of such methods.

Lustig rejected the typical literary solution that summarized a book through one generalized image. "His method was to read a text and get the feel of the author's creative drive, then to restate it in his own graphic terms," wrote James Laughlin, the publisher of New Directions, in "The Book Jackets of Alvin Lustig" (*Print*, Vol. 10, No. 5, October 1956). Laughlin hired Lustig in the early 1940s giving him the latitude to experiment with graphic forms. New Directions' eccentric list of reprinted contemporary classics, which featured authors such as Henry Miller, Gertrude Stein, D. H. Lawrence, and James Joyce, was a proving ground for Lustig's visual explorations and distinctive graphic poetry. While attaining higher sales was always an issue, Lustig believed that he should not "design down" to the reader. Although mindful of the fundamental marketing precept that a book jacket must attract and hold the average book buyer's roving eye, Lustig crossed over into taboo marketing territory with his introduction of abstract images and small, discreetly typeset titles, influenced by the work of Jan Tschichold and other European moderns.

Lustig's first jacket for Laughlin, a 1941 edition of Henry Miller's *Wisdom of the Heart,* eclipsed the previous New Directions books, which Laughlin described as jacketed in a "conservative, 'booky,' way." At the time Lustig was experimenting with nonrepresentational constructions made from slugs of hot metal typographic material, suggesting the influence of architect Frank Lloyd Wright, with whom he studied for three months at Taliesin East. While decidedly unconventional, some years later Laughlin noted that this particular jacket "was rather stiff and severe. . . . It scarcely hinted at the extraordinary flowering which was to follow."

Laughlin was referring to the series of New Directions New Classics that Lustig designed from 1945 to 1952. With few exceptions, the New Classics seem as inventive today as they were when they first appeared almost fifty years ago. Lustig had switched over from typecase compositions to drawing distinctive symbolic "marks" that owed more to the work of artists like Paul Klee, Joan Míro, and his friend Mark Rothko, than to any accepted commercial style. Although Lustig rejected painting as "too subjectivized" and never presumed to paint or sculpt himself, he borrowed liberally from modern painting and integrated the abstract sensibility into his total design.

Each of his New Classic jackets is a mix of expressionistic and analytical forms—sophisticated doodles, really—that interpret rather than narrate the novels, plays, and poetry. For Franz Kafka's *Amerika,* Lustig used a coarsely rendered five-pointed star divided in half by red stripes and out of which emerges childlike squiggles of smoke—a reference to Kafka's intemperate critique of a mythic America. For E. M. Forster's *The Longest Journey,* he used stark black bars that suggest a labyrinthian maze. It does not illustrate the author's romantic scene; instead the symbolism alludes to the emotive tension of the story. "In these as in all Lustig's jackets the approach is indirect," wrote C. F. O. Clarke in *Graphis* (No. 23, 1948), "but through its sincerity and compression it has more imaginative power than direct illustration could achieve."

The New Classics succeeded where other popular literary series, including the Modern Library and Everyman's Library, had failed. Each New Classics jacket had its own character, yet Lustig maintained unity through formal consistency. However, at no time did his style overpower the book. Lustig's jacket designs for New Directions demanded contemplation; they were not quick-fix visual stimulants.

Lustig was a form-giver, not a novelty maker. The style he chose for the New Classics was a logical solution to the specific design problem. The New Classics did not become his signature style any more than his earlier typecase compositions did, for within the framework of modernism Lustig varied his approach, using the marketplace as his laboratory. "I have heard people speak of the 'Lustig Style,'" wrote Laughlin in *Print*, "but not one of them has been able to tell me, in fifty words or five hundred what it was. Because each time, with each new book, there was a new creation. The only repetitions were those imposed by the physical media."

Lustig's design appeared revolutionary (and so unacceptable) to the guardians of tradition entrenched at the AIGA and other book-dominated graphic organizations, but he was not the radical that critics feared. He stressed the formal aspects of a problem, and in matters of formal practice he was devout to a fault. In "Contemporary Book Design" (*Design Quarterly*, No. 31. 1954) he wrote, "The factors that produce quality are the same in the traditional and in the contemporary book. Wherein, then lies difference? Perhaps the single most distinguishing factor in the approach of the contemporary designer is his willingness to let the problem act upon him freely and without preconceived notions of the forms it should take."

Lorca: Three Tragedies exemplified Lustig's versatility and was, moreover, one of many covers for New Directions that tested the effectiveness of inexpensive black-and-white printing as it pushed the boundaries of accepted modern design. For with this and other photo-illustrations (done in collaboration with photographers because he did not take the photographs himself), Lustig customized the modern visual language to fit his preferences. Of course, he was not alone. Paul Rand produced art-based book jackets, but Lustig's distinction, wrote Laughlin in *Print*, "lay in the intensity and the purity with which he dedicated his genius to his idea vision." While the others may have been graphic problem-solvers, Lustig was a visual poet whose work was rooted as much in emotion as in form.

In the early 1920s, when William Addison Dwiggins (1880–1956) was in his forties—an age by which many of his contemporaries had already done their best work and were ossified in their ways—he was at the peak of his form and open to all possibilities. He did not subscribe to avant-garde theory or any other theory that held sway in the 1920s and 1930s. He was never dogmatic regarding the ideological rightness of form. On one occasion he wrote disparagingly about the typographic antics of those modern American designers he referred to as the Bauhaus boys, while on another he attacked the rigidity of narrow-minded traditionalists.

Dwiggins, WAD, Dwig, or Bill—take your pick—grew up in Cambridge, Ohio, and at nineteen studied lettering with Frederic Goudy at the Frank Holme School of Illustration in Chicago, Illinois. He was weaned on the ideals of the aesthetic movement, of which proponents imitated fine printing of the past. In 1912 Dwiggins and T. M. Cleland were singled out by the preeminent posterist and typographer Will Bradley for work that had brought taste and skill back into a field that had "sunk to the lowest possible depths before their appearance."

But Dwig did not follow the rules. His longtime friend and collaborator Dorothy Abbe once said that he had arrived at his own determination of fine printing, and it differed very considerably from that of Goudy, Updike, and Rogers. While these stalwart keepers of the classical rejected mass production as anathema to fine design, during the course of his life Dwig witnessed the passing of individual craftsmanship and the substitution of bigger, faster machines in all phases of typesetting and printing. He saw no reason why new technologies should not produce quality work, and he proposed that photoengraving, for example, made calligraphy more widely available, which would increase popular appreciation of good design.

Dwiggins practiced advertising design, type design, book design, and marionette design. He even designed a working puppet theater in his clapboard studio across the street from his home in Hingham, Massachusetts. But to appreciate Dwig's obsessions for work and therefore his contributions, one must know that he was driven to accomplish as much as possible before succumbing to the dire prediction of an early death. "He was handicapped by the clock and the calendar," says a biographical notation. Diagnosed with diabetes, an often fatal disease at that time (1922), Dwiggins exhibited an intense drive to get on with life. Dorothy Abbe explained: "He resolved thenceforth to satisfy himself." A year later Dwig announced to the world: "Me I am a happy invalid and it has revolutionized my whole attack. My back is turned on the more banal kind of advertising and I have canceled all commissions and am resolutely set on starving. . . . I will produce art on paper and wood after my own heart with no heed to any market." However, fate intervened: Insulin soon became available, giving Dwiggins another thirty-three years of life.

Tossing aside his lucrative advertising accounts, he concentrated on the not-so-profitable business of book design and page ornament. His earliest book commissions were from the Harvard University Press, for whom he designed the now-rare volume *Modern Color* (1923), and from Alfred A. Knopf, for whom, beginning in 1924 and continuing for almost two decades, he designed 280 books of fiction and nonfiction as well as almost fifty book jackets. "Bill enabled us to produce a long series of trade books that for interest and originality of design are unequaled," writes Mr. Knopf.

In addition to his uniquely composed (and sometimes illustrated) title pages, two features characterized his design: The text was always readable, and the bindings (and especially the shelf backs) were adorned with his calligraphic hand lettering and neo-Mayan ornament. Every piece of lettering and typography—down to the minutest graphic detail—was rendered by hand; given the extant physical evidence, many were done without a single mistake (when mistakes did occur, he simply redrew them rather than touching up the errors). Dwiggins's calligraphic display letters, a marriage of classical typefaces and invented scripts, set the standard for Knopf's books and influenced many other publishers, who employed Dwig or one of his many imitators.

Book jackets, however, fell into the category of advertising that Dwiggins initially wanted to avoid. Yet, due to his special relationship with Mr. Knopf, when asked, he did them. Nevertheless, his method was a form of denial. He refused to pictorially illustrate most covers, as was the common practice, but rather applied Dwigginsian ornament and calligraphic lettering. Hence, there was a great formal similarity between all his jackets. The image area of his most common jacket format was cut in half, with the title on top and a subtitle or other type below. Sometimes he used an excessive amount of ornamentation, but only with his self-authored books did he ever use a drawing. A typical approach—found in his jacket for Willa Cather's *Lost Lady*, which includes a hand-lettered title and byline and characteristic Dwigginsian ornament printed in pink, green, and brown—is something like a souped-up title page. Compared to the designers of many of the lettered jackets of his day, Dwiggins had a unique flair, wedding balance and harmony with quirkiness. The jackets rarely evoked the plot or theme of the book but were essentially decoration—a "dust wrapper" in the purest sense of the word. One of his most alluring jackets—for James M. Cain's *Serenade* (1937), the design of which is a bouquet of abstracted flora—is akin more to beautiful wrapping paper than an advertisement for the book.

Given the choice, Dwiggins preferred using his hands to make things; hand lettering was more satisfying than type design. He did not begin to design complete type alphabets until 1929, when, at the urging of C. H. Griffith, marketing director for the Mergenthaler Linotype Corporation, he designed his first typeface for continued reading. He did not attempt to replicate his calligraphy. In fact, the initial undertaking (the first of eighteen typefaces), had no relationship whatsoever to his lettering. Metro Black was a uniform sans serif letter that Dwiggins designed because he saw a need for a strong gothic that did more for display advertising than Futura and other European gothics. Ironically, Dwig never used this typeface on any book jacket.

"There are few American designers whose work can be revisited after decades with more pleasure and instruction," an admirer wrote about Dwiggins a decade after his death. When viewing examples of his printed work or the original drawings that surface at exhibitions, much of Dwig's work stands up not as nostalgia, but for its invention. Even the book jackets, which are stylistically locked in time, could, with some typographic modifications, be used today. By the 1950s, however, with the advent of the international style and the sweeping success of corporate modernism, Dwig was virtually ignored. Moderns, who tended to disclaim as crass commercial art anything that preceded modern design, eschewed Dwiggins for being folksy, arts-and-craftsy, and, of course, passé.

Though he challenged tradition, he attempted to reform the old school not abolish it. Curiously, his work, including the book jackets, is gaining appreciation among makers of so-called distressed type; even Emigre Fonts sells Dorothy Abbe's book of Dwig's stenciled ornaments, the same decorations used in his book and book-jacket design.

Merle Armitage (1893–1975) taught himself to design sets and costumes for the theater in New York. Next he became a theatrical impresario, managing concert tours for Will Rogers, Martha Graham, and Igor Stravinsky. Later he segued into the role of publicity and advertising director for Diaghilev's Ballet Russe before cofounding the Los Angeles Grand Opera Association, followed by a stint as manager of the Philharmonic Auditorium in Los Angeles, where he presented concerts with conductor Leopold Stokowski and the first staging of *Porgy and Bess* by composer George Gershwin—all before his thirtieth birthday.

An avid attraction for the arts, and especially modern artists like Picasso, Klee, Kandinsky, et al., inspired his ultimate and total immersion into typography and book design, often for books he authored, edited, or published about progressive artists of his time, many of whom became his friends. Armitage mined everything from his early career as inspiration for authorship and book design. However, he is perhaps best known for his book design (especially among book art aficionados), although he is considerably less celebrated than his modern contemporaries. Although his books are seriously collected today and his writings are occasionally cited, owing to his stylized "period" typography (which even he admitted became "outmoded"), he is nonetheless rarely taught as an exemplar or discussed as a member of the orthodox modern clan. Many of his over one hundred books evidence a formal bridge between celebrated classicists, like Bruce Rogers and T. M. Cleland, with modernists like Herbert Bayer, Paul Rand, and Alvin Lustig. In terms of current design history, however, Armitage's work is a rather wobbly bridge.

Rand grumbled that Armitage "overdid it," referring to his signature mammoth type treatments, usually on double-page title pages (which he "invented"), extremely generous margins, and often widely leaded serif body texts. Other orthodox moderns further accused him of being modernistic. Armitage considered himself modern, however, and even admitted with just a hint of false modesty in *A Rendezvous with the Book* (George McKibbin & Son, 1949), a treatise on book design, that each one of his books was "unsuccessful." Yet there was a caveat: "I believe, [they were] failures in the right direction . . . for they represent attempts to speak to readers in a contemporary language of design . . . and to close the gap which now exists between the written word and the manner of its presentation."

The alleged ham-fisted typographical treatments that characterized Armitage's design were resolutely contemporary—the result of a mission to demolish antiquated tenets and reflect his time. He angrily wrote that the books of his era were "anonymous among their fellows and are becoming comparatively impotent as a means of communication." Referring to the book field in general, he wrote, "the grand escalator that has brought us all up from darkness and slavery into light and freedom, has, in our time, lost its leadership, and is uncertain of its function and its direction." Sure, his prose often provided as much melodrama as his type, yet he was convinced that mediocrity had so contaminated book design that what he called "the stammering books of today" had to be totally cleansed. So, mustering self-taught skill and homegrown bravado, he took it upon himself to stem the tide, transform the medium, and leave a significant body of work, even if it doesn't always pass the test of time.

Born in Mason City, Iowa, in 1893, the son of a cattle rancher, Armitage's passion for design may not appear to be genetic, but it definitely consumed him throughout his entire life. He developed a keen ability for making type reflect the Zeitgeist when, as an impresario for progressive composers and musicians, he found himself habitually disappointed that the circulars and posters advertising his concerts misrepresented his clients' avant-garde practices. He deplored ersatz William Morris and other antique graphic forms used to promote the likes of Anna Pavlova, George Gershwin, or Igor Stravinsky. Thus, "the duties of writing copy and designing printed material for these attractions were therefore added to my general responsibility of building careers," he wrote in *A Rendezvous*. Armitage replaced run-of-the-mill and inappropriate graphics with modern sans serif typefaces, custom-made hand letters, and bold pictorial images. He imbued in each book a certain monumentality that underscored the words and enhanced the pictures.

He soon realized that the French were more successful in "marketing" the works of contemporary artists because they published beautiful and intelligent books explaining the theory that underscored progressive art. This astute observation encouraged Armitage to create (and often write) his own books, to both enlighten the public and foster greater appreciation for the new vanguard. "My aim was a synthesis of text, picture and design . . . a revealment of the general attitude expressed by the subject." In practice, this meant books that were contemporary in form, structure, and pacing, that served to mirror their subjects' unique sensibilities. "The book must be an outward expression of its content," he wrote, not reflexive reproductions of Olde English, Renaissance, or other period styles.

When Wassily Kandinsky first exhibited at a gallery in Hollywood in 1939, Armitage was asked to write an essay that explained the unprecedented work to a befuddled public. And when requests for the essay turned into a small deluge, the publisher E. Weyhe (New York) invited Armitage to design a slender book called *So-Called Abstract Art*, which not only shed light on the idea of abstraction, but did so with stark typography that echoed the new artistic sensibility. Similarly, with his self-published *Martha Graham* (1937), Armitage developed a typographic scheme and pictorial pacing using dramatically lit photographs that became the visual identity for this visionary dancer. "Taking Martha Graham on her first transcontinental tour convinced me that she was the greatest dancer of our time," wrote Armitage in *Merle Armitage, Book Designer* (University of Texas Press, 1956). "Through subtle handling I attempted to make the book 'dance' in a most contemporary manner."

For his 1938 memorial book *George Gershwin* (Longmans, Green and Co.), Armitage infused the project with what he called "some of the vitality, color, and excitement that were so manifest in this great American composer." He later followed up with a second book on his friend titled *George Gershwin* (Duell, Sloan and Pearce, 1958), with a simple sans serif "GG" on the cover, which included the art that influenced the composer and he in turn influenced.

New approaches to book design coincided with modern innovations in other arts; for Armitage, Frank Lloyd Wright, Serge de Diaghilev, and Raymond Loewy were among the leading progenitors. He wrote that what men like Loewy had done for the machine must be similarly applied to publishing. Of course, the streamlined aesthetic developed by Loewy and other industrial designers in the 1930s was as concerned with veneer as with function, and that was echoed in Armitage's work, too. Nonetheless, even given his typographic excesses, on the whole Armitage's books goosed book design out of complacency. He was unforgiving when in came to "publishers who purchase manuscripts they have never read and assign them to designers who will never read them," he wrote. To the contrary, he conceived of a book as a whole entity, not the sum of disparate parts. In fact, the publishing convention that dictated (and still dictates) an artificial division between cover and interior designers prompted Armitage to assert, "We read that 'dust wrapper and title page have been designed by so and so' . . . but a Cadillac advertisement proclaiming, 'front fenders and steering wheel have been designed by so and so' would be an impossible absurdity." While jackets on many of his own books were usually more neutral than the startling cover or interior typography, everything was designed as one totality, and thus evoked an unmistakable identity.

Designers throughout the late 1920s and 1930s copied the elegant calligraphic scripts and Mayan-influenced decorations of W. A. Dwiggins, yet few if any pilfered Armitage's style. Perhaps his approach was just too idiosyncratic or maybe too horsy for some. Whatever the reason, his distinctive method was exclusive to the few independent publishers—including the famed Ward Ritchie Press in Los Angeles, which also published Alvin Lustig's early type-case experiments—who realized that book design had to reflect the times. Consequently, his personal fingerprint is the explicit graphic force of his type and the prominence he gives to illustrations, art, and photographs.

Despite Armitage's preference for modern aesthetics rooted in what he called the "tension" of demonstrative letter and color combinations (i.e., black and red and some yellow were his favorites), he did not promote a single method or ideology. "No system is readily at hand to solve the problem; it is not a matter of formulas," he wrote. "'Modern' is not something you can put on or take off as you would a hat." But it is something that has various interpretations and his, while at odds with other Modern practitioners, was for type to emote rather than stay neutral. Armitage's timely books were designed to be unashamedly theatrical, just like the concerts and plays he promoted so successfully on the big stage.

About U.S.

Lester Beall, Brownjohn Chermayeff Geismar, Herb Lubalin, Gene Federico

In 1955 Aaron Burns (1922–1991) was the Composing Room's type director and quality-control expert, responsible for facilitating the difficult hot metal settings demanded by agency art directors. Burns, who later cofounded the International Typeface Company, was also "a seeker-outer of people who were cutting edge," recalled Ivan Chermayeff. This was more than the typical designer and supplier relationship; Burns developed formative outlets and forums for graphic designers to express themselves through typography. Under his direction the term *cutting edge* had at times a very literal meaning. This was the period when the constraints of hot metal composition made it difficult to achieve such now common effects as tight spacing, touching, or overlapping without the designer cutting with a razor blade, repositioning the proofs, and then making an engraving of the mechanical. Burns explored any reasonable ways to push the limits of typography. One of his most satisfying attempts was a series of four sixteen-page booklets produced in 1960 titled *About U.S.*, which gave four American designers an opportunity to wed type and images without any conceptual constraints and push the edges of production in any way possible.

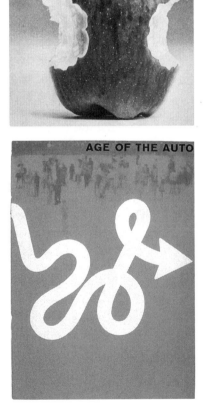

The four booklets (written by Percy Seitlin) were: Lester Beall's *The Age of the Auto*, where type was laboriously composed in long, thin, and contoured lines to suggest the path (or tire tracks) of an automobile ride; Herb Lubalin's *Come Home to Jazz*, a pictorial jam of jazz instruments photographed in high contrast with drop-out type in different sizes and weights running in and out of the images, suggesting the discordance of the music itself; Brownjohn Chermayeff Geismar's *That New York*, which flirted with typographic abstraction against a New York cityscape; and

Gene Federico's discourse on the *Love of Apples,* an exercise to see how close he could touch slugs of type without using a razor blade. "I wanted to try something where I used metal type in extreme ways without having to cut it—without cutting up proofs or playing with stats," explained Federico. "For some time I had known that if you stacked title gothics they would have a different look than traditional types. So the whole book was based on that simple idea."

The designers' motivations for solving the problem of filling sixteen pages were different, but each followed his own muse, not a client's. Beall, who was coming to the end of his career as a designer of corporate identity, was interested in returning to his early inspirations, which borrowed from dada and surrealism. His "essay" was concerned with the tension between typographic precision and a free-form environment. Lubalin, who was beginning to have influence on contemporary typography with visual puns and type-pictures, was attempting to bust through the confines of hot metal (which he would later do with phototype). Brownjohn Chermayeff Geismar, which had been doing conceptual design in a modern idiom since the late 1950s and was about to split up, leaving Robert Brownjohn on his own, was seeking the nexus of art and design. "Ours was impossible typesetting and useless prose," added Chermayeff. "But it was also an attempt to use typography as paint, and to explore relationships that were based on texture not language. We were doing no less than what David Carson is doing today. However, for us to be completely irresponsible required a sympathy with language." In addition to overlapping and layering through intricate film processes that were made into engravings, this typeplay mixed numbers with letterforms to make words. For Federico, an advertising art director with a special interest in type, *Love of Apples* was an excuse for a poetic polemic about nature's beauty being radically altered, as is exemplified by the line: "When we, in business, industrial America, began to get smart about apples, we packaged them and packaged them and packaged them until the apple itself became the package," which he illustrated with a photograph of an apple with a string tied around it.

About U.S. is one of modern American design's most important artifacts, both as a chronicle of the end of hot metal and as a clarion of impending photo composition. It is also one of the first public displays of conceptual and expressionistic typeplay that would alter advertising and editorial practice in the 1960s and usher in the method (or style) of design known as the Big Idea—noted for witty copywriting wed to smart conceptual typography, illustration, and photography. *About U.S.* is a snapshot of the moment when type first talked.

Ha Ha Ha: He Laughs Best Who Laughs Last

Lou Dorfsman

The Columbia Broadcasting System (CBS) was the foremost American television network from the 1950s to the 1980s. No other network had such intelligent news and entertainment programming, nor had earned such public confidence. During its golden years, the "CBS eye" was a proud emblem that stood for a reputation of service and

quality built by William Paley, founder and former CEO, and later, Frank Stanton, former chief of the broadcast division. Yet even inherently great programming required an equally great corporate image, an identity born of memorable graphics and compelling advertising. It can be argued that if not for the originality of its promotion CBS would have had to slug it out much harder against ABC and NBC, whose advertising rarely reached the same heights.

CBS management understood the value of a strong graphic identity, which is why in 1937 Paley hired William Golden, who created the venerable CBS trademark, and why after Golden's death in 1959 Paley and Stanton named Lou Dorfsman (b. 1918), then the promotion art director of the radio division, to take his place. Dorfsman earned the job through inspired trade advertising designed to sell advertisers on the viability of radio at a time when television was decidedly the more compelling market.

Dorfsman was the engine that drove the company's most successful advertising campaigns, and ultimately its entire graphic design program. He wrote much of his own copy and practiced the art of visual persuasion with rare wit. What his ads lacked in typical hyperbole was made up for in uncommon intelligence. He never lowered himself or his company to hard-sell tactics. He was a master of the Big Idea, a conceptual strategy characterized by understatement, self-mockery, and irony, and noted for clean design and strident copywriting wed to intelligent illustration and photography. In the more than forty years that Dorfsman managed CBS's visual identity there is not a single example where he used a typeface as novelty or decoration simply to grab attention, or abused a photograph, painting, or drawing merely for shock value. The audience was never treated as visually illiterate, and by making the public feel good about CBS's intrusion into their lives, Dorfsman instilled a pride of viewing.

Among the ads that still resonate—indeed could be reprised today without changes—"Ha, Ha, Ha: He laughs best who laughs last" is economical yet eye-catching. The word *ha* grows larger according to the Neilson's ratings response to the comedy shows of the three television networks, turning into the largest *Ha,* which represents CBS's high standing. Without the benefit of a hard-sell slogan or sensational image, but by harnessing the power of irony, Dorfsman let type alone to do the persuading. For an ad entitled "Worth Repeating, CBS News" Dorfsman used bold, disproportionately large quotation marks sitting majestically upon a pedestal of copy. These curiously abstract marks have greater shouting range than any single line of type or picture. "Dominate," a series of four advertisements used to convince potential advertisers that CBS enjoyed dominance in the ratings, was an example of "talking type." Once again, without the benefit of an image, Dorfsman used four words— "Captivate!" "Elucidate!" "Fascinate!" "Exhilarate!"—each set in a different typeface with an exclamation point dotted with the CBS eye. The copy suggested the range of CBS's programs in a market it totally controlled. Yet another exemplar was a soft-sell idea entitled "A Glossary of Television Terms," an illustrated lexicon of words such as *fish bowl, one shot,* and *audio,* that were introduced to the public through television. Cleverly illustrated, this compendium of trivia captured the interest of even the casual reader. After holding the reader's attention it smartly climaxed with the word "Leadership: The quality invariably associated with the CBS Television Network."

These ads did more than remind, inform, and persuade potential clients of the network's virtues, they increased the recognition of CBS by giving it a uniform identity, which in turn underscored the value of its corporate culture. Rarely were any of Dorfsman's designs, even the more decorative logos and trademarks, lacking an idea. In fact, if an idea was not readily apparent, he went to great lengths to concoct one. Without Dorfsman CBS would have had its eye, but with him the eye became the most positive logo in America.

Going Out

Gene Federico

Good graphic design was long an exception to the rule in American advertising. Beginning at the turn of the century, copywriters were allowed to rein over designers and nuances of type and image were secondary to the hard sell of a product or message. Unlike European advertising of the same period, which was aggressively visual and pictorially innovative, in America it was virtually inconceivable that an art director would be much more than a glorified layout man subservient to the needs of the text. This changed in the 1930s when the advertising pioneer Earnest Elmo Calkins discovered that the effective marriage of word and picture could produce startling results. Prefiguring the "creative team" and creative revolution by more than three decades, he brought copywriters and designers together, forging a creative union. By 1939, when Gene Federico (b. 1918), a twenty-one-year old Pratt Institute graduate with a special interest in typography, entered the advertising field, a few exceptional designers had already begun to change the look (and often the content) of mainstream advertising, paving the way for a distinctly American modern style.

"Lester Beall opened my eyes to the idea that type could be used to emphasize the message," Federico said about one of American advertising's leading modern typographers. "One of his ads had the great line, 'To Hell With Eventually. Let's Concentrate On Now.' The *e* in *eventually* was very large and *now* was the same size. The simple manipulation of these letterforms allowed the reader to immediately comprehend the message." Federico's method was also based on the integration of text and image. He always worked intimately with a copywriter and played with the nuances of language. He looked for those simple elements in copy that expressed or emoted, and suggested that when a designer doesn't read the copy to catch the sound of the words, he or she runs the risk of misconstruing the typography. "If the rhythm of the words is disregarded, the copy is likely to be broken incorrectly," he continued.

Federico was more concerned with attitude than with style. Despite Lou Dorfsman's assertion that he was the prince of Light Line Gothic (admittedly one his favorite typefaces), few of his ads conformed to a single formula or evoked stylistic déjà vu. Nevertheless, one trait was dominant; his love of type. Letters served as sculptural forms placed on or against an image. Type both communicated messages and evoked a time and place.

Federico's series of advertisements for *Woman's Day*, which appeared in the *New Yorker* magazine in 1954 and were targeted at media buyers, typified his rhythmic sensitivity. One of the most well known had the catch-line "Going Out," and showed a photo of woman riding a bicycle with wheels made from the two Futura *O*s in the headline—a visual pun in the modern tradition. The goal of the ad was to persuade potential advertisers that three million-plus devoted readers went out of their way to buy this check-out counter magazine. The ads apparently did well for the client, but more importantly proved the power of persuasive visual simplicity in a field that often erred on the side of overstatement.

Man with the Golden Arm

Saul Bass

There are two Hollywoods. One, the land of fantasy and glitz. The other, the land of formula and convention. It was into the latter that Bronx-born Saul Bass (1920–1996) arrived in 1945 intent on producing unconventional advertising for the movie industry. But the odds were against him. In those days Hollywood promotion was mired in formula. Convention dictated the look and feel of posters, foyer cards, and ads. Romantic realism was a conceptual and aesthetic panacea, and the common poster showed something for everybody whether it was in the movie or not—bits of romance, action, drama, and, of course, unblemished portraits of the stars.

Bass, who had read and was influenced by Gyorgy Kepes's *Language of Vision* (1944), became a reductionist designing in a modern idiom. When he worked in the New York office of Warner Brothers, he toyed with the picture and text components of movie ads, mostly playing with scale, which was the only latitude he was allowed. Of course, it was a dead end. "I could only carry it so far, because the other ingredients had to be there," he recalled in *Graphic Design America* (Harry N. Abrams, 1989). So he packed up for Hollywood and went to work for Buchanan & Co., the agency that handled Paramount Pictures. Finally, in 1949 he designed his first breakthrough ad for *The Champion,* Kirk Douglas's seminal motion picture.

The ad was totally black with a tiny halftone and a little lettered scrawl below it. It took up about an inch and a half in the center of the page. In contrast to cluttered conventional ads, it was a real eye-opener. It was also the auspicious beginning of what evolved into Bass's expressionistic approach to Hollywood publicity, the precursor of the innovative advertising and film title sequences that he created first for Otto Preminger and, later, for Alfred Hitchcock.

In 1954 Bass designed the titles for Preminger's *Carmen Jones,* which were decidedly unique compared to the mundane lettering superimposed over backgrounds common in Hollywood movies at that time. In 1955 he made a bolder leap with the print advertising for *The Man with the Golden Arm,* which eschewed a picture of its star, Frank Sinatra, in favor of a pattern of black bars that framed a primitive woodcut-like rendering of a crooked arm. Theater owners were not pleased with the absence of the one-two punch of star portrait and heroic vignette. But one incident tells the story of Bass's subsequent success: "[Preminger] was sitting with his back to me—he didn't know I was there—talking on the phone, obviously to an exhibitor somewhere in Texas," Bass recalled in *Graphic Design America.* "The exhibitor was complaining about the ads and saying that he wanted to have a picture of Sinatra. . . . And I heard Otto say to him, 'Those ads are to be used precisely as they are. If you change them one iota, I will pull the picture from your theater.' And hung up on him." Rather than hype the film, the graphic reduced the plot, the story of a tormented drug addict, to an essence—a logo really—that evoked the film's tension.

Jumping at the opportunity to animate this simple graphic form as the title sequence for the film, Bass created a series of moving white bars on a black screen, which was transformed into an abstract ballet of erratic shapes. After a few moments the bars metamorphosed into the arm. "There was a tendency, when I did the title for *The Man with the Golden Arm* to think it worked because it was 'graphic,'" Bass explained in *Print* (1960) "but that was incidental. If it worked, it was because the mood and feeling it conveyed made it work, not because it was a graphic device." Nevertheless, by creating a graphic symbol that was effective for use in both the print campaign and the opening title sequence, Bass had introduced a new design form.

Actually, he returned to the essence of motion pictures before sound, Technicolor, Cinemascope, and other pyrotechnic advances upped the ante of filmmaking. Movies began as a purely visual medium. "We've come full circle," Bass once explained, "[we] went to a theatrical stage approach with inordinate reliance on dialogue, and now we're back again to a greater reliance on the visual, but in a way that is more real and more current with our lives today." Not surprisingly, Bass was often called upon to direct certain sequences within films where the visual scheme was more important to moving the story along than the dialog.

The Man with the Golden Arm was more than a fine piece of abstract animation. It was Bass's first movie within a movie, and it had less to do with specific aesthetics of design than a sense of the story (a key trait in Bass's later work). Yet it was not an independent effort; he believed that all aspects of a movie should fit together like pieces of a puzzle. "In every title I've done, I've been very conscious of the fact that the title has a responsibility to the film, that it is there to enhance the film, to set it up, to give it a beginning—and not to overpower and preempt it," he asserted in *Print*. For Bass the title was only the beginning of something, never the thing itself.

He continued making title sequences for four decades, many as memorable as the films themselves. And his work evolved from "mood-setting" animation into what he called "metaphorical live action" in *Walk on the Wild Side* (1962), where a black cat and a white cat meet, have a fight, and then part, as a metaphor for New Orleans street life. Later he pioneered the film prologue with John Frankenheimer's *Grand Prix* (1966), for which Bass traveled around the world directing camera crews in the shooting of racing sequences.

Forty years after challenging the studio's conventions and taboos, creative movie title sequences are facts of motion picture history. Indeed every designer who has ever designed film titles owes a debt to Bass. As a coda to the breadth of his influence, in 1995 director Spike Lee paid dubious homage when he copied Bass's logo for *Anatomy of Murder* as the print graphic for his own film, *Clockers*. Although Bass did not appreciate the larceny, it vividly illustrated the extent of Bass's contribution to the movie industry.

The Area Code (Parenthesis)

Ladislav Sutnar

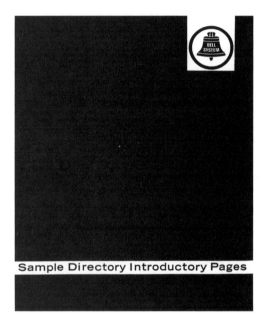

Sample Directory Introductory Pages

If recognized at all, graphic designers earn cultural kudos for work that has a direct impact on society. Yet even under these circumstances the world is usually oblivious. Which is why Ladislav Sutnar (1897–1976), a Czech modernist graphic and product designer who emigrated to the United States in 1939 and worked in New York until his death, has not received even a modicum of credit for a unique graphic innovation that has had far-reaching effect. Although it may well be considered arcane, his invention was the parentheses around American telephone area code numbers when the system was introduced in the early 1960s.

Sutnar is not credited for the appearance of the area code because the concept was so integral to the design of the Bell System's new calling apparatus that it was instantly adopted as part of the vernacular. Moreover, Ma Bell never offered or gave Sutnar credit; for this company, graphic designers—like the functional graphics they produced—were invisible. Nonetheless, Sutnar's other contributions to information architecture, the commissions that brought him to the Bell System's attention in the first place, are milestones not only in graphic design history but of design for the public good. Sutnar developed logical and hierarchical graphic systems for a wide range of American businesses that clarified and made accessible vast amounts of complex, often ponderous information. He took on the thankless job of transforming routine business data into digestible and understandable forms.

Before most designers focused on the need for information organization, Sutnar was in the vanguard, driven by the missionary modern belief that good design applied to the most quotidian products had a beneficial, even curative effect on society. In his role as a pioneer of information design and progenitor of the current trend in information architecture, Sutnar's sophisticated data-management programs, which he designed during the late 1950s and early 1960s for America's telecommunications monopoly, allowed customers to scan directories more efficiently. The Bell System was engaged in the technological upgrade of its huge network, and Sutnar's brand of functional typography and way-finding iconography made public access to both emergency and regular services considerably easier while providing Bell with a distinctive identity. But in the history of graphic design, Saul Bass received more attention for his late-fifties/early-sixties redesign of the Bell System logo, which had little direct consequence for the public, than Sutnar did for making user-friendly graphic signposts. In recent years information architect Richard Saul Wurman has also utilized Sutnar's model in developing the California Bell telephone directories known as "smart pages."

Although it was a small part of the overall graphic system, the parenthesis was one of Sutnar's signature devices, among many used to distinguish and highlight various kinds of information. From 1941 to 1960, as the art director of the F. W. Dodge Sweet's Catalog Service, America's leading distributor and producer of trade and manufacturing catalogs, Sutnar developed an array of typographic and iconographic navigational tools that allowed users to efficiently traverse seas of data. His icons are analogous to the friendly computer symbols used today and were inspired, in part, by El Lissitzky's iconographic tabulation system in Mayakovsky's 1923 book of poems, *For the Voice*. In addition to designing grid and tab systems, Sutnar made common punctuation, including commas, colons, and exclamation points, into linguistic traffic signs by enlarging and repeating them, which was similar to the constructivist functional typography of the 1920s. These were adopted as key components of Sutnar's distinctive American style.

While he professed universality, he nevertheless possessed graphic personality that was so distinctive from others practicing the international style that his work did not even require a credit line, although he almost always took one. Nevertheless this graphic personality was based on functional requisites not indulgent conceits and so never obscured his clients' messages (unlike much of the undisciplined commercial art produced during the same period).

"The lack of discipline in our present day urban industrial environment has produced a visual condition, characterized by clutter, confusion, and chaos," writes Allon Schoener, curator of the 1961 *Ladislav Sutnar: Visual Design in Action* exhibition, which originated at the Contemporary Arts Center in Cincinnati, Ohio. "As a result the average man of today must struggle to accomplish such basic objectives as being able to read signs, to identify products, to digest advertisements, or to locate information in newspapers, books, and catalogues. . . . There is an urgent need for communication based upon precision and clarity. This is the area in which Ladislav Sutnar excels." If written today, this statement might seem like a critique of current design trends, but in 1961, it was a testament to progressivism. Sutnar introduced the theoretical constructs that for him defined "good design" in the 1940s, when such definitions were rare in American commercial art. Design was one-third instinct and two-thirds market convention, and the result was eclectic at best, confused at worst. Such ad hoc practice was anathema to Sutnar, who was stern about matters of order and logic, fervently seeking to alter visual standards by introducing both American businessmen and commercial artists to "the sound basis for modern graphic design and typography," which he asserts in his book *Visual Design in Action* (Hasting House, 1961) is ". . . a direct heritage of the avant-garde pioneering of the 1920s and 1930s in Europe. It represents a basic change that is revolutionary."

Sutnar synthesized European avant-gardisms, which he says "provided the base for further extension of new design vocabulary and new design means" into a functional commercial lexicon that eschews "formalistic rules or art for art's sake." While he modified aspects of the New Typography, he did not compromise its integrity in the same way that elements of the international style became mediocre through rote usage over time. "He made Constructivism playful and used geometry to create the dynamics of organization," observes designer Noel Martin, who in the 1950s was a member of Sutnar's small circle of friends. Despite a strict belief in the absolute rightness of geometric form, Sutnar allowed variety within his strictures to avoid standardizing his clients' different messages. Consistency reigned within an established framework, such as limited type and color choices as well as strict layout preferences, but within those parameters a variety of options existed in relation to different kinds of projects, including catalogs, books, magazines, and exhibitions as well as the Bell System's instructional materials.

In the field of information design, it is arguable that contemporary missionaries Edward Tufte and Richard Saul Wurman are really just carrying the torch that Sutnar lit decades before. Many design students, either knowingly or not, have borrowed and applied his signature graphics to a postmodern style. Nevertheless, Sutnar would loathe being admired only as a nostalgic figure. "There is just one lesson from the past that should be learned for the benefit of the present," he wrote in 1959, as if preempting this kind of superficial epitaph. "It is that of the painstaking, refined craftsmanship which appears to be dying out."

Armin Hofmann

A successful advertising poster must be able to be clearly viewed from a distance of one hundred feet, suggesting that if such a prominent image cannot instantaneously attract the attention of harried passersby, then even an exquisitely beautiful design is ineffectual publicity. This idea has been tested throughout the twentieth century with methods ranging from the unambiguous *sachplakat* (object poster) in the early 1900s to optically challenging psychedelic posters in the late 1960s. Some are effective with more and others with less visual noise, but one thing is certain: Every poster must have the kind of graphic impact that intimate printed materials do not. This impact is best experienced (for it is indeed a visceral experience more than an intellectual one) in the work of Swiss graphic designer and teacher Armin Hofmann (b. 1920). His posters have uniquely bridged the divide between representation and abstraction. Few other designers have produced more vivid work, which can be seen from one hundred feet or one foot away.

Hofmann created a great many poster icons over a six-decade-long career. These include but are not limited to the multiple hands for the Municipal Theater Basel, the huge "C" for the Cavellini Collection, the spiraling ballerina for "Giselle," and the bold apple for "William Tell." However, the appropriately titled *Die Gute Form* (Good Design), for a 1954 exhibition at the Swiss Industries Fair in Basel, is perhaps the designer's quintessential contribution to the poster field. This stark typographic design is at once concrete and abstract, simple and complex, conventional and radical. It does everything a poster should do—attract the eye, pique curiosity, impart a message—all, incidentally, without benefit of an explicit picture or clever slogan.

Yet the headline *Die Gute Form* is, in fact, a picture, and the picture is a headline that can be read either as words or symbols—or as both at a single glance. To make this poster indelible, Hofmann designed geometrically precise yet thoroughly novel letterforms that are so harmonious when composed into the three words and then partially obliterated that they phenomenally retain their readability. The viewer is indeed asked to take a second or two to decode the lettering, but once accomplished, the mysterious beauty and overt significance of the poster is obvious.

I have used many words in the above paragraph to explain what Hofmann so effortlessly achieved with just a few strategic marks on paper, which just goes to underscore the very essence of his achievement.

Hofmann is a master of eloquent economy, not the cold stereotypical reductionism associated with the 1950s- and 1960s-era corporate variation of the Swiss Style (which is used on generic packages, traffic tickets, and business forms), but rather a graceful complex simplicity that combines purely aesthetic and distinctly functional values. While his graphic language, comprised of radical shifts in scale (never superfluous), precisionist type arrangement (at no time predictable), and stark symbolism (by no means clinical), is rooted in what is referred to as "Swiss rationalism," it is nonetheless imbued with a particular personal dialect underscored by emotion. I have often heard critics of orthodox Swiss design who call it unrepentantly cold and formulaic, but Hofmann both defies and transcends this tunnel view.

Die Gute Form is anchored on a rigid grid, yet the armature is invisible to the naked eye thanks to the resolute fluidity of Hofmann's typography. The same is true with his other purely typographical posters, wherein custom designed letterforms are constructed with sculptural character to be both conventionally read and intimately experienced. *Temple and Tea House in Japan* (1955), *Wood as Building Material* (1955), and *Karl Geiser* (1957) have more personality and actually tell more story with only a few smartly stacked, constructed, and interconnected words than most pictorial narratives. As with *Die Gute Form*, Hofmann has produced in these posters abstract entities that are immediately recognizable as both pattern and word. When each individual poster is viewed in a repeating sequence on a wall or display case, the viewer experiences the aesthetic virtues—a dramatic arrangement of form—but when viewed individually, the message is clearly readable as a conventional missive.

The drama Hofmann could achieve with just a few words is even more intense when he uses only two letters. Indeed, one of Hofmann's recurring leitmotifs is the employ of two bold capitals—a Modernist monogram—for a series of art exhibition posters at the Kunsthalle Basel. Each exhibition features two curiously and sometimes harmoniously matched artists, and so for the poster, Hofmann has two immense initials sharing the same bill, such as "CL" for Fernand Leger and Alexander Calder

(1957), "SJ" for David Smith and Horst Janssen (1960), and "KJ" for Franz Kline and Alfred Jensen (1960). The monogram motif is an elegant idea that transforms the traditional art poster into a kind of linguistic game. Rather than predictably reproduce two representative pieces of the artists' art, resulting in a clash of styles, Hofmann makes the initials of the two exhibited artists into a trademark that not only "brands" the exhibit but forces the viewer to play along in a sport of deciphering. Since these curatorial pairings of representation and abstraction are surprising, Hofmann's solutions were surprising too. Which, actually, is not very surprising.

Hofmann's work repudiates routine. When seen as an entire body, there are the inevitable consistencies that reveal Hofmann's style, but nothing in his oeuvre—certainly at the time he began his string of emblematic designs in the early 1950s—was in any way customary. Indeed, nothing supports this claim better than his collected theater posters for Stadt Theater Basel, to which the designer gave an indelible identity during the late 1950s and 1960s. These are not the typical theater bills laden with titillating teasers or obligatory credits, nor are they sensational or romantic depictions of the company's theatrical offerings. Hofmann's posters are symbolic summations and iconic interventions that serve to introduce the audience to dramatic or musical fare while offering a visual challenge. Rather than give only the facts, these posters require that the audience interpret the meanings of the images. It is not a complicated puzzle but the questions posed by such pictures as a huge ear and eye (for the 1961 season), a laughing clown (for the 1960 season), or a scowling/maniacal face (for the 1967 poster) demand that the audience interact with the stimuli rather than remain passive receivers.

Passivity is not what Hofmann demands of his viewer, nor is it part of his own visual vocabulary. One need only to look at (and later read, of course) his classic *Graphic Design Manual: Principals and Practice* (Reinhold Publishing, 1965) to understand that Hofmann's design is purposefully animated, requiring that the viewer's eye navigate various pathways that he's carved through his field of type and image. I've always felt that his otherwise static work is equally suited to paper or screen, and I venture that if he were starting his career over again today, motion might very well be his key occupation. If there is any doubt that Hofmann's static imagery is not jumping madly—though logically—around a mental screen, simply scan the multiple rows of geometric layout options reproduced in his handbook. Then look at his posters together on a wall or turn the pages of this book (paying special attention to the posters for Gewerbemuseum Basel) to experience unbridled kinetic energy and cinematic power.

Hofmann has designed type and image for the print medium

throughout the better part of his life, so naturally he would not exactly choose to describe his work in terms of its relationship to film. But it is nonetheless clear that a distinct kinetic sensibility has contributed to making posters that transcend the inert confines of the medium. It is also the trait that makes his work so unequivocally modern.

Of course, "modernism" is an imprecise term that connotes the radical overhaul of artistic standards by mid-twentieth-century avant-garde artists, and Hofmann is certainly influenced by the great advances of this time. Yet Hofmann's modernism, like his friend Paul Rand's, is a uniquely personal interpretation that reflects more than the ideological requisites of the key movements and schools. Rand was known for playful humor that ironically acknowledged the comic strips and show card advertisements that were positive and negative influences on him while growing up in Brooklyn, New York, as well as the imported dada and Bauhaus notions of form and content to which he was later exposed. Hofmann, born in Winterhur, Switzerland, in 1920, studied graphic art in a different aesthetic and philosophical environment in Zurich under Alfred Willimann and did not have the exact same influences as Rand, yet the play instinct bound to European modernism was (and is) every bit as intense. Nonetheless, unlike Rand, there is a hushed quality to Hofmann's play, as evidenced in his color palette, which rarely changes from black and white or red and white.

His most stunningly playful and playfully serious series of posters for the Gewerbemuseum Basel and the Herman Miller Collection (1962) use abstraction in the same way that Jackson Pollack dripped paint: expressively. Hofmann's amorphous shapes and solid color fields shake and wiggle, thrust and parry, lunge and recede, in a kind of expressionistic improvisation. The Helvetica type, however, is an anchor of consistency that keeps these posters from being too anarchic. And yet I see these as free-form posters, like no others that come close to being an independent genre of expression—neither fine nor applied art—a theory I suspect that Hofmann, the quintessential applied artist, might refute.

Hofmann's posters collectively epitomize mid-century modernism not because ornament is rejected and mechanical methods (i.e., photographs) are used in place of hand-drawn decoration or illustration, but because they touch the soul of their times. I know that it is probably difficult to look at large typefaces in black and white and sometimes red, or bold geometries, or crisp photographs, and then conjure the word "soul." I realize that Hofmann's work might better be characterized as a kind of well-ordered clinical beauty, but there is also something so incredibly soulful in the posters for Stadt Theater Basel 1958 Season (1958) and Brahms Requiem (1986) that it is hard not to use the word or be accordingly moved. I marvel at their formal purity, yet also feel the designer's passion for the material.

And although as a writer of manuals and teacher at Basel School of Design and Yale University, Hofmann established standards and formulas for design, it seems apparent from the work of his most able students that he did not simply preach the gospel of standardization as a catechism for all design. He gave his students tools and a solid armature on which to build classical or "timeless" typography, but he also imparted a sense of passion (or soul). Hofmann could not produce the work found in this collection—posters that not only formally stand the test of time but also continue to resonate with viewers such as me on an emotional level—without a total commitment to his art and design. So, in addition to his expert ability to manipulate type and image, this soul is what gives this work and his legacy its impact.

Back in high school during the late 1960s, existentialism fed a ravenous adolescent appetite for self-indulgent despair, and the covers of two angst-ridden paperback books, *Nausea* by Jean-Paul Sartre and *The Stranger* by Albert Camus, did for me what religious iconography triggers in devotees. Only, rather than provide spiritual uplift, each cover made me melancholic. Book covers should, of course, create an intellectual bond with a reader, but rarely do they tap as deeply into a psyche as these did.

In the 1950s and 1960s, during the nascent period of what in the United States was (and still is, for that matter) called "quality paperback publishing," many covers for so-called serious fiction and nonfiction were designed as signposts that grabbed the eye and sparked the imagination. They further branded the identity of individual books more profoundly than most hardcover jackets, which were so predictably formulaic that little room was left for the reader's personal interpretation.

The covers of *Nausea* and *The Stranger* were cleverly symbolic and disturbingly mysterious. *Nausea,* designed by Ivan Chermayeff, is a high-contrast, double-exposed black-and-white photograph of a dyspeptic man, which so keenly illustrated the title that over four decades later, the original is still in print. The cover for *The Stranger,* with a surreal line drawing by Leo Lionni of abstract faces, was a perfect evocation of anonymity and loneliness. (However, it is no longer in print.) Both of these covers defined existentialism, yet merely hinted at the books' contents. When compared to most hardcover jackets, with their turgid literal illustrations, or mass-market paperback covers with tawdry sensationalist vignettes, the vast majority of quality paperback covers exhibited a high degree of subtlety, sometimes cut with wit, that demanded the reader's interpretive participation.

The designers and illustrators most identified with this genre, including Chermayeff, Lionni, Paul Rand, Alvin Lustig, Milton Glaser, Seymour Chwast, and Rudolph deHarak, were encouraged by their respective publishers and art directors to inject Modernist notions of minimalism, abstraction, and symbolism to signal a more serious publishing genre. And so, they challenged entrenched marketing conventions that proscribed such minute details as type size and color palette.

Following World War II, the mass-market paperback industry decreed that appealing to the "masses" meant that cover art must reduce all content, even William Shakespeare's most emotional dramas, to romantic or sentimental pulp realism with movie matinee typography. On the other hand, quality paperbacks—initially developed by Anchor Books in 1947 as a vehicle for reprinting classics and serious out-of-print books on better paper and with sturdier bindings—sought a new market of college students as well as earnest general readers. Consequently, quality paperback covers required an urbane visual language that included abstract illustrations and spare modernist typography—a scheme that elevated books but did not rarify them.

Arthur A. Cohen, an audacious twenty-three-year-old cofounder of Noonday Press (in 1951) and of Meridian Books (in 1954), noted, "It would have been quite easy for me—in deference to the conventions of the publishing industry—to have resisted the seductions of 'good design.'" He was referring to the widespread tendency among established hardcover publishers to squander book jacket real estate with mediocre design solutions that sensationalized rather than edified. So, Cohen commissioned Alvin Lustig (and after he died in 1955, Elaine Lustig) to design the majority of the Noonday and Meridian covers in a modern manner, which effectively raised the overall level of design for most quality paperbacks.

Cohen had proclaimed, "Paperbound publishing seems destined to obliterate cloth trade publishing as we presently know it." And the "paperbound book revolution" of the late 1950s and early 1960s, while not an absolute overthrow of old standards, was a sea shift in the publishing industry's customs that exerted unprecedented influence on Americans' reading habits. College students, for example, could now afford their own portable classics (and received what Cohen called "a paperback education"). Many important books once relegated to out-of-print purgatory had another shot at immortality. Some publishers also originated new titles as quality paperbacks rather than first launch them in hardcover, which made innovative design and typography even more essential.

As a leader in paperback books, the English publisher Penguin introduced a much-celebrated though inflexible typographic format, designed in 1946 by Jan Tschichold, that replaced design excess with Spartan solemnity. While this established a strong identity, the Penguin scheme nonetheless reduced all titles, regardless of content, to a single typography with limited color. Cohen wrote that this "simple and often painfully boring design" had one virtue: "Everyone who can see and read knows that two swathes of blue bisected by a white area containing the title and author means Penguin." In a market where all publishers hawk books "with clamor and stridency, the soft-sell conservatism of Penguin Books communicates an impression of solidity, impassableness, and confidence." Yet for his own books, Cohen avoided what he called Penguin's "monolithic conservatism" as well as the greater tendency for repetitive fashion. As much as he objected to Penguin's "stoic self-discipline," he also refused to succumb to "sleek photographs which look as though they were cut out of terribly chic *New Yorker* advertisements, woodcuts which become so important in the jacket that typography becomes an afterthought, and clichés which go on endlessly." Cohen's vision of the quality paperback relied strongly on an exclusive look defined by modernist graphic design.

Alvin Lustig, who in the late 1940s introduced surreal photomontage and abstract glyphs (influenced by Paul Klee and Miró) to New Directions Books' hardcover jackets, switched over to using eclectic nineteenth-century wood and metal typography for Meridian and Noonday paperback covers. Akin to earlier typography by Lester Beall, Lustig's book covers' typography were a mix of slab serifs and railroad gothics, sometimes paired with antique engraver's scripts and often set against unusual flat color backgrounds, including rich purples, oranges, and maroons, some with contrasting bars and stripes.

Simplicity was a virtue, since these books had to withstand strong visual competition in bookstores from bestseller book jackets, children's books, and in some cases record album covers and greeting cards. Rather than try to out-shout the more flamboyant designs, Lustig's goal, he explained in a collection of unpublished notes, "was to create the effect of a special object which is only incidentally a book." The method of display required viewing all the books together face-out on shelves and "would be very important in creating the proper isolation and emphasis for the books." He further noted that the titles were purposely kept small rather than try to "compete with the large lettering of hardcover book jackets and thus lose their sense of quality." But most important in Lustig's overall plan, "The designs, although non-representational, would have an emblematic character and would possess overtones of a traditional sense of order. They would strive for freshness and a rather unclassifiable quality rather than try to seem either modern or traditional in the usual sense of those words."

For graphic designers of the 1950s and 1960s, quality paperbacks were what CD packages are today—wellsprings of a certain kind of design innovation that was perhaps best characterized by a statement made at the

1957 AIGA symposium on the role of the designer (reported in *Publisher's Weekly*): "Books of today are read today. So let's not design for all eternity." And one of the foremost quality paperback publishers at the time was Vintage Books, with covers ministered by art director Harry Ford and production manager Sidney Jacobs. Paul Rand was commissioned to design Vintage covers that paradoxically stand the test of time because he employed abstract forms, expressive collages, and witty sketches that were dictated not by fashion but by modernist preference for play and economy. His covers were mini-posters that interpreted rather than illustrated content.

By the mid- to late 1950s, when the golden age of modernist Vintage covers was produced by Rand, Lionni, Chermayeff, Ben Shahn, Bradbury Thompson, George Guisti, and others, most bookstores had become used to displaying more quality paperbacks than a few years earlier, when Lustig's covers were virtually the only ones on the shelves. This meant that cover design could not afford to be as uniform as in Lustig's graphic scheme, and eclectic solutions were increasingly more common.

Ivan Chermayeff—who in his student days was an assistant to Lustig and followed through on some covers and designed other original covers—also made formidable contributions to modern and eclectic design. In addition to *Nausea*, he explored the range of photomontage for New Directions' covers. He composed others for art director Frank Metz at Simon & Schuster using typographic puns, including the *Art of Dramatic Writing*, where exclamation points are substituted for all the instances of the word "is." Wordplay was an effective way of illustrating otherwise un-illustratable ideas by making titles of the books into word games. In this way, Chermayeff made the cover into a laboratory for his developing work.

Likewise, Rudolph deHarak experimented with the nearly 350 paperback covers created for McGraw-Hill Paperbacks during the early to mid-1960s. His basic systematic format, based on a rigid Swiss-inspired grid, was a tabula rasa where symbolic and allegoric imagery interpreted a wide range of nonfiction themes including philosophy, anthropology, psychology, and sociology. The format offered deHarak a control with which to test limits of conceptual art and photography as he introduced approaches inspired by dada, abstract expressionism, and op-art movements. The McGraw-Hill covers, which epitomized a late-modernist purism, were subsequently copied by many other paperback cover designers at various publishers.

In 1964 Milton Glaser, Push Pin Studios cofounder, was given the enviable assignment to develop a series of contemporary illustrated covers for a popular mass-market paperback line of Shakespeare's plays. Art director Bill Gregory wanted the Signet Shakespeare series to have interesting covers, and as Glaser recalls, "They made an impact partially because they were done in sequence, and could be grouped together in-store." But there was another, more arcane breakthrough, explains Glaser: "At the time, hardcovers were not usually printed in process color, but the paperbacks could exploit full color." So he framed a subtly colored ink drawing of Shakespeare's characters on a white field with a color band on top to identify the books and hold the logo.

Glaser understood that "the form of address had to be more illustrative, and it was my presumption that it couldn't be abstract or typographical. But it could still stand out and didn't have to be banal-looking, like most mass-market books." The cover illustrations helped popularize Shakespeare's works, and the affordability of these books made Signet a mainstay in high school and college classes.

Following Signet's lead, during the mid-1960s, other mass-market paperback publishers reprinted serious literature and nonfiction, and adopted more sophisticated design and illustration for new markets. Like Glaser, Push Pin Studios cofounder Seymour Chwast employed an eclectic array of graphic styles on covers for a wide variety of themes and authors. "Paperbacks provided creative opportunities," Chwast recalls. "I was not told what to do, just given the parameters and a free hand." Accordingly, each style was integrally matched to the subject: "If it was something about the South Seas, for instance, I'd do a primitive drawing." For *The Plague*, another of Albert Camus's lugubrious existential dramas, Chwast introduced a stark woodcut painted in an expressionist manner. "I couldn't do anything too fancy," he says about the morose visage that spoke directly to Camus's angst. For a biography of the mystic Gurdjieff, he blended Middle Eastern–inspired calligraphy with his eclectic, personal style. Chwast's variegated designs signaled that anything was possible in this genre.

When mass-market paperbacks were first introduced during the 1940s, the publishing industry shamelessly acknowledged that they were ephemeral and destined for the junk heap. Although the advent of quality paperbacks did not immediately change prevailing attitudes toward the genre's overall disposability, the quality of graphic design signaled more serious (and perhaps more durable) content, and this did have a positive impact on readers. Hardcover books will always be more prestigious, but during the 1950s and 1960s the quality paperback cover as a wellspring of innovative modern design—and even as icon—surpassed hardcover jacket design in freedom and ingenuity. Ultimately paperback covers earned the respect that the designers brought to them, and influenced the state of all book jacket and cover art today.

"If I was born to do something," states Paul Bacon, "it was to design book jackets." And that's exactly what he did for about fifty years. But not just any old jacket for any old book. Although he did his share of obscure titles, his jackets have adorned some of the most prestigious bestsellers of the second half of the twentieth century. In fact, Bacon can be said to have invented the bestseller jacket as we know it: His designs have been emblems for such eminent works as E. L. Doctorow's *Ragtime*, William Styron's *Sophie's Choice*, Philip Roth's *Portnoy's Complaint*, Joseph Heller's *Catch-22*, Ken Kesey's *One Flew Over the Cuckoo's Nest*, James Cavell's *Shogun*, and Robert Caro's *The Power Broker*. And while each of these covers was distinctively designed, they all shared three traits that in the early 1960s fused into something known as the "Big Book Look": large title, large author's name, small symbolic image.

The "look" had its inception in 1956, when Bacon was commissioned by Simon & Schuster's art director, Tom Bevins, to design the jacket for *Compulsion* by Meyer Levin, a roman à clef about two young men who systematically plan and carry out the cold-blooded murder of a young boy to see if they can get away with the crime. The publisher knew that the highly publicized real-life killing of Bobby Franks by Loeb and Leopold would popularize the novel, but was uncertain how to devise a jacket that would be suggestive without being lewd, and evoke a sense of mystery without resorting to clichés. Bacon sketched out a number of ideas until he came up with the rough, hand-scrawled word "Compulsion," which he positioned at the top of the jacket, taking up a fifth of the space, while below it, an empty taupe rectangle bled off the field, and below that, at the bottom, was scrawled "a novel by Meyer Levin." Sparse and dramatic—yet Bacon felt something was missing.

That "something" became two small, nervously drawn figures printed in red, running on the vacant expanse upward toward the title. Although the cover calls to mind Saul Bass's 1955 expressionistic film poster for *The Man With The Golden Arm,* it was more likely influenced by the jazz albums Bacon had designed starting in the late 1940s. Whatever the influences, the book became a huge bestseller and the jacket, displayed everywhere, caught the publishing industry's attention.

Other publishers lost no time contacting Bacon to request similar jackets for their potential bestsellers. But few of them really understood what made *Compulsion* so successful. Bacon remembers, "I'd get calls that started like this: 'We have a book we'd like you to do, and it's called *Darkness on the Highway at High Noon,* and it's set in Tulsa, Oklahoma,' or something like that, and I'd say, 'Wait a minute; what you like about *Compulsion* is that big, powerful one-word title.' But it's hard to dissuade people from their titles. Nonetheless, I took the jobs, and I started to work for literally everybody."

Bacon estimates he designed about 6,500 jackets from the late 1940s through early 2000 for all the major houses—but most consistently for Simon & Schuster for over forty years. The Baconesque approach became pervasive throughout the trade book world, yet his signature style was not always instantly recognizable because Bacon characteristically subordinated ego to function. He explains: "I'd always tell myself, 'You're not the star of the show. The author took three and a half years to write the goddamn thing and the publisher is spending a fortune on it, so just back off.'" Robert Gottlieb, an editor at Simon & Schuster during the 1950s and later editorial director at Knopf for twenty-one years who often worked with Bacon, comments, "He had a bestseller look but he came up with other looks as well, some of which helped books become bestsellers."

In fact, when you look at Bacon's jackets en masse, you realize that you're looking at a history of late twentieth-century commercial book cover design, a virtual legacy of eclectic lettering, illustration, and typography prior to the digital revolution. Bacon was, after all, a product of an era of hand-drawn lettering, handmade illustration, and type that was cut and pasted in order to achieve precise spacing. While this sounds archaic in a time when layered Photoshop imagery is the order of the day, Bacon's work was appealing precisely for its handcrafted precision (as well as minor imperfections) and spot-on conceptual acuity that evoked the story rather than an isolated passage.

Born in Ossining, New York, in 1923, Bacon grew up in Union Beach, New Jersey, attended Arts High School in Newark, and started his jacket career by accident in New York after he was discharged from the

Marine Corps in 1946. Unable to get into the course he wanted at New York's Art Students League, he took a job with the former promotion art director of *Fortune,* Hal Zamboni, who had started his own Bauhaus-influenced studio in Manhattan. Bacon was given a $30-a-week job making laborious scratchboard drawings of, among other mundane items, bottles of pills for advertisements. However, from doing such tasks he developed a better-than-average drawing style, along with a certain stylistic flair.

At the time, a friend's father—who had written a book titled *Chimp on My Shoulder,* about venturing into Africa to round up monkeys for the Dennis Roosevelt Chimpanzee Farm in Florida—asked Bacon to do the illustrations. The witty, impressionistic drawings were, Bacon recalls, "pretty good for a novice"—good enough that the art director for E. P. Dutton, the book's publisher, requested that he do the jacket, too. The jacket, a photograph with type, is "nothing to send to the Hall of Fame, but it got me started," he says.

But Bacon's real passion was jazz, certified by his membership in the Newark Hot Club, a hyper-serious bunch of fans that included Alfred Lion and Frank Wolff, founders of the legendary Blue Note Records. Bacon had known the two before the war and soon started designing 10" album covers for their label. He simultaneously wrote record reviews for *The Record Changer* magazine, edited by Bill Grauer and Orrin Keepnews, who eventually started Riverside Records, for which Bacon also designed albums. Today, many jazz aficionados know Bacon exclusively for his contemporary-looking record sleeves.

But record albums alone did not insure a viable living, and during the early 1950s, Tom Bevins at Simon & Schuster gave Bacon a quirky grouping of titles to work on, including an album of cartoons from *Punch* and some science fiction novels. It wasn't until the *Compulsion* jacket, however, that Bacon realized that books were going to be his lifelong vocation. The S&S advertising people liked the idea of using an icon or a logo on a jacket as opposed to the conventional treatments of just type or literal illustration. And Bacon discovered he was good at "finding something that would be a synthesis graphically of what the story was about." Moreover, since he had had no formal training in illustration, he felt free to explore in this realm. "I was not encumbered by having to work from models," he says. "Many of the things I did, I just did strictly from memory and without any reference at all. Unless I needed something specific, like a German airplane or something—then I'd look it up. But it was very liberating to realize that I didn't have to do something that looked like Norman Rockwell did it."

If he was decidedly not Rockwellian, neither was he a follower of the modernist principles pioneered by Paul Rand, Alvin Lustig, and Leo Lionni, who imbued their work with theories of European art. While Bacon admired these designers, he points out that as the book covers they did were generally for "heady" works of criticism, analysis, and literature with small print runs, they could do virtually anything they wanted with little interference. His orientation, on the other hand, being resolutely commercial (heavy-hitter books with big runs), required that he navigate around sales and advertising people and countless others with numerous opinions.

This he did—with the help of staunch supporters like Frank Metz, art director at Simon & Schuster for over forty years, and Harris Lewine, iconoclastic art director at Harcourt Brace and various other houses. Having editors as allies was also a plus; Robert Gottlieb, for example, when he was at Knopf, not only kept the merchandising people at bay, but kept authors at a distance too. According to Bacon, writers make literal suggestions that result in dumb illustrations. He recalls one occasion when Norman Mailer managed to get through to him. "Mailer was very diffident," Bacon remembers. "He called me 'Mr. Bacon.' We both sort of bowed and scraped to each other. And it turned out that what he wanted— he actually loved the jacket—was to know if a very tiny postage stamp of his girlfriend could go somewhere on the front. As it turned out, there was no way it could hurt, so I said, 'Sure, why not?'"

Bacon didn't do thumbnails or multiple sketches—just one iteration of any idea. But he was accommodating. "If people didn't like something about a Cole Porter tune, he just tore it up," he says. "And I did the same thing with the jackets." For the 1961 publication of Joseph Heller's classic *Catch-22,* he did as many as eleven versions. "I did a jacket that just said 'Catch-22' in very large lettering, and underneath, I can almost remember how [the subtitle Heller wrote] goes: 'A novel wildly funny and dead serious about an Assyrian malingerer who recognized the odds.' Gottlieb liked it but didn't do it. Then I did one that had [the protagonist] Yossarian bull's-ass naked, but with his back to you, saluting as a flight of planes went over. I liked that one. Then I did the finger. Then I did a couple of modifications of those. Then at some point I came up with the little guy that I tore out of a piece of paper, representing Yossarian in full flight from everything." The finished jacket doesn't conform to any of Bacon's other book jackets, but it became a true icon, which makes it a typical Bacon after all.

Bacon designed most of the jackets for Heller's other books, an association that Heller once commented on: "The coverage of my life as an author, from *Catch-22* to *Closing Time* thirty-three years later, may be unique in publishing; in my case, Paul Bacon did it for me, and I've been lucky and glad!"

The cover for Philip Roth's *Portnoy's Complaint* (1969) was also characteristically uncharacteristic. Though the vast majority of Bacon's covers are built on some conceptual idea or image, this one consisted solely of pure type against a yellow background; no fancy touches, except for the swash capitals in the title and author's name. Asked why he avoided his signature conceptual image, Bacon says it was because of the difficulty in portraying the book's most prominent element: masturbation. But also, "In color, it was just so simple and raw," and this was one of the things "I started to do for books like *Sophie's Choice* that were strictly lettering covers, which in some ways I suppose was a coward's way out. But it just seemed appropriate for these enormously complicated books." Given the epic plots of *Sophie's Choice* and *Ragtime,* Bacon felt that attempting to do anything other than a solution that proclaimed, "Important book—read it!" would not work. "I guess that's kind of a dumb thing to say, but it was at the back of my mind," he admits.

Ragtime, with its Victorian sheet music–inspired, hand-lettered title, was not only symbolically astute; it also indelibly evoked the book's character. About his increasing use of illustrated lettering, Bacon explains that he didn't try to be "too accurate in a time sense" and did not, as a rule, go after a face that was used during the period of the story. He simply would write the title and author's name out to see what they looked like in upper- and lowercase and in caps, and then see if there was some interesting feature, like a double consonant, that could be manipulated. "I did all that stuff by hand and I wonder why I didn't go crazy," he comments. E. L. Doctorow himself says of the *Ragtime* cover, "I believe it's a classic of book jacket design—simple and immensely evocative at the same time."

No trend follower, Bacon confides that he did what seemed feasible at the time. "I had a feeling for the art directors and the editors of a given house," he says. "If they had certain prejudices or if they were going to be resistant to something I had in mind, I wouldn't waste my time with it, even if I thought it was fundamentally good." Yet he was so highly regarded that editors often would just send him a manuscript with the mandate to "figure it out" for himself. Except that every so often, Bacon would get a note saying, "Please, no swastika,"—this because he had been justifiably dubbed "King of the Swastika," having done many books about World War II that incorporated the Nazi emblem.

To Bacon, a successful jacket is one that the reader makes sense of. "If after you've read the book, you then look at the jacket and say, 'I wonder why he did that,' that doesn't make it for me," he states. These days, ambiguity is much more frequent in book jackets, which may explain why Bacon's past and recent work seem dated to some. While the "Big Book Look" is not precisely obsolete, it is no longer a design code for readers, who today are drawn to fragmented and vague pictorial jackets with skewed type.

Time and fashion have changed, and Bacon has officially retired from the book jacket business, though he still gets calls for assignments. He has returned to designing his first passion, jazz albums. "I certainly believe that anything in the arts is a track meet, and when you run 10 flat and somebody else can run 9.8, your day is done. To some extent, that happened to me," he admits, adding, "I still like the last things I designed—they're good—but they're not competitive in that multigrained way that the things being done now are." There's another reason, too. "I was seventy-eight last December—I'm too goddamn old," Bacon says. "But I'm lucky, in one sense. I got phased out by myself and by publishing at the same time."

If Robert Massin (b. 1925) had not done anything else during his extended career as typographer, art director, and editor, the frantically kinetic book he designed in 1964 for Eugene Ionesco's absurd "anti-play" *La Cantatrice Chauve,* which is known in its American edition as *The Bald Soprano* (1965) and in the English edition as *The Bald Prima Donna* (1966), ensures his place in the pantheon. He pioneered a kind of expressive typography that just two decades later would be common and easy to achieve with the aid of computer programs, but in 1964 Massin only had the digits on his two hands to work with. Influenced by the metaphoric and kinetic *parole in liberta* endemic to futurism, dada, and constructivism, *The Bald Soprano* was Massin's attempt to capture what Laetitia Wolff, curator of "Massin in Continuo," a retrospective exhibition at the Herb Lubalin Study Center of Cooper Union, New York (Winter 2002), calls, "the dynamism of the theatre within the static confines of the book."

Massin loved live performance and saw this play over twenty times. So, what he wanted was to project in print all the nuances, inflections, and ticks that the actors experienced on stage. He assigned to each character a specific typeface that represented a personal voice, and the type was combined with photos of the actors that were taken using high-contrast film. Through this process they were literally transformed into black-and-white symbols that replaced their typewritten names in the original script. The layout of the book is akin to a large storyboard used to block out a film, but rather than typing the dialogue neatly underneath the images—as was the custom—the text was integrated throughout. In this sense there is also a faint resemblance to a comic strip without speech balloons. Stage directions were replaced by the actual gestures and movements of the actor/icons as the type spewed from their respective personages across the pages in varying sizes and configurations. The dueling dialogue became increasingly chaotic as more actors appeared on the stage/page.

Massin's graphic interpretation was conceptually in sync with Ionesco's existential satire of language and logic, but technically speaking it was a big mess. Every element was not only arduously composed and pasted up (remember the days of glue and photo-mechanicals?), but it was also produced in three different versions for the French, English, and American editions. Even more extraordinary was the way in which Massin distorted the type to distinguish soft and loud conversation. He stretched the text (which today is a simple keyboard operation) by transferring the type onto soft rubber—using three dozen condoms, to be exact—which he pulled and tugged to bend and warp, then photographed the result as line art. It was hard enough doing this for the original French edition, but he also had to do iterations for two separate English translations. The end result, however, was a tour de force of interpretative typography.

At the time it was published and for almost a decade thereafter, *The Bald Soprano* was a veritable textbook that influenced many designers, especially those working with minimal budgets. In fact, I am well aware of one such influence on mid- to late-1960s American "underground" newspapers. Under the constraints of working with primitive materials, high-contrast (or Kodalith) film eliminated the need for costly halftones because veloxes (or paper prints) could be directly pasted upon the mechanical, reducing the expense of negative stripping. As evidence of Massin's impact, my very own tattered copy of *The Bald Soprano,* which remains on my bookshelf, was "borrowed" from the chief art director of one of these papers. Stylistically speaking, Massin's method further introduced both a noir aesthetic to eclectic underground design and a kinetic dynamism found in the purposeful, if messy, clash of type and image on a single page.

In addition to this influence, *The Bald Soprano* also directly inspired a small group of book artists working with pictorial narratives—most notably the work of American typographer and performance artist

Warren Lehrer, who added color, textures, and even more chaotic typographic interplay to the Massin model. In recent years neo-expressionist and deconstructive typographers have furthered the "type-as-voice" idea. But Massin's work, despite the ignorance of many artists and designers who perhaps unknowingly stand upon his shoulders, remains the hallmark of these typographic contortions.

Massin's second significant work, *Letter and Image*, is an encyclopedic anthology of illustrated and expressive letterforms that took him fifteen years to compile and edit, and incidentally was one of the first volumes to address the history of eclectic type before the widespread, postmodern interest in design history starting in the 1980s. When first published in America by Van Nostrand, the book was a fixture on many designers' bookshelves, though few actually made the connection between this and *The Bald Soprano*. Dover Books had long published clip-art collections of lost and found passé typographic specimens, but *Letter and Image* was the first treatise to provide the historical context and intellectual underpinning to truly understand how metaphoric letterforms in Western culture developed into distinct languages that were more than mere accessories to pictures.

Moreover, "the publication provided an alternative to the rationalist history of typography propagated by the Bauhaus-influenced Modernists," writes Latetia Wolff. And though many who bought the book did so to "borrow" ideas (as I did), the anthology of over one thousand examples, including Apollinaire's *Calligrammes* (the wellspring of expressive typography), Medieval illuminations, and sign, graffiti, advertisement, and package lettering, articulately describes the holy marriage of the pictorial-letterform and its roots. Massin was not the only designer of his time to be interested in this relationship—certainly in America, Push Pin Studios prefigured postmodern pastiche by decades—but he was the first to codify the history, if not the tenets, of what might be labeled "typographic pictorialism." Therefore, what Jan Tschichold did for the New Typography, Massin did for a new eclecticism through *Type and Image*.

The word "pastiche" means imitation, takeoff, or spoof, and the connotations are not always positive. The modernists abhorred pastiche as nostalgic artifice, but Massin built a vocabulary (not simply a style) on the reapplication of vintage graphic forms, which he applied to books and book covers when he was art director for several postwar French book clubs, including Club Français du Livre and Club du Meilleur Livre, among others. Some designers argue that even the most classical texts and their covers should be reinterpreted in a contemporary design idiom. But Massin, whose interest in classical letters dated back to his boyhood when he learned engraving from his father, a stone engraver, believed that pastiche "always extracts the essential character of a period, thus acknowledging the course of graphic history," writes Wolff. For Massin, matching the content and context of a book was more than a problem-solving exercise; it was his responsibility to readers to afford them a comfortable reading environment. Arguably, all his bookwork is concerned with the reader's relationship to literature, rather than how design must sell a product.

Massin was never taught design—either form or history—yet he developed a fervent ethic concerning the role of type and image as a vessel of meaning. Nonetheless, he did not have a fixed ideology (Modernist or otherwise) or methodology rooted in a single truth. "I had no methods, because I didn't attend courses at the specialized schools," he relates. But what did govern his work was curiosity, which caused him to practice design, in part, was the experimental manipulation of form and the exploration of materials. In his role as book designer and art director, he continually played with new binding materials, "like linen cloth, gunny, silk, velvet, wood, etcetera," he says about what he uses to transform a conventional cover and pages into a tactile object. During the 1950s, designing for book clubs (which routinely published high-quality limited editions) gave Massin an opportunity to produce *livre-objects* (book objects), but even he acknowledges that after some time the tropes became less interesting to members.

Furthermore, by the late 1950s, mass distribution of trade books throughout France had reached prewar efficiency and the book clubs were not as popular. In 1958 Massin joined Gallimard as the first art director. Prior to this, the printer created all the cover, jacket, and interior designs. In return for a freehand, Massin offered to design everything using an exclusive typographic standard. Over the next twenty years he produced a distinct visual character through individual books and various series for Editions Gallimard. During this time, Wolff notes, "The book jacket replaced the decorative hardcover of the club era, following a model explored earlier by Italian and American publishers of popular literature. Again, French publishers were stylishly late." But Massin was not a slave to his or any other's style. Sure, some of his late jackets were similar to the American bestseller look (devised by Paul Bacon and featuring a big byline and title with a small illustration), but Massin's strength was with series, and his ability to at once have uniformity and surprise within a continuous imprint. His most visible was the Gallimard Folio series.

In less than six months he redesigned over three hundred covers in one pop, using the same format with changing elements. (He eventually designed over one thousand covers in all.) The type was Baskerville Old

Face on a white background for about one-third of the cover image, with a unique illustration filling the rest of the space. For the illustrations, he hired the best: Andre François, Folon, Ronald Searle, and Roland Topor, among over two hundred others. But each series had its own character. "My favorite period is the first age of typography," he injects, "Garamond and Venetian Italic—and Didot too." So, for Gallimard's Soleil Collection, each cover was a simple setting of Didot on a flat color background—nothing that would drive the fashions of the day, but the formal subtlety that underlined the classical nature of the texts was a perfect fit.

Massin is more than a book designer; he is intimately involved with the organism of books, and it has made him acutely aware of how writing functions in the world. Therefore, it came as no surprise that by 1979, after leaving Gallimard Editions, he was offered an editorship at Hachette, France's other leading publisher. In recent years the concept of designer as author or auteur has been debated and critiqued in some graphic design circles, yet decades earlier, Massin accomplished the feat. Under the imprint Atelier Hachette/Massin, he conceived, often wrote, edited, researched, and designed various books on popular culture. And later he became a publisher as well, with Proust—a selection of excerpts from *A la recherché du temps perdu* conceived as a hypertext. He also published a volume of Robert Doisneau's elegant photographs of French street life, and is currently working with the Emile Zola family to bring Zola's rare photographs into public view.

In 1989, *L'ABC du Métier,* an illustrated biography of Massin's own collected work, was published in France. As he states, it is a "résumé of a career, where is demonstrated the interaction of different arts." Despite the requisite reprise of a lifetime's artifacts, it is not only a retrospective, but also a chronicle of a self-taught artist and artisan who markedly influenced attitudes of graphic design. Yet most practicing designers have never heard of Massin. A few recent articles about *The Bald Soprano* in the design press have only served to spotlight one of the twentieth century's most significant typographic artifacts, not the breadth of the designer's contributions. Not until the exhibition at the Herb Lubalin Study Center did I understand that *The Bald Soprano* is only one appendage in an entire body of design.

Electric Circus

Ivan Chermayeff

DARLING DAUGHTERS
SWEET MOTHERS DANCE
BLACKLIGHT DYNAMITE
ACROBATS ASTROLOGERS
JUGGLERS FREAKS CLOWNS
ESCAPE ARTISTS VIOLINISTS
GROK GRAPES GRASS
UPS DOWNS SIDEWAYS
COFFEE THINK TANK
AIR-CONDITIONED
IN MORE WAYS THAN ONE
THE ULTIMATE LEGAL
ENTERTAINMENT EXPERIENCE

THE ELECTRIC CIRCUS.
OPENS JUNE 28, 1967
23 ST. MARKS PLACE, N.Y.C.,
EAST VILLAGE
THINK ABOUT IT.

In the mid- to late 1960s, the East Village in Manhattan, especially St. Mark's Place between Third Avenue and Avenue A, was the epicenter of the East Coast hippie movement. Bars, coffee houses, dance and concert halls, and headshops, with names like Psychedelicatessen and Peace Eye, mixed politics, drugs, and rock and roll with art and culture. Alternative theaters, like Channel One, radiated a kaleidoscope of sounds. On Second Avenue and Sixth Street the Fillmore East, the East Coast branch of Bill Graham's rock palace, headlined a youthful Grateful Dead, Jefferson Airplane, and Janis Joplin. Psychedelia stimulated by drugs like LSD and peyote was transplanted from Haight-Ashbury and acquired a New York accent.

On the West Coast, Victor Moscoso, Wes Wilson, Rick Griffin, and other rock poster artists translated music into images. Encrypted by hand, nearly illegible type became a signpost, a code that conveyed the message to the young and confounded the Establishment. Hallucinogens slowed the passage of time and rendered it plastic. They transmogrified sensory modes. Feel orange! Taste purple! The psychedelic posters spoke the same undulating dialect in holistic compositions whose chromatic vibrations nonetheless took advantage of Albers's color theory.

The Electric Circus was a popular rock club in an old Ukrainian social club with a huge dance floor. Chermayeff (b. 1932) and Geismar (b. 1931) first designed the interior of the club then the poster announcing its grand opening on June 28, 1967, with words strung together in a stream-of-consciousness, ". . . darling daughters sweet mothers dance black light dynamite acrobats astrologers jugglers freaks clowns escape artists. . . ." Chermayeff was intrigued by the rambling, poetic language written by the owners of the club. Did the words describe the entertainment inside or invite the neighbors in by name?

Although not as visually elaborate as Moscoso's posters, the *Electric Circus*'s kinetic typography nevertheless reverberated with visual cues that fused form and content and added impact to the word-pictures jarred loose by the colorful language. Chermayeff's jiggly, hyperventilating alphabet wed word to image, too. At the same time, other designers like Gene Federico, Lou Dorfsman, and Herb Lubalin coaxed typeset words into visual and verbal configurations and took new liberties that the introduction of widespread phototypesetting afforded in the 1960s.

Chermayeff and Geismar met as students at Yale in the mid-1950s while doing research for papers on typeface design. In the spring of 1957 they teamed up with Robert Brownjohn to form Brownjohn Chermayeff Geismar. Brownjohn had studied with Moholy-Nagy at the Chicago Institute of Design and Chermayeff worked with Alvin Lustig in New York. They called themselves a design office instead of an art studio, which signaled a new professionalism based on problem solving and utilization of broad aesthetic resources. In those early years, before Brownjohn left the firm in 1960, the partners found inspiration in sorties to Coney Island and other urban hinterlands, immersing themselves in the sumptuousness of street vernacular. In text accompanying a photographic essay formalizing what he and his friends discovered, Brownjohn wrote, "everything of interest in this wide-open area of social uplift [the city] has been done by dead men or by amateurs, or vandals or politicians or accident or neglect or dirty old men or the makers of big, busy neon signs" ("BJ", *Eye*, Vol. 4, No. 1).

The alphabet for the *Electric Circus* poster began as an exploration of typographic expression in hot metal composition. In a booklet titled *That New York,* designed as an experiment for the Composing Room, Brownjohn, Chermayeff, and Geismar pushed the limits of typographic invention. They explored type as texture, stretched and distorted words and letterforms, created incongruous typographic hybrids, and layered words to the point of illegibility. If all this sounds vaguely familiar, "This and other works utilizing rubber stamps, wrong fonts, and fragmented letters preceded David Carson by thirty-five years," observed Ivan Chermayeff.

For the title, *That New York,* the designers began with a sans serif typeface whose letterforms were overlapped and manipulated on film, in both positive and negative formats. The effect was a double-exposed image. New letterforms appeared—the *A, O,* and *R* had double counterforms and additional legs, and the *N, Y, W,* and *K* had new spiky protuberances. Using all capital letters afforded maximum play in the interstices with additional strokes added for vibrational energy.

In 1959 the firm designed the jacket for the book *Toward a Sane*

Nuclear Policy. The type on the cover is stacked with uppercase sans-serif letterforms, one word per line. The top word, *Toward*, is printed twice with the second imprint offset dramatically from the first. Each of the following words is gradually more off register, culminating with the word *Policy*, which stands alone. The overlapping letters hint at the later-developed alphabet. But Chermayeff dismisses the *Sane* cover as an antecedent, saying the solution was purely conceptual and achieved through overprinting and not through the manipulation of films at all.

The alphabet was designed for the *That New York* booklet in 1960. Although it appeared in an advertisement entitled "Modern Banking is Electronic Banking" in *Fortune* magazine in 1961, it wasn't until it was applied to the *Electric Circus* poster in 1967 that it found its proper place. Chermayeff said it was "the first totally appropriate client to come up to take advantage of it." The poster won awards and was published often. Of course, it helped to have a client who intended it as an image builder for the club, not a ticket sales generator, and who neither expected or needed direct results. Although not born of the radical fringe, the *Electric Circus* poster nonetheless established an image for a club in the heart of New York hippiedom and stands as a bridge between alternative and establishment cultures.

Blues Project

Victor Moscoso

Victor Moscoso's psychedelic *Blues Project* poster is as illegible today as it was in 1967 when it, and scores of other vibrating rock posters advertising the San Francisco rock scene, first appeared. It is also as electrifying. Moscoso's posters did for graphic design what bands like the Grateful Dead, Jefferson Airplane, and Big Brother and the Holding Company did for rock music: turned up the juice and broke all the rules.

During the mid-1960s San Francisco was the vortex of the counterculture. The hippies prevailed, hallucinogenic drugs were plentiful, and rock and roll knew no bounds. Brooklyn-raised, Spanish-born Victor Moscoso (b. 1939) stumbled into this milieu and became a defining force in the distinctly American design genre known as the psychedelic poster. Characterized by illegible typefaces, vibrating colors, and antique illustrations, psychedelia was a rebellious visual language created to communicate with an exclusive community. Within a year, however, it was usurped by entrepreneurs who turned it into a trendy commercial style that appealed to a new market of youthful consumers. Before ceding the field to the so-called culture vultures, Moscoso created some of the most emblematic images of the 1960s, of which the *Blues Project* poster is one classic.

Most of the more than sixty posters Moscoso designed during a frenetic eight months in 1967 rejected publicity photos in favor of found images. For the *Blues Project* poster he used a vintage photograph of a nude Salomé. Following her contour, he hand-lettered the concert information in a typeface that Moscoso called Psychedelic Playbill (an adaptation of a Victorian woodtype). Because he drew the letters out of negative space (whiting out all the areas between the bodies of the letterforms rather than drawing them directly), they look as if they have been carved onto the page. The figure was printed in bright orange against an acid green background; the lettering was printed in process blue. The slightly off-register trapping gave the letters a three-dimensional look in addition to the vibrating sensation produced by the juxtaposition of similar chromatic values.

The *Blues Project* poster defined a Moscoso style. Other leading contemporary poster artists, including Wes Wilson, Rick Griffin, and the team of Mouse and Kelly, had distinct visual personalities, but Moscoso's use of vibrating color was the most emblematic of the group. His brand of chromatic vibration was surprisingly derived from strict modern principles. Moscoso was schooled at Cooper Union in New York and Yale in New Haven before migrating west, and he credited his Yale professor Joseph Albers, a master of modernism, for this key discovery. Likening Albers's famous Color Aid paper exercises to the futility of learning algebra in high school, Moscoso admitted that color theory drove him crazy, but ultimately proved to be an invaluable resource. "Albers's impact really didn't show until the psychedelic poster . . . when I found myself in a situation where all I had to do was reach back to my dusty shelf, so to speak, and pull out what I had learned."

Compared to rock posters by Rick Griffin and Mouse and Kelly, each of whom practiced an obsessively precisionist, macabre comic style, Moscoso was a master of simplicity. Despite what appeared to be layers of graphic complexity, his visuals were strategically composed and purposefully designed. While being stoned may have added to the enjoyment of the *Blues Project* poster, the design was not drug-induced chaos. Moscoso was a highly disciplined rebel. He consciously rejected all the rules he learned during his time at college when he admired Paul Rand, won a cash prize for designing a roman alphabet based on the Trajan inscription, and rendered Chancery Cursive and Caslon from memory just for kicks. But the *Blues Project* poster was indicative of a complete understanding of balance, proportion, and color. The poster may not directly conform to any modernist theory, but it was influenced by contemporary design thinking.

Moscoso's first rock poster for The Family Dog dance hall, a picture of a gargoyle on the top of Notre Dame with psychedelic type overprinting the image, was an admitted flop. "I had seven years of college— I could have been a doctor," he said about the process of self-reevaluation that resulted in a creative epiphany. He realized that none of the self-taught poster artists were encumbered by the rules of good design, so Moscoso reversed everything he had formally learned. The rule that a poster should transmit a message simply and quickly became how long can you engage the viewer in reading the poster? Five, ten, twenty minutes? "Don't use vibrating colors" became "use them whenever you can and irritate the eyes as much as you can." "Lettering should always be legible" was changed to "disguise the lettering as much as possible and make it as difficult as possible to read." Moscoso called this "a world turned upside down." But by acting on these ideas he created a body of work that altered the language of a generation.

With the *Best of Jazz* poster, Paula Scher
(b. 1948) introduced young American designers
to forgotten design languages and inadvertently
unlocked the floodgates for unknowing
designers to pilfer historical artifacts as
decontextualized scrap. With the Reagan
presidency in 1980 national sentiment turned
toward nostalgic and old-fashioned feel-good
graphics that fed a longing for past innocence.
This provided, consciously or not, a fertile
environment for a new wave of historical
derivation in design, which ultimately became
known as "retro." For a generation of designers
and consumers disconnected from their visual
past, the *Best of Jazz* poster appeared fresh and
unprecedented.

Early in her career, Scher was inspired
by Push Pin Studios' reprise of passé styles such as Victoriana, art nouveau,
and art deco. She turned to type from illustration shortly after coming to
New York, citing a self-assessed inability to draw well. As an art director at
CBS Records from 1975 to 1982, Scher commissioned conceptual illustrators
and combined their surrealist styles with eclectic and often historic
typography that echoed the illustration. The effect was a holistic
integration of type and image in the manner of nineteenth-century posters.

In the late 1970s, the record industry hit the skids economically—
sales slumped, costs soared, and inflation took its usurious bite. "I could no
longer put all of our money into imagery," Scher stated in an interview in
Mixing Messages (Princeton Architectural Press, 1996), "so the type came
forward." About that same time Russian constructivism was being revisited
in books and exhibitions. Scher, who had long collected and admired old
graphic styles, quickly assimilated the revolutionary language.

Scher may have begun the *Best of Jazz* poster with an
anthropological dig through the Russian avant-gardists' visual vocabulary,
but she ended up with a distinctive tapestry woven of personal affinities,
problem-solving pragmatism, and New York derring-do. The letterforms
are not Cyrillic, but, oddly enough, nineteenth-century sans-serif

woodtypes borrowed from old Victorian type catalogs. The Russian artists had located their constructions in the weightlessness of white space even as they concretized that same space as a formal element. Scher, conversely, confines this poster within a border then packs it with a feverish riff of letterforms that energize the surface plane and metaphorically mimic the improvisational nature of jazz itself.

Scher borrowed the constructivist's strong geometric composition, thrusting diagonals, and signature colors: red and black. High contrast is apparent between the bold, black capitals that spell out *BEST* and the smaller, busier typography. Overlapping colors, surprints, and knockouts make the most of the limited color palette. These elements may explain why the poster was popularly perceived as constructivist, but there was also an unmistakable resemblance to Victoriana in the tightly packed, nearly cluttered arrangement of type, the woodtype typography itself, and the slant toward ornamentation. Although it was a hybrid of two historical forms, the result was fresh-faced, decidedly contemporary, and, yet, eerily familiar, much like a child whose genetic code descends from but ultimately transcends that of its parents.

Effectively reinterpreting historical style is harder than it looks. To create unique graphic imagery inspired from the past involves juggling a number of currents: the inspiration and historical context of the original work; the resonance of the source material in its original time frame and the interpretations it might be given when restaged in a contemporary setting; and the designer's own personal style and taste. But where are the boundaries when designers treat past aesthetic vocabularies as a storehouse of motifs to be used willy-nilly for their gratuitous impact on contemporary audiences? Far from any universal agreement, historical appropriation ranges from the clearly ethical—inspiration, influence, homage, reinterpretation, quotation, and parody—to the blatantly unethical—mimicry, copying, imitation, and plagiarism.

Some of Scher's historically inspired inventions have veered perilously close to copying an original, as with the 1986 Swatch advertising parody of Herbert Matter's 1938 poster for the Swiss Tourist Bureau. With tongue in cheek, Scher assembled most of the same visual elements as Matter did, with the notable addition of a hand and wrist wearing two Swatch watches, which are, not incidentally, made in Switzerland. The capricious nature of the product dramatized in the monumental style of Matter's poster created a humorous juxtaposition and sense of absurdity that appealed to Scher's wit. It was a chance to play with the 1950s this-will-change-your-life type of advertising. In an interview with Dick Coyne of *Communication Arts* (May/June 1986), Scher explained, "Whether or not people get the joke or understand the basis of it—I hope they do—that's the fun for us [Scher and then-partner Terry Koppel], and one reason why we both love to design." They acknowledged Matter in a credit line at the bottom of the ad.

Historical reprise has been a mixed blessing. At once it serves to educate designers about history, making them more open to learn about past eras and epochs, but also sanctions easy formal solutions devoid of originality. While some critics argue that overt borrowing from the past tends to trivialize both past and present by promoting rote design, others argue that the introduction of these reprises serves to enliven the field by offering more creative options. Where history is intelligently absorbed the results are invisible. Where history is used effectively as a model, a sense of appropriateness is usually apparent. But where history is just a cut-and-paste procedure, the result is almost always a cliché.

Basel Kunstkredit 1976/77

Wolfgang Weingart

"By itself, typography is as boring as hell," stated Wolfgang Weingart, the man who stood Swiss typographic design on its head. "What makes it exciting is how you interpret it." The tenets of Swiss design, later the International Typographic Style, emerged from the traditions of the Bauhaus, the New Typography of the 1920s and 1930s, and de Stijl. Sans-serif typography and objective photography—photographs that do not seduce or make exaggerated claims—were positioned on an underlying mathematical grid of verticals and horizontals in a harmonic relationship derived from objective and functional criteria.

Switzerland's neutrality in World War II provided a sanctuary for pioneering designers Max Bill and Theo Balmer to continue their explorations begun at the Bauhaus. A booming postwar economy heightened industry's demand for publicity and the rationalist design ethic prospered, spreading to Germany, Basel, and Zurich, and eventually to the design community at large. Emil Ruder and Armin Hofmann began teaching at the Allegemeine Gewerbeschule (Basel School of Design) the same year, 1947, establishing their own version of typographic principles based on a correct balance between form and function, the sanctity of readability, and the belief in an absolute and universal graphic expression.

After a three-year apprenticeship as a hand typesetter with a small printer in Stuttgart, Wolfgang Weingart met Armin Hofmann by chance in 1963 when he inquired about his and Ruder's classes at the School of Design in Basel. Although he studied briefly with both teachers a year later, Weingart considers himself an educational orphan, a failed student of Ruder's and underexposed to the teachings of Hofmann, who left for India shortly after Weingart arrived. "I had a special understanding with Ruder and he let me use the workshops whenever I wanted," Weingart said in an interview in *Eye* (April 1991).

In this pristine academic environment, the perpetually restless Weingart began to question: Why does type need to be flush left and ragged right? Why do paragraphs need to be indented? He didn't want to reject all that came before, just expand it. In 1968 the Advanced Course for Graphic Design was started, and Weingart was offered a position on the typography faculty. His contributions to graphic design's lexicon are considerable: wide letterspacing, layering of photographic and typographic imagery, solid bands and blocks of reversed type, grids implied then violated, underlining, unconventional mixing of type sizes and weights, diagonal type, and using geometric shapes and typographic units as illustrative devices—all elements that would later be adopted as contemporary mannerisms. Is Weingart pleased? Hardly. He would condemn this list as "design cream" that has been skimmed off and used as disembodied fragments by designers who don't think for themselves. "I never intended to create a 'style,'" Weingart said. He did intend to discover a new visual attitude and method of experimentation based on a solid teaching foundation.

Weingart's posters for the Basel Kunstkredit (art fair) document his investigations. The *1976/77* poster is a hallmark of typographic and spatial play, and visual proof of his philosophy that typography exists in a triangular relationship between the design idea, typographic elements, and printing technique. Photographic fragments of a building and interior architecture allude to illusionistic space, a snippet of reality. The camera lens image is photographic, too, but frontal and flattened in space. For contrast Weingart used the tools of print technology, enlarged halftone dots and moiré patterns, as aesthetic elements to interrupt the reading of the "reality" of the photographic images and reinforce the true nature of the poster—ink on paper.

Diagonals draw the viewer into the space, both through the perspective of the architectural references and the directional nature of the geometric shapes. Graphic devices, grids, and solid blocks of typography are embedded in the graphic imagery, sometimes overlapping other images, other times tucked behind. The effect is one of layering, or put another way, of spatial dialogue between illusionistic three-dimensionality and the two-dimensional activity of the surface. The result is disorienting, complicated, and dynamic, but it is not chaotic. A solid vertical and horizontal axis underpins the geometric thrusts and girds against the photographic allusions to spatial depth, reminding the viewer of the surface plane. Weingart tinkered with visual pathways, tested readability by partially obscuring letterforms, and left the viewer with a nonlinear, holistic conglomeration.

Weingart is not a theorist, but a practitioner for whom technology is the ultimate challenge. He embraced it as both a partner and a friend, garnering techniques from his own investigations and experiments. He pioneered sandwiching and juxtaposing film positives in the darkroom to form a seamless union between imagery, typography, and technology, a technique that prefigured the computer. He acknowledged the computer has "speeded things up," but with an ironically peevish attitude for an alleged technophile. He still maintains that basically "there's nothing it can do that can't be done by hand or film montage. It hasn't produced a new visual language."

As a teacher, Weingart's influence radiates beyond his own oeuvre. In 1972 he organized a lecture tour through Switzerland, Germany, and the United States, illustrating his threefold manifesto to expand typographic alternatives through syntactic, semantic, and pragmatic considerations. Prophetically, he concluded his remarks by confessing his program completely neglected the study of texts, which would find full flower in the next decade's passion for semiotics, the study of signs and sign function. Early students like April Greiman, Willi Kunz, and Dan Friedman, after studying with Weingart in Basel, returned to the United States to teach and practice. This extended spirit of aggressive exploration eventually coalesced as the new wave in America.

Weingart's style was appropriated during the late 1980s and early 1990s. At first he said imitation was a stimulant, an incentive to keep one step ahead. Now he says, "My work is a quarry. People see a stone they like, appropriate it and work it until there's nothing left." He still teaches but no longer designs. He is far from distraught, though. "No, I had to stop, in order to let the things that I produced sink in, and wait until the next, real explosion comes, so that designers in the new decade can copy me again."

Cranbrook

Katherine McCoy

Accused of being a cloistered atmosphere polluted by its own freedoms, the graphic design program at the Cranbrook Academy of Art was certainly in the forefront of design criticism from the late 1970s through the 1990s. One might expect to find guerrilla theoreticians lobbing graphic cherry bombs at mainstream modernism, but, in fact, Cranbrook's influence did not come from launching manifestoes; it developed by creating a stimulating environment where graphic experimentation altered the conventional practice of graphic design. According to Katherine McCoy (b. 1945), chairwoman of the graphic design program from 1971 to 1995, the work done during that time can be loosely organized into three

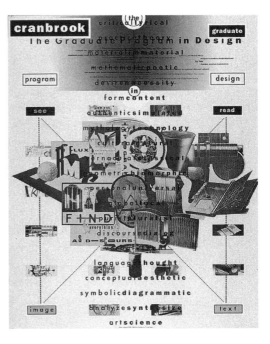

"clusters of concerns": the expansion of modernism's formal language (1971–1979), a short middle phase characterized by "high formalism" (1980–1981), and a third, poststructuralist stage (1982–1995). Criticism notwithstanding, Cranbrook's explorations served as fodder for rigorous discourse that helped define and expand the profession during the 1980s.

Although Cranbrook embraced the Bauhaus notion of unity between art and industry, as early as 1940, when Charles Eames became chairman of the department of industrial design and Eero Saarinen and Harry Bertoia were on the faculty, Cranbrook had replaced the rigidity of Bauhaus ideology with a more complex, eclectic approach in which personal directions were encouraged. It was in this context that Katherine and Michael McCoy became co-chairs of the design department in 1971. In what started out as a part-time position, Katherine was responsible for two-dimensional design and Mike the three-dimensional design of furniture, interiors, and products.

How did the institution that Paul Goldberger described in the *New York Times Magazine* (April 1984) as "part artist's colony, part school, part museum, and part design laboratory" become an experimental crucible for American typography during the 1970s and 1980s without a plan, much less a manifesto? In this unstructured environment the focus and impetus for learning came directly from the students, who were highly motivated self-starters. "We always encouraged students to read," explained McCoy (*Eye*, No. 16, Vol. 4). McCoy kept an ever-expanding department bibliography, but texts were not assigned; students were encouraged to research, ruminate, and formulate with an eye to developing their own conceptual strategies. Cross-fertilization was a way of life between departments (art, photography, and architecture) and people. Students worked cheek by jowl in studios with faculty and each other as dorm rooms and cafeterias became laboratories for high-spirited discussions.

McCoy was reluctant to describe the evolution at Cranbrook as a progression. It was more like spontaneous combustion, but there was an overarching philosophy that confronted graphic design's traditional dilemma—form versus content—head on. "Form is not the enemy of content, and form can become content as well as a container of content," she explained. For McCoy, her 1989 *Cranbrook Design* poster symbolizes this reconciliation and pluralism. Visually, word pairs stretch the length of the poster anchored to the center, their dialectic reinforced by color and layout. Layered beneath the word pairs are collaged image-fragments of student work, echoing the bilateral symmetry with two-dimensional design projects on the left and three-dimensional projects on the right. The deepest information layer is the See-Read-Text-Image diagram that unites the poster formally, and semantically suggests multiple interactions between the elements.

To structure the phases during her tenure at Cranbrook, McCoy used a simplified communication model based on a 1949 linear-progression schematic developed by Shannon & Weaver. Although Shannon's model was later replaced by more sophisticated ones, "the sender › message › receiver" chain identified the core elements of communication as a basic linear interaction. McCoy, whose background is in industrial design, came to Cranbrook as a problem-solver and modernist. In the early years, 1971–1980, the program focused on the message part of Shannon's equation, expanding the modernist notion of the transparent designer communicating a clear and precise message to an audience. The entire lineage of Swiss work was examined, from Karl Gerstner and early Müller-Brockmann, Hans Neuberg and Emil Ruder to the later "high Swiss" of Ruedi Rüegg, Odermatt & Tissi, and Wolfgang Weingart's "mannered Swiss." Despite this thoroughness, the Swiss vein was just one of many being explored at the time.

As a result of working with Ed Fella, a self-taught commercial artist with a highly personalized graphic style, McCoy's modernist tendencies expanded to include an understanding and sympathy for the "low end" of commercial art and the vernacular. McCoy brought Fella into the program at Cranbrook to participate formally in critiques and informally in spontaneous interactions with students. This sparked investigation into other commercial vernaculars and books like Robert Venturi and Denise Scott Brown's *Learning from Las Vegas*.

In 1978, *Visible Language*, a scholarly journal devoted to exploring the role and properties of written language, dedicated a volume to contemporary French literary aesthetics and engaged Cranbrook in a collaborative effort to design the volume, titled "French Currents of the Letter." Daniel Libeskind, head of Cranbrook's architecture department, worked with McCoy and select students, giving them a crash course in French linguistic theory.

Deconstructionism, a term that would later become Cranbrook's albatross, is a part of poststructuralism, which, in turn, is a response to structuralism, an earlier movement in French literary theory. Led by Ferdinand de Saussure, structuralism posited that signs, rather than being isolated elements with self-contained meanings, are culturally interdependent parts of an overall network whose meaning is derived from the relationships between the parts. Deconstructionism was introduced to the United States through the writings of Jacques Derrida, which were translated into English in the late 1970s. Derrida suggested that a cultural construction, such as an idea, a value, or a sentence can be disassembled, or taken apart, and decoded—its parts examined for "meaning." The parts can be reassembled into another whole that may, then, take on a different meaning. The rearrangement of the parts into various wholes opens a way of exploring the complex nature of signs and moves communications into the complicated landscape of multimeaning, layered contexts, thus marking a shift from binary, yes–no signification to a more subjective, multidimensional interpretation of meaning.

For the *Visible Language* project, McCoy and students Richard Kerr, Alice Hecht, Jane Kosstrin, and Herbert Thompson created a typographic analog to the text. The essays began with traditional layouts. Progressively the space between the words and lines was expanded and footnote material was repositioned to interact unconventionally with the text. The final essays appeared to be pages of floating words visually punctuated by black horizontal bands of marginalia that so dislodged conventional reading order that the viewer was forced into alternative reading patterns. Vertical and diagonal pathways opened up, causing words and phrases to reassemble themselves through new juxtapositions that jarred conventional meanings. It offended almost everyone, drawing rage and ridicule from designers still committed to the modernist canon of simplicity, legibility, and problem solving.

The investigation of formalist expression culminated in 1980–1981 with the high formalist phase. Here the emphasis shifted, in Shannon's model, from the message to the sender. The classic student exercise in typography, to take a semantically neutral message like a weather report or recipe and explore its presentation through typographic and compositional variations, had evolved into what became known as the "label" exercise. After some classic warm-ups, the projects started with a Yellow Pages ad or a product label that was subjected to visual analysis, typographic variations, and most controversially, subjective interpretations of the original object or ad. The designer was no longer just a translator, but a commentator, partner, and participant in the delivery of the message.

The third, poststructuralist phase (1983–1995) grew out of a restlessness and dissatisfaction with mannered formalist manipulations. Although the *Visible Language* project in the late 1970s touched on deconstructionism, it wasn't until the mid-1980s, with the classes of 1985/87 and 1986/88, that an active interest in linguistic theories really flourished. Driven by student inquisitiveness, McCoy called this period the "theory-of-the-week-club—structuralism, poststructuralism, deconstruction, phenomenology, critical theory, reception theory, hermeneutics, letterism, Venturi vernacularism, postmodern art theory." McCoy resisted, asked questions, and challenged both students and theories. As Jeffery Keedy, a student at the time, recalled (*Eye*, No. 16, Vol. 4) that McCoy kept saying, "But what does it look like? How you do make it work as a design tool?" She admitted to being skeptical at times, but always remained committed to the mutual search, if not the mutual conclusions.

In the poststructuralist period at Cranbrook, the emphasis in Shannon's model of communication changed again, now from sender to receiver. The traditional notion that text was to be read (a linear, encoded, left-brained activity) and images were to be seen (a holistic, experiential, right-brain activity) was questioned. Text became cross-functional and took on an expanded capability to communicate beyond its functionality, moving into the realm of the illustrative (type as image), atmospheric, or expressive. Similarly, images could be "read," sequenced, and combined to form more complex information patterns.

Concepts like multiplicity, layers of embedded information, viewer-controlled text and imagery, and nonlinear progression, which were characteristics of Cranbrook's experimental design in the late 1980s, have become bywords of multimedia, the new graphic design frontier. McCoy saw graphic design as a pluralistic activity, one in which the components of Shannon's model still apply, but no longer in a linear fashion. The imperative was for integration and cross-functioning of all the elements. "I think this approach fits modern society because the contemporary world is subtle and complex. Simple black-and-white dualisms no longer work."

Is graphic design graduate school a hermetically sealed research and development laboratory or a pseudoprofessional environment with training wheels? Those who would attack Cranbrook for being the former need to consider the impact on the design profession of alumni like Lorraine Wild, Nancy Skolos, Tom Wedell, Lucille Tenazas, and Jeffery Keedy. Cranbrook didn't intend to launch a revolution in theory-based graphic design. In fact, Katherine McCoy didn't even want to teach. So why did she stay for twenty-four years? "Because it is such a flexible situation. . . . If you want change you can change. The only real requirement from the administration is that you attract good students and produce strong graduates who find their way in the profession."

The Discreet Charm of the Bourgeoisie

Yuri Bokser

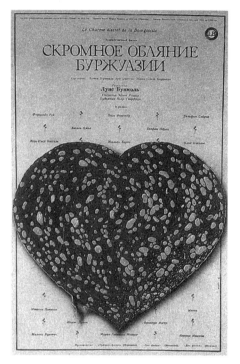

On August 19, 1991, the day that hard-line Russian communists ousted Mikail Gorbachev in the famous short-lived coup, Yuri Bokser, a thirty-seven-year-old Russian poster artist, boarded an Aeroflot jet at New York's Kennedy International to return to his besieged Moscow knowing that he might be arrested. Bokser—one of Moscow's leading film-poster designers, who also designed unpublished political posters critical of Lenin, Stalin, and Gorbachev—had just finished a short stay in New York where he received assignments from the *New York Times* and *Rolling Stone*. Warned against returning home, he had little choice: his wife and children had been left behind because temporary entry visas to the United States were difficult to get in those days, and his life's work was there, too.

Bokser, born in Tashkent in 1954 into a Jewish family with roots deep in the Russian soil, had drawn cartoons for exported Soviet magazines that had looser restrictions than internally distributed media, but he wanted to do something more meaningful, like posters. "This was impossible because I could not make the kinds of posters that the official publishing houses would print," he once recounted. "I made two or three attempts at that and failed miserably." It was not his plan to become a nonconformist, but through the underground artists at the Moscow Art Institute he had seen Polish magazines like *Projekt*, the Swiss *Graphis,* and some American design journals. "I was inspired by the freedom in that work, and also in American art in general," he said.

Bokser made his first unofficial poster around 1981, a few years before *perestroika* (the new openness) took hold. It was for rock-musician friends and was printed in a small quantity. "But after that I didn't make another poster for a long time," he recalled. Bokser's first success came when Reklamfilm, the USSR's oldest film promotion company, changed leadership when its chief art director was caught taking kickbacks from artists. His replacement decided to use new artists. Bokser was the first of the newcomers, then, one by one, came his friends. Nevertheless, having an art director who was sympathetic to expressive and symbolic art—surreal, allegorical imagery with hidden references and meanings—did not immediately change the way things were done. "It was very difficult in the beginning because Reklamfilm had to get permission to print each poster from the department of film distribution, which demanded that everything be conventional." Ironically, the films did not have to sell or make money, so in any other context more freedom would have been possible.

Bokser's breakthrough came when an editor at Reklama Cine did what Bokser referred to as "a very strange thing" by printing a small quantity of one of his formerly prohibited posters. The image for Luis Buñuel's *The Discreet Charm of the Bourgeoisie,* showing a slice of salami in the shape of a heart, was exhibited both in- and outside of the USSR—the first time since the constructivist art of the 1920s that such a symbolic treatment had replaced the official Russian pedantic representation. The public response was so positive that it encouraged a shift in the policy of the film distribution department. As if by waving a magic wand, a new style of conceptual film posters, which owed more to the Polish tradition of illustrative poster art than to Russia's constructivist legacy, were produced at prodigious rates. Each of the regular Reklamfilm artists produced between twenty and thirty posters annually. For a few years, the posters were printed in quantities that exceeded one hundred thousand and could be seen everywhere, providing a festive atmosphere to the otherwise drab Soviet cityscapes.

Bokser was not, however, content just to do film posters. He turned to social art that rejected the style known as socialist realism, which he argued was really "socialist romanticism." His satiric jabs at the Soviet establishment, especially the failings of perestroika, became well known. "I was skeptical about perestroika almost from the beginning," he explained at the time. "It quickly became merely a new slogan. Of course, it's better than Stalinism." Indeed under Gorbachev the promised freedoms were rationed; the majority of Bokser's social commentaries were prohibited from being printed by the official publishing house and in many instances could not even be shown in exhibitions. Leaders of the Artists Union, to which Bokser belonged, would not allow certain critical representations of Lenin and, especially, Gorbachev to hang since they feared losing their positions. "In our country it is normal," he said. "I do not feel offended by these people. I can understand the pressures brought to bear." Yet Bokser continued to do unpublished critical works for a small coterie of friends.

Bokser insisted that he was always free to do his work as long as he did not expect the controversial works to be published. But he also admitted that exercising total freedom in the USSR was never easy. So he remained true to the ideals of reform, despite the fact that the inevitable shift to a market economy proved deleterious to his art. Shortly after returning to Moscow in 1991, he wrote that "there has been less work during the past two years, and I am afraid that the great cinema period of Soviet posters will be over. With capitalism everything depends on money, including film. And now the film distributors want *Rambo* movies and *Rambo*-styled posters, which is really socialist romanticism all over again. My fellow artists and I deceived the system for five years. Now, some younger artists will come along and do the *Rambo* posters, but not us."

| Radical Modernism |
| Dan Friedman |
| |

Like "Ultrasuede," the term "radical modern" sounds like a dubious synthetic, or worse, another arcane subdivision in an already pretentious taxonomy of art that includes such updates as neo-dada and postexpressionism. But even if one is skeptical about new and improved art movements, the terminology should not get in the way of appreciating Dan Friedman's

(1946–1995) graphic design, which, infused with his self-defined principles of radical modernism, is neither synthetic nor pretentious.

Radical modernism originated as a twelve-point manifesto at the AIGA's 1989 "Dangerous Ideas" conference in San Antonio, Texas, where Friedman proposed the unfashionable idea that modernism—as developed in 1920s Europe before evolving into a corporate language—remains the basis for socially relevant *and* formally diverse design. What he calls "radical Modernism" is "a reaffirmation of the idealistic roots of our modernity, adjusted to include more of our diverse culture, history, research, and fantasy." Rather than turning to postmodernism, Friedman calls for a post-corporate modernism that rejects cold universal systems and clichéd solutions. *Radical Modernism* (Yale University Press, 1995), a monograph published months before his death at the age of fifty, is a manifesto that critiques modernism's failures and perpetuates—indeed celebrates—its triumphs. But most important, it is a record of a stimulating body of contemporary work that convincingly blurs the traditional boundaries between art and design.

Friedman, who was schooled in both the science-based rationalism of Germany's Ulm school and the intuitive logic of Wolfgang Weingart's convention-busting typography program at the Basel school, rejected the International Typographic Style that dominated American design in the 1960s and early 1970s. As a teacher at Yale and the State University of New York at Purchase during the early 1970s, he introduced students to linguistic and perceptual theory as a way to expand design thinking.

Friedman challenged corporate modernism in both theory and practice by creating an oeuvre that adapted original modern humanist ethics while transcending the functional blandness that had turned the younger generation against it.

By the late 1970s he began to propose the idea of having students make "dysfunctional" messages in order to measure the true limits of communication, a method that has had exponents in many other design institutions. He wrote, "[G]raphic designers should work past some rather naïve positions. It may be an illusion that the newest orientation to typography is automatically better and has more layers of meaning than previous experiments that were either more or less concerned with formalistic possibilities. It may also be an illusion that the new digital technology . . . has a higher authority and represents a kind of progress, considering that technological progress has often caused some erosion of human values."

Friedman wed formalism to activism. Whether for an AIDS project or for a cultural institution, his work displayed a passion for play with color, composition, and contrast. He was deeply motivated by the spiritual. "Landscapes have always been a theme in my work because they suggest a source for transcendental reflection," he wrote. His nongraphic design, including furniture and sculpture, appear most naturally to incorporate activism, formalism, spiritualism—and eccentricity. Friedman's tour de force was his own apartment in an otherwise nondescript postwar building on lower Fifth Avenue in New York, which he regularly redecorated with abstract forms and bright cartoon-like colors inspired by East African art contrasted with elements of the New York street.

Graphic designers who practice fine art are usually separatists, preferring not to taint one with the other. Apart from the physical differences, Friedman's art and design are compatible, if not in application, then in spirit. Even his most visible corporate campaign for Citibank, created in 1975 while working for Anspach Grossman Portugal, is evidence of his artistic evolution that followed. In this campaign, he adapts and synthesizes the experimental typography introduced at Basel, the result being a refreshingly lighthearted image for a conservative corporation. After the success of Citibank, Friedman could easily have made pseudo-experimental work for corporate clients, had he not realized its limitations. Instead, he decided to veer toward the margins "to avoid being eaten up by the center."

There's an old garment center joke that goes like this: Moe, a coat manufacturer suffering from a steep decline in business, is so consumed by despair that he jumps from his twentieth-floor ledge. Plummeting to the ground, he chances to look into the window of his competitor a few floors below, and shouts up to his partner, "CUT VELVET!"

One does not have to be a coat-maker to know that the fashion industry is predicated on mimicry. What a hot designer originates today is invariably "knocked off" tomorrow. In fact, all mass-market, ready-to-wear manufacturers dutifully follow styles and colors that have been deemed au currant in the fashion press. Moe realized a tad too late that velvet was the next big fashion code.

Similarly, most mass-market product packages are graphically designed to conform to specific codes or "trade dress" established by leading companies and then copied by all others within that genre until the next big thing emerges. All cereal boxes look like cereal boxes; all pain relievers look like pain relievers; all laundry detergents look like laundry detergents, and all lottery tickets look like lottery tickets, because producers agree that Pavlov was right—dogs and consumers are behaviorally conditioned to respond to recurring stimuli. Woof, woof.

Therefore, major alterations to mass-market packages are as cautiously watched as Saddam's weapons of mass destruction, since new and novel tropes could easily disrupt consumers' mass buying habits. This means that we should not underestimate the power of graphic design and typography in moving the masses, yet it also underscores that originality is not always welcome in consumer culture.

Most consumer products are market-tested to the hilt before being released into the nation's malls. In the 1950s, the Container Corporation of America, duly celebrated for producing some of the most progressively modernist institutional advertising in the country, was also largely responsible for establishing some of the mass graphic codes still used today. Its researchers developed pseudo-scientific devices for testing an average consumer's ability to recognize packages at certain distances, identify and distinguish logos, and retain various visual impressions of a product's identity. One such invention was a shadow box that opened and closed at incremental speeds to test the time needed to hook a customer with a particular product image. Since this required considerable time and money, it was obvious to less enterprising companies that the cheaper route was to simply copy CCA's research rather than invest in its own. Widespread genre code mimicry started with the rationale that spending money on research and development was unnecessary when their product was already a knock-off, and those same dollars would be better spent promoting the brand instead.

Inventing a brand mythology is essential to the success of any product, which means a knock-off could easily be touted as an original through an effective ad campaign. Whether, for example, Tostitos, Chipitos, or Nachos* lead the current salsa chip marketing bonanza is really unimportant. Whoever and whichever company initially designed the colorful Mexican rectilinear motifs and stereotypical cha-cha-like lettering imprinted on the originator's bags probably understood that every other product in the genre would ultimately adopt the same look. Customers might ask for a brand by name, but are easily duped into buying whatever looks similar and familiar. Redundant design is a strategy that enables rivals to trespass on another's market share. Although promotion blitzes emphasize unique qualities of each chip, using common graphic characteristics on packages doubtless confuses most consumers at the point of sale.

Confusion is, therefore, one of the strategies for capturing buyers' hearts and minds.

Take another classic example: At most supermarket checkout counters, buyers are confronted with the confluence of gothic headlines in colored boxes and overprinting photographs of celebrities. The tabloid weeklies—the *Star,* the *Globe,* the *Examiner,* and *National Enquirer*—come off as a congealed blob of typefaces and imagery, and even their mastheads are ostensibly the same—set in gothic faces, either as white dropped out of red or red on white. Each periodical is also bathed in yellow, which on newsprint apparently has the same allure for *Homo sapiens* as bananas for monkeys. This sameness rests on the idea that while waiting on a supermarket line, customers in a weakened state don't really care which one or how many of these periodicals they buy—one is as good as the next and all are better than one.

---

*Actually, it was probably Fritos. Remember, the currently defunct Frito Bandito gave the corn chip the allure of Mexico.

Nonetheless, unique brands should theoretically maximize their uniqueness to corner their respective markets. But try telling that to the makers of all those pregnancy tests. About a year or two ago, a clever TV commercial for one of the leading tests showed a woman at home waiting for her test results; sitting next to her on the couch is presumably her husband, but he is actually a delivery boy whom she hugs profusely upon learning she is pregnant. Okay, so I don't remember the brand. (In fact, it wasn't an ad for a home pregnancy test at all, but for a dot-com delivery system.) The point is that it was more distinctive than the package itself, which follows rather lackluster conventions: white box with a red or pink airbrushed hue overall, with a photograph of two or more of the testing devices situated in the lower right-hand corner of the box. (Why they are all in the same place, I have no idea.) Eschewed are drawings or photos of babies, because the testing stick apparently has more allure. The logos for E.P.T., First Response, and Confirm are set in different typefaces, but the general "trade dress" takes generic to a new level of mediocre sameness.

If you're wondering, however, why babies are totally absent on a product devoted to making them, perhaps it is because the baby is a big "if" at this juncture and suggests false advertising—but it might also be because they appear in abundance on many leading brands of toilet tissue. Charmin, SoftPak, Quilted Northern, and Angel Soft packages all use different colors and typeface combinations, but each features an infant or toddler to suggest the quintessential softness of this essential product. Of course, there are dedicated wipes for babies (on which infants are also featured), but the heated battle for toilet tissue market share demands that these young combatants appear as an ersatz seal of approval—and anyone who has ever used the sandpaper-coarse Scott Tissue knows why a baby is not on that particular package.

One expects certain products like toothpaste, denture cream, and even preground coffee to have repetitive packaging tropes since they are sold in supermarkets, where competition demands they conform to the respective genres that people are used to. What's more, the huge amount of advertising dollars invested in promoting them efficiently impresses the brand name on the consumer, making the package design slightly less critical. Yet, a surprising but no less derivative product, is the common road atlas. Although sold in bookstores, where the time for browsing and contemplation is usually longer than in supermarkets, most atlases are imbued with the same fundamental properties. Sure, all atlases look the same anyway—a map is a map—yet the covers for different publishers, which could be more creatively designed, are all bathed in that supermarket tabloid yellow. Rand McNally apparently launched the yellow trend, and

Hagstrom, Arrow, and American Map have followed suit, perhaps to signal to the consumer that they are each as authoritative as the original. And this is also a key reason for institutional mimicry. Not only does an inferior product want to look as superior as the big guys, but even a distinctly good product that wants to cut into the market of the big guys must play by the leader's rules.

Nowhere is this more obvious than blue jeans design. Aside from the denim material, the single most familiar design characteristic on all popular brands is the leather belt-loop label with the brand's "branded" logo. Originally created by Levi's in the late nineteenth century, this piece of real or ersatz cowhide is such a common genre accessory that every manufacturer from Armani to Old Navy (and all the mid-range brands in between) wouldn't think of producing jeans excluding the identifying accoutrement. And customers are so used to this as endemic to the jeans gestalt that unless they are antisocial (and anti-branding) snobs, they would not buy a pair without the label.

So, what does the law say about this plethora of mimicry? Trademark infringement is frowned upon, while trade dress is accepted. For example, no other fast food restaurant can use McDonald's Golden Arches, yet another can refashion its red and orange color palette or secondary typefaces in ways that might be similar yet not the exact same as the original. (Even the name could be changed to McDoodle's, as long as it is well over six degrees of separation from the original.) In the land of free markets and mandatory competition, companies are allowed considerable leeway in how they conform to the trade dress of a particular genre. And this does not only apply to major mass-market goods; the more sophisticated or subtle design of so-called boutique products like specialty bottled waters and expensive packaged foods are continually impinged (but not infringed) upon. Although designers and design competitions celebrate originality, the fact is that many producers could care less. Indeed, how often have you heard a client say, "I want my product to look just like this one"? And, you know, it would make perfect sense to Moe.

IDENTITY

Edward ("Ted") McKnight Kauffer (1890–1954) was one of Europe's most prolific and influential advertising artists of the 1920s and 1930s, certainly as innovative as his more celebrated French counterpart, A. M. Cassandre. In England, where he lived and worked, Kauffer brought advertising art into the twentieth century, yet in America only a few knew of the Montana-born expatriate's achievements.

Kauffer was sent abroad at the behest of Professor Joseph McKnight (the young man's mentor from whom he took his middle name). If he had not gone he might never have become a poster artist and graphic designer, and if he had not been introduced to Ludwig Hohlwein's poster masterpieces in Munich and attended the Academie Moderne in Paris, his life would have taken a much different turn. Before crossing the Atlantic he stopped in Chicago where he was profoundly influenced by the Armory Show, the landmark exhibit that gave Americans their first exposure to the burgeoning European avant-garde—it had opened first in New York and then Chicago to critical, if not dismissive, reviews. Kauffer didn't know what to make of the unprecedented Picassos, Cézannes, Duchamps, and Matisses on view: "I didn't understand it. But I certainly couldn't dismiss it," he wrote some years later. Eventually, these paintings would inspire his own benchmark work entitled *Flight* (1916), which in 1919 was adapted as a poster for the London *Daily Herald* with the title *Soaring to Success! The Early Bird,* the first cubist advertising poster published in England.

The art capitals of Europe beckoned, but the clouds of war loomed, and in 1914 Kauffer became a refugee with just enough money in his pocket to return to America. Instead of sailing straight home, however, he discovered England, and with it a tranquillity he had not experienced in America. "I felt at home for the first time," he wrote. Kauffer volunteered to serve in the British army but was ineligible because he was an American citizen. Instead he did a variety of menial jobs while waiting for painting commissions to come along.

At this time Kauffer met John Hassall, a leading English poster artist, which led to a meeting with Frank Pick, the publicity manager for the London Underground Electric Railways. Pick was responsible for the most progressive advertising campaign and corporate identity program in England. He had the vision to both unify the Underground's graphic system and diversify its publicity, thus making it more efficient and appealing. He commissioned Edward Johnston to design an exclusive sans-serif typeface and logo for the Underground (both are still in use) as well as England's finest artists to design posters for its stations. Kauffer's first Underground posters, produced in late 1915, were landscapes rendered in gouache or poster paints advertising picturesque locales. These and his 140 subsequent Underground posters, spanning twenty-five years, evidence Kauffer's evolution towards modernism.

During his first year in England, Kauffer became a member of the London Group, a society of adventuresome painters who embraced cubism. He refused to abandon painting for his new advertising career, but rather questioned the growing schism between fine and applied art. "He could see no reason for conflict between good art work and good salesmanship," wrote Frank Zachary in *Portfolio* #1. In fact, he was dismayed by the inferior quality of English advertising compared to work being done on the continent. During the 1890s there had been a period in which the "art poster" flourished in England, exemplified by Pride and Nicholson (known as the Beggarstaff Brothers), yet this flicker of progressivism was soon snuffed out by nostalgic fashions. Although Kauffer's earliest posters were picturesque, they were hardly sentimental; he intuitively found the right balance between narrative and symbolic depiction in prefigurations of his later abstract images.

It is likely that Kauffer saw the first exhibit of the vorticists in 1916, and that this avant-garde movement of British futurists, who worshipped the machine, had an impact on his own work. *Flight*, in its minimalism and dynamism, echoed the vorticist's obsession with speed as a metaphor for the machine age. This is "Kauffer's major work," wrote Kauffer biographer Hayward Haworth-Booth, "[and] also the finest invention of his entire career." The image departed just enough from direct quotation of cubist form as to become the basis for a personal visual language. "He had a child-like wonder and admiration for nature," continued Haworth-Booth referring to how Kauffer based this image not on imagination, but his first-hand observation of birds in flight. However, *Flight* might not have become an icon of modern graphic design if Kauffer had not submitted it in 1919 to *Colour* magazine, which regularly featured a "Poster Page" where unpublished maquettes were reproduced free-of-charge as an inducement for businessmen and advertising agents to employ talented poster artists. The poster was seen as one means of helping England get back on a sound commercial footing after the war. *Flight* was bought by Francis Meynell, a respected English book publisher and printer who organized a poster campaign for the Labour newspaper, the *Daily Herald*. Meynell interpreted that the soaring birds represented hope, and Kauffer's novel design somehow suggested renewal after the bloody world war. The poster was hung everywhere, and soared its maker into the public eye. Kauffer soon received commissions to design campaigns for major English wine, clothing, publishing, automobile, and petroleum companies, most notably Shell Oil and Shell Mex.

Kauffer argued that nonrepresentational and geometrical pattern designs "can effect a sledge hammer blow if handled by a sensitive designer possessing a knowledge of the action of color on the average man or woman." He believed that the artist's job was to foster an appreciation of diverse visual stimuli that transcended the conventional marketing tricks. Nevertheless, even Kauffer had to lead clients by the hand: "In most cases it has not been possible to give me full freedom," he wrote, "and my clients have gone step by step rather than by leaps, but by this slow process we have argued and discussed each advance until our opposite points of view have reached a synthesis, and it is because of this mutual understanding that I confidently expect England to progress to international distinction, not because of myself but through the new talent that is making way in many directions. . . ." His own productivity is evidence that certain businessmen appreciated the communicative power of unconventional form, but even in such a receptive milieu (particularly when compared to American advertising) there were hostile critics who referred to Kauffer's abstract designs as "McKnightmares."

Despite these occasional barbs, critics realized that Kauffer made significant inroads in the applied arts, first in the application of cubist form, and then after 1923 when he realized that vorticism no longer offered viable commercial possibilities and he entered his so-called jazz style, in which he created colorful, *art moderne* interpretations of traditional form. In 1927 he took a three-day-a-week job at Crawfords, the largest advertising agency in England, which lasted two years and marked the end of his jazz style and the move towards modernist photomontage, influenced by German and Russian advertising of the time. Kauffer expanded on this revolutionary vocabulary, and in his own work he replaced diagonal with rectilinear layouts, crushed his type into parallelograms, used positive/negative lettering frequently, and most importantly took up the airbrush to achieve the streamlined effect that characterized his work of the 1930s. Kauffer was further involved with the popular new medium of photomurals, and developed the "space frame" to give an illusion of multiple vantage points on a single picture plane.

Kauffer was called the "Picasso of advertising design." Critic Anthony Blunt wrote: "Mr. McKnight Kauffer is an artist who makes one resent the division of the arts into major and minor." And in the introduction to the 1937 Museum of Modern Art exhibition catalog of Kauffer's posters, Aldous Huxley praised Kauffer's primary contribution to modern design: "Most advertising artists spend their time elaborating symbols that stand for something different from the commodity they are advertising. Soap and refrigerators, scent and automobiles, stockings, holiday resorts, sanitary plumbing . . . are advertised by means of representations of young females disporting themselves in opulent surroundings. Sex and money—these would seem to be the two main interests of civilized human beings. . . . McKnight Kauffer prefers the more difficult task of advertising products in terms of forms that are symbolic only of these particular products. Thus, forms symbolical of mechanical power are used to advertise powerful machines; forms symbolical of space, loneliness, and distance to advertise a holiday resort where prospects are wide and houses are few. . . . In this matter McKnight Kauffer reveals his affinity with all artists who have ever aimed at expressiveness through simplification, distortion, and transposition. . . ."

No longer are postage stamps staid icons of officialdom, they are outlets for exceptional design, striking imagery, hilarious wit, even biting satire. Yet no other form of graphic design is as sacrosanct or more indicative of a nation's character. With the exception of a national flag no other official design is more politicized. Postage stamps are more than mere currency, they are a nation's signboard. They commemorate the most important issues and events, and they are potent instruments for propaganda when they carry messages designed to influence, inspire, and move.

What appears on stamps is usually determined by committees. In the United States a citizens advisory panel comprising experts in various areas of popular culture, sports, and art advise the Postmaster General on what stamps to issue. Special interest groups are known to lobby as vociferously for stamp recognition as for congressional legislation. Stamps are the most widely recognized collectible, and in certain nations the field of stamp collecting is a major industry. The postal agencies of larger nations have become veritable stamp dealers either to supplement their national budgets or to subsidize their postal services. In countries where the postal service is privatized, such as the Netherlands, brisk sales can mean the difference between profit and loss.

Designing postage stamps is not easy. With the eyes of a nation focused on the result, these images are intensely scrutinized. When the Croatian artist Boris Bucan designed his nation's first air mail stamp he came under fire. Since this breakaway Yugoslav republic had very few commercial airplanes, he designed a stamp that showed a paper airplane against a blue sky. Although the stamp was published, his sarcasm went unappreciated by countrymen who petitioned for its recall. Conversely, there were few if any notes of displeasure when the Dutch designer Rick Vermullen, of Hard Werken Design in Rotterdam, designed a preprinted paid postcard for the

Royal PTT Nederlands on which he included a picture of himself in a comic pose. Vermullen was commissioned to design a stamp that somehow represented the users of such cards. After conducting research, he determined that ninety-five percent of preprinted postcards were used by sweepstakes players and contestants to enter quizzes and games. He therefore decided to show a quiz master (Mr. Vermullen himself) standing over a TV screen that projects the seventy-cent value of the stamp in large numerals. The seven is decked out like a crossword puzzle, while the zero is a dart board, representing a game of chance. The quiz master holds up two prizes: in one hand money and the other hand flowers. The image is printed outside of the formal stamp area, giving it the appearance of a coupon.

The Royal PTT Nederlands is one of the most progressive postal agencies. Back in the early 1930s its visionary director, Jean François Van Royen, commissioned avant-garde designers Piet Zwart and Paul Schuitema to create advertisements and stamps that transcended convention by employing their distinctive use of typofoto (collage and New Typography). Under Paul Hefting, art director of the art and design department, the PTT continues to push the limits of the postage stamp tradition in terms of marketing, management, and design. Since the PTT was privatized less than a decade ago, emphasis has been placed on increasing the amount of stamp sales by creating designs that people are compelled to buy for utilitarian and aesthetic reasons.

In addition to the conventional postage stamps, PTT encourages designers to take unique approaches to commemorative, cautionary, and information stamps. They lead the way in commissioning internationally known graphic artists to extend the boundaries. French designer and former principal of Grapus design collective Pierre Bernard designed a series of Red Cross stamps; British designer Neville Brody designed stamps for a national flower exhibition; Belgian cartoonist Ever Mullen designed a series of child welfare stamps; and American Robert Nakata of Studio Dumbar in Den Haag designed stamps commemorating 150 years of travel on the Dutch railways. Nakata's design is indicative of the creative license afforded by the PTT. To suggest the idea of travel, Nakata used the famous *Kiss* by Rodin to signify both arrival or farewell. To ground this metaphor behind the sculpture the roof of a railway station platform is visible.

To stimulate sales to collectors and users stamps must elicit intellectual or emotional responses. That distinctive stamps are designed annually indicates that the world's postal services understand that the public has tastes that can be served by stamps. That many of these are designed by inventive graphic designers proves that this art for the masses is by no means crass.

If modernism imposes coldness and sterility, as critics have argued, then Rudolph de Harak (b. 1924) must have done something wrong. A devout modernist, his work for public and private institutions has been uncompromisingly human. For proof take 127 John Street, a typically modern skyscraper in New York City's financial district. Before de Harak designed its entrance-level façade it exuded all the warmth of glass and steel on a winter's day. But with the installation of his three-story-high digital clock (composed of seventy-two square modules with numerals that light according to hour, minute, and second), the mysterious neon-illuminated tunnel leading to the lobby entrance, and the bright canvas-covered permanent scaffolds that serve as sun decks, 127 John Street was transformed from a modern edifice into a playground.

De Harak's innovative addition to the John Street building enlivened a faceless street; likewise his inspired exhibition designs for museums and expositions have transformed didactic displays into engaging environments. Dedicated to the efficient communication of information, he used detail the way a composer scores musical notes, creating melodies of sensation to underscore meaning. His exhibits were indeed symphonies that both enlightened and entertained. His exploded diesel engine, the centerpiece of the Cummins Engine Company Museum in Columbus, Indiana, in which virtually every nut and bolt of this complex machine was deconstructed in midair, was evidence of the designer's keen ability for extracting accessible information from even the most minute detail. And yet while his exhibition design explored the rational world, his graphic design uncovered the subconscious.

Although de Harak deliberately employed neutral typography to anchor his design, the hundreds of book jackets, record covers, and posters he created between the opening of his design office in 1952 and its closing in 1990, are evidence that throughout his career he expressed *emotion* through type and image. While not the raw expressionism of the most fashionable designers of the 1990s, de Harak employed abstract form ever so subtly to unlock alternative levels of perception. He related this practice to abstract expressionism, which in the early 1950s he wholeheartedly embraced, and while this may be difficult to see amid his orthodox, systematic design, the nearly four hundred McGraw-Hill paperbacks he designed in the early 1960s bring this relationship into clear focus. De Harak's rigid grid was, in fact, a tabula rasa on which both rational and eccentric imagery evoked ideas. The subjects of these books—philosophy, anthropology, psychology, and sociology, among them—offered de Harak a proving ground to test the limits of conceptual art and photography. At the same time he experimented with a variety of approaches inspired by dada, abstract expressionism, and, ultimately, op-art.

His on-the-job research helped push the design practice towards an art-based theory. With one eye on the international typographic style, the other was focused on pushing the bounds of letterform composition. Following in the tradition of poetic typography of the 1920s, de Harak imposed his own levels of legibility through experimentation with various forms of letter and word spacing.

He built his typographic scheme on Berthold's Akzidenz Grotesk from Berlin. This bold European typeface effectively anchored de Harak's design and gave him a neutral element against which to improvise with a growing image repertoire. His early experiments, including fifty covers done for Westminster records, were the basis for the decidedly modern book jackets that he designed for Meridian Press, New Directions, Holt Rinehart and Winston, and Doubleday. And all the approaches he developed during the late 1950s led to his opus, the McGraw-Hill paperback covers that became laboratories for his experiments with color, type, optical illusion, photography, and other techniques. More important, these covers would define his design for years to follow.

McGraw-Hill paperbacks were emblematic of 1960s design. At this time the international typographic style and American eclecticism were the two primary design methodologies at play in the United States. The former represented Bauhaus rationalism, the latter 1960s exuberance. De Harak was profoundly influenced by the exquisite simplicity of the great Swiss modernist Max Bill, but as an American he wanted to find a vehicle for reconciling these two conflicting sensibilities. Just as he resisted the hard-sell approach in advertising, he also rejected the eclectic trend to make typography too blatantly symbolic. "I never saw the need to put snowcaps on a letterform to suggest the cold," he offered as an example of the extreme case. Instead he worked with a limited number of typefaces, at first

Franklin Gothic and News Gothic, preferring it over Futura, then Akzidenz Grotesk, and ultimately Helvetica. De Harak believed that Helvetica gave him all the color, weight, and nuance he required to express a variety of themes and ideas.

The McGraw-Hill covers were pure visual communication. Since de Harak did not allow for anything extraneous, each element was fundamental. Yet as economical as the covers were, each was also a marriage of expressionistic or illusionistic imagery and systematic typography, the same repertoire of elements that de Harak would use in other graphic work where he was known for reducing the complex without lessening meaning.

| **Dylan** |
| Milton Glaser |
| |

Bob Dylan arrived in New York in January 1961 at the age of twenty-one. In five years he produced seven albums and came to symbolize a generation caught between the unprecedented consumer prosperity that followed World War II and the Cold War's chilling rhetoric of mutually assured destruction. The 1960s generation adopted Dylan, projecting onto him its collective hope and cynicism. On July 29, 1966, it was reported that while riding his motorcycle on the back roads in Woodstock, New York, the back wheel locked, and Bob Dylan was thrown over the handlebars and seriously injured. Rumors abounded. Some thought he was dead, and some thought it was a ruse to cover up a recovery from an overdose. Whatever the truth, the words and the music stopped.

After six months without any new Dylan material, Columbia Records was in a nervous panic. To fill the gap, Columbia unilaterally decided to issue a greatest hits album pieced together from previous album cuts. Creative director Bob Cato and art director John Berg had a dramatic, backlit photo by Roland Scherman of a closely cropped profile of Dylan playing the harmonica, his wild hair bathed in a corona of light. Dylan had previously rejected it as cover art. But because he was in breach of contract, Dylan could no longer control what his recording studio did.

It was further decided to include a free poster in each new greatest hits album. Columbia decided to use the Scherman photographic profile on the album cover, but needed someone to design the poster. The Scherman profile triggered Berg's memory of Milton Glaser's (b. 1929) playful and inventive silhouettes that captured the essence of gesture and content through minimal means.

The hallmark of Glaser's work was an aggressive mining of visual artifacts and archetypes from diverse and unexpected sources. In addition to silhouettes, Glaser was working with black-ink contour lines, creating flat shapes and enriching them with adhesive color films, echoing the simple iconography and directness of comic books. He was interested in Islamic miniatures and was intrigued by the psychedelia emerging from the West Coast. Long before postmodernism, Glaser understood that design is essentially a vernacular language, and he delighted in discovering obscure typographic forms. On a trip to Mexico City he was so captivated by the letterforms on a small advertisement for a tailor that he photographed the sign and returned home to invent the remainder of the alphabet, which became the typeface Baby Teeth.

When the request came from Berg to design the poster of Dylan along with a package of pictorial reference, including copies of the Scherman photograph, it didn't strike Glaser as anything extraordinary—and time was short. So he did what he was already doing, rather effortlessly and entirely intuitively.

First, the memory of a powerful icon surfaced, a self-portrait by Marcel Duchamp—a profile torn from a single piece of colored paper and placed on a black background. Dylan's hair became an inductive mélange of Persian-like forms. Dylan's name, executed in Glaser's own Baby Teeth typeface, rested in the bottom right corner of the poster, a warm brown against a black background, unusual in its subtlety. The geometric letterforms contrasted sharply with the mellifluous hair and sinuous profile. Glaser admitted to being consciously intrigued by the notion of opposites: the hard, reductive edge of Dylan's profile contrasts with the expressive nature of the hair; bright, whimsical color reverberates off the dense, solid black.

In the original sketch (his only sketch), Glaser positioned a harmonica in front of Dylan's mouth, as in Scherman's photograph. When Berg saw the sketch, Glaser recalled, he said "Simplify, simplify." What he meant was, "Get rid of the harmonica." Eliminating the harmonica created a white negative space nearly equal to the black silhouetted profile. This increased the visual vibration of the whole piece and focused more attention on the "coastline" of Dylan's profile. Glaser went directly to finish. Six million *Dylan* posters were printed and included in the album, making it the single most reproduced image Glaser ever created, aside from his I ♥ NY™ campaign.

NeXT

Paul Rand

It is difficult enough to invent a meaningful corporate logo, sign, or mark to express conventional business issues without having to depict the future as well. However, that is what was demanded of Paul Rand (1914–1996) when in 1988 he was commissioned to design a logo for NeXT, an educational computer company headed by Steven Jobs, the founder of Apple Computer Company. Although NeXT's new product was cast in secrecy, the corporate name alluded to its futuristic positioning—not simply a *new* computer, but the *next* wave of information processing for the educational market. With only a few clues, Rand was given a month to devise a logo that would embody as much symbolic power as the memory of a silicon chip.

Rand had made identity systems out of whole cloth many times before. He created time-honored marks for IBM, UPS, and ABC. In each he found the most identifiable graphic forms: stripes for IBM, a gift box atop a shield for UPS, the repetition of circles for the lowercase letters *abc*. Designing such charged—and lasting—logos is not magic, but it does take an acute understanding of the nature of perception and the ability to translate that into a visual form. "Logos are *aides de mémoire* that give you something to hook on to when you see it, and especially when you don't see it," explained Rand. And the problem with the word NeXT was that it was not depictable. "What are you going to show? A barber shop with somebody pointing, 'You're next'? It's simply not describable in typographic terms."

Graphic devices that represent the future, such as the arrow, were made meaningless by overuse, but the NeXT computer was contained in a black cube, which gave Rand the idea he needed. He decided to frame the word in a cube to evoke the product itself. However, at the time the logo was introduced to the public, the computer's shape and form were completely secret. "It was understandable only as a cube, nothing else," he explained. "But without that reference point, I would have had to devise something out of the blue." In fact, for Rand it was not so much a question of having a reference point as using that reference point. "The client mentioned the cube to me when I was given the problem, and I'm sure the other designers who worked on the logo must also have heard about it," Rand presumed.

The NeXT logo was successful in part because the cube was symbolically related to the product itself, but Rand insisted that the shape was only important in sparking the idea. "Some reference was made to it being like a child's block," he continued. "I really think that is one of its virtues and part of its charm. However, the logo is not designed to be charming, it is designed to identify."

Before the logo could do the job, however, Rand had to sell the mark to Jobs. For this he had a pronged strategy. The first was to present only one logo. This underscored his own confidence in the solution and deflected indecision on the part of the client. The second was to "speak" only through a presentation booklet that concisely explained the rationale and showed the applications of the logo. Jobs had seen all the timeworn futuristic clichés—arrows, clouds, lightning bolts—in the book. However, he was unprepared for Rand's twenty-page book, entitled "The Sign of the Next Generation of Computers *for Education . . .*"

From the beginning of this limited (fifty copies), Platonic document, Rand announced his premise: "What should a logo for NeXT look like?" he asked in text set in Caslon, which led into a concise narrative that condensed decades of communications history into ten minutes of reading time.

First he introduced the concept of type itself: "Choosing a typeface as the basis for the design of a logo is a convenient starting point. Here are two examples: Caslon and Bifur. Caslon is an alphabet designed as far back as 1725 by William Caslon. It appears to be a good choice because it is both elegant and bookish, qualities well suited for educational purposes. . . ." He described the nature of his faces, their quirks and virtues, and concluded by admitting, "Attributing certain magical qualities to particular typefaces is, however, largely a subjective matter."

Next he defused the client's need to sample a variety of typefaces: "One reason for looking at a number of possible typefaces is to satisfy one's curiosity. Another, and perhaps more meaningful one, is to study the relationship of different letter combinations, to look for visual analogies, and to try to elicit ideas that the design of a letter or group of letters might inspire." He offered some examples that were intended to pique the reader's interest, and offered this warning: "Personal preferences, prejudices, and stereotypes often dictate what a logo looks like, but it is *needs*, not wants, *ideas*, not type styles which determine what its form should be. . . ."

Then Rand took a representative typeface and set it in caps to explain why this particular iteration was unsuccessful: "Set in all capitals, the word NEXT is sometimes confused with EXIT, possibly because the EXT grouping is so dominant. A combination of capitals and lowercase letters alleviates this problem." And after winning the argument, he provided a textbook example of a more successful application: "Here are some possibilities which explore the use of lowercase letters. The *e* is differentiated so as to provide a focal point and visual contrast among the capital letters which, otherwise, consist only of straight lines. Happily the e also could stand for: education, excellence, expertise, exceptional, excitement, $e = mc^2$, etc."

This brief lesson in typographic style segued into an explanation of how a mark should function: "Ideally, a logo should explain or suggest the business it symbolizes, but this is rarely possible or even necessary. There is nothing about the IBM symbol, for example, that suggests computers, except what the viewer reads into it. Stripes are now associated with computers because the initials of a great computer company happen to be striped. . . ." And then he introduced the idea underlying his version of NeXT: "A logo takes on meaning, only if over a period of time it is linked to some product or service of a particular organization. What is essential is finding a meaningful device, some idea—preferably product-related—that reinforces the company name. The cube, in which the computer will be housed, can be such a device because it has visual impact, and is easy to remember. Unlike the word NEXT, it is depictable, possesses the *promise of meaning*, and the *pleasure of recognition*."

Understanding that questions would arise concerning the application of the cube, Rand talked about versatility: "This idea in no way restricts its application to any one product or concept. The three-dimensional effect functions as an underscore to attract the viewer's attention." Once established that the cube was the appropriate form, Rand addressed the basic structure of the logo: "Splitting the logo into two lines accomplishes several things: it startles the viewer and gives the word a new look, thus making it easier to separate from common usage. And even more importantly, it increases the letter size two-fold, within the framework of the cube. For small space use, a one line logo would have been too small to fit within this same framework." Rand showed that readability was not affected because the word was too simple to be misread. "Moreover, people have become accustomed to this format with such familiar four-letter word combinations as LOVE."

He concluded his primer with a down-to-earth analysis: "The adaptation of this device to miniaturization—tie tacks, charm bracelets, paper weights, stickers, and other promotional items is endless. It lends itself as well to large-scale interpretation—signs, exhibits in the shape of cubes, in which the actual exhibit is housed, as well as exhibit stands. For printed matter, its infinite adaptability and attention-compelling power is self-evident."

Upon presentation, Rand did not utter a word, he just sat silently watching as Jobs read. "The book itself was a big surprise," Jobs recalled. "I was convinced that each typographic example on the first few pages was the final logo. I was not quite sure what Paul was doing until I reached the end. And at that moment I knew we had the solution. . . . Rand gave us a jewel, which in retrospect seems so obvious." Moreover, as it turned out, Rand's user-friendly teaching aid underscored Jobs' own commitment to the process of education.

Dr. Strangelove

Pablo Ferro

As an attack on Cold-war hysteria, there was no more biting comedy than Stanley Kubrick's 1964 doomsday film, *Dr. Strangelove: Or How I Learned to Stop Worrying and Love the Bomb*, in which an overzealous U.S. general, Jack D. Ripper, launches an A-bomb attack against the USSR. This send-up of nightmare scenarios depicted in the nuclear dramas *Fail Safe* and *On the Beach* fiercely lampooned the era's hawkish fanaticism, suggesting that the world was close to the brink of the unthinkable.

The film's frightening absurdity is established in the very first frame of the main title sequence designed by Pablo Ferro. As the ballad "Try a Little Tenderness" plays in the background, a montage of B-52 bombers engage in midair coitus with their refueling ships, underscoring the subplot that sexuality is endemic to all human endeavor, especially the arms buildup. Surprinted on these frames, the film's title and credits are full-screen graffiti-like scrawls comprised of thick and thin hand-drawn letters, unlike any previous movie title. The sequence brilliantly satirizes the naïve pretense that America was protected from nuclear attack by oversexed flying sentries. It also contrasts beautifully with the film's concluding montage, edited by Ferro, which shows atomic bombs rhythmically detonated to the accompanying lyric, "We'll meet again, don't know where, don't know when. . . ."

This was not the first time that a movie title sequence added narrative dimension to a film. During the brief history of modern film titles, which began with Saul Bass's 1954 *Carmen Jones*, a handful of designers (among them, Maurice Binder, Steven Frankfurt, and Robert Brownjohn) established film identities by compressing complex details into signs, symbols, and metaphors. By the time that Ferro made his 1964 debut, the stage (or rather the screen) had already been set for ambitious artistry. Although the *Dr. Strangelove* titles were a distinct departure from Bass's animated, geometric forms in the German expressionist manner, they were consistent with the experimental film-within-a-film concept that gave title sequences momentary independence while serving the practical needs of a motion picture. Moreover, this film launched the long career of Pablo Ferro as title designer, trailer director, and feature filmmaker.

Yet, before he started designing film titles, the Cuban-born Ferro (b. 1935), who had emigrated to New York City when he was twelve years old—quickly becoming a huge film fan and aficionado of UPA cartoons—had earned a reputation for directing and editing scores of television commercials.

After graduating from Manhattan's High School of Industrial Art, Ferro began working at Atlas Comics in 1951 as an inker and artist in the EC-horror tradition. A year later he began learning the ropes as an animator of UPA-styled cartoons and worked for top commercial studios, including Academy Pictures, Elektra Films, and Bill Stern Studios (where, among other things, he animated Paul Rand's drawings for El Producto cigars). In 1961 he founded the creative production studio Ferro Mogubgub Schwartz (later changed to Ferro Mohammed Schwartz, Mohammed being a mythical partner invented only to retain the cadence of the studio name). As a consummate experimenter, Ferro introduced the kinetic quick-cut method of editing, whereby static images (including engravings, photographs, and pen and ink drawings) were infused with speed, motion, and sound.

In the late 1950s most live-action commercials were shot with one or two stationary cameras. Conversely, Ferro took full advantage of stop-motion technology as well as shooting his own jerky footage with a handheld Bolex. Unlike most TV commercial directors, Ferro maintained a strong appreciation and understanding for typography such that in the late 1950s he pioneered the use of moving type on the TV screen. He had a preference for using vintage woodtypes and Victorian gothics not only because they were popular at the time but because they were vivid on television. In 1961 he created an eclectic typographic film sequence for Jerome Robbins's stage play *Oh Dad, Poor Dad, Mamma's Hung You in the Closet and I'm Feeling So Sad,* an innovative approach that, similar to a film title sequence, preceded the opening curtain and announced the different acts within the performance.

After seeing Ferro's commercials, Kubrick hired him to direct the advertising trailers and teasers for *Dr. Strangelove* and convinced him to resettle in London (Kubrick's base of operations until he died there in March 1999). Ferro was inclined to be peripatetic anyway; ever anxious to bypass already-completed challenges, he agreed to pull up stakes on the chance that he would get to direct a few British TV commercials, which he did.

The black-and-white spot that Ferro designed for *Dr. Strangelove* employed his quick-cut technique—using as many as 125 separate images in a minute—to convey both the dark humor and the political immediacy of the film. At something akin to stroboscopic speed, words and images flew across the screen to the accompaniment of loud sound effects and snippets of ironic dialogue. At a time when the bomb loomed large in the fears of the American public (remember, Barry Goldwater ran for president promising to nuke China) and the polarization of left and right—East and West—was at its zenith, Ferro's commercial was not only the boldest and most hypnotic graphic on TV but also a sly, subversive statement.

Dr. Strangelove was key to Ferro's eventual shift from TV to film. And working with Kubrick was the best possible introduction to the movie industry, since this relationship allowed Ferro to bypass the stultifying Hollywood bureaucracy. Ferro was free to generate ideas, and Kubrick was sufficiently self-confident to accept (and sometimes refine) them. For example, once the sexual theme of the opening title sequence was decided upon, Kubrick wanted to film it all using small airplane models (doubtless prefiguring his classic spaceship ballet in *2001: A Space Odyssey*). Ferro dissuaded him and located the official stock footage that they used instead. Ferro further conceived the idea to fill the entire screen with lettering (which, incidentally, had never been done before), requiring the setting of credits at different sizes and weights, which potentially ran counter to legal contractual obligations. Kubrick supported it regardless. On the other hand, Ferro was prepared to have the titles refined by a lettering artist, but Kubrick correctly felt that the rough-hewn quality of the hand-drawn comp was more effective. So Ferro carefully lettered the entire thing himself with a thin pen. Yet only after the film was released did he notice that one term was misspelled: "base on" instead of "base*d* on." Oops! Incidentally, Kubrick insisted that Ferro take "front credit" rather than "back credit," a rare and significant movie industry protocol.

Ferro's work is not always immediately identifiable, although he has reprised his signature style from *Dr. Strangelove* a few times since 1964. *Stop Making Sense,* the Talking Heads concert film (1984), *The Addams Family: Family Values* (1993), and *Men in Black* (1997) all employ his distinctive hand lettering. But Ferro is less concerned with establishing a personal identity than he is with creating titles that support the movie they frame. Ferro defines each problem according to the ethos of the specific film; hence, titles for *The Thomas Crown Affair* (1968), with its quick cuts and innovative multiple-screen technique, or *Midnight Cowboy* (1969), with its lyrical narrative sequencing, are individual works born of the same vision and purpose—to introduce another artist's work.

In 1986 a chef named Florent Morlet opened an inexpensive French restaurant in New York City's unsavory meatpacking district. Without any investors and little capital, he rented a funky old luncheonette that had recently gone out of business. His intent was to remain unpretentious (and still appeal to an exclusive clientele), yet Restaurant Florent did require the basic promotional materials, such as menus, business cards, and a sign. For these graphics he hired M&Co., a New York firm known for experimental commercial art. Tibor Kalman (1949–1999), M&Co.'s creative director, suggested that Florent keep all the fixtures, furniture, utensils, and the sign that the previous greasy spoon had left behind. "Let the restaurant design itself," said Kalman.

The menu designed itself too. Kalman decided that to be consistent with the restaurant's overall ambiance the menu should look like a printer had thrown it together. He would have gone to a place where they print typical Greek coffee shop menus, "but we felt that the result wouldn't be quite as effective as what a job printer might do, because those other printers are imitating designed things," he explained. Instead the menu looks as though it had been pieced together in a few hours using random type from a letterpress type case. Nevertheless, it took two months to design. "If we weren't trained designers it would have taken less time," said Kalman. "The difference between something really wonderful and really horrible is very close."

M&Co. designed Florent's first announcement using a mundane exterior photograph of the restaurant (the kind used for common diner postcards). For the second they made an original design and printed it on a coarse chipboard paper stock. Kalman decided to illustrate the idea of a restaurant through little pictographs lifted straight from the Manhattan Yellow Pages. The result was a kind of rebus with a chair representing the restaurant, a truck representing the address, a gun representing New York

City, and an old Bell Telephone Company logo representing, well you know. "Our vocabulary was based on dumb, really obvious, generic images used for most commercial advertising," explained Kalman. But the goal was not nostalgia. In fact, Kalman insisted that the difference between nostalgia (or kitsch) and appropriation is ultimately how the finished product is filtered through the designer. Nuance is the key.

Early versions of advertisements for Florent employed quirky iconography, too. One showed a raw steak, another a simple salt shaker (both had the restaurant's name but no address or phone number). As Restaurant Florent's popularity increased additional funds were available for larger ads. M&Co. created a different ad every week, all orchestrated to create a distinct mythology. Inexpensive stock photos and studio shots of found objects conveyed a variety of ideas, the most emblematic of which was a common three-dimensional menu board left over from the greasy spoon days, complete with misspellings of the day's specials. Others showed arrows pointing to the shirt of a customer, humorously indicating what specials had been spilled that day, a parody of an ecological chart. The most fashionably design-conscious ad used words in the manner of dadaist typography of the 1920s to illustrate Florent's food and drink menu.

Many restaurants and businesses have consistent identity campaigns, but Restaurant Florent stands out for two reasons: it was a pioneering effort in vernacularization (the return to commonplace elements of commercial art), and it was a successful performance of various talents brought together as a repertory producing the equivalent of scripted and improvisational graphic design.

Walt Disney World in Orlando, Florida, is not a Mickey Mouse operation. It is as large as San Francisco and as diverse as New York's five boroughs. By comparison it reduces the original Disneyland in Anaheim, California, founded in 1955, to the status of mere amusement park. Disney World is the escapist capital of the world with attractions like the Magic Kingdom, a fantasy theme park modeled after Disneyland; Walt Disney Village and Pleasure Island, a mammoth resort and shopping mall; Epcot Center, a world's fair–scaled projection of the future; and UA/MGM Studio, a Hollywood movie set come to life. These realms are separated by large greenbelts and connected by a north-south axial highway and arterial road system, which like any interstate requires precise way-finding management. But precision is only one concern of Michael D. Eisner, Walt Disney Inc.'s chairman and chief executive officer.

Eisner's widely publicized strategy of growth brought with it a Medicean patronage of art and architecture. His commissions to postmodern architects Michael Graves, Frank Gehry, and Arata Isozaki reflected a commitment to the unique and unusual. Paul Goldberger, architecture critic of the *New York Times*, called Disney Inc. "a corporate patron like no other." Hence, the commission given to Sussman/Preja and Company—the creators of the carnival-modern graphics of the 1984 Los Angeles Summer Olympics—to design Disney World's road signs, buses, and gateways underscored Disney's commitment to distinctive design, down to the smallest detail.

In 1986 Eisner thrust Walt Disney Inc. into a developmental frenzy that included expansion of its film, publishing, and resort operations in the United States and Europe. Unlike most American cities of comparable size, where poor planning has ruined skylines and made ingress and egress confusing at best, Disney believed in coordinated development.

A responsibility for the total comfort of visitors, both in the attractions and on the roads, meant that as Disney World grew, a new environment that facilitated mobility and identified Disney World as an integral and accessible entity was needed.

"In the beginning our signage was like everywhere else in the country," said Eisner about their original "liver-colored" road signs that also serve as the National Park Service standard. But beyond his apparent preference for nonconformity, Eisner admitted, "I drove myself around Disney World but routinely got lost. If I couldn't find my way, who could?" The desire for a contemporary look, plus the development of new hotels and attractions were good enough reasons for Eisner's decision to change the entire system. But he also offered a more fundamental rationale: "When Walt Disney World was originally built, the Magic Kingdom was up at the extreme north of our property. I'm told that the [development group] felt that if they signed at the beginning of the property, kids would get so excited about going to the Magic Kingdom they'd be frustrated to find a fifteen minute drive ahead of them." With the new growth it no longer took fifteen minutes to get to a Disney attraction, making a uniform signage system not only more appealing but, in fact, quite necessary.

Based on their success with the graphics program for the 1984 Summer Olympics, Deborah Sussman (b. 1931) and Paul Preja (b. 1930) of Sussman/Preja and Company were invited to propose ideas. When they were awarded the commission, Wing Chao, senior vice president of planning, architecture, and engineering of Disney Development (the division administering to all areas other than the design of the thematic attractions) had one simple request: "I wanted their wildest ideas and craziest notions. They shouldn't hold anything back." Sussman was glad to oblige. "We showed them a hundred ideas for the one that got built, but that was part of the fun," she said.

Understanding how the signs could be more efficiently used was key to an effective design solution. Sussman took charge of the design team, Preja led the analytical phase, Scott Cuyler did much of the initial creative work, Robert Cordell was the in-house project manager for all Disney work, and Debra Valencia worked on the typography during the refinement stage. April Greiman, a frequent collaborator with Sussman/ Preja, consulted on various aspects of the signage. The design problem was also opened to other designers in their office.

At the outset the designers needed to be familiar with the rather complex layout of Disney World. "We didn't know what Epcot was," admitted Sussman. "Or that the Magic Kingdom was essentially the same as Disneyland. Or what Pleasure Island was and how it related to the

Magic Kingdom." Indeed most outsiders are also unaware that these diverse attractions fall under one umbrella. After their initial research was completed, Sussman issued a statement that became the blueprint for her vision. In it she said, "there is the world and then there is Disney World," suggesting the scope and limits of the problem.

The first planning decision was to simplify the signage requirements yet attend to every complex detail. "We decided to establish a series of discrete districts, similar to boroughs," Sussman said about the initial stage, "which affected how many of the previous signs we could effectively eliminate. Instead of having to erect a separate sign for every component of Disney World, we could group them into discrete categories that were headed by these districts. That, of course, affected things like size, typography, and nomenclature. Before this, every sign began with 'Walt Disney World,' followed by the name of the attraction and other pertinent information. It was like reading a long menu—by the time you get to the end you forget what the other entrées were. Similarly, by the time you've finished reading the road sign [if you can read it at all] what you probably remember is the heading. That indicates a tremendous amount of redundancy."

The new plan reduced the number of messages under the district name, which then was eliminated on the signs nearer to the attraction. A hierarchy of signs was established and designed accordingly; it included large highway signs, secondary message markers (like what frequency to turn the car radio to for Disney World's exclusive channel), off-highway directionals, and so on. The next step involved the three basic aesthetic components: color, typography, and form. "We agreed with the Disney people who felt that they had enough images in Disney World already," Sussman continued. "But we did, however, want to evoke the spirit of Disney. Our challenge was how to do it without imitating or, as Frank Gehry said 'co-opting, or being co-opted by' these famous Disney icons. Our answer was to look at the simplest vocabulary possible."

Sussman selected Univers type because of its numerous size and weight variations. As for color, "Mickey is black and white, plus red and yellow. Yet from these colors you can't make a whole signing system—at least we didn't think that we could," she said. Ultimately green was introduced, as well as purple for its playful spirit. As for form, Sussman played around with various cut-paper configurations, and Scott Cuyler devised the angular post used for some of the highway signs, which took on a kind of postmodern, or Disney Deco, flavor. But in the end it was Mickey's profound influence that made the difference. Without literally looking like Mickey Mouse, the addition of a black circle (in which directionals were placed) onto the otherwise rectangular signboards became an indispensable graphic signature. "It worked immediately," Sussman said about the simple yet brilliant composition. "And when we made the signs that had two circles, it was unmistakably Mickey."

The concept went to Eisner for final consideration, who, according to Sussman, said upon first glance "'If I had to make a decision today, I'd say yes.' But since this was a major commitment, he wanted to test it out while looking at some other ideas." Eisner loved the colors, and even suggested they be copyrighted so that no one else could use them. But he also wanted to know what else could make the signs "more Disney." An obvious suggestion was to put Mickey's hand in the black circle in place of the arrow. "We tried it out as a full scale, on-site sign," Sussman explained, "but we felt strongly that it didn't work. The hand just does not want to become an arrow." Since Eisner liked the idea, Sussman was a little worried that he would insist on going with it. "But," she said, "when we showed it to him he admitted that we were right." Another option was to use a silhouette of a Disney character or part of one sticking out of a diagonal sign for off-highway use. However, the feeling at Disney was that visitors would either steal them or stop to have their pictures taken next to them, which would ultimately impede the flow of traffic. In the end they decided on one special series of highway messages featuring Mickey on three sequential overhead signs spread over a few miles. The first showed two yellow gloved hands reaching over the sign, Kilroy style; in the second, two round black ears peeked up; and finally, in the third, Mickey's smiling face peered over.

Like an old Burma Shave sign, these teasers span Disney World's main highway. Elsewhere, other signs of all descriptions, even the commonplace markers indicating stop, yield, and speed, are set atop colorful stanchions and pylons that are not only efficient, but also playfully decorative. How have the signs fared with the public? "They have gotten good response," Eisner said proudly. "I don't know whether it's because people now know where they're going or that they really like the look." In creating an environment that reflects its time, communicates a purpose, and defines a corporation that since its inception has devoted itself to celebrating the imagination, Sussman/Preja joined other architects and designers who transformed Disney World into a festival of late twentieth-century design.

The revolution was already in full swing when, in the late 1950s, Paul Davis (b. 1938) entered the fray. Some renegade illustrators and art directors had already begun to revolt against the saccharine realism and sentimental concepts in most American magazines and advertising. Although Davis was not among this first wave, he was swept up by it. By the early 1960s he had developed a distinct visual style—a unique confluence of primitive and folk arts—that brought a fresh, American look to illustration. In a relatively short time he was among the most prolific of the new illustrators, and his style had a staggering impact on the field.

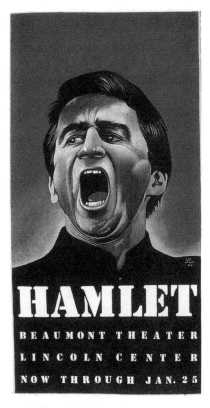

Davis developed an interest in American primitive painting and folk art as well as in the hand-lettered wooden signs that defined eighteenth- and nineteenth-century American commerce. "An artist of the caliber of [the nineteenth-century Pennsylvania primitive] Horace Pippin, whom I still think is one of the most undervalued American painters, was making honest observations of American life," he said about the search for a native culture. "The 1950s were a particularly nationalistic time, especially in the arts. People were talking about what is American. Europe was still the acknowledged leader in the arts, and many people did not believe that Americans even had a culture." In 1959 Jasper Johns showed his flag paintings for the first time. They were unmistakably American. Davis remembered going to the Whitney Museum biennial exhibitions where Larry Rivers and Robert Rauschenberg were shocking people with their new American visions.

One of Davis's many stylistic evolutions occurred between the late 1960s and early 1970s with a cover for the left-wing arts and politics journal *Evergreen*. He rendered a religious depiction of Cuban revolutionary Ernesto "Che" Guevara, whose exploits in South America had become mythologized by the American New Left. In this image Davis eschewed the Early American conceit for a synthesis of Italian religious art and socialist realism. "I was trying to make the image of a martyr," said Davis about this artifact of the era. "I didn't realize the potency of the symbol at the time. But when the cover and later the poster appeared, *Evergreen*'s offices were firebombed [by Cuban émigrés]."

With this image he began a formal shift from the stiffness and motionlessness of his primitives to a more photographic sensibility. "I tried to erase the traces of American primitive art because it was becoming a trap," he admitted. "I wanted to rid my work of all the elements that referred to other styles. And within a year or two after this, I had eliminated a lot of self-consciousness from my work." Soon Davis began to "depend more on the beauty of objects," and depicted scenes rather than ideas.

Davis's most significant contribution to American graphic design is his theater posters. His rendition of *Hamlet* and subsequent posters for Joseph Papp's New York Shakespeare Festival done during the mid-1970s challenged the conventions of contemporary theater advertising. First, they were not encumbered by the usual bank of "ego" copy. "Those early posters didn't say anything: No Joe Papp; No Shakespeare Festival; No actors. I didn't even sign them at first (and only self-consciously used my initials when I first began to do so). The only lettering was the title of the play and the name of the theater, though we realized later that it wouldn't hurt to mention that this was, in fact, a Shakespeare Festival production and began to include a logo." Second, without mimicking style, Davis's posters referred to the late nineteenth-century European tradition of poster art, which was ignored by contemporary posterists.

His Public Theater posters were stark, employing a central image with simple type either stenciled or silkscreened directly on the artwork (as he did on *Hamlet* in collaboration with art director Reinhold Schwenk) or seamlessly integrated into the composition (as with the *Three Penny Opera*). "The history of the Shakespeare Festival posters says a lot about the way the posters are used," he said. "I have often made comments in the posters about the way posters look on walls and in the environment in which they are hung. Many of my posters for the festival have had that self-conscious quality about being a poster." One example, *For Colored Girls Who Have Considered Suicide When the Rainbow Is Enuf*, showed the main figure with the title lettering scrawled on a tiled subway wall where, in fact, the poster was intended to be hung. The third, and final challenge to conventional theater posters was his basic methodology. Davis read the play, went to the rehearsals or readings, and talked to the actors and directors. "They seemed to think," he said, "that I was doing this revolutionary thing by actually reading the scripts."

Paula Scher (b. 1948) is not a native New Yorker, but she has acquired the self-assured, sarcastic, and abrupt elocutions of one. Scher believes that the best way to communicate to New Yorkers is to shout. "What better way to get a message across than for someone to yell something like 'I'm pregnant!' down a corridor; it's better than the Internet," she said. And this is exactly how she designs for The Public Theater. She shouts with type—boldly and unmistakably.

Scher's posters for The Public's 1995 season, only a component of a larger shouting campaign, have been included in virtually all the design annuals and shows, but one has to be a New Yorker (or at least from the environs) to truly appreciate the impact of The Public's language on the public. This is not the typically benign illustration sandwiched between layers of billing and flowery hyperbole. Rather, Scher's cacophony of disparate woodtypes, silhouetted photos, and bright, flat colors is more akin to the two-color rag bond or oak tag bills produced by job printers or run off at Kinko's to advertise circuses, county fairs, prize fights, and dance bands—the kind that are stapled and wheat pasted every time the New York sanitation authority's back is turned. Scher's scheme, inspired by today's street graphics and yesterday's Victorian playbills, was purposefully designed to appeal to a broad audience, from the inner city to the outer boroughs, especially those who have not been attracted to the theater before and for whom the typical "Broadway style" of advertising says exclusion.

Scher's street-based campaign supported the vision of The Public's creative director, George C. Wolfe, the director of such plays as *The Colored Museum*, *Angels in America*, and *Jelly's Last Jam*. After taking over in 1993, three years following the death of impresario Joseph Papp, The Public's director for more than twenty years, Wolfe has completely reshaped the institution—its season, staff, lobby, advertising, and mission—to be more inclusive of those persons and communities for whom theatergoing has not been an option. "I want to have the kind of plays in The Public where the whole building becomes a giant snapshot of where America is," he said in his rapid, syncopated cadence. Although Papp, who coined the name The Public Theater, welcomed the public during his significant tenure, and introduced a diversity of plays and playwrights, such as David Rabe, Caryl Churchill, Miguel Pinero, Ntozake Shange, David Mamet, and George C. Wolfe, the theater's traditional audience was still essentially what one critic described as "uptown white." Wolfe, on the other hand, wanted total inclusivity. "I want to take populist culture and elevate it, and bring elitist culture to a populist level," he stated with missionary zeal. So to change both the perception and the reality, as an adjunct to producing plays that addressed the experiences and lore of African-Americans, Hispanics, Asians, and gays, Wolfe dramatically changed The Public Theater's distinctive visual persona, which for twenty years had been based on Paul Davis's iconic painterly posters. "I was looking for someone who could give The Public an in-your-face unity," he continued. "I wanted something combustible and dynamic."

Scher's debut was somewhat of an improvisation. The day she learned that she and her Pentagram/New York team had been selected, she was also informed that Wolfe immediately needed to begin advertising The New York Shakespeare Festival, The Public's long-running, free summer performances of Shakespeare in Central Park. With little time, Scher had to create a coherent scheme that not only advertised the plays, but also signaled both the beginning of Wolfe's era and the Shakespeare Festival's relationship to the whole Public institution, comprising Central Park's Delacorte Theater, five separate theaters in The Public's headquarters in the old Jacob Astor Library, its Broadway productions, and additional public events, which, Wolfe explained, "were originally tied together by Papp's personality," but now required an organized system. Rather than ponder the virtues of one design scheme over another, Scher was forced to create what would become The Public's visual identity based on one of its many component parts. Nevertheless, she turned a necessity into a blessing. The idea to focus solely on typography as the organizing principle was a response to Wolfe's mandate to "cleanse the visual palate" and thereby eschew illustration entirely. Wolfe liked Scher's earlier Victorian- and constructivist-inspired compositions done in more or less appropriate contexts, but nothing could have been a better fit than this assignment; for here she could revive her favorite Victorian woodtypes—the ones that can be seen from a block or more away—on real playbills, posters, and billboards, not as mere pastiche, but as functional design elements.

The Shakespeare Festival graphics were based on a simple format. Key words like *free* and *live* were greatly enlarged, satisfying Wolfe's desire to address the public in a direct, no-nonsense manner, like sale signs in supermarket windows. Likewise, enlarged fragments of the titles of plays set in bold gothics, like the words *wives* for *The Merry Wives of Windsor* and *gents* for *Two Gentlemen of Verona*, drew attention to a linguistic mystery and provided a distinct contemporary identity that Evan Shapiro, director of marketing for The Public, said was like giving a news report rather than an ad spiel. "The approach is not complacent," he added, "it says we're here, come see us, or we're coming to get you." The typographic posters were placed on telephone stalls around New York, hung in commuter railroad stations in the environs, and on a few select billboards. They were intended to draw passersby into a visual game of deciphering the meaning of the words. If they missed on the first try, the ads were positioned close enough that on second glance the message was revealed. Flyers and handbills with this ersatz call-to-arms typography were also sniped around town in a blitz of paper promotion that is typically New York.

Language by its very nature is a communal thing, and Wolfe and Scher, who have their own personal shorthand, believed that the syncopated sounds formed by the truncated titles and phrases communicated through bold type, dark rules, and bright colors would develop into a conversation between the people of New York and The Public Theater.

The cornerstone of The Public persona was its logo, a combination of Scher's visual/linguistic elements that shouted the word *public,* which was spelled out in a sampling of black woodtype letters in weights ranging from heavy to light set against a white field; the words *The* and *Theater* are there, but subordinate to the dominant word/idea. In addition to the main logo, Scher designed round logos, or what Wolfe called "tokens" (The Public is built over the Astor Place subway station) for individual theaters. The next level in the hierarchy of communication were accordion-folded flyers that when completely unfolded (to a length of around two feet) revealed the entire season's programs in a typographic array reminiscent of Victorian theater bills, a sharp contrast to the usually quiet treatments of most mainstream theatrical subscription materials.

An exception to the pure typography rule were the posters for the individual plays, many of which included photographs—such as the emblematic silhouette of tapmaster Savion Glover on the poster for that tongue-twisting titled musical, *Bring in da Noise, Bring in da Funk,* which sandwiched him between a jumble of letterforms, somewhat akin to a wall of graffiti.

Wolfe wanted his posters to be like old LP album covers, and Scher, who designed albums for CBS Records in the 1970s, has certainly obliged by making them very graphic. But while most of her posters owe a spiritual debt to street graphics, they do not look like anything else on the street. One needs only to look at construction hoardings where sniped posters for *Blade to the Heart* and *The Diva Is Dismissed* were hung; both had the allure of untutored street graphics, but stood noticeably apart. The *Blade* poster, for example, featured an enlarged process-color photo of a boxer in a typical fighting stance with the large dots of the color plates knocked out of register in a pun on the punch drunk nature of the play's protagonist. The *Diva* poster showed the huge face of Jennifer Lewis, whose one-person show this was, with a kinetic propeller of type coming from her open mouth. The forms were somewhat vernacular, and therefore beckoned, but it was the subtle wit that gave them resonance and fostered memorability.

When the Philip Morris Company changed its corporate name in January 2003 to Altria, it introduced an abstract logo that is diametrically different from its former heraldic coat of arms, still used on its cigarette packages. Since big business is so reverent toward logos—especially venerated ones—to reinvent an entirely new corporate identity raises a flag, which is exactly what Philip Morris has done in its battle against negative public perception.

In fact, the new logo, a colorful mosaic grid conceived by Landor Associates, New York, looks incredibly similar to the 1994 "Earth Flag" by a Danish designer, Torben Skov, for a conference in Ostend, Belgium. It is also reminiscent, in concept though not form, to the post-apartheid South African flag, with clashing colors symbolizing the nation's diverse tribes. Likewise, Altria's luminescent grid represents Philip Morris's brand diversity, from its cigarette line (Marlboro, Virginia Slims, Benson & Hedges, Parliament, Chesterfield, English Ovals, L&M, and dozens of others in the U.S. and Europe) to Miller Brewing Co. and Kraft Foods (Cheez Whiz, Kool-Aid, Maxwell House, Oscar Mayer, Sanka, Tang, Velveeta, and more).

The logo is inspired (if one squints) by a display of varied packages. Nonetheless, compared to the imperial lions framing Philip Morris's original monogram, this contempo symbol is fairly generic and applicable to scores of different companies, which vividly shows how graphic abstraction can make even the most simplistic concept into a mark of authority.

And yet, Altria's logo is actually more similar to one of those vibrating pixelated distortions used on Court TV or *60 Minutes* to obliterate a witness's or whistle-blower's face than it is to a national flag. It is therefore designed more to camouflage than to illuminate, which is not surprising, since one of the jobs of CI (corporate identity) is to hide or remove stains from a questionable corporate image.

Ever since smoking was officially deemed hazardous and addictive by the Surgeon General, Philip Morris's tobacco divisions have cast long dark shadows over both its more benign product lines and its aggressive cultural philanthropy. According to *www.identityworks.com,* a Web site that reviews new CI programs, this switch from emphasizing Philip Morris's more negative possessions, regardless of how profitable, to its more acceptable corporate assets was overdue: "At long last, management accepted the obvious need to distinguish the corporate brand from its tobacco businesses." Or, as the official corporate literature opines: "The name 'Philip Morris' is truly a tobacco name—a name associated with a remarkable history as a leader in that industry, both in the United States and around the world. But we also have come to own a number of companies that are not tobacco-based . . . Altria Group will clarify its identity as what it is: a parent company to both tobacco and food companies that manages some of the world's most successful brands." As articulate as the above may be, and however naïve I may sound, something is still disturbing about an identity intended to conceal complicity in one of society's most dreaded health risks.

Incidentally, the name "Altria" derives from the Latin word *altus,* meaning "high," which the corporate literature states, "connotes an enterprise that aims for peak performance and constant improvement. Our goal is that, over time, the name also will reflect the seven attributes that we believe define who we are and how we grow our businesses: performance; marketing excellence applied by our consumer packaged goods companies; commitment to responsibility; financial strength; innovation; compliance and integrity; and dedication to people." So, reading between the lines, to distance itself from secondary smoke and other related issues, this corporation selected ecclesiastical Latin for repositioning itself, because it is both enigmatic *and* spiritual.

Many other corporations have likewise adopted Latin- or Greek-sounding names not only because they are attempting to concoct new mythologies for themselves, but also because everyday English words and names are becoming something of an endangered species. The diminishing pool of common identifiers that are available for use as trademarks is the result of two trends, according to Frank Martinez, a trademark and intellectual property lawyer: "First is the growing practice of filing applications to federally register a trademark based upon a bona fide intention to use the trademark sometime in the future. Corporations like to know that they own the right to use the proposed trademark prior to devoting valuable resources to building a brand."

The second reason grows directly out of the emphasis trademark law places on the "distinctiveness" of a trademark: "The made-up business name is considered 'fanciful' or 'arbitrary,' and is considered 'inherently distinctive' by the U.S. Patent and Trademark Office." As competition gets fiercer in a dwindling economy, Martinez predicts we should expect an increase in unusual business and product names, "since the success of a new product may be directly related to the novelty of its trademark."

This concept is not, however, a novel one. Almost a century ago Kodak was an invented "inherently distinctive" name, which still sounds and looks good today. But the problem with Altria is that its made-up-ness has a false ring. Today, there are myriad strained product and business names that start with "A" and end with "A," like Acura, Altima, Achieva, Adapta, and Accela. Or names like Maxima and Previa, which sound like Russell Crowe's buddies in the movie *Gladiator*. Then there are names like Consignia—a reinvented title for England's Royal Mail that was abandoned shortly after its introduction—which sounds like a medicine for stopping flatulence. It also turns out the Altria is not entirely original either. In 2002, a Denver venture capital firm called Altria Group LLC tried to legally enjoin Philip Morris from instituting the change, but lost its case because trademark law doesn't ban company names that sound alike unless the similar names would cause confusion among consumers.

Made-up names are not, however, a priori bad, notes Brian Collins, Senior Partner, Executive Creative Director of the Brand Integration Group at Ogilvy & Mather: "I truly hated Verizon at first. It sounded too desperate. But at some point, I started thinking the name was sorta okay—maybe even good." Of course, names get their real meaning from what they represent, and Verizon has become a successful brand (despite a clumsy logo now seen on countless phone booths and stalls) because it efficiently serves its clientele.

But back to Altria: Collins was originally suspicious of the Altria name, though he now says, "In all of the advertising work they've done to launch the new name, they've actually gone out of their way to say it represents the two divisions of the Phillip Morris Company. They are not really hiding behind anything, as Phillip Morris remains the name of their big flagship tobacco company, [which] they have made very clear." He further believes that the graphic identity is a memorable, fair representation of a giant company that is in several different businesses. "The logo is a distillation of the colors of their many, varied brands. I think the identity is beautiful and powerful—especially when it's animated."

Granted, the color grid is alluringly hypnotic when morphing on the computer screen, yet on the printed page it is just vague and clumsy, in large part because the Altria logotype is not integrated into the mark and sits untethered to one side, as if it were a typographic afterthought. When used on the four magazine advertisements, created by Leo Burnett USA that launched Altria—which feature pleasing, though enigmatic, color photographs of (respectively) a tree, a bridge, an architectural column, and a waterfall—the grid appears like a misplaced scrap of paper, something a designer or printer neglected to remove from the layout before sending it off to press.

But the copy on the print ads is not ambiguous. For example, the one with the tree reads, in part: "From these branches grow many brands each worth a billion dollars or more, like Marlboro, Nabisco, and Oscar Mayer. Along with hundreds of other household names such as Altoids, Parliament, Post, and Ritz." The cageyness of the ad is the nonchalant inclusion of cigarettes with lunchmeats and breath mints. Likewise, the logo blends the products together in one chromatic blur under the inscrutable name. The ads are not aimed at the general public, who certainly know the difference between butts and bologna, but rather at investors, who doubtless need to be encouraged to feel more comfortable about supporting a company that in addition to processed food markets hazardous and addictive products. During these times of raised health awareness, it is easier to feel ethically sanguine about earning dividends from something called Altria (which sounds curiously like "altruist") than something called Philip Morris. And that is the real inspiration behind the name and logo change.

INFORMATION

Before its transformation into a corporate theme park, New York's Times Square was the world's largest and gaudiest carnival midway. Replete with dazzling lights, boisterous barkers, and frightening freak shows, the Great White Way was a hugely popular attraction with a reputation that spanned the globe. Until the 1960s, Ripley's Believe It or Not! Museum was one of the most famous of Times Square's destinations. For displayed in a dark and cavernous dungeon one floor below street level on teaming

KLM ROYAL DUTCH AIRLINE
OFTEN TRANSPORTS ELEPHANTS - *AND ALWAYS*
SENDS ALONG A HEN *AS A CALMING INFLUENCE*

The University of Utrecht, after extensive studies, informed the airline that "Elephant Girl," the hen, which has occasionally laid an egg en route, has a decided calming effect on the elephant. She has accompanied over 30 elephants traveling to the U. S. by air.

Broadway, illuminated by faint colored spotlights, were myriad oddities guaranteed to raise hackles *and* tickle funny bones. Shrunken heads from Africa, human skulls pierced with hundreds of nails, stuffed vampire bats with demonic eyes, South American birds with multiple wings, and domestic canines with extra legs and tails were all splendiferously on view. The world's weirdest phenomena were presented with such sublime verisimilitude that the visitor could only believe it . . . or else.

Walt Disney discovered gold in Anaheim, California, in the early 1950s, but he was not the first to get rich through cartoon creation. During the 1940s, Robert Leroy Ripley gave his name to, and earned riches from, a chain of enticingly titled Odditoriums inspired by his popular cartoon, "Ripley's Believe It or Not!," a daily diet of odd and entertaining factoids (before that word was coined) which ran in hundreds of American newspapers, to the delight of millions.

Ripley had a lifelong passion for rooting out the bizarre and the grotesque, as well as the rare and the uncommon, which he discovered while on globetrotting expeditions that took him to 198 different countries and across a total of 585,000 miles in the course of forty years. Ripley was dubbed the "Modern-Day Marco Polo" by the Duke of Windsor. Unlike Mr. Polo, he recorded his findings in crayon using the common realistic cartoon style. But despite this tame presentation, Ripley's comic was decidedly surreal in its plumbing of the unusual. All irony was curiously suppressed as it tested the public's capacity to believe the incredible. And believe they did.

The cartoon was imbued with a distinct character, both from the lettering and from the drawing styles. Moreover, Ripley's signature, while typical of the way contemporary cartoonists signed their works, was a powerful brand: The flourish or end-line after the "Y" gave it a particularly witty look. The "logo" for Believe It or Not!, reminiscent of the typeface Cooper Bold with a shadow, was an unmistakable identifying mark as well. Real type was never used for body text—only a somewhat crude, speedball hand-lettering. And the drawings, done in pen and ink and grease crayon, were also somewhat primitive. Nonetheless, the overall graphic impact was impeccable. Together, all the elements got the message across and gave the work a singular personality. Had the cartoon looked any different—had the overpoweringly garish red been a soothing yellow—it might not have succeeded as it did.

A self-taught artist, Ripley sold his first drawing in 1907 to the American humor magazine *Life* when he was only fourteen. Nonetheless, he was a natural-born athlete who dreamed of pitching in Major League baseball. A freak injury during his first professional game brought an end to his career, so he quickly turned to cartooning for his livelihood and landed a job as a sports cartoonist for the *San Francisco Chronicle*. Ever peripatetic, he moved to New York, where he worked on the sports desk of the *New York Globe*. In 1918, while drawing sports cartoons, he created a feature called "Champs and Chumps," a comic sampler of individual athletic highs and lows and odd sporting feats. His editor, however, rejected the title as too limiting, and ultimately Ripley settled for the more encompassing "Believe It or Not!" The cartoon was such an overnight sensation that soon after its debut, he decided to expand the scope. The cartoon ultimately developed into a regular radio show on which he would regale his audience with exotic discoveries and fantastic claims. Eventually, Ripley turned to television.

Ripley reveled in oddities and lived the life of an eccentric. A millionaire a few times over, he filled his houses and apartment with artifacts from Europe, Asia, and South America. A colleague once said "the most curious object in the collection is probably Mr. Ripley himself." Among his many quirks, he is said to have drawn his comic strips, while holding them upside-down; he did so every morning without fail. He dressed in the brightest colors and most sensational patterns, and wore bat-wing ties and two-toned spat shoes. He collected automobiles as though they were toys, but never learned to drive. Even though he often used complicated recording equipment for his broadcasts, apparently he was afraid to use a telephone for fear he would be electrocuted. A non-swimmer, he owned an odd assortment of boats, including dugout canoes and even an authentic Chinese sailing junk. Such were the rewards of cartooning that many others were inspired to seek riches plying the same trade.

Believe It or Not! became such a common household phrase that its potential as an advertising tool was well exploited. The tremendous amassed backlog of cartoons was licensed for virtually any promotional use. For a modest fee, Ripley's unmistakably recognizable graphics were frequently used to represent everything from auto parts manufacturers to coffee shops.

Ripley's Believe It or Not! is an American cultural icon that has been exported around the world. Although the cartoon has ceased, the museums and Odditoriums continue to draw in crowds in the United States in Florida, Texas, and Missouri, as well as in Juarez, Mexico; Queensland, Australia; Lancester, England; Kyonggi-do, Korea; Chonburi, Thailand; and others. Today, Ripley's is quaint given how the media offers exposure to the weird and the ridiculous, but where else can one learn about "The Island Made of Soap," "The Hardest Working Stenographers in the World," or "The Accidental Soap Bubble by which Ibn Al Haitam of Iraq Discovered the Science of Optics"?

Catalog Design Progress

Ladislav Sutnar

Even before the advent of the "information age" there was information. Masses of it begging to be organized into accessible and retrievable packages. In the 1930s American industry made an initial attempt to introduce strict design systems to business, but the Great Depression demanded that the focus be on retooling factories and improving products, which spawned a new breed of professional: the industrial designer. In Europe the prototypical industrial designer had already established himself, and the graphic design arm of the modern movement was already concerned with access to information as a function of making the world a better place. The mission to modernize antiquated aspects of European life led directly to efficient communications expressed through typographic purity. This revolutionary approach to design began simultaneously in Germany, Russia, and Holland, and swept through Eastern Europe as well. Ladislav Sutnar (1897–1976), a graphic, product, and exhibition designer, led the charge in Czechoslovakia years before emigrating to the United States.

Sutnar was such an enthusiastic propagandist for industrialization that he was introduced to Karl Lönberg-Holm, the publicity director of the Sweet's Catalog Service, the largest American industrial catalog publisher, who instantly arranged for Sutnar to become his art director. Löndberg-Holm quickly became the other half of Sutnar's brain. Their collaboration was to information design what Gilbert and Sullivan were to light opera or Rogers and Hammerstein were to the Broadway musical. Together they composed and wrote *Catalog Design* (1944) and *Catalog Design Progress* (1950). The former introduced a variety of radical systematic departures in catalog design, the latter fine-tuned those models to show how complex information could be organized and, most importantly, retrieved. More than forty years after its publication, *Catalog Design Progress* is still an archetype for functional design. Sweet's Catalog Service was a facilitator for countless, disparate trade and manufacturing publications that were collected in huge binders and distributed to businesses throughout the United States. Before Sutnar began its major redesign around 1941, the only organizing device was the overall binding, otherwise chaos reigned. Lönberg-Holm had convinced his boss, Chauncey Williams, the president of F. W. Dodge, to order an entire reevaluation from logo (which Sutnar transformed from a nineteenth-century swashed word, *Sweets,* to a bold *S* dropped out of a black circle), to the fundamental structure of the binder (including the introduction of tabular aids), to the redesign of individual catalogs (some of which were designed by Sutnar's in-house art department).

Sutnar was one of the first designers to design double spreads rather than single pages, an aspect of his methodology that is so common today that in retrospect the fact that it was an innovation could easily be overlooked. A casual perusal of Sutnar's designs for everything from catalogs to brochures from 1941 on, with the exception of covers, reveals a preponderance of spreads on which his signature navigational devices force the users to follow logically contiguous levels of information. Through these spreads Sutnar was able to harness certain avant-garde principles and therefore injected visual excitement into even the most routine material without impinging upon accessibility. While his basic structure was decidedly rational, his juxtapositions, scale, and color were rooted in abstraction. Underlying Sutnar's modern mission was the desire to introduce aesthetics into, say, a plumber's life.

The Medium is the Massage by Marshall McLuhan and Quentin Fiore (b. 1920) is the touchstone of media lore and doctrine from the 1960s. It was required reading for everyone concerned with what McLuhan dubbed the "electric age," or how technology in general, and new communications media specifically, would alter people's lives. McLuhan was a philosopher and prognosticator whose books *The Mechanical Bride*, *The Gutenberg Galaxy: The Making of Typographic Man*, and *Understanding Media: The Extensions of Man*, explored the evolution of technology and its effects on the way mankind thinks, acts, and reacts. He was revered by some, attacked by others. Critics called him a fake, charlatan, and savant, arguing that his ideas were simplistic, obtuse, and contradictory. McLuhan countered that contradiction was endemic to contemporary life; contradiction was the metaphor for television, a medium that allowed a person to ponder two or more ideas at one time.

McLuhan believed that the invention of printing had shattered community by destroying the oral tradition. He argued that writing and reading were solitary acts that conflicted with tribal unity, memory, and imagination. Electronic media, television mostly, was destined to return us to a global village, allowing individuals once again to take an active role in the communications process. Media were extensions of human activity (e.g., the wheel was an extension of the foot). Television, he insisted, would allow for greater individual participation.

Was this genius or hocus-pocus? Critic Marvin Kitman referred to this book as "The Tedium is the Message." Indeed *The Medium is the Massage*'s contents by McLuhan and graphics by Fiore came under harsh criticism. But this should not eclipse the historic nature of Fiore's work.

The Medium is the Massage (the title comes from mass-age, a double-entendre used to underscore McLuhan's notion that media are so pervasive that they work people over like a masseuse) was the first book for the television age. *New York Times* critic Eliot Freemont Smith wrote that the large format of the hardcover took on "the aspect of a TV screen." Fiore, who initiated the project with the help of Jerome Agel, a book packager, designed it as a kinetically flowing collection of word bites and iconic images set in economical (Helvetica) type. He underscored McLuhan's ideas with what might be called a series of literary billboards—double-page spreads with large call-outs and blurbs. McLuhan described them (perhaps sarcastically) as "collide-oscopic interfaced situations."

    The Massage heralded a number of firsts: the first time that a paperback preceded the hardcover version into the marketplace; the first time such cinematic visual pacing was applied to American book design; the first book coordinated by a "producer," Jerome Agel, who takes credit for orchestrating its "sound and music." And although not a first, most important, was the close conceptual relationship between the designer and writer—like those of Lazar El Lissitzky and Vladimir Mayakovsky, John Heartfield and Kurt Tucholsky, Guylas Williams and Robert Benchley. Although the collaborators were not in constant contact during the creation of the book, Fiore was in tune with McLuhan's thinking so that the concrete presentation of McLuhan's often complex (and contradictory) ideas was made accessible.

    Fiore was born in New York in 1920. He had been a student of George Grosz at the Art Students League and of Hans Hoffman at the Hoffman School. He was a devotee of classical drawing, papermaking, and lettering and began his career before World War II as a letterer for graphic designer Lester Beall (for whom he designed many of the modern display letters used in ads and brochures before modern typefaces were available in the United States) and for Condé Nast, *Life,* and other magazines (where he hand-lettered headlines for editorial and advertising pages). He left lettering to become a graphic designer, and for many years designed all the printed matter for the Ford Foundation in a modern but not rigid style. Since he was interested in the clear presentation of information, he was well suited as a design consultant to various university presses, and later to Bell Laboratories (for whom he designed the numbers for one of Henry Dryfuss's rotary dials). In the late 1960s he also worked on Homefax, an early telephone facsimile machine developed (but never marketed) at RCA/ NBC, where he coordinated an early electronic newspaper.

    Fiore predicted the widespread use of computer-generated design, talking computers, and home fax and photocopy technologies. He also predicted the applications of the computer in primary school education long before its widespread use, and accordingly in 1968 he designed two hundred computer-like "interactive" books for school children to help increase literacy skills. McLuhan's philosophy was a logical extension of Fiore's own practice.

The second coproduction with McLuhan was, by Fiore's own admission, less successful than *The Massage*. *War and Peace in the Global Village: An Inventory of Some of the Current Spastic Situations that Could Be Eliminated with More Feedforward* was assailed by one critic as a crankish, repetitive, and disjointed tome in which McLuhan's puns had become a nervous tic. McLuhan based his book on the bewildering idea that war is a result of the anxiety aroused when changing metaphors in perception fail to yield up familiar self-images. Fiore's design was a mosaic of disparate imagery and text, which struggled with little success to reign in McLuhan's humorless meanderings. Fiore next worked on a book with Buckminster Fuller, entitled *I Am a Verb*, which could be read from front to back and back to front. Each is emblematic of the times.

Jerry Rubin's *Do It!* was also designed in the manner of *The Medium is the Massage*. Although universally panned by the critics, it became a bible of the 1960s. Fiore worked directly with the former yippie leader, typographically emphasizing certain ideas in a manner vaguely reminiscent of the dadaists and futurists. Photographs were also used as icons and exclamation points and strewn through the text to add sight and sound to an idea or pronouncement. Fiore was as anarchic as possible while still working within the constraints of bookmaking. His design was ahead of its time, but he believed that the methods he adopted were simply the most appropriate ways to convey the information. "They were just jobs, each requiring special treatment," he said.

At the end of a meeting in the early 1990s where Vignelli and Associates presented a comprehensive redesign of the subway train interiors for the New York Transit System, one of the members of the selection committee asked, "Mrs. Vignelli, you once said in your book [*Design: Vignelli*] that it is not pleasant to work with the Transit Authority. Why do you want to be involved in a project like this again?" Without hesitating Lella Vignelli responded, "Because we are socially responsible." The unpleasantness referred to was the design of the New York City subway map in 1970, one of Vignelli and Associates' most well-known and difficult achievements.

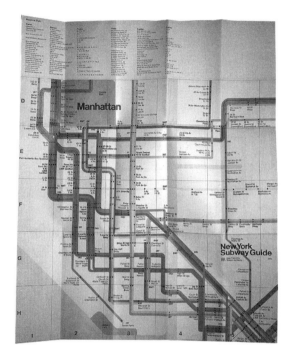

In 1965 Massimo Vignelli (b. 1931) moved to the United States from Italy and cofounded Unimark with Bob Noorda, a Dutch graphic designer and former art director at Pirelli in Milan. In the early 1960s Noorda designed informational graphics for the Milan subway system, which helped Unimark get the job to create signage for the New York Subway in 1966, and which later led to designing the map.

Vignelli's training as an architect in Italy in the mid-1950s and his study with the Swiss graphic designer Max Huber made him a veteran of the grid. In those early years Vignelli also began a long-lasting friendship with Umberto Eco, author of *The Name of the Rose*, and one of the top semioticians in the world. "We were analyzing everything according to a semiotic grid. It was just natural for us, like the ABCs." Semiotics is the study of symbology, the notion that every sign (word, letter, image, number, etc.) is arbitrary and has meaning only when it represents an idea or thing. Vignelli sees the semiotic grid as a relationship between semantics (the meaning of the information), syntactics (its visual representation), and pragmatics (the effect of the sign on the receiver). It's a closed-loop system to make sure a design clearly and consistently represents the proper message and that the audience receives that message as intended.

For Vignelli the semiotic grid is the *sine qua non* of communication design and the perfect tool to untangle the jumble the subway system had become by the 1960s. The IRT, BMT, and IND had grown sporadically into 714 miles of track with some 465 stations. The signage project began with an analysis of the traffic flow to identify points of decision and levels of information. From that, Vignelli devised a modular system of signs each designed as individual units, like the letters of an alphabet, which were then hung together to form informational sentences. Mathematical precision and rationality informed every part of the system from the prefabricated signs in lengths of one, two, four, or eight feet, to the typography that was similarly modulated with the smallest type on the informational panels one-half the size of the type on the directional panels, and that one-half the size of the typography on the station identification signs.

Vignelli wanted to hang the signs from thick black support bars that he believed would unify the information. This echoed his earlier work for the Piccolo Teatro (1964) in Milan, a poster that featured his signature style of tightly spaced sans-serif typography and introduced the concept of "information bands," information separated by wide black rules, which became characteristic of his designs in the following years. The Transit Authority never installed the black support bars, but rather painted black bars across the tops of the panels.

In 1971 Massimo Vignelli left Unimark and with his wife Lella established Vignelli and Associates and Vignelli Designs in New York. Lella was named president of Vignelli Designs, the branch of the firm responsible for product and furniture design. Vignelli and Associates was commissioned to design a map for the subway system that would untangle the web of train lines on the existing one. Vignelli had initially envisioned an interrelated system of maps: an overall system map, a geographic map indicating the relationship of the subway to the geography, a detailed neighborhood map to re-orient the traveler upon arrival at a new destination, a pocket map, and what Vignelli called a "verbal map"— intended for the main stations that featured written directions from point *A* to point *B* in language that Mama would use, "Take train #6 to 59th Street, transfer to train RR and get off at Times Square." Pointing out that 50 percent of the population is verbally oriented and 50 percent is visually oriented, Vignelli's verbal map directly addressed the needs of the public. Although one was implemented in Grand Central Station, the verbal maps were shelved, along with the neighborhood and geographic maps, victims of budgets and bureaucracy.

But the overall system map and the pocket map survived. Researching and learning from previous underground system maps, like Beck's London Underground map, Vignelli, too, organized his subway map on a grid, orienting the "spaghetti work" of the railways to the verticals, horizontals and forty-five-degree angles of the page. Each line had a different color, bright primary colors, and either a number or letter designation appearing at the beginning, at the end, and at intervals along the route. Every station was listed. Every stop had a dot. A dot on the line indicated the train stopped at that station. No dot, no stop. The web of lines dominated the background of white abstracted land masses, with the surrounding waters a mid-range gray, and parks designated with geometric forms in a darker shade of gray. The map was distorted, with the central, more congested areas larger and the outlying areas truncated. Vignelli used layering, separation, and color to differentiate the planes of information. This system of representation clarified what was important to the traveler: how to go from point A to point B. The map bypassed the literal and focused on the relationships inherent in the information and at the same time exemplified the essence of orthodox modernist principles.

Soon after the system map was put into effect, the official at the Transit Authority who originally commissioned Vignelli and Associates retired. His replacement called for a new map. He criticized the Vignelli map for lacking reference to the natural geography: the water was not blue, the parks were not green. Vigorous campaigning to retain the award-winning map eventually failed to convince this new official who, as Vignelli described, "had the knife by the handle." The map was replaced in 1979.

ICONOGRAPHY

Few symbols have had as much impact on humankind as the swastika. No other known symbol in the primitive or civilized world is as old; scholars argue that it predates the Egyptian ankh (the symbol for "life"). No other mark has turned up in so many distant and different cultures, suggesting an enormous migration or diaspora of peoples joined by a common belief or understanding. Yet no symbol in recent memory elicits such fear and loathing while at the same

time such reverence and respect. Arguably not even the Latin (or Christian) cross exerts as much raw emotional power throughout the world today.

This hooked cross, also referred to as a sun-wheel, which gets its name from the Sanskrit word *svastika*, meaning "well being," "good fortune," and "luck," and resembles the Indian mystic figure *svastikaya*, a "sign of benediction," was adopted by Adolf Hitler in the summer of 1920 as the emblem of the nascent National Socialist Workers Party (the Nazis). Refashioned by Hitler to maximize its inherent graphic power, the *Haken-kreuz* (the German word for hooked cross), emblazoned on armbands and flags, represented this nationalistic political and social movement. From that moment, this venerable symbol was forever associated with the most heinous crimes perpetrated by man.

"The fact that an ignominious fanatic placed a swastika on his battle flag is insufficient reason for ignoring this symbol's historic significance," wrote Henry Dreyfuss in *Symbol Sourcebook: An Authoritative Guide to International Graphic Symbols*. He suggested that the swastika must not be totally rejected because it was co-opted by a madman and embraced by a blind nation. Indeed, the swastika has not entirely lost all of its former mystic significance. It is still employed in rituals in some Eastern and Far Eastern cultures. But more important, as the single most charged symbol of the twentieth century its history should not be overlooked by designers who can learn valuable lessons from how and why it was used.

Before 1920 the swastika's symbolism was convoluted, but was at all times benign. Even in the United States it was indigenous to cave dwellers—one was found in the excavation of a prehistoric tomb in what is now Ohio. During the nineteenth century certain native American tribes embroidered the mark on blankets and ceremonial attire, and decorated pottery and ceramics with it. It was adopted as a ubiquitous design motif and was still in currency until a few years after the Nazis came to power in Germany in 1933. The swastika as a good luck symbol was adopted by American merchants and manufacturers on packaging, wrappers, and in advertising. It was frequently used as an architectural ornament, and was also popular as an ornament or border in prewar typeface books. The swastika was as common a graphic design motif in the 1920s and 1930s as the lozenge, leader dot, and sawtooth rule are in contemporary design.

Hitler was a wannabe architect, painter, and dabbler in commercial arts, but as leader of his movement he was the quintessential art director too. His understanding of symbolism, propaganda, and design is clear upon reading excerpts from *Mein Kampf* ("my struggle"), in which—though it was written in stupifyingly formal prose replete with euphemisms and epithets that enforce his own self-styled heroism—he convincingly argued the need for a powerful symbol/emblem/logo for his nascent party. "The lack of such symbols," he wrote, "had not only disadvantages for the moment, but it was unbearable for the future. The disadvantages were above all that the party members lacked every outward sign of their belonging together, while for the future it was unbearable to lack an emblem that had the character of a symbol of the movement and that as such could be put up in opposition to the communists." Hitler recalled the first time he witnessed a large communist party rally, where he saw a sea of red on flags, scarves, and flowers among the one hundred thousand in attendance. "I personally could feel and understand how easily a man of the people succumbs to the suggestive charm of such a grand and massive spectacle," he wrote.

It is uncertain who actually suggested that the swastika be adopted by the Nazis—Hitler likes to take the credit—but its redesign as the party emblem and flag are documented fairly well in *Mein Kampf*: "Suggestions were made from all sides which, however, were better meant than they were successful," wrote Hitler. "For the new flag had to be as much a symbol of our own fight as, on the other hand, it had to have an effect as great as that of a poster. . . . In hundreds of thousands of cases, an effective emblem can give the first impetus for the interest in a movement." Hitler's brief color analysis in *Mein Kampf* read like a term paper on semiotics: "White is not a color that carries people away. It is suitable for associations of chaste virgins, but not for the overpowering movement of a revolutionary time. . . . [Black] is also not thrilling enough. . . . White and blue was out of the question, despite the wonderful effect from the aesthetic point of view, as the color of a German individual state and of a political orientation directed at particularistic narrow-mindedness that did not enjoy the best of reputations. . . . [Black, white, and red] this color composition . . . is the most resplendent harmony that exists."

Hitler was never satisfied with the results of his open competition to design the flag, in which all party members were invited to take part: "I had to reject, without exception, the numerous designs that in those days were handed in by circles of the young movement and that mostly had placed the swastika on the old flag. I myself—as leader—did not want to come forth immediately with my own sketch, as it was quite possible that someone else would produce one that was just as good or even better." In fact, according to Nazi lore the form that the party adopted was ostensibly designed by Dr. Friedrich Krohn, a dentist from Starnberg whom Hitler never acknowledged by name in *Mein Kampf*, but about whose design he wrote, "[it] was not bad at all, and besides that approached my own design very closely, except that it had the mistake that the swastika was composed in a white circle with curved hooks. Meanwhile, I myself, after innumerable attempts, had put down a final form: a flag with a background of red, with a white circle, and in its center, a black swastika. And this then was kept."

Although Hitler gave credit to a Munich goldsmith, Herr Füss, for designing the party's badge (similar in design to the flag) he neglected to credit Wilhelm Deffke, a leading German logo and trademark designer for having refined and stylized a version of the swastika before 1920. According to a former assistant, Deffke was branded a "cultural bolshevist" by the Nazis, but in a recent biographical note on her employer she wrote: "Deffke came across a representation of the ancient Germanic sun-wheel on which he worked to redefine and stylize its shape. Later this symbol appeared in a brochure which he had published, [the Nazis] chose it as their symbol but reversed it. . . . Needless to say, this was done without any thought of copyright or compensation to the 'cultural Bolshevist.' In September 1935, this symbol was incorporated into the Third Reich's flag. It is ironic that the design chosen for the national emblem and the ruling party was rediscovered and refined by a man whom the regime later persecuted. . . ."

The swastika would not have been adopted if Hitler did not want it, nor would it have been applied so effectively. Even the most vociferous opponents of Nazism agree that Hitler's identity system is the most ingeniously consistent graphic program ever devised. That he succeeded in transmuting an ancient symbol with such a long-lasting historical significance into one that was even more indelible is attributable to his mastery of the design and propaganda processes. Yet, the Nazi emblem's good design does not redeem the corruption of a party and a nation that embraced it. "As National Socialists we see our program in our flag," wrote Hitler in *Mein Kampf.* "In the *red* we see the social idea of the movement, in the *white* the national idea, in the swastika the mission of the fight for the victory of the idea of creative work which in itself is and always will be anti-Semitic."

Hitler's death and Germany's defeat in 1945, twenty-five years after the symbol was adopted, may have stopped the Nazis' crimes against humanity, but no amount of cleansing can wash the blood off the swastika. Unless the history of the Nazi era (1933–1945) is totally rewritten—and the danger of that is ever present—the swastika will remain forever the most powerful logo of the age, the manifestation of evil and hate.

Despite the resurgence of hero worship after 9/11, heroic iconography has long adorned canvas and poster for reasons as varied as patriotism and paternalism, valor and ego. "Hero" is, after all, the highest of human distinctions, a status to which everyone, at least subconsciously, aspires. The true hero is born with or acquires real virtues, while the synthetic hero is a composite of these ideal attributes. But in either case, the heroic image has considerable sway over public perception, which makes it such a commanding propaganda tool. Paradoxically, a real hero is not always ideally heroic in appearance or stature, so designing heroes that conform to accepted models necessitates creating symbolic beings that are bigger and bolder than life.

In heroic art, the diminutive Napoleon was depicted as taller, while the impuissant Hitler was stronger than nature had originally intended. The exaggerating lens is routinely used to elevate rulers and warriors, as well as sports and media stars. Micheal Deaver, Ronald Reagan's chief "image maker," once explained that placing the former president in heroic light relied, quite literally, on effective lighting to smooth out the gnarled parts and give an aura to his countenance.

Lights, camera, hero! Indeed, filmmakers routinely create larger-than-life, live-action characters whose heroic personas the public unquestioningly embraces simply because of a few special effects. But the grandest fictional heroes—the superhero comics variety—are not made of flesh and blood at all, but paper, ink, and myth. Take Superman, created in 1939 by Joe Seigel and Jerry Shuster, a pair of Depression-era American Jews who, having learned about the Aryan Superman, wanted to show that not all supermen were Nazis. By imbuing him with otherworldly superhuman powers to defeat evil and bullies (not unlike those Nordic myths that gave rise to Nazism), they tapped into the universal desire for invincible heroes to uphold, in this case, "Truth, Justice, and the American Way."

It is no mystery why the powerless conjure white knights, demigods, or supermen to defeat their foes; similarly, it is expected that the powerful will consolidate real strength through heroic manifestation too. "The chief business of the nation, as a nation," wrote H. L. Mencken, the petulant American critic and journalist, "is the setting up of heroes, mainly bogus." And the job of the illustrator and graphic designer in this particular business is to bolster false heroes with graphic façades.

Whether in the service of democracy or dictatorship, during the twentieth century, artists and graphic designers have been responsible for the lion's share of hero-mongering. They have painted the paintings, drawn the drawings, and designed the icons that impress a leader's likeness on mass consciousness. Heroism relies on establishing credible myths that sustain heroic legend. In the West heroic figures are, in addition, the moral equivalent of commercial trade characters, and function on a similar level. A heroic figure must at once prompt recognition, engender response, and forge indelible bonds.

The depiction of Uncle Sam is a good example. As he appeared in 1917 on recruitment posters created by the American illustrator James Montgomery Flagg, he was the Armed Forces' rendition of the Campbell's Soup Kids, Armour Meat Man, and Aunt Jemima. Flagg himself was the model for the famous "I Want You" poster, but he purposely exaggerated his naturally rugged features for heroic affect. To truly be inspiring, a heroic figure must start with a human visage, and in 1914 Alfred Leete designed the first of such modern images: "Britons [Lord Kitchener] Wants YOU" poster, with a silhouette of England's highest-ranking general as pitchman, pointing his finger directly at the viewer. Kitchener was a real person, but Leete transformed him into a romantic symbol.

While Flagg's rendering of Uncle Sam was not yet a real part of the American consciousness, he was a composite of the historical Uncle Sam and his own heroic visage. Similarly, in 1917, 1919, and 1920 respectively, the Italians, Germans, and Russians issued recruitment posters with the exact same "I Want You" motif showing renderings of idealized soldiers beckoning the viewer to follow the leader into war.

Nations use heroic representation to unite their citizenry behind an idea or ruler. Democracies heroicize the common man; dictatorships worship leaders. But both engage in necromancy through representations of fallen heroes because there is no better way to capture hearts and minds than to promote heroic martyrs. In Nazi Germany, "the fallen become part of the 'eternal German,'" wrote historian George L. Mosse in *Masses and Man* (Howard Fertig, 1980), and "those who preserve their basic nature from all contamination with the passage of time." The Nazis called this "heroic sacrifice," and the idealized images of men and boys giving their lives for the leader were almost as common as the swastika itself. Those who heroically sacrifice for any nation or ideal pass on their souls for what is presumed to be a greater good, and are thus afforded the equivalent of sainthood, with the visual tribute that comes with it.

But from where does the heroic image derive? Clearly, portrayals in stone of Greek gods and Roman centurions, as well as Renaissance paintings of noble kings and princes in robes and armor riding upon their noble steeds gave rise to the paradigm. And official court portraits of seventeenth-, eighteenth-, and nineteenth-century monarchs also influenced the modern stereotype. Frankly, it does not take a genius to create a heroic image. A hero is one who rises above the ordinary and must therefore appear to be extraordinary. Hence, age-old *and* contemporary visual lexicons of heroism are essentially the same the world over, barring fashionable styles that connote specific periods. Realism is the primary method, and this approach involves romanticizing and ultimately beatifying those depicted in such a way that after the warts are removed and the muscles are fleshed out, what remains is a heroic shell.

Soviet Socialist Realism was, however, more than a shell; it was a shroud. Instituted in the late 1920s as reaction to abstract Revolutionary art that was deemed suspiciously perplexing to the masses, it became the official language for representation of a system based on a sacrificing proletariat. Official images—realistic painting or photomontage—showed an elevated stature and forward-looking visage. At the 1939 New York World's Fair, "Joe Worker," as he was known to Americans—a huge statue of a laborer with muscular, rolled-up shirt-sleeved left arm raised to the heavens, holding a red star—stood atop the monolithic Soviet pavilion, representing the heroism of the state and its people. Inside hung scores of blemish-free portraits of Marx, Engels, and Lenin, and the most omnipresent of all, the nation's absolute leader, Joe Stalin. Yet in the annals of hero depiction, Stalin was clearly outdone by Adolf Hitler, Benito Mussolini, and later Mao Tse-Tung.

The Führer Principal (or cult of the leader) on which Hitler fashioned his rule demanded the distribution of a ubiquitous image, though it varied from firm to benevolent, from statesman to god. In fact, one poster portrays him as a Nordic knight replete with armor and flag. Hitler was omnipotent in multi-storied billboards and wallet-sized snapshots. Borrowing his guise from Imperial Roman history, he made sure his face was engraved in profile on countless stamps (for which he received a hero's royalty every time one was used in occupied countries). But he was not the sole hero.

The master German poster artist Ludwig Hohlwein, whose Munich style (or *Holhweinstil*) eventually dominated German advertising throughout the late 1920s, 1930s, and into the 1940s, created the most effective heroic realism. His depictions of Nazi Youth and SS Police were given monumental stances and lit to accentuate their grandeur. He did not engage in negative stereotypes, preferring to mythologize rather than demonize. But he did set a standard against which Nazi poster iconography must be judged. It is difficult to say definitively that Hohlwein invented National Socialist (or Nazi) Realism, but his work was the paradigm. In a 1933 issue of *Gebrausgraphik*, he stated how such art must operate in the service of his nation:

> Today, art, as a cultural factor, is more than ever called upon to take a leading place in building up and conserving cultural values. It must take its place in the front ranks of the legion, which Europa has gathered to preserve her individuality against the onslaughts from the East. Art is the best possible disturbing agent for ideas and intellectual tendencies. Commercial art is doubly effective in this sense for it stands in the very forefront, giving form and expression to the daily panorama and forcibly dominating even those who would ordinarily remain impervious to artistic influences. May the best among us realize fully the significance of what is at stake and their own responsibility and may labor creatively and with conviction at the preservation of our cultural civilization and its restoration to perfectly healthy conditions.

Nazi heroic realism recalled ancient Rome, but it owed a debt to Italian Fascism, which had taken its cues from Caesar. No one was more ubiquitous than Mussolini—and not just in his embellished regalia, but shirtless for the world to see. Hitler wouldn't dare show his chest in public, even if it were magically grafted onto a perfect Aryan body. When it came to propagating the heroic image of the Italian leader throughout society, Mussolini had no reservations about being the virile Roman man, and with the graphic bravado unequaled by any national figure, his bald visage became the logo for his regime. Even when reduced to its most elemental form, the round, usually helmeted and domed head, protruding lip, and searing eyes formed the quintessential icon—the biggest of "Big Brothers." Which is why, after his capture and execution, his beaten body dangling from the hangman's scaffold was an indelibly powerful symbol against his regime.

Every period creates unique heroic imagery conforming to specific events and needs. America's most famous monument to heroism, the World War II memorial at Arlington, Virginia, sculpted by Felix De Weldon, was based on a photo of a flag-raising after the bloody battle with Japanese troops for Iwo Jima. Just two days after the photo was published, the United States Senate called for a national monument modeled on the picture. Thousands of ordinary Americans wrote the President appealing for a monument, and a clay replica was sculpted within seventy-two hours. Although commemorating a real event, the original image was nonetheless re-posed by the photographer to achieve the most dramatic stance, and later the monument itself was based on a recreation in the sculptor's studio. Certainly one reason for such image management was to capture the most opportune moment. But the monument's theme, "Uncommon Valor Was a Common Virtue," like most heroic sentiment, is best expressed through the absence of gore, and while heroes arise from adversity, revealing these conditions does not make for the most effective heroic image. Imagery showing the dead and wounded—heroes all—from that awful day's battle would have never become the indelible icon that it did. Arguably, the most effective heroic depictions are sanitized.

Whether called Socialist Realism, National Socialist Realism, Heroic Realism, or just plain Realism, the design of heroic imagery is carried out with similar components for the same effect. While the Chinese certainly have a unique visual culture, when Mao's regime prevailed over the Nationalists, the official art of Communist China was Socialist Realism. On the one hand, Mao appeared on everything glowing like a beacon of hope, the father of his nation. On the other, soldier, worker, peasant—men and women—were cleansed of every blemish in sanctified posters and banners that heralded the glories of the nation. Chinese propaganda art also transformed people of all Third World nations—from Cuba to Africa—into heroes of an international people's revolution.

Indeed the Third World—Palestine, Vietnam, Angola, Mozambique—was ripe for heroic representation. And in the 1960s, there was no more recognizable heroic figure than Che Guevara, the Cuban revolutionary, whose Christ-like visage adorned stamps and posters, flags and billboards as the exemplar of people's revolt in countries outside Cuba. Even in the United States, an avowed enemy of Cuba, the Che myth was perpetuated by the Left through iconography—and notably American illustrator Paul Davis's 1968 iconic portrait of Che as cover and poster for the left-wing magazine *Evergreen Review* (which prompted the bombing of the magazine's offices by anti-Castro loyalists).

Davis, in fact, made his method of heroic depiction into a style that he applied to more benign figures and events. For another cover of *Evergreen Review*, he celebrated presidential candidate Robert F. Kennedy in much the same iconic way as he had rendered Che. But for the most part, in the United States, heroic imagery is often dubiously employed in the service of commerce rather than politics. Some illustrators have created personal styles on heroic conceits of Nazi and Socialist realism applied to the idolatry of movie, music, and athletic stars. Sometimes this is ironic, but not always. How many times has the classic "Atlas balancing the world" image been used to represent everything from soft drinks to continuing education programs (among others)? Heroic depiction is simply too effective to relegate entirely to parody and satire—especially since audiences have been perpetually susceptible to its allure.

Artists and designers filter heroism through their subjective lenses, but the photographer captures it through an objective one. While this does not imply the absence of prejudice or of predisposition for heroic stereotypes, it means that photographers on the field generally record real heroism in all its nuances. War photographer Don McCullin's pictures from Vietnam, for example, vividly revealed the essence of men under fire—the meeting of bravery and fear. And in the photographs shot by Magnum photographers in the aftermath of the 9/11 terrorist attacks on the World Trade Center (*New York September 11*, Magnum Photos/Powerhouse Books), Steve McCurry records a lonely hero, a New York City fireman, stalwartly climbing a ladder over the devastation of Ground Zero. This and other such photographic images are real life.

However cynical one may be about the manipulating power of heroic imagery, after the attacks on Washington and New York, it is clear that the new heroes—the rescuers—needn't be designed or improved upon. The set pieces of this current wave of heroic imagery have not been re-posed or composed with artificial lights. The photographs of Ground Zero are candid and true. Sure, out of this new hero-imagery old clichés will doubtless emerge, but for now the real images will also prevail. Over a hundred years ago, Elbert Hubbard, the founder of the Roycroft Arts & Crafts Community, wrote, "The heroic man does not pose; he leaves that for the man who wishes to be thought heroic."

"Sometimes at night I lie awake in the dark and try to recapture the vision and the sound of the World of Tomorrow," wrote Meyer Berger in 1940, shortly after the World's Fair closed. "I try to remember how the pastel lighting glowed on Mad Meadow in Flushing: soft greens, orange, yellow, and red; blue moonglow on the great Perisphere and on the ghostly soaring Trylon. I think with a sense of sweetened pain of nights when I sat by Flushing River and saw the World of Tomorrow reflected on its onyx surface, in full color, and upside down. . . . "

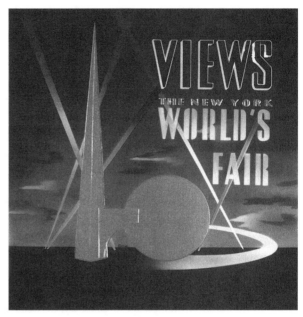

The 1939/1940 New York World's Fair was an extraordinary experience for the reported fifty million visitors who passed through its futuristic gates and gazed at its majestic centerpiece, the Trylon and Perisphere. It was the most ambitious international exposition since the phenomenal Crystal Palace housed the first New York World's Fair in 1853. Not just a trade show, it was endowed with mythic qualities; it was the "Fair of the Future," the "World of Tomorrow," and the "Dawn of a New Day." It was a masterpiece of showmanship, the epitome of stagecraft—a real-life Land of Oz indelibly etched in the memories of those who attended and in the imaginations of those who did not. It was more than a collection of exhibits; it was a wellspring of innovation in corporate identity and promotion.

In 1935 the fair's 121 incorporators decided to put an end to a decade of municipal malaise, marked by the stock market collapse and subsequent economic depression, with the most elaborate demonstration of scientific, technological, and human ingenuity that the world had ever seen. As the guidebook announced: "This Fair of Tomorrow is a promise for the future built with the tools of Today, upon the experience of Yesterday."

Towards this end New York's park and highway czar, Robert Moses, gave his blessing. The fair corporation took as its site the once beautiful tidal basin of the Flushing River, which had been turned into a festering bog and ash dump by one Fishhooks McCarthy and his Brooklyn Ash Removal Company. Miraculously it was transformed into Flushing Meadow, the park of the future. Heralded as a "scientific victory," it was the most ambitious environmental reclamation project of its time.

Consistent with the theme committee's precept that "super civilization . . . is based on the swift work of machines, not on the arduous toil of men," the fair was a mélange of provocative, often symbolically designed pavilions (some representing *architecture parlante,* or billboard architecture—a building whose exterior look revealed its interior purpose, such as the Aviation Building shaped like a dirigible hanger) that were organized into thematic zones covering all aspects of human activity in which man and machine were somehow wed: Transportation, Production and Distribution, Communications, Community Interests, Government, Business Systems, Food, Medicine and Public Health, Science and Education, and Amusement.

Democracity, the Fair's central theme exhibit, designed by Henry Dreyfuss, was an idealized projection of America in 2039, an interdependent network of urban, suburban, and rural areas. Viewed from two moving circular galleries, the viewer was given a bird's-eye view of Centeron, a perfectly planned, modern, riverside metropolis that could accommodate a million people but, in fact, had no inhabitants because it was used exclusively as the hub of commerce, education, and culture. The mellow yet authoritative voice of H. V. Kaltenborn in a recorded narration, underscored by music written by William Grant Still and conducted by Andre Kostelanetz, told visitors about a population that lived in commodious high-rises amidst suburban garden developments, or Pleasantvilles, and in light-industrial communities and satellite towns called Millvilles, rimmed by fertile and profitable farming zones or greenbelts— all linked, of course, by modern express highways and parkways. "This is not a vague dream of a life that might be lived in the far future," wrote Robert Kohn, chairman of the Fair's Board of Design, "but one that could be lived tomorrow morning if we willed it so."

Democracity was suitably housed in the Perisphere, an enormous white futuristic temple that also served as the fair's indelible, architectural trademark. Designed by Wallace K. Harrison and J. Andre Foulihoux— who had also been involved in the design of Rockefeller Center—the Perisphere was the largest "floating" globe ever built by man: 180 feet in diameter and eighteen stories high, twice the size of Radio City Music

Hall. The theme center emerged after more than one thousand sketches and models, and despite its new forms, the design was not without precedents, including Bauhaus and constructivist references.

Each hour more than eight thousand spectators entered the Perisphere through the Trylon, a triangular obelisk 610 feet high, larger than the Washington Monument, ascending on the two largest escalators ever built to a 65-foot-high bridge that led directly into this visionary extravaganza. Six minutes later they would exit down the Helicline, an 18-foot-wide ramp with a stainless steel underbelly. Ironically, this futuristic trademark was built with common steel and clothed in the imperfect materials of the day, including gypsum board that would flake and crack, and required continual maintenance. Even Harrison commented that "in many ways, it was more beautiful when it was just steel."

Selling the public on modernity, and more importantly on coming to see it incarnate in Flushing Meadow, was a task as monumental as building the Fair itself. No sales pitch was as persuasive as the one extolled by the view from the Perisphere as visitors left *Democracity*. That first elevated view of the fairscape was a stunning advertisement for the rightness of the future—or so the planners hoped. Laid before Mr. and Mrs. Average American in all its colorful splendor was the World of Tomorrow today. Equivalent to more than 370 city blocks, it included more than two-hundred modern and moderne buildings curiously laid out according to a nineteenth-century *beaux-arts rond-point* system of radiating streets and fanlike segments extending like spokes from a central hub.

The Fair vividly represented and profoundly utilized the new, distinctly American field of industrial design. Industrial designers were industry's predominant form-givers, whose "faith was . . . based on moral conviction," wrote historian Francis V. O'Connor, "that the public good was to be attained by the universal adoption of a certain rightness of form in all matters from the design of cities to the styling of pencil sharpeners." The lighting stanchions, monumental fixtures, and most of the kinetic exhibits were imaginatively designed by these gifted proponents of the new streamline aesthetic. Among them were Raymond Loewy, Walter Dorwin Teague (who was an original member of the design board), Henry Dreyfuss, Donald Desky, Egmond Arens, Russell Wright, Gilbert Rohde, and Norman Bel Geddes.

Loewy, who before establishing himself as an industrial designer was a commercial artist following the dominant *moderne* style, conceived of the Chrysler Corporation and Transportation exhibits; Teague, who was also a skilled but pedestrian commercial artist, designed seven exhibits including those for Kodak, U.S. Steel, Consolidated Edison, DuPont,

National Cash Register, and Ford; Desky applied surrealism to the Communications exhibit and Russell Wright did likewise for Food. Of all these, however, the most memorable was the brainchild of a one-time scenic designer, Norman Bel Geddes. His theatrical extravaganza for General Motors, called *Futurama*, was housed in architect Alfred Kahn's seven-acre-square streamline monument, and was the most ambitious and visionary multimedia educational entertainment built for any fair.

The Fair was also the most crassly merchandised event the world had ever known. Among the thousands of souvenirs were toys and games, ranging from kazoos to paint sets, all emblazoned or molded in the shape of the Trylon and Perisphere. Despite the predominance of cheaply manufactured trifles, the fair committee insisted in their press releases that the quality of these articles was guaranteed by the "artistic prominence and skill of their designers."

The efforts of the World's Fair's planners should not be dismissed as merely a vain effort to predict the future. Despite its failures, the 1939/1940 New York World's Fair was not an empty metaphor, but rather a colorful, though temporary, beacon of hope. The Trylon and Perisphere symbolized the real world of tomorrow for a nation about to enter a storm of conflict and gave its visitors the stuff of memories that neither war nor time could erase.

The modern poster had its start in Paris a few years before Viennese designer Joseph Binder (1898–1972) was born. Yet he became one of its later pioneers, introducing a cubist-inspired style that employed sharp edges of color to define forms. Binder emigrated to the United States in the late 1930s. His long-running campaign for A&P Coffee (1939) and emblematic posters for the New York World's Fair (1939) and particularly the U.S. Army Air Corps (1941) defined a modern American graphic style.

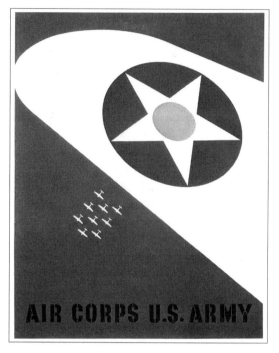

Binder rejected any direct influence from his contemporaries: "I always worked alone—no one ever influenced me," he claimed. But he was inspired by industrial progress. He was born in Vienna a year after the secessionists disrupted the complacency of the bourgeois art establishment. His hometown became a wellspring of modern art and design. At the beginning of the twentieth century the influence of industry was reflected by the contemporary Austrian architects Otto Wagner, Joseph Maria Olbrich, Josef Hoffmann, and Adolf Loos. Nourished in this environment, Binder was instinctively drawn to and understood the requisites of posters. "We live in modern times of life and mind. Everything moves faster today," he wrote in an unpublished memoir. "In poster design we need the same speed to put the message across effectively."

Binder opened a design studio in Vienna in the early 1920s. It was large because the original drawings for the six-foot-four-inch by twelve-foot-seven-inch posters had to be produced in actual size and covered a whole wall. From 1925 to 1929 he was a freelance designer for the Julius Meinl Company, Vienna's leading importer of coffee, tea, and related products, for whom he created advertising, trademarks, and labels. His unifying vision, dubbed the Meinl style, was celebrated by the leading design publications, the *Studio* and *Gebrauchsgraphik*.

Binder believed that style was a transmission code. He developed an emblematic hard-edged style that he encouraged others to freely mimic. "I am here to introduce this style," he announced at a lecture in New York City in 1938. "In the short weeks I am [here] I want to furnish an explanation of exactly what 'modern commercial art' means." But at the time his mission was difficult. American advertising was governed by copywriters who preferred the word to the image and distrusted modern graphic approaches. Binder's first major assignment for the J. Walter Thompson advertising agency was a successful, albeit lackluster, series of billboards for Ballantine's beer, and many of his early American assignments were to comp experimental ideas that never saw the light of day. Undaunted by the reluctance of American business, Binder eventually secured some profitable accounts.

Among his most well-known commissions, the *Air Corps U.S. Army* poster, which won first prize in a Museum of Modern Art competition, signaled a new utilization of space. Noteworthy for its minimal imagery and simple graphic forms, today it is dated only by the silhouettes of propeller-driven aircraft. A yellow wing set against a grayish blue sky offsets the red, white, and blue Air Force logo. The entire image is stylized to ensure memorability. Binder did not self-consciously try to "be of his time," a trap that many lesser stylists fall into, but his works are nevertheless clearly tied to their epoch.

Binder built his design philosophy on the fundamental idea that "the artist should contribute to the development of the modern style instead of indulging in realistic representation of past periods and vain attempts to imitate the works of former times." He believed that the new industrial style was descended from painting, but its function was "to convey the essence of the advertising message in the shortest and most impressive way. . . . It is the artist's task to transfer the clear and constructive shape of the objects as he sees them to the two-dimensional surface. . . . Realism should be left to photography. The artist must not compete with the camera. . . . Therefore the artist must abandon realistic representation and take up styling." Modern design was, therefore, not in competition with technology, but enhanced what the machine could achieve.

Stylization was chiefly based on geometric forms—which is necessary for reducing and abstracting any object from a tree to a human head. "Every form in nature has a very strong and definite construction for it has 'grown,'" Binder wrote. "Every plant has gradually and organically developed. . . . The fine artist renders in his picture the atmosphere and pictorial value of a pine or a palm. But the designer must understand its proportions and emphasize its natural construction. On the other hand, he must reduce the complicated details of the object which make the picture distinct." Binder also believed that color was an important aspect of styling, and taught his students that the artist must "surpass the optical effects of nature with a limited number of colors."

Binder wed cubist form and Bauhaus theory, and wrote frequently about these issues. On shapes: "The sphere and cube are selected as they will simplify the possibilities in design. [As artists we] like to bring the visible world into rules, as scientists have always done. A design will be most attractive when it gives the essentials in a concentrated form." On color: "The same concerns the use of color. Planes of pure color are placed side by side, characteristic of the object. The perspective must not upset the balance. Light and shade must be kept simple." On perspective: "If we draw perspective as it appears in nature, then the effect is too weak. We must strengthen this effect. This will be obtained by simplifying, for which two possibilities can be applied; the orthogonal or the parallel perspective." On proportion: "The individual differences between similar forms are determined by proportion. Height and width create opposites." And on *surprise*: "[Everyone will say that they] saw a blue cow. Such are the enormous possibilities not yet explored. What is small render large, and vice versa. Space adds legibility."

Today Binder's works may appear dated, but his method is an appropriate learning tool. In 1964 the psychologist Rollo May, Binder's longtime friend, summed up his practice: "Most artists have an antagonistic point of view toward Western society and its civilization. Binder's work has the feeling of relationship with modern sciences. . . . Binder always had a positive point of view toward modern science and technical development in relation to his aims in artistic achievement . . . where all established conceptions are stripped from word until the essence of the word is clarified. I feel it is this essence in Binder's art which is so apparent."

One need not be a marksman to appreciate the simple beauty of shooting targets. For function and utility they are among the most perfectly designed graphic forms; nothing could be more economical than the black concentric circles surrounding a bull's-eye. If the archetypal target did not date back to antiquity it would epitomize the modern marriage of form and function—as designed by a Bauhaus master perhaps. The fact is, no form is more modern than geometric form. A circle is a circle, an oval is an oval whenever it is produced.

The target was a visually eye-catching device used in Russian constructivist ads and posters during the 1920s. In the 1930s Western advertising-arts magazines referred to "scoring a bull's-eye" with stark, modern graphics. Such mainstream products as Odol, Tide, and Lucky Strike use targets on their packages. And the vivid geometric form continues to be used in contemporary design and illustration. However, the standard shooting target was not originally, nor has it been subsequently, designed by any individual designer. Its formal attributes were born of necessity. In ancient times the *targe*, as it was called, was a light circular shield protecting the foot soldier from arrows. The shooting target, which simulated that shield, was made from a bundle of wood formed into and painted with circles and hung from a tree or easel.

Jasper Johns transformed the target into pop art in 1960, and today antique dealers sell shooting gallery targets as naïf art. Yet targets have primarily served a utilitarian function. Wade Jackson who oversees the firearms training program at the FBI Academy in Quantico, Virginia, said, "the target is a tool that helps perfect the fundamentals of marksmanship."

In the 1930s and 1940s the classic FBI target was a cartoon version of the stereotypical criminal; a pug-faced, Caucasian male of undetermined ethnic origin aiming his pistol at point-blank range. The central shooting area of this target, from the chin to the diaphragm, was lightly shaded to guide the shooter's aim to that part of the body where he could effect what law enforcement terms a "cessation of voluntary activity." In the 1980s the "FBI Silhouette," an outline of a male torso that stands upright either at attention or with one hand on hip, replaced the caricature and has been more or less officially adopted by most American law enforcement organizations. Scoring numerals are positioned along contoured rings, akin to a topographic map, indicating the various hit zones resulting in "rapid incapacitation."

"The numbers on the targets," explained Agent Jackson, "are worked out in ballistic workshops where scoring agenda take the arbitrary nature out of the process." But it is not necessary for a target to be a human figure. "The fundamentals of marksmanship," Jackson asserted, "will get you where you want regardless of the target itself." Actually, in the 1980s the FBI switched to the FBI-Q, or the so-called "Coke bottle," a simple rendering of a thin neck and fat body that eschewed human resemblance but provided a proper hit zone. Jackson speculated that since there is no FBI design department dedicated to target research, the redesign of the FBI-Q and Federal Firearms QIT (Quick Incapacitation Target) was probably the work of "one persuasive guy in the organization."

Targets are designed to be ripped, torn, and shot apart. In this sense even the basic circular target evokes an eerie quality that is difficult to detach from its graphic grace and elegance. Yet it is this very tension between the target's form and function that makes it so intriguing, indeed hypnotic. In the hands of a marksman it is an efficient tool, but in the eyes of the designer a target is harmony and balance.

Darkie was the bestselling toothpaste throughout Asia. Manufactured in Hong Kong and Taiwan by Hawley & Hazel, part-owned by the Colgate-Palmolive Company, its leadership was challenged in 1990 not by a new and improved competitor, but by the Interfaith Center on Corporate Responsibility, which argued that the trademark of a grinning black minstrel promoted racial stereotyping. Spokespersons for Colgate-Palmolive initially insisted that the product name and design were not offensive to Asian people. However, the company ultimately gave in to mounting protest from the West and ordered Hawley & Hazel to change the image. The redesign featured a young, well-dressed black man in a top hat and a new name, Darlie.

An American visiting a Far Eastern metropolis might well be shocked by the sight of billboards showing the original smiling, bug-eyed minstrel advertising Darkie toothpaste. Since the mid-1960s Americans have become sensitive to derogatory stereotypes. Yet these deep-seated images have been difficult to extinguish even here. Racial and ethnic stereotypes have no higher purpose than to simplify, dehumanize, and degrade people, yet many such stereotypes have been used for mass market product identification, advertising, and as trade character mascots. Although the Darkie controversy occurred continents away, it recalled a period in American history when stereotypical images of Jews, Irish, Italians, Chinese, and African and Native Americans were exploited by manufacturers and merchants to sell products.

From the cigar-store Indian to the Gold Dust Twins (two comical African pygmies who were trademarks for a leading detergent), stereotypes have pervaded popular art. The practice has all but ceased, but vestiges of benign racist trade characters remain, including Aunt Jemima, the former plantation mammy who over the years has been transformed into a housewife, and the Cleveland Indians logo, the comic heathen with the foolish grin.

In the early twentieth century, ethnic and racial trade characters were accepted symbols of national brand campaigns. A 1915 issue of the trade journal the *Poster* reported that among American housewives, the most popular, indeed friendly, brand identifiers were the Armour Meat Company and Cream of Wheat chefs, both black men, and Aunt Jemima, precisely because of the customer's identification with them as warm character trademarks. Today Aunt Jemima is so positively engrained in the popular subconscious that rather than retire her entirely, her handlers have taken the bandanna off and given her a mainstream persona.

Stereotyping was common from the end of the Civil War through the 1890s, when the population expanded in urban areas and more goods and services were required to feed and clothe them. Enterprise and competition grew at a fast pace; numerous advertising techniques were employed to make a large consumer base aware of mercantile options. The earliest forms were typographic space ads, bills, and broadsides composed by job printers. Then, as printing technology improved and color printing became economically feasible, more specialized commercial artists took responsibility for the design of advertising, including trade cards, posters, and collateral ephemera. Racial and ethnic caricature was one of the most commonly practiced graphic leitmotifs. Comic physiognomic distortion was used with impunity for both political and social satire, and as entertainment in forms such as Currier and Ives print series *Darktown*, *Judge's Blackville*, *Puck's* mildly Jewish humor book *Pezneez* (a transliteration of *business* in a Yiddish dialect), to name a few. Comic artists, including Thomas Worth, F. W. Opper, R. F. Outcault, F. M. Homrath, A. B. Frost, and E. W. Kemble, also developed character trademarks to sell soaps, patent medicines, writing inks, and washing machines. Racial stereotyping in the service of commerce was a benign graphic convention not intended to deride, or so the artists may have believed. It was a right-of-passage, a tax levied upon all entrants to the melting pot.

The process might be called democratic. Every major immigrant group was indiscriminately pilloried by caricaturists—a curious badge of distinction. Ultimately, however, most immigrant groups were allowed to enter the mainstream, stereotype in tow. Often the groups themselves used similar self-caricatures in their own media. But not so for African and Native Americans. Stereotypes of the Native American "heathen" or "noble savage" continued unabated, while African Americans were saddled with various slave images (Uncle Tom, Mammy, etc.). The black minstrel image, the birth of black face, was so popular that white performers would put on burnt cork to entertain in theaters that otherwise restricted black people.

The grain of truth on which stereotypes were developed made

racial and ethnic caricature both dangerously insipid and useful to merchants. Blacks, for example, were used to identify certain food staples because on the plantation they were either cooks or picked similar crops in the field. Playing off skin color, they were also used to advertise soap products, like the Pears Soap ad showing a black child being scrubbed so thoroughly that he turned white. Images of the "noble savage" adorned patent medicines and tobaccos, the former because they were hyped as Indian remedies and the latter because Indians grew the weed. Although the noble savage was not as denigrating as other racial caricatures, it was, nevertheless, a false stereotype that oversimplified the plurality of Native American tribes and nations. While caricatured Jews, Italians, and Irish were not as gainfully employed as trademarks, they appeared often on "soft-sell" trade cards that showed generic vignettes on the front side with more specific advertising copy on the back, and were given away with merchandise. Usually in these often comical scenes, hooked-nosed Jews were shown with pawnshop balls, Italians were organ grinders, and Irish had simian characteristics.

Some historians argue that racial and ethnic stereotypes represent early indigenous American humor. With the different waves of immigration each new group threatened the previous one, making hostility inevitable. Humor was a means of letting off steam. By extension, product identification was an even more widespread means of assimilation. Yet over a long period of use graphic symbols come to represent certain truths. Such is the case with racial and ethnic stereotypes. Artists who simplify, distort, and exaggerate physical or behavioral characteristics have significantly influenced popular perception. Early American myths of race and ethnicity developed, in part, from the popular arts. While contemporary graphic artists and designers are more inclined to understand the ramifications of their work, the lessons of the not-so-distant past underscore the potential power of graphic design. The Darkie controversy proved that the strength of stereotypes must not be underestimated.

Design Quarterly #133 (1986) was no
ordinary magazine. Although
disguised as a common thirty-two-
page magazine format, upon opening,
the issue unfolded accordion style
until, when finally extended and
opened, it metamorphosed into a
single-page poster, measuring
approximately two by six feet. *Design
Quarterly,* then edited by Mildred
Friedman, was a publication of the
Walker Art Center in Minneapolis
directed toward the international
design community. Each issue focused
on a single theme, and, in 1985, *Design
Quarterly* invited April Greiman
(b. 1948), a pioneer of computer-
generated design, to design an issue
of the magazine about her work.

Instead she transformed
the magazine into a poster, a life-size
digitized, nude self-portrait. Greiman's
eyes are closed and her left breast is cloned onto the right side of her
body. Another close-up of her head, this one with eyes wide open, projects
from the vertex of her feet under the heading "the spiritual double."
Superimposed type and image ideograms were dispersed over the surface of
the poster, and photographs of dinosaurs, outer space, hieroglyphs, formulas,
weather pattern symbols, and disembodied miniature hands performing
mysterious acts all orbit around the meditative, naked Greiman. A tally
stick, simultaneously suggesting a time line and growth chart, underscores
the length of the poster and emphasizes the physicality of the oversized
page. In addition, time line entries mark major scientific innovations,
including "Electricity 1831," "Relativity Theory 1905," and "Man on the
Moon 1969" as well as "Birth of April Greiman 1948." The scale below the
hash marks reads in ticker tape fashion: "proton·neutron·electron·moron·

milli·micro·nano·pico·kilo·mega·giga·tera·order·chaos·play·dream·dance·make sounds·feel·don't worry·be happy."

The reverse side renders tales of dreamlike narrations in floating text boxes, a Zen koan, ambiguous, large-scale photographs, and an agonizing step-by-step record of the process of working with the new computer technology.

Flight of fancy or logic puzzle? Did it make sense?

Greiman's poster was a compendium of the preceding decade—a nation bloodied by the Vietnam War saw the rise of feminism, Eastern religion, consciousness-raising, spiritual awakening, and reinvigorated interest in Jungian archetypes and dream symbology. It was also a formalist autobiography. Graphically, designers grew restless with the absolute order and clarity of the reigning classic Swiss modernism. In the early 1970s Greiman studied with Wolfgang Weingart and Armin Hofmann at the Basel School of Design in Switzerland where a spirited climate of innovation and research nourished inventive typographic experiments: extreme leading, wide letterspacing, typographic weight changes mid-word, alternative text divisions—pushing typographic expression toward the personal, expressive, and, occasionally, humorous. Technically, *Does It Make Sense?* was dazzling.

As director of visual communications at CalArts in 1982, Greiman had early access to state-of-the-art video and digitizing equipment formerly used by Nam June Paik. The Macintosh computer was introduced in 1984. By 1986 the collage in *Does It Make Sense?* involved no conventional paste-up; it was composed and assembled as a single document in MacDraw and printed out as it was designed on screen, tiled out on 8½" × 11" sheets of bond paper. It was a feat only dreamed of until then—the ability to bypass conventional paste-up production methods. The text function of the MacDraw program for the first time allowed direct composition of text in relation to the digitized video images.

Before *Does It Make Sense?* bit-mapped type and imagery had been an anathema to designers; the computer was arcane, expensive, and unfriendly. With its publication, the design world was challenged to take another look. Decontextualized images, thematically mixed texts, apparent non sequiturs, floating text blocks, typography set in mirror image, humor, and personal juxtapositions were all recontextualized and revoiced as Greiman's own in a pyrotechnic meld of form and content. It was rendered coherent by the digital medium.

The personal computer would eventually open opportunities for new levels of authorship for designers. Although the role and legitimacy of personal expressiveness in graphic design is still being evaluated, *Does It Make Sense?* is a touchstone: the creation of self-referential statements and compositions through the medium of professional graphic design

Design organizations are the short-order cooks of printed ephemera, and the posters and flyers that they produce announcing myriad events—from competitions to conferences—are the graphic designers' equivalent of two eggs, bacon, and side of whiskey down. Served up at such a prodigious pace, design for designers could constitute its own industry within an industry. Since members of these organizations are asked to donate their talents, their payback is a license to experiment. But despite the latitudes in designing for designers, one requisite is absolute: the need to visually represent *design* itself. Can anything be more mundane?

      Unfortunately, unique solutions to this problem have diminished as clichés have risen. And the most common of these are the tried-and-true, including light bulbs, pencils, T squares, drawing tables, loupes, and computer monitors—as well as combinations thereof, such as pencils with light bulbs as erasers, or computer monitors with light bulbs on the screen, or light bulbs with pencils for filament. Add to this a lexicon of somewhat more abstract symbols—like babies (birth of ideas), rainbows (variety of ideas), sunbursts (the dawn of ideas), and picture frames (framing ideas)—and it is reasonable to conclude that design creativity is difficult to represent creatively.

As Mies van der Rohe once said, being original is not as important as being good. But to be good under these circumstances a designer must find alternative ways to express the nature of design without resorting to hackneyed concepts. This, of course, is the very essence of creativity: creating something unexpected. However, surprise is not always a virtue. Sometimes it can be as cloying as a cliché and as annoying as any distraction. Effective surprise—the kind that does not merely shock but influences perception and understanding—is not as simple as shouting *Boo!* in a dark room.

Stefan Sagmeister (b. 1962), a native of Austria with a New York design studio, encountered this problem when he was commissioned to design a mail-poster announcing Jambalaya, the 1997 AIGA National Conference in New Orleans. Although designers covet such assignments for the visibility and prestige afforded them within the design community, the requirement to pack both an iconic image and an enormous amount of information onto the front and back of the missive creates challenges that often limit license. Information architects may be stimulated by the problem of clarifying layers of names, times, and places, but often the results, though well ordered, are too reductive to be stimulating. Finding a balance between clarity and the unexpected is difficult. And since this particular AIGA conference situated in the mecca of Mardi Gras was a veritable gumbo of speakers and events, the pressures to accommodate *and* innovate weighed heavy. Sagmeister's art school training taught him discipline, but his instinct demanded raucousness.

After starting his own New York studio in 1994, Sagmeister, who worked for two years at the Leo Burnett advertising agency in Hong Kong and later for eight months at M&Co. in New York, earned attention for CD covers for the Rolling Stones, David Byrne, Lou Reed, and others that were conceptually startling and eschewed stylistic consistency. "Style = Fart" reads a banner over Sagmeister's desk, which for him means that trendy surface alone is hot air. Instead of adhering to contemporary conceits, Sagmeister builds his design on ideas that, although quirky and contentious, are very logical, ultimately producing work that grabs the eye and disrupts the senses while satisfying his own atavistic need to agitate.

When considering the metaphors for this AIGA poster, Sagmeister made lists of various design references and New Orleans clichés —everything, he notes, "from silly jambalaya recipes to stupid Mississippi steamboats. And I hated them." But when the conference coordinator gave him a list of the eighty participants speaking in eight different auditoriums over three days, Sagmeister says, in his lilting Viennese cadence, "it sounded like one big happy chaos that had everybody running around like headless chickens." This reference to domestic fowl was the egg that hatched into an idea. Indeed, a picture of a couple of headless chickens with its reference to voodoo ritual was just the perfect off-center illustration that Sagmeister needed as the focus for a wealth of information on a dense but dynamic poster.

The probability that such an image would be offensive to some, including the client, did not really concern Sagmeister, who prostrates himself to avoid making things good, clean, and ordinary—or what he dismisses as "nice design." "There is so much of this well-done, competently designed fluff around," he observes, "that doesn't bother anybody, doesn't annoy anyone, and is rightfully ignored." He refers to design in which form rather than concept prevails and ornamental layering triumphs—like slick paper-company promotions where designers are engaged in orgies of stylistic excess. "Tons of this stuff was given away by paper manufacturers in New Orleans," he chides, "gorgeously produced beautiful fluff designed by people who have no opinions on nothing whatsoever."

Sagmeister objects to experimental work that is really dysfunctional. While some may apply the word "experimental" to Sagmeister's own work, he insists his design solutions are built on equal parts intuition, play, and the desire to rise above the mundane. For example, he once defiantly designed the logo, labels, and shopping bags for Blue, a chain of blue-jeans outlets in Austria, using only gold and black. Sagmeister maintains that he has no interest in hiding in a laboratory while his work is tested; rather, he is on a crusade to pump untried ideas into the real world. The Jambalaya poster was one way of announcing that he was an enemy of the safe and sanctioned.

"I refused to do it in any of the 'hot' mannerisms, like Euro-techno, the new simplicity, or tiny type in boxes," he explains. In fact, his real influence comes from a Swiss outsider artist named Adolf Wölfli, who in the 1920s covered his own imagery with bits and pieces of found detritus. Sagmeister acknowledges that at the time he was given the AIGA poster assignment, he was also working on album covers for the Rolling Stones and the Pat Metheny Group, which demanded very exacting effort. The Stones cover required months of tiresome research and the Metheny cover involved creating very intricate visual codes. As a respite, he says, "I was happily and mindlessly doodling."

In addition to the headless chickens, which were deliberately composed so that they would emerge as the poster was unfolded, the front and back of the piece is comprised of hundreds of small labels featuring the handwritten names (and self-portraits) of the conference speakers. Some were pasted ad hoc on top of the image on the front side, while the rest (along with all the registration information and sender's reply coupon) were affixed willy-nilly on a board that was photographed and used as the back side. Sagmeister asked all the participants to sign their names in ballpoint pen or draw comic portraits. Naturally, scores of mistakes were made, which, after copyediting, were corrected in a rather unorthodox manner. "Some of the corrections were done directly on the poster while on the phone with the client," Sagmeister says, explaining how he crossed out words and phrases and replaced them with his own handwriting. Rather than leave empty space, Sagmeister wrote additional text as much to enhance the chaotic nature of the poster as to offer conference lore. "I hid a lot of small inside jokes and stories all over the poster, and I actually talked to a number of people who read the whole thing start to end." In fact, now it can be told: One of the small hidden images, Sagmeister confesses, "is a photograph of my testicles (I told the client that it was a picture of a monkey's knee)."

When the poster arrived in AIGA members' mailboxes, it caused the stir that Sagmeister had hoped for. Some recipients were enraged that the AIGA, long the keeper of America's modernist design tradition, condoned such abhorrent, anarchic work. National headquarters in New York received a few letters of protest, and even a membership was canceled. But positive sentiments far exceeded the dissent. Viewed as an enticement for prospective conferees to register for an event that promised to broaden the design discourse, the poster served its purpose well. It effectively promoted AIGA's Mardi Gras and signaled that the event was not just a staid congress of self-important old-timers. But most the "headless chicken poster," as it has come to be known, proved that when designing for designers nothing is worse than resorting to clichés.

STYLE

Goudy Stout was designed in 1930 by Frederic W. Goudy, one of America's otherwise foremost type designers. Why the equivocation? Because Goudy Stout was a frivolous typeface. "In a moment of typographic weakness I attempted to produce a 'black' letter that would interest those advertisers who like the bizarre in their print. It was not the sort of a letter I cared for . . . ," admitted Goudy.

Even luminaries blunder when they succumb to the unpredictable tastes of the marketplace, consequently a rather long list of talented designers have perpetrated typographic crimes and misdemeanors, placing many ill-advised typefaces into currency. Among them are Hermann Zapf's Sapphire, Emire Reiner's Floride, Morris F. Benton's Hobo, J. Hunter Middleton's Plastica, A. M. Cassandre's Acier Noir, and Roger Excoffon's Calypso.

Benton's Hobo, which has been on typositor for many years, has aged poorly. When issued by the American Type Foundry and Intertype in the early 1920s, Hobo had fashionable characteristics that made it a viable advertising display face. Its vertical strokes and curved bars with the variation of stress on different letters gave it a quirky character and eye appeal; the elimination of all lowercase descenders saved on space. In the right designer's hands Hobo isn't half bad as a decorative alphabet, but used incorrectly, which is usually the case, the results are abominable.

With all the elegant typefaces extant, why are so many of the ugly specialty faces used? Or more to the point, why were they designed in the first place?

Typography is a handmaiden to commerce, and as Goudy suggested, pleasing the client is at least one of the typographer's raisons d'être. Decorative, ornamented, or novelty typography dates back to the early nineteenth century and the Industrial Revolution. Commerce was expanding its boundaries. A primitive form of print advertising replaced the tradesman as the primary hawker of goods. In *Printing Types: An Introduction* (Beacon Press, 1971) Alexander Lawson wrote: "Early in the nineteenth century English type founders produced a variety of embellished types designed to emphasize their unique characteristics for the single purpose of attracting attention. Fat faces, grotesques, and Egyptians—decorative types when compared to the romans that had undergone but minor changes since fifteenth-century Italy—were not flamboyant enough for the new requirements of advertising display."

Type founders discovered that virtually any unusual design would be purchased by job printers for advertising, broadsides, and packages. Initially the ornamented types were inline or outline versions of the Didot and Egyptian styles, but designers soon switched from altering existing faces to creating more unique and outlandish inventions. Letterforms mimicked the appearance of Gothic architecture, and were intricately designed with filigree like that applied to cast-iron machinery. Type echoed the Victorian's penchant for extravagant decoration.

Some of these alphabets were reproduced from letters in ancient manuscripts, but most were conceived by artists and produced at great expense. A somewhat arcane, but nevertheless important, distinction must be made between ornamented typefaces and the so-called fancy faces. Since designers of the latter were prone to derive inspiration more from common sign painters than from monastic scripts, fancy faces did not resemble book illumination, but rather vernacular lettering.

Concerning fashions in typefaces, an 1879 issue of the *Typographic Advertiser* offered the following: "We change, tastes change, fashions change. The special furor is now for bric-a-brac—antique pots and platters, Japanese oddities, and Chinese monstrosities. But fashion's rule is despotic, and so, yielding to her commands, we have prepared and show in this number some oddities to meet the taste of the times. . . . As printers no doubt desire to be in fashion, we trust they will approve our course by sending in orders for them, that their patrons also may catch the infection . . . "

The infection eventually disappeared. As the Victorian era came to an end the passion for extreme ornament faded. A renewed interest in typography of classic origin contributed to the demise. In *The Practice of Typography* (1900), Theodore Low De Vinne offered this eulogy: "Printers have been surfeited with ornamented letters that did not ornament and did degrade composition, and that have been found, after many years of use, frail, expensive, and not attractive to buyers." However, De Vinne further noted that "more changes have been made in the direction of eccentricity than in that of simplicity. Fantastic letters were never in greater request, but they rarely appear as types in books. To see the wildest freaks of fancy one must seek them not in the specimen books of type founders, but in the lettering made for displayed advertisements and tradesman's pamphlets." Although traditional typographers now eschewed ornament, a new breed of professional, the commercial artist, was creating hand-drawn, often one-of-a-kind, novelties for use on a plethora of printed matter.

At the turn of the century, designers working in the art nouveau style rejected the nineteenth-century excesses, but replaced it with "floriated madness," which was eventually rejected by those designers who sought yet another style. The vogue for the decorative letter was somewhat eclipsed during the 1920s by the canon of purity and functionalism espoused by the Bauhaus and described by Jan Tschichold in his book *The New Typography* (1928). However, despite the proliferation of functional sans-serif types like Futura, advertisers required eye-catching type to appeal in an increasingly competitive market.

During the 1920s and 1930s, the era of *art moderne,* a multitude of quirky types were issued by the major German, American, English, Dutch, and French type foundries and promoted through extravagant type specimen sheets. Many of these faces symbolized modernity.

Type design has traditionally been based on past models, and typographers today are archaeologists digging through antique typebooks for faces suitable for revival or adaptation. While the revivalists pay homage to the past, the computer mavens are looking towards the future. But the future of quirky typography is déjà vu. Primitive, low-resolution bitmap forms have offered numerous possibilities for quirky typography equaling the worst produced during the nineteenth and early twentieth centuries, but in the right designer's hands, there is also an unlimited variety of fascinating concoctions.

Design is a religion for the Japanese. Even the most everyday objects are imbued with elegance. Economy is a sacrament. And this may explain the fervent embrace of European modernism by Japanese designers during the early 1920s. The Japanese fascination with things Western is not just a late twentieth-century phenomenon. The Bauhaus and Russian Constructivist ideas were taught in art schools and universities by graphic artists, architects, and painters who had studied in the Western capitals. They translated the documents of modernism, including F. T. Marinetti's *Futurist Manifesto* (published in 1909 in *Suburu*), and filtered these works into popular and commercial cultures. Modernism as substance and style developed over two decades through the design of magazines, books, logos, posters, and even movie tickets.

From the Meiji era (1868–1912) to the present, Western aesthetics have influenced Japanese popular arts in various ways. James Fraser, coauthor of *Japanese Modern* (Chronicle Books, 1996), notes that the Japanese people value anything new that came by way of the sea. "Modernist ideas came thick and fast in ships (and planes) . . . Some designers were successful in assimilating and transforming Western design concepts and style that were perceived as being modern. Others appropriated Western styles badly . . ." Devout Japanese moderns advanced the "form follows function" ethic in publications that echoed their European counterparts, while the opportunistic commercial artists simply appropriated the surface, void of its utopian doctrines. The principal purveyor of the new graphic style was a multivolume manual titled *The Complete Commercial Artist,* published by the Association of Commercial Artists. This manual provided art directors and designers with templates for copying both modern and modernistic approaches. Different volumes were devoted to posters, logos, shop signs and display windows, advertisements, and package design. It encouraged commercial artists to reject the traditional for the nouveau. Owners of stores and shops, and designers who worked for them, found theoretical guidance and practical models. In addition to examples of orthodox modernism, *The Complete Commercial Artist* reproduced many pieces by the exemplars of European art deco or "commercial modernism," including Lucian Bernhard, A. M. Cassandre, Jean Carlu, and others. Their respective works were icons. In fact, overt copying of their most well known designs was encouraged.

The most visible manifestation of Western influence was in advertising posters for the major Japanese retailers. The Mitsukoshi Department Store established a design department in 1909, and almost immediately adopted cubism as a house style. It continued to foster a modernistic sensibility for decades following. Shiseido Company Ltd., known for its cosmetics, was a major proponent of the new style in posters and packages that employed stylized illustrations of the sleek (and void of ethnicity) deco women. Advertisements for the Tokyo Subway Company, South Manchurian Railway, Japan Tourist Bureau, and Minori Cigarette Company, among other major businesses, also employed artists who understood the Western idioms.

It took more ingenuity to adapt, or modernize, Japanese type characters to the model of Europe's New Typography, but designers and typographers invented ways to streamline traditional forms. They even developed Futura-like equivalents. The airbrush was a prime method of giving characters the illusion of motion so common in contemporary Western letterforms. And Japanese type specimen books included many pages of Western "novelty" alphabets alongside Japanese characters that were similarly composed. In fact, many of these hybrid decorative character sets look as though they could have been designed today by digital fontographers.

During the 1920s and 1930s, as it was preparing for war, Japan was a thriving commercial nation with Western trading partners. So, aside from the indigenous designers' formalist fascination with modern design methods, commercial imperatives demanded that popular graphics be more cosmopolitan, if not universal. The decorative European style ultimately won over stoic modernism, and was used for every kind of visual communication, large and small. Movie tickets are perhaps the most surprising of all the ephemeral media to be seriously (and ambitiously) designed. Yet they provided the perfect venue.

The advertising industry was booming in pre-war Japan, and business leaders understood that every empty structure, object, and material was a potential conveyer of an advertising message. Movies were so popular in Japan that there was no more efficient way to reach a filmgoer than the imprinting of messages on tickets. It is unclear who started this practice, but printing companies acted as advertising agents, so probably the leading ticket printer in Tokyo developed the idea and sold space to advertisers, thus developing two sources of income.

Japanese movie tickets of this type were produced in the late 1930s in standardized formats that different theaters could use, regardless of what they were showing. The illustrations on the front side did not attempt to reflect the movie at all, but were personality portraits or vignettes with no literal significance. They were colorful and pleasing to the eye, and conformed to the dominant styles of the day. The ticket-taker snipped off a small corner to validate the ticket, leaving unsullied the main, full-color image and the one or two color advertisement on the reverse side. Moviegoers were encouraged to retain their tickets as receipts for possible prizes—a good advertising ploy.

An admirer said of William
Addison Dwiggins (1880–
1956): "There are few
American designers whose
work can be revisited after
decades with more pleasure
and instruction." Dwiggins
was a renaissance man:
typographer, type designer,
illustrator, author, puppeteer,
marionette designer, book
jacket and book designer. He
was the missing link between
the aesthetic movement and
commercial art, an auteur in
that he developed an

unmistakably distinctive graphic style that informed the practice of his
epoch, from the 1920s to the 1950s. To give further buoyancy to his
reputation, on August 29, 1922, in an article in the *Boston Evening
Transcript*, Dwiggins was the first to use the term *graphic design* to describe
his broad design practice.

Dwiggins's passion for design pervaded everything he touched
(and wrote). His work was an extension of his self. "One stood quietly apart
waiting for him to look up," recalled Dorothy Abbe, his long-time
colleague, about his intensity, passion, and humanity. "Presently he swung
from his stool. With a final glance at the piece that absorbed him, he
reached for tobacco and, filling his pipe, slowly turned toward you, smiling
his welcome. This was ever his way—the smile, the slow unhurried steps,
emphasized by the simplicity of his dress, always in white. Not only did he
move slowly, but he worked slowly in the sense that the first effort was
usually discarded, to be written, or drawn, or carved, again and again. And
yet in this quiet, patient manner he brought into being more than most
people even dream of."

Among the countless projects completed during his long career,
the shelf backs (or spines), title pages, and illuminations for a five-volume
boxed set of Rabelais's *The Great Gargantua and Pantagruel* (1936) reveals

his virtuosity. In this book Dwiggins wed respect for tradition with passion for the new. In Dwiggins's work, the classics served as foils for a contemporary decorative vocabulary that synthesized medieval, oriental, and Mayan visual forms. Although his motifs are described as *art moderne* (art deco), they were only remotely related to this machine age international style. Actually, Dwiggins developed a distinctive manner that was later adopted by other purveyors of commercial style. Dwiggins did not conform to the times, rather the times conformed to him.

The Limited Editions Club publication of *The Great Gargantua and Pantagruel* is certainly one of the finest on Dwiggins's own shelf. Even when compared to the unique spines he designed for numerous other classics, these exuded a certain magic through their composition. Every aspect of the books' conception, production, and manufacture from the deep green color of the cloth bindings and slipcase to the conceptual acuity of the lighthearted illustrations to the composition of neo-baroque ornament to the curvaceous hand lettering on the title and chapter breaks made this a readable confection. Over time it has become a kind of fetishistic design artifact.

George Macy, the irascible publisher of the Limited Editions Club, commissioned a three-volume set; Dwiggins urged him to divide the text into five separate volumes (*The Great Gargantua and Pantagruel* was written as five books under one cover). This number gave Dwiggins the opportunity to create a virtual stage on which the characters in the books could play. Dwiggins tied the five volumes together through the spine illustrations. Separately each spine had its own integrity, but together they became a frieze of the book's leading characters. Dwiggins further created individual title pages, which he precisely hand lettered in pen and ink in actual-size layouts, often in more than one version, as if titles for a play or film. Title page design was a time-honored part of bookmaking, and Dwiggins respectfully played with the medium by busting through the rigid constraints. Inside the books he designed vignettes that illuminated the text, but not in the conventional mimicry of a passage or line. Personally inscribed on the flyleaf of Dorothy Abbe's copy Dwiggins wrote: "Although the . . . vignettes might be considered gothic I tried to avoid a gothic overtone in this book." He succeeded in designing a book that, though set in another time, was not merely relevant, but vital.

In Hingham, Massachusetts, far from the capitals of commercial art and design, Dwiggins remained an iconoclast for his entire life. But few mavericks were ultimately as influential. He inspired imitators, yet none were able to recreate his panache. Dwiggins was the quintessential designer and experimenter of his time. "Modernism is not a system of design—it is a state of mind . . . a natural and wholesome reaction against an overdose of traditionalism," he wrote. "The graphic results of this state of mind are extraordinary, often highly stimulating, sometimes deplorable." Dwiggins pushed the boundaries when necessary, while standing for tradition. He once wrote that he lived for a single purpose: "the game is worth the risk."

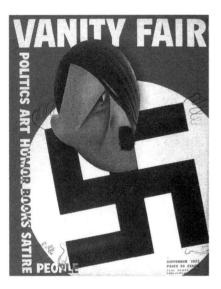

Paolo Garretto (1903–1983) was a prolific cartoonist, caricaturist, and poster artist who worked for magazines from the mid-1920s to the late 1940s. During his peak in the mid-1930s, every week at least one major periodical or poster hoarding featured an image that he produced. For *Vanity Fair*, just one of his primary outlets, he designed more than fifty covers and was known as one of *Vanity Fair*'s graphics triumvirate, which also included Miguel Covarrubias and William Cotton.

Although he was friends with *Vanity Fair*'s legendary art director M. F. Agha (1896–1978), Garretto was originally commissioned in 1930 by one of the magazine's editors, Claire Booth Brokaw (later Claire Booth Luce). His caricatures for *Vanity Fair* were uniquely styled and defined the times when they were made. Overtly influenced by cubism and futurism, his style grew more out of a naïve instinct than premeditated borrowing. Which came first, a dominant style or a personal one? Garretto was a leader not a follower. His covers for *Fortune*, the legendary finance magazine that pioneered poster-like covers, veered from caricature/design to pure design in an illustrative mode. These were grand visual statements.

Garretto's graphic approach was based on simplification of primary graphic forms into iconic depictions and loose but poignant likenesses. Vibrant, airbrushed color was his trademark, and he also experimented with different media to create exciting new forms, including experiments with collage and modeling clay that proved fruitful. Without his superb draftsmanship, what is now pigeonholed as deco styling would surely have been a superficial conceit, but his conceptual work was so acute, and his decorative work was so well crafted that he eschewed these pigeonholes. Writing in a 1946 issue of *Graphis*, Orio Vergani described Garretto's ingenuity this way: "Once the constructive theme of his images is discovered Garretto proceeds to the invention of the media necessary for executing them. I believe he has painted, or rather, constructed his images with everything: scraps of cloth, threads of rayon, with the bristles of his shaving brush, with straw, strips of metal and mill board, with iron filings and sulfur, tufts of fur and wings of butterflies. His colors are born of a strange alchemy of opposed materials in the light of an artificial sun, he seeks for the squaring of shade as others have sought for the squaring of the circle."

Garretto was born in Naples, Italy, in 1903 but had a peripatetic childhood because of his father, a scholar and teacher who traveled extensively. When he was twelve years old his family moved to Philadelphia where, before he mastered English, he would communicate with his teachers through drawings. At the outbreak of World War I he returned to Italy and moved to Florence because his father was a reserve officer in the army. After the war, and amid the throes of great social upheaval, the family moved to Rome—a hotbed of cultural activity and political revolution. In Rome, Garretto would go nightly to the Caffe Aragno where the intelligentsia assembled; there he would sketch portraits on the marble table tops. One portrait of F. T. Marinetti, the founder of futurism, and another of the thespian Pirandello served to get him a job doing cartoons for a local newspaper.

The postwar years were marred by struggles between communists and fascists. Garretto hated the bolsheviks, he said, somewhat romantically, for the murder of the Czar and particularly his little son Prince Alexei. But, closer to home, the bolsheviks had attacked his father at a veterans rally, beaten him, and stole his medals. Although his father "turned the other cheek and forgave his enemies," Garretto was not so forgiving. At the age of eighteen he joined the Vanguardists, the fascist youth organization. In those days fascism was an antiestablishment movement and an alternative to communism. Although he has since renounced those years as childish folly, at the time he was committed to the cause. He even designed the fascist uniform (because he said that he disliked the disheveled look of the fascist partisans). And when Mussolini saw him and a few of his friends in a formation dressed in their spiffing splendor, Il Duce appointed Garretto one of his personal bodyguards. And a great honor it was too until he learned that the position was for life. The elder Garretto, who was adamantly opposed to Paolo's involvement with the fascists, eventually helped obtain a permanent discharge, allowing him to go back to school, earn his architectural degree, and ultimately travel to England, where he became a sought-after caricaturist.

At age twenty-two Garretto received steady work from Dorland, Europe's largest advertising agency. His work was published regularly in the eight major British pictorial magazines, including the *Tattler* and *Illustrated News*, and frequently appeared in the major German weeklies. In Paris, where he had married, opened a studio in his apartment, and eventually sired a son, he was commissioned to do numerous advertising projects. One such was the result of a meeting with Alexey Brodovitch, who was art director for the department store Trois Quartiers. He was also asked to become a member of Alliance Graphique, a loosely knit advertising cooperative that included poster artists A. M. Cassandre, Jean Carlu, and Charles Loupot, for whom Garretto did an Air France campaign.

By the 1930s his friendship with publisher Condé Nast was so close that this corporate chauvinist allowed Garretto to work for the competition. In the meantime the war broke out and Garretto wanted to return to Paris to be with his wife and child. Being Italian he was not allowed to cross the border, and after various attempts at entry he returned to New York. In 1941 Garretto was interned in the United States with other German, Italian, and Japanese enemy aliens. He was eventually deported, having agreed to an FBI proviso that he not make any anti-American artwork for the duration of the war. This was certainly a little far-fetched and unenforceable, but he did refuse to do caricatures for the Nazis with whom he had no sympathy. Moreover, his stylized but critical caricatures of Mussolini and Hitler did not make him very popular among party officials. In 1944 he was assigned to Budapest to develop a literacy project so that "defeated and conquered peoples" could learn the Italian language through pictures. But when Italy capitulated to the Allies later that year, he was interned as an enemy alien in Hungary for the duration of the war.

After the war he continued to make political and social caricature; he also did fine art in the same style. Paul Rand, who called Garretto a master of illustration, hired him to render the Dubonnet man. He continued to do caricatures well into the 1970s, but he stopped working for American magazines in the 1940s because after the war, he said, the art directors who knew him had changed or died and his kind of design was eclipsed by photography. In 1982 Lloyd Ziff, then design director for the newly revived *Vanity Fair*, located Garretto at his home in Monte Carlo and asked him to do some covers. He did a few, but they were rejected by the editors in favor of a contemporary caricaturist whose drawing was influenced by Garretto's style. Although he was active until his death at the age of eighty-six, Garretto never altered the style that defined his time.

Artone

Seymour Chwast

The curvilinear style known as art nouveau in France and Jugendstil in Germany was revived by Push Pin Studios during the early 1960s and prefigured the postmodern reappraisal of passé forms by well over a decade. Push Pin, founded in 1955 by Seymour Chwast (b. 1931), Milton Glaser, Edward Sorel, and Reynold Ruffins, was a pioneer of stylistic sampling, known for combining traits of Victorian, arts and crafts, art nouveau, and art deco approaches with contemporary typography and illustration that underscored the influential "Push Pin style." This approach was a model for other American designers interested in decorative form and, as a byproduct, fostered a return of drawing to the design process. The prevailing modern ethos rejected historicism as quaint and unresponsive to contemporary business needs. But Push Pin's eclecticism was based on the idea that historical form could be revitalized and given currency with certain mass media, including book and record covers, advertising, magazines, and package design. There is probably no better example of the appropriateness of this method of historical quotation than Seymour Chwast's 1964 design of the Artone Studio India ink package, the logo of which was the basis for his display typeface called Artone, released that same year by Photolettering Inc.

In 1963 Push Pin Studios was commissioned to repackage the Artone ink carton by the new owner of the art supply company, a Wall Street businessman named Louis Strick. Since his company was small, Strick rejected costly market research and customer profiles. Rather, he left the problem entirely in the hands of Chwast and Glaser (then the two remaining principals of Push Pin). As was often their procedure, each made sketches independently and only later came together for reaction and critique. "We'd talk about it, do our own ideas, and then talk about it again," Chwast recalled. Glaser's proposals are lost and his ideas forgotten, but Chwast recalled doing a few variants on his best sketch showing a large *a*, which, though not directly copied from an existing alphabet, echoed the fluid art nouveau/Jugendstil lettering he had seen in vintage issues of *Jugend*, the turn-of-the-century German art and satire magazine. In fact, the letterform was based more on the idea that "marks had to be simple and straightforward," than on replicating art nouveau conceits.

The curvilinear *a* was contrasted by a delicate, lightline banknote script used to communicate the other pertinent information. Unlike typical art nouveau/Jugendstil packages known for a preponderance of florid decoration, Chwast favored an unencumbered box. The only decoration was three rows of nine smaller *a*'s—designed with a Zen-like simplicity—on the box top. Chwast insisted that using the *a* by itself was not a radical idea since making a simple, identifiable mark on a package was a proven way of establishing the identity for a product. "I knew it had to be something with graphic impact," he said. "In contrast to Winsor-Newton [a competing brand], which took a different approach by having full color paintings on their packages."

Printed on a white background, the *a* was the most identifiable element. In addition to being the first letter in the alphabet, and therefore memorable in its own right, its curved form was at the same time reminiscent of the Artone ink bottle and a drop of ink. Chwast, however, had acted entirely on blind intuition since he admitted that he did not even realize the strong symbolic relationship until another member of the studio pointed it out to him before the client ever saw it. "Somebody said 'its sort of like an ink drop,' and I thought that was a pretty good way to sell the idea to the client."

Chwast used an existing script as the secondary typeface but realized it would be useful for future advertising and promotional purposes to have a complete alphabet and a set of numerals. So he sketched out the capitals, lower case, and numerals over the course of one week and had a designer in the studio render the finished drawings. Chwast said the *a* was easy, while the idiosyncratic nature of some of the other letters made them more difficult to work out. After the design was resolved, it was offered to Photolettering Inc. as a display face and was immediately accepted. Yet a potential problem having to do with fashion arose in Chwast's mind. "The art nouveau thing had reached its peak [by 1964]," Chwast recalled, "and I thought it might be too late to put this alphabet on the market." He was wrong. Artone became very popular, if not overused. It was so popular that at least two pirated versions were issued by other phototype houses. And the pioneer psychedelic poster artist Victor Moscoso credits Artone specifically, and Chwast generally, as influencing his own distinctive style of design.

Chwast used the upper- and lowercase alphabet on the Artone counter display box and eventually applied it to other projects, including posters and book covers. Strick was not troubled that his logo was being reused as a commercial alphabet because it furthered his product's identity. By the 1970s the popularity of the Artone alphabet was on the wane, but it continues to be emblematic of an era of graphic design when eclecticism was at its peak.

The Lover

Louise Fili

According to marketing wisdom, the book jacket designed by Louise Fili (b. 1951) for *The Lover* by Marguerite Duras could never propel the book to the bestseller list. The vignetted portrait of a young woman set against a soft-hued background and titled with delicate typography that casts a gentle shadow was bound to fail the rule that a jacket must strike the viewer's eye from a bookshelf ten feet away.

But *The Lover*, Duras's memoir of being a fifteen-year-old French schoolgirl who becomes the lover of a Chinese financier in prewar Indochina, did become a bestseller. Tales of forbidden sexuality may be commercially appealing, but Duras's story, like its jacket, is subtle and more complicated than it appears. It is filled with contradictions. She recalls the past with knowledge of the future, creating a tableau of memories superimposed one on another like double-exposed film. The prose is spare and unerotic, yet the words trigger imaginative pictures of this girl-woman who at fifteen struggles with sexual awakening amid cultural and familial taboos.

For the jacket, Fili chose a deceptively simple composition that characterized the writer's mix of the intangible and the real. The photograph was of the author at precisely her age in the memoir. Although the head-on pose is direct and engages the viewer, Duras's half-smile is enigmatic and elusive. The jacket's muted tones and feathered background added emotional subjectivity to the photograph's apparent objectivity. The thin-stroke typography complemented the spareness of the composition, but its shadow suggested weight and presence. Published by Pantheon in 1985, *The Lover*'s success was a vindication of Fili's artful style, which marketing people often criticized as too low key to be commercially viable. Readable or not at ten feet, it stood out because of its understated countenance, not in spite of it.

Since the 1960s, consolidations and takeovers in the book publishing industry have increased competition for shelf space and put greater emphasis on the marketing and promotion of books. Book jacket and cover design in the 1960s was typified by Paul Bacon's jackets that featured large type for titles and author's names and small, illustrated scenes intended to summarize the book.

In the mid to late 1970s Fili—then art director at Pantheon—and others departed from modernist aesthetics and approached their designs as miniposters with integrated type and image in the spirit of the late nineteenth-century advertising posters. They researched typographic styles of the past and drew inspiration from movements like futurism, Jugendstil, and constructivism, incorporating them into contemporary work. This style, called "retro," was similar to postmodernism in its eclecticism and reliance on past motifs; postmodernism, however, drew more from Greek, Roman, and Renaissance sources. Fili's work was distinguished by a conceptual underpinning and an ability to set a mood appropriate for literature that superseded postmodernism's tendency toward a cut-and-paste pastiche of passé forms.

At Pantheon, a trade division of Random House that published fiction and popular nonfiction titles that leaned toward the academic, Fili was given a comparatively small list of books, which allowed her to design most of the covers herself. Initially little attention was paid to her covers, just like those of the other designers before her. She soon realized what great opportunity for change lay in this environment where no one had high expectations. Fili recalled a comment made to her by an art director colleague, "You're lucky. My editors have bad taste; yours have no taste."

How did she create an environment conducive to innovation and inspired design? "Slowly, very slowly." Fili recalled. "I set out to educate them, albeit very slowly and continuously, with incremental changes and innovations: matte laminations, unusual paper stocks, different types of photography and illustration, and, of course, experimentation with type." She broke new ground graphically but always spent less than any of her colleagues, so no one complained.

By 1985, when *The Lover* was published, Fili had used hundreds of typefaces devised from reinventions or interpretations of existing typefaces that were either outdated, overlooked, or from a different era. In Fili's hands they came alive. Her long-time love of letterforms found a home at Pantheon, where for Fili the best part of designing jackets was that "every day I could use a different typeface." Since college she had frequently traveled to Europe to collect all types of printed ephemera, to photograph signage, and to study poster and type design. She clipped faces from old printing manuals and saved even just a few letters from old books or posters if they caught her eye.

When it came time to design, Fili drew tissue after tissue until just the right letterforms evolved to capture the particular mood or emotional tone of the book. Then, she hunted for a typesetter who carried the typeface. "Usually no one did, so I had to start from scratch and rebuild it, letter by letter, for my needs," Fili told illustrator Dugald Stermer in an article in *Communication Arts* magazine (September/October 1986). With the typeface reconstructed or redesigned, she then hired a professional to render the new letterforms (this was before Fontographer). Occasionally, as was the case with *The Lover*, the title and author's name were rendered exactly as they would appear on the jacket, complete with any special effects like the shadow. She has altered the stress, weight, slant, or width of typefaces to achieve an unusual effect. Her combinations of letterforms and juxtapositions of type styles within a single composition were rarely safe, but the unexpected combinations resulted in work that while respectful of a book's content nevertheless projected a highly intuitive, expressive style.

Considered tame by today's standards, which, thanks to the computer, present custom typography and unexpected visual juxtapositions as the norm, Fili's jackets and covers nevertheless opened the door for further innovation. In the late 1980s art director Carol Carson and designers Barbara de Wilde and Chip Kidd for Alfred A. Knopf, and, later, Michael Ian Kaye for Farrar, Straus, & Giroux in particular have expanded the ways books present themselves in the marketplace. Unusual materials and textures have transformed books into intimate objects. Imagery made of visual fragments, quirky typography, and aggressive compositions have pushed the limits of conceptual interpretation, occasionally providing only tangential clues to the content of the book. Over the eleven years she was at Pantheon, Fili's precisionist covers, with their typographic sensitivity and conceptual illustration, moved beyond mimicking content.

French Paper

Charles Spencer Anderson

Some call the current trend in revivalist design postmodern, vernacular, or retro; Charles Spencer Anderson (b. 1958) once called it *bonehead*, a word that conjures up goofy cartoon characters and self-mockingly describes a design mannerism that draws heavily on 1930s and 1940s stock commercial art. But Anderson's design is anything but goofy. Sentimental? Maybe. Nostalgic? Possibly. Silly? At times. But *ironic* is more to the point. His is a highly polished graphic style that has evolved into a distinct dialect rooted in American vernacularism. Rather than a trendy trope intended to exploit a popular fashion for quaint pastiche, this is a consistent formal vocabulary, featuring a lexicon of repeatedly used images, typefaces, and dingbats, which signifies both an attitude in contemporary design and this designer's particular obsession with pop visual culture. What began as parody is raised to the level of art, much in the same way that pop artists of the 1960s elevated the artifacts of commercial culture to icon status.

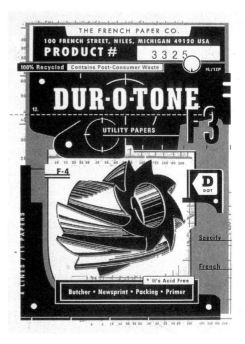

Anderson's long-running campaign for the French Paper Company borrowed the iconography of early commercial printing and incorporated it into witty rebus-like compositions that critiqued the mindless ubiquity of these once anonymous materials by placing them in a comic light. If postmodernism is a reappreciation of passé forms as a critical commentary of modernism, then Anderson's approach is the humorous arm of this graphic design movement. His quotation of common visual advertising clichés and sampling of gothic commercial typography uncovered a lost aesthetic that had been dismissed as artless by the masters of orthodox modern visual communications. By the 1960s the cartoony printer's cuts and trade characters that would later form the corpus of Anderson's work had sunk to the nadir of graphic achievement and were repudiated by modern formalists whose mission was to raise the level of visual beauty and literacy.

Although Anderson did not set out to be a counter-revolutionary, he discovered the graphic integrity woven into the crude innocence of time-worn vernacular images, appreciated them for their nonsensical qualities, and promulgated their use as design imagery. Here the various elements of the French Paper campaign, including paper specimens that were developed as toys, playing cards, and other graphic playthings, exploited the more camp characteristics for the purpose of engaging the viewer in a distinct visual world. Since Anderson was not of a generation that fought the war to make the world safe for universal design, he did not harbor the same aesthetic prejudices as these designers. For him, discovering artifacts in old printing catalogs, type manuals, and other industrial ephemera was like uncovering a Pharaoh's tomb. Yet Anderson did not merely display his archaeological finds, he revived their components by distorting, reshaping, and otherwise transforming vintage iconography into a distinct style that was applied to a range of packages, brochures, books, posters, advertisements, and products.

Anderson's bonehead style began in the mid-1980s when President Ronald Reagan made nostalgia into national policy. It was a time when, as critic Natalia Ilyin writes, "nostalgia twisted truth out of its socket" by forcing the public to accept the false simplification of a vague, mythic past. The earliest iterations of Anderson's design were consistent with retro trends, but it was not the graphic design analog of, say, the nostalgic TV show *Happy Days*. Anderson's was never a totally nostalgic conceit aimed at exploiting that momentary fad. On the contrary, much like the folklorist who discovers lost or forgotten stories that tell grand tales, Anderson's images became the basis for multiple narratives. While the style was used to promote the wares of companies like French Paper, Urban Outfitters, and the Turner Network, among others, it simultaneously told a story of commercial design itself.

Anderson and his design staff position products, establish allure, and attract audiences through precisionist designs. It is noteworthy that such an identifiable design signature succeeded in a field where most graphic designers avoid a single specific stylistic mannerism. But Anderson does not practice monolithic design. Within a proscribed framework there is formal and conceptual range. Over the years much of the vintage advertising sampling has been replaced by original still-life photographs and conceptual illustration, which allows Anderson to communicate with various voices. Still, Anderson's work is governed by an aesthetic that rules the color palette and conceptual thrust. His spirit is equal parts irony, history, and the down and dirty visual effluvia of the twentieth century.

Through the flagship CSA Archive Catalog of Stock Art, Anderson has both reintroduced and laid claim to many of the forgotten artifacts of American commercial printing, and in doing so he has made a ragtag collection of random forms into a regiment of disciplined artworks. Or put another way, he has made a variety of generic visual idioms into an accessible design lexicon. In popularizing these forms Anderson has also contributed to the continuum of design by building on what designer Art Chantry referred to as American commercial folk art—the anonymous artifacts of the commercial era. In the original forms that Anderson draws upon the customer was never aware of the human hand, the images just matter-of-factly materialized in newspapers, "shocards," and flyers. In Anderson's work, however, the presence of the artist/designer is always apparent, and it is this intervention that makes his appropriation (and ultimate invention) into a commentary of sorts on the state of design, past and present.

Propaganda

Art Chantry

When Art Chantry (b. 1954) started designing posters in the late 1970s, a time when corporate design budgets were high and slickness was the vogue, he appropriated found art and printed his work on cheap paper. The untutored look was a preference born of a youthful interest in surfer and hot rod culture, psychedelia, comic books, and monster magazines. As an adult, Chantry revisited these pop culture influences as the basis for his personal iconography. Sampling vernacular imagery was an old idea, dating back to 1920s dada and 1960s psychedelia, but Chantry was not being nostalgic. He distilled the salient points and developed a cut-and-paste style that reveled in quirky typography, silly lettering, and absurd collage. "I'm basically an artist masquerading as a graphic designer," he explained. "I have a degree in painting, though my teacher used to scream because I put type on my paintings." When he left school in 1978 the punk scene was in full pitch, and scores of posters by seasoned unprofessionals were plastered everywhere. "I thought, well, here is someplace I can fit in," he continued.

Chantry defines commercial art as America's true folk art, not so much the work of individuals as the work of culture itself. "This seems to be kind of an aberrant idea to the design community, because it rejects the 'great man' theory of history," he said. "Although certain individuals are great practitioners, the things I tend to champion are subculture design styles that have been lost or forgotten." He found a fresh vein of vernacular gold in a lost industrial graphic design style that was prevalent from 1945 to 1955 in tool catalogs and trade journals for the steel, nuclear, and other heavy industries. He designed advertisements and catalogs for an alternative Seattle arts group by lifting entire pages from old precision machine and tool catalogs and adding only new type. Like the 1960s pop artists, Chantry paid homage to commercial and industrial art, but unlike them he did not merely sanctify these lost artifacts of popular culture; he recycled them as functional graphic designs.

The crude quality achieved by craftsmen isolated from international design movements held great appeal for one who regularly undermined the canon. Years before the vernacular became an official 1980s graphic style, and before the progressive design academies affixed cultural theories to such things, Chantry became a design archaeologist. "I unearthed the work of naïfs and then tried to ape it," he admitted. "Ultimately it became part of my general vocabulary and all of a sudden my language expanded." Other "outlaw" or anti-canonical styles, such as tattoos and "the Hallmark card idea of what hippie stuff looked like in the 1960s" informed his work, too.

A large number of Chantry's posters for alternative theater companies in Seattle were done amidst considerable competition because as he put it, "everyone here seems to be a graphic designer. So it becomes a supply and demand thing; prices are usually low and quality must be high." One of his most memorable projects was the design for a small run of three hundred posters for *Propaganda*, a production of the New City Theatre Company, one of Seattle's most avant-garde independent groups. Although the play opened in 1990 to lukewarm reviews and closed soon afterward, the poster left an indelible image. For this low-budget job, Chantry took a photograph of a man's tormented face from a 1950s clip-art book. It was enlarged and flopped, and printed over itself twice to give the sense of three dimensions. The cheapest way to print it was on a web offset newspaper press, and therefore Chantry produced the original artwork on a smaller scale than the finished, ordering the printer to enlarge it five times to give it an even cruder surface. The poster symbolized the plot of the script but avoided a literal interpretation. "I rejected the billboard school of poster design which says the message should be given and received immediately. I don't think that anyone is going to go to the play based on the poster anyway," Chantry said.

Generally, Chantry comes up with a concept and sells it to the client as an idea. "I became acquainted with the work of the late Robert Brownjohn [Brownjohn Chermayeff Geismar] who during the early 1960s was such a brilliant conceptualist that he could sell ideas to his clients over the telephone. He believed that if it wasn't good enough to talk it out, then it wasn't good enough to take to completion. I try to get so well versed with the client's needs that my concepts fit the problem, and I too can verbalize them before putting them to paper," he explained. If a client demands a more visible interpretation, Chantry sketches things out, but most of his composition is done in the mechanical stage. That's where he does his best work because his art *is* the mechanical. "When I depart from the direct hands-on approach my work gets somewhat rote and sterile, but being that the mechanical is only a step away from reproduction it is closer to fresh than other methods," he said referring to the nineteenth-century method of working directly on the litho stone.

When Chantry began he did not have access to typesetting facilities, so he generated type by photocopying it from books, cutting it out letter by letter, and pasting it into place with glue sticks. Each early project, therefore, had its own personality. Some were image heavy/type light and others were all type, enabling him to learn about the expression of different letterforms. "When I make type decisions that interplay with an image it is usually based on gut reaction. I might scan all my old type books—or comic books and things like that—until I find something that just feels right. I try to avoid type that clashes with my image."

Sooner or later, the immediate advertising function ceases and a poster becomes an artifact. Understanding this, Chantry has designed certain posters, *Propaganda* included, that change over time—inks that fade to reveal other aspects of the work, papers that deteriorate quickly. Sometimes they included thematic ideas that changed with time. "I would love for my posters to have an archaeological function, so that twenty years from now, when people are researching certain aspects of this culture they will be able to refer to my posters for reference to a historical moment."

COMMERCE

The show card (or sho-card) was the quintessential form of early commercial art. It embodied essential design attributes of balance, harmony, and proportion that enabled unsophisticated designers, primarily job printers, to produce effective advertising. But even such modern pioneers as El Lissitzky, Jan Tschichold, E. McKnight Kauffer, Herbert Bayer, and Paul Rand adhered to the same design truth associated with the show card: Primary colors and sans serif typefaces resulted in eye-catching design.

Starting in the late nineteenth century, the show card was a piece of bristol board on which a letterer or artist would draw or paint a message or image. The quantities that were produced were invariably limited. Eventually show cards were printed on multilith presses, and stereotype plates were designed by art service agencies, which distributed to printing companies large and small. Standard show cards were produced by printers and sign makers, who inserted their own wood and metal types into the empty mortised sections on the printing plate.

Various styles filled sample books, but around 1920 the now classic format was initiated by Empire Litho, a printing firm in Massachusetts, and was quickly adopted by job printers throughout the nation. These predominantly type-based posters printed against one or two stark primary colors became the most ubiquitous medium of advertising for all kinds of regional events, including county fairs, vaudeville and movies, prize fights, square dances, and political campaigns.

3 Color Design No. 159

Functional design was essential: gothic type, flat colors, and sometimes the split-fountain technique—where two colors at the top and bottom of the card mix in the middle to give a multichromatic effect. The occasional stock line cut or halftone might be used for decoration, and a variety of eye-catching borders were required. "The border demands full consideration in card design," wrote F. A. Pearson in the 1925 edition of "Ticket and Showcard Designing." "Its effect is that of a frame round a picture. It limits attention within its bounds." In addition, bull's-eyes, stripes, and other geometric patterns, not unlike Russian constructivist and Bauhaus compositions, guided the viewer's attention to the message.

The genre has been both parodied and used as inspiration for contemporary work. Paula Scher's New York Public Theater posters, for example, with their bold gothics of varying sizes set against yellow or red backgrounds, are admittedly influenced by the show card. In its original form, it is still used for carnivals, circuses, auctions, and concerts. The classic show card has survived shifts in trend and fashion because it is the essence of good design.

Some celebrities collect paintings and others, sculptures. Aga Kahn, Persian billionaire and husband to 1940s movie star Rita Hayworth, was a razor blade wrapper collector. Given his untold wealth, he could have anything in the world—in fact, each year he was literally presented with his weight in gold and diamonds—yet in

addition to cars, homes, and art, he was inexplicably drawn to the graphics of an inexpensive, everyday commodity. Filling scores of bulging albums with blade wrappers from around the globe, he amassed what may be the largest collection of its kind (part of which is currently held by the Wolfsonian Institution in Miami, Florida). But he was not alone. During the 1920s, 1930s, and 1940s, razor blade wrappers were among the most sought-after ephemerally designed objects of consumer culture. And it is safe to say that even with the thousands that Aga Kahn amassed, he did not collect them all.

The safety razor and blade was more convenient than the straightedge and strop, and caused fewer cuts, too. So, since the introduction of the double-edge blade in the late nineteenth century, and its widespread adoption during the twentieth, every industrial country prior to the age of multinational conglomerates produced its own unique brands. Nonetheless, the product was always based on the same form. The classic double-edge blade—made from thinly stamped steel and designed with slots on the front that could be snugly sandwiched between the tight-fitting layers of the razor—had not changed during much of the century, until the advent of the double- and triple-blade cartridges of today's "super razors." At the outset, therefore, little distinguished one blade from the next, although Swedish steel was a grade above German steel, which was thought to be more durable than Italian steel. Yet in truth, most were made at the same few foundries and exported to hundreds of companies that packaged and distributed them.

The key factor that distinguished one blade from another was the brand name and the package design. Like cigarettes, razor blades were impressed with heroic, romantic, ironic, and nonsensical mnemonic names, such as Mac's Smile, Merlin, Super Gam, 7 o'Clock, Tre Teste, Carezza, Honor, Stormo, and Eclipise. Each was adorned with a mini-poster design—sometimes bold novelty typography, other times drawings of elegant men, sensuous beauties, and goofy mascots. The blades themselves were made from white, blue, and gold steel, and were differentiated from each other with such superlatives as "extra," "superior," and "super extra," although the same traits were really common to all. A few were touted as flexible, and at least one was said to be "magic."

In the early days of what is now called branding, any verbal and visual trick was used to capture attention. Once purchased, a good clean shave would presumably ensure the customer's loyalty.

Why were there so many brands and wrappers? Well, during the 1920s and 1930s when these packages were current, razor blades were fairly easy and inexpensive to produce, so one company could issue half a dozen mini-brands in the hope of hitting big with just one. Every basic safety razor model accepted the same double-edge blades, which would last for between five and ten shaves before turning dull, thus adding to the widespread need to replenish supplies. Since consumers were not necessarily loyal to any one blade—except in the United States and England, where Gillette was long a major brand—it was incumbent on producers to distribute enough new products to maintain the sense of novelty that seduced most buyers.

Blades are Lilliputian, so manufacturers had to find visible means to attract the consumer. The most common sales devices were easel-back point-of-purchase displays (or "risers") on which tiny individual boxes containing five to ten blades were attached to cardboard hooks. These countertop "standees" were colorful, eye-catching, and cheap. Another common form was the countertop box with die-cut panels that, when raised off the surface of the box, highlighted the logo or trademark of the product.

Blade packs were anonymously designed by commercial artists in printing plants that specialized in this and other forms of consumer packaging. The format was obviously proscribed, but within the limitations, anything was possible. Color was a requisite, and many blade wrappers were printed with metallic inks or multiple primary hues. Simplicity was the watchword for obvious reasons, yet a few brands—such as Apollo No. 10, a German blade—were designed with an engraving of the Greek god framed by classical filigree, and Lama Italia, an Italian brand, had Novocento-styled graphic iconography. Most of the wrappers were as colorful as posters and as visually spirited as book jackets.

Trademarks were necessary for promoting the leading brands—and some not-so-famous ones, too. The Gillette Blue Blade company invested all its equity in a simple package, colored in two shades of blue with a stark black-and-white photograph of the founder, Englishman King C. Gillette (captioned with his signature). This remained the company's design for well over fifty years. For the Italian product Tre Teste, three look-alike, stylishly coifed female heads float above the brand name. Souplex, a German product, features the happy, well-fed face of a burgher mortised inside a circle. One brand even used a topsy-turvy head as a mascot—turn it one way he is unshaven; turn the other way and the face is clean as a baby's behind.

Blade wrappers range from commercially sophisticated to amateurishly naïve. A case in point is the Hamburg Ring Blade (made in Germany), featuring a distortedly drawn ocean vessel heading on a collision course with a life preserver that bears the brand name. By current standards this, and indeed all the specimens from this timeframe, are quaint. Today, packages have scant personality but a lot of marketing surveys to back them up. Many fewer products are on the market, while those that remain have heaps of high-visibility brand recognition. These vintage wrappers and displays are not, however, simply nostalgic artifacts; they are remnants from a time when a recognizable package design could shave a few customers off the competition.

Don't ask me why collecting matchbox labels is called "phillumeny." It is not in most dictionaries yet, but just type the word into an Internet search engine, and entries abound with phillumeny Web sites replete with colorful matchbox labels assembled by presumably obsessive phillumenists.

Personally, I do not fit this obsessive profile. However, I do admit to collecting my fair share of these so-called light boxes for their exquisite craft and artistry, as well their particular wit and beauty. And I suspect that these are some reasons why they are so popular among the truly avid collectors. But the other reason people are obsessive about collecting them, I suspect, is that so many were produced over the span of almost two centuries—in more than a score of nations, which resulted in an extraordinary variety of designs—that the utter quantity gives the genre incredible allure. Of all the minor popular arts, matchbox-label design was certainly one of the most major. And out of all the countries that produced matchboxes, the Japanese were at the top of the form.

Modern matchbox labels follow the invention of the safety match, in 1844, when Swedish chemist Gustaf Erik Pasch developed a phosphorous compound that was stable but would combust when friction was applied on contact. The first matchboxes were designed with a small strip of striking material on its narrow side. Pasted on the wider top was a relatively intricate woodblock design, or an illustration printed with the brand name and reference to the country of origin (e.g., "Made in Japan"). Matches became profitable export businesses for Sweden, Thailand, Russia, Italy, and Japan, to name a few, as each produced its own graphics, which were both unique and universal.

During the early twentieth century, matchbox art from around the world began to share many of the same graphic conceits, among them comic animals, imaginary coats of arms, intricate ornamentation, and portraits of real and mythical beings. These were common naturalistic images for a good many packages before the age of pseudo-scientific branding. Matchboxes made at the turn of the century used English as the common language, indicating the broad scope of international trade. But each nation also maintained a distinct iconographic accent that revealed its unique visual heritage and national preoccupations (e.g., the samurai or Mt. Fuji for Japan).

Japan's match industry was exceptionally prodigious, and the designs produced were various, plentiful, and consistent with the early twentieth-century expansion of the nation's heavy industries. Commercial art played an important role, in general, as it developed brand recognition and sales for new industrial products. It put Japanese graphic designers at the forefront of what is now called "branding." The designers were clearly influenced by imported European styles such as Victorian and art nouveau, and later by Art Deco and the Bauhaus, which were introduced through Japanese graphic arts trade magazines and incorporated into the design of matchbox labels during the late 1920s and 1930s. Western graphic mannerisms were harmoniously combined with traditional Japanese styles and geometries from the Meiji period (1868–1912), typified by both their simple and complex ornamental compositions. Since matches were a big export industry, and the Japanese dominated the markets in the United States, Australia, England, France, and even India, matchbox design exhibited a hybrid typography that wed Western and Japanese styles into an intricate mélange. The domestic brands, however, were routinely designed in a more reductive—though typically Japanese—manner, solely using Kanji characters.

In Japan, matchboxes were a mainstay of daily, vernacular culture. Safety matches became an important staple in part because they satisfied a primal social need (fire), and because of the nation's substantial lumber industry, which supplied a near endless supply of material. The largest Japanese match manufacturers, including Shungen & Co., Mitsui & Co., Seiryukwan, and Koyoukan Binnaka Seizo, from Osaka, Koshi, and Himeji, Japan, were all well known, but the artists who created their respective designs were purposely kept in the shadows—like most commercial artisans in other quotidian fields.

Anonymity was the fate for those who produced the most vibrant, as well as the most ephemeral, products of the Japanese popular arts. Nonetheless, certain manufacturers were known for certain styles designed to appeal to different aesthetic tastes. Nisshinsha's labels often featured a central "trademark" (a rabbit suggesting good luck) or a vignette (two-winged cherubs framing a globe), while Shiyosegumi Seizo's labels were heavily typographic, with tiny images integrated into the overall design. But for the most part, the labels followed a standard template that was developed in the late nineteenth century and was maintained for decades.

Phillumenists explain that the extraordinarily large number of diverse matchbox labels had to do with the sophisticated marketing ruse of cultivating a collector's mentality among their consumers. This kind of thinking is not unlike the strategy for selling razor blades (where one brand issued various collectible packages and wrappers) or cigarettes (where serially collectible cards were incentives).

During this period, matchboxes were sold indiscriminately through all kinds of stores and vendors as a necessity not just for lighting the ubiquitous smoking materials, but also for routinely igniting fires in ovens, grills, and heaters. Not until the 1930s were matchboxes and matchbooks—the newer, more compact invention—produced as vehicles specifically to promote and advertise restaurants, shops, and businesses. In fact, the comparatively early stage of Japanese matchbox manufacturing and design seemed bent on making its profit by satisfying the public's desire for the purity of their design. Back then, the only thing that these labels promoted were their matchboxes.

The *Priester Match* poster is so startling that it grabs the viewer's eye in an instant. Of course, the aim of all good advertising is to make the unmemorable memorable by mythologizing the commonplace products of daily life. However, before the *Priester Match* poster first appeared on the Berlin poster hoardings in 1906, most advertising was ornate and wordy. The persuasive simplicity of the Priester poster was rare indeed. Moreover, no one had yet heard the name of its eighteen-year-old creator, Lucian Bernhard (1883–1972), or the genre of advertising he invented, which became known as the *Sachplakat*, or object poster.

Bernhard's early object posters are ubiquitous in poster anthologies. The most striking excel in terms of their graphic eloquence, simplicity, and strength. The method he defined, and the style that ultimately emerged, was predicated on an unadorned, bold-outlined, centered representation of the product being advertised, like a typewriter, spark plug, or piano, placed against a flat color background of forest green, bright purple, or deep orange. The lettering was reduced to a few words, usually the brand name alone. The object in the *Sachplakat*, rendered much like a woodcut, grabbed the attention of passersby as it aesthetically and unambiguously hawked its message. The virtue of this invention was that viewers didn't have to navigate through tedious selling copy, confusing graphics, or other visual distractions. The image was clear, concise, and downright pleasing to the tired eye.

Bernhard's formative years coincided with the explosion of art nouveau in France and Jugendstil in Germany. Munich was the center of the "radical" German graphic arts, but he decided to settle in Berlin where the wonders of industrial production and commercialism were manifest. Like most turn-of-the-century industrial capitals, Berlin bustled with vehicular traffic, was bathed in electric lights and signs, and exalted in the progress of the industrial age. Berlin businesses routinely sponsored poster competitions as a means of identifying new talent for the expanding advertising industry. When Bernhard was around sixteen he decided to enter a competition sponsored by the Priester Match company and judged by some of the leading promoters of the burgeoning poster movement. Two hundred Marks (about $50) would be awarded to the winner, but more important, the winning entry would be printed and pasted around Berlin. Bernhard jumped at the opportunity, and, with little time to produce his entry, he reportedly made some crucial, instinctive design decisions.

Using paint and brush, he laid down a brown/maroon background—an unusual choice at that time; most posters used either black or bright primaries—on which he rendered an ashtray with a pair of wooden matches along the side. Seeing that the ashtray needed some additional graphic device to balance the composition, he drew in a cigar. Logically, from the cigar wafted smoke, and from the smoke, what else, but a few scantily clad Jugendstil dancing girls. The ashtray needed grounding, so he painted in a checkered tablecloth. At the top of the poster in block letters he rendered the word *Priester*. The original sketch does not exist, but what a mélange it must have been. Nevertheless, proud of his work, he showed it to his mentor at the time, a political caricaturist, who congratulated Bernhard on the wonderful *cigar* poster. Bernhard immediately realized his error and proceeded to remake the poster by painting out the cigar, then the smoke, then the ashtray, then the tablecloth, leaving only a pair of red matches with yellow tips and the brand name, Priester, in gothic lettering. He met the competition deadline without a moment to spare.

Upon seeing it for the first time, the judges, feeling it was too empty, threw it unceremoniously into the garbage can, where it would have remained had not the most important judge arrived late. Burly, bald, and jocular, Ernst Growald was the sales manager for the Hollerbaum and Schmidt lithography firm, which was widely admired as Berlin's leading advertising poster printer—a kind of proto-advertising agency. Growald was a man of unique vision who understood the critical role that advertising could play in Germany's expanding economy. He also had good taste, and, not seeing any other noteworthy entries on the judges table, turned his wayward eyes to the artwork in the trash. Removing it, he hung it on the wall, and was reported to have exclaimed: "This is my first prize. This is genius!" Bernhard won the contest. With Growald as agent and broker, Bernhard never again wanted for paying work.

The Priester poster was a great success for the company, too. In a highly competitive marketplace the message was so simple that it emblazoned the brand in everyone's memory. By chance, Bernhard tapped into the power of simplicity and created a paradigm of modern functionality. Later Bauhaus inventions were hardly more reductive. He modeled much of his subsequent work on that poster, and though many of his designs were good, he never really surpassed Priester for ingenuity. And why should he? The *Sachplakat* was not merely a style, it was a tool for spreading the word. It would become dated over time, but only in the same way that one tool might be superseded by a better tool.

As the one who discovered Bernhard, Growald felt he had the right (and certainly he had Bernhard's permission) to encourage others to work in this manner. He formed a loose-knit "school" of kindred artists known as the Berliner Plakat. Some members followed Bernhard to the letter; others veered off in their own directions, adding a touch of humor or a typographical flourish. As a charter member, indeed the school's foremost innovator, Bernhard became involved with many of what was also known as the *Plakatstil* (poster style).

Bernhard's *Sachplakat* might very well be credited with providing the model of objectivity that was ultimately adopted later by the progressive segments of the advertising industry. In the 1930s dramatic still life photography, responding to the call for a machine art for a machine age, heroicized the industrial product in much the same way that Bernhard celebrated mere matches, spark plugs, and gear shafts. Photographers took Bernhard's notion a step beyond the sentimentality endemic to the drawn or painted image and were therefore even more modern in the formal sense. But Bernhard also prefigured pop art in his popularization of the object. The success of the *Priester Match* poster rested on figuratively rubbing two sticks together that ignited a new methodology. Without Bernhard's pioneering effort, it is possible that objectivity as method and style would have taken much longer to catch on.

| **Golden Blossom Honey** |
| Gustav Jensen |
| |

In promotional advertisements Gustav Jensen (1898–1942?) called himself a "Designer to Industry." He designed some of the most appealing packaging and advertising of the late 1920s and early 1930s. "His peers called him a Designers' Designer," recalled Paul Rand, who, in his early twenties, fruitlessly tried to get a job at Jensen's one-man studio. Rand later borrowed Jensen's *beaux-arts* style before developing his own modern vocabulary. Jensen developed the elegant identity for Charles of the Ritz and other stylish companies, but his most enduring design was the packaging for Golden Blossom Honey, which has kept virtually the same label for some fifty years.

Enigma shrouds Gustav Jensen's life. He is known to have been born in Copenhagen, Denmark, in 1898; his father was a banker and lawyer, and his mother came from a long line of ministers. He studied philosophy at the University of Copenhagen, but with his deep bass voice he wanted instead to become an opera singer. He developed an interest in architecture, however, and architecture somehow led to an absorption in art, and art caused him to pursue aesthetic beauty in typography and printed design. Jensen produced a large body of work for companies like General Motors, Westvaco, DuPont, Edison, American Telephone and Telegraph, Morrel Meats, Gilbert Products, and more. He brought a special elegance to a marketplace obsessed with fashionable conceits. Although making purely functional merchandise was not his primary concern, Jensen believed that the designer had a responsibility to provide the public with appealing products. "The public," he wrote, "is being imposed upon all the time, given stones for bread; the kind of bread we artists can give the public is hard sincere work straight from ourselves. Never mind what the style racketeers say."

Jensen's approach was decorative but not ornate. His work is characterized by economically applied textures derived in part from the

Weiner Werkstatte (Vienna Workshop) and the Glasgow School, whose products were imported through Danish retailers. Jensen was a proponent of neither the modern nor the *moderne*: he did not believe in functionalism as an end in itself. Utility is what designers begin with, he said. "The useful tools of civilization come first and then beauty is added. If a thing is to satisfy modern man, it must be beautiful as well as useful." But for Jensen, beauty could be separated from function and simply please the mind and all its mysterious senses. Advertising, he suggested, is only useful when it is beautiful, and Jensen took great pains to see that the many small newspaper ads he designed were eye-catching in the most provocative ways. This aesthetic requirement was apparent in much of his work, even everyday packaging, as exemplified by the Golden Blossom Honey container with its typographic purity and decorative personality.

Jensen based his process on elimination; it was simple but exhaustive. *PM* magazine noted that "he does not make one sketch only, he makes hundreds." Jensen's individuality was expressed as much in the visible style of his wares as in his overall approach. One friend wrote about him this way: "Gustav Jensen has a grand vision. He is a man who has the courage of his own convictions. A lover of everything in nature, he is impatient with fakes, fads, and fashions; he is extremely sensitive to beauty that is noble and poetic; and he is a master of design."

In the 1930s his packaging filled the annuals. But during the war, owing in part to a cessation in the manufacture of nonessential goods, he was underutilized. Nevertheless he continued as a one-man studio, making design and sculpture until he died in the early 1940s.

Portable, collapsible, and durable. Before air conditioning, handheld fans were a necessity. In the hotter climes neither man nor woman would be caught without one. During the late nineteenth and early twentieth centuries fans became the ideal vehicle for advertisements. The fan had two sides—perfect for displaying two messages at once—one aimed at the holder and the other, the beholder. It could be argued that the advertising fan prefigured promotional T-shirts and shopping bags.

Advertising fans were used in many commercial cultures. In the United States they were common in the South, promoting social events, local businesses (undertakers were among the most frequent users of advertising fans), and political parties. Certain job printers specialized in fans and offered a variety of standard shapes and stock designs, but none was as widely used as the fattened oval on a wooden stick given out by local merchants for free on unbearably hot summer days. Like all American advertising of the time, however, the typical American advertising fan was essentially utilitarian; devoid of artistic flourish, it conveyed a message clearly and simply.

Compared to French fans of the same period, the American specimens were dreary. Compared to French publicity in general, America appeared to be a backwater rather than a bustling commercial culture and the world's most progressive industrial nation. The French were always ahead of Americans in the marriage of art and commerce, and this was true of their advertising fans, often designed by famous designers to complement their poster campaigns for France's most prestigious industries.

The exact year that advertising was first placed on fans is not known, but the earliest advertising fan has been traced to 1880 when a stylish specimen, like those fashion accessories from the time of Louis XIV, was imprinted with a romantic scene and swash type that announced a

French industrial exposition. The French pioneered a variety of formats for advertising fans that ranged from the classic folded and gathered form to a splayed peacock-like version called a "Jenny Lind" and the *coccarda* printed on very thin vellum and glued to two sticks, which when pulled apart and joined in a 360-degree turn revealed a brilliant circle of color. Other classically based formats included the *fontage,* a folded half oval, and the *palmette,* a smallish boxy-shaped pleated type; both were attached to foldable spokes. Conversely, the poor-man's fan was usually either a piece of cardboard pasted on a stick or a single piece of die-cut cardboard that formed a handle and paddle.

In France, fans were the premium of choice for manufacturers and businesses, notably the department store Galleries Lafayette, which complemented each seasonal merchandise campaign with a new fan much the way Bloomingdales does with its thematic shopping bags. Most of the store's fan designs from the 1920s and 1930s were rendered in the elegant *moderne* style popularized in Paris at the 1925 *Exposition Internationale des Arts Décoratifs et Industriels Modernes.* The liquor industry regularly employed advertising fans to complement its various other means of product promotion. Fans for Amer Picon, St. Raphaël, Cognac Sorin, Amourette, and other well-known brands and distilleries were distributed, usually during the summertime, to customers at myriad French cafés. A profusion of colorful fluttering was often seen along the boulevards on the hottest days of the year.

While some mimicked famous posters, notably A. M. Cassandre's well-known Dubonnet sequence, *Dubo, Dobon, Dubonnet,* most fans were custom designed for a specific purpose. Some were quite painterly, showing an elegant vignette or highly stylized characterizations. Usually the fronts had a strong image while the backs were reserved for selling copy; some fans had different images on front and back. Common visual themes included romantic and nostalgic scenes from the eighteenth and nineteenth centuries, but the most common, indeed the most beautiful images were rendered in the contemporary *art moderne* style. The rays of the unfolded fan provided the ideal canvas for *art moderne,* which used radiant lighting patterns borrowed from cubism as the basis for many decorative motifs.

Since their inception, critics have assailed billboards as a blight on the American landscape. Although legislation has been passed limiting them, outdoor advertising is much too important for business to be outlawed entirely. Moreover, billboard art is the cornerstone of America's poster history. Before radio and television, the billboard—strategically situated on roadways, buildings, and city streets—was the primary mass-advertising vehicle. Although many were produced by anonymous studio artists, leading illustrators and designers such as Lucian Bernhard (Rem cough syrup, Amoco gasoline), N. C. Wyeth (Coca Cola), Otis Shepard (Doublemint gum), A. M. Cassandre (Ford motors), and others applied their talents. Today, some of these mammoth images are important artifacts of the material culture.

The earliest recorded leasing of outdoor signboards in the United States occurred in 1870; they were on a fence around a post office under construction in New York City. Noting the increased need for advertising media, in 1872 the printing firm of Kissam and Allen began to lease its own poster panels. Soon poster-stands (as the billboard was first called) dotted the landscape. In 1891 a standard printed sheet (28" × 42") was offered in combinations ranging from one to twenty-four-sheets. And in 1912 the standard twenty-four-sheet poster (8' 10" × 19' 8") was the industry choice as the preferred size for its "Double A" poster panels—the ones still used today. Initially, billboards were sold by solicitors or agents often connected to a printing firm. In the 1920s advertising agencies assumed responsibility. From a handful of independent suppliers grew the Outdoor Advertising Association, which soon became the regulatory group employing inspectors to check on the construction and distribution of panels and the appearance of posters. By 1917, $350,000,000 was spent on outdoor advertising. By the mid-1920s, twice that amount. But according to critics, the quality of the American twenty-four-sheet poster was generally inferior to the smaller yet more innovative English, French, and German posters.

During the 1920s and 1930s, the golden years of American outdoor advertising, artistry was of secondary importance. Both the artist and designer in American advertising (where copywriters were the kings) were less important than in Europe (where the image was dominant). Stark communication, the need to steal viewers's attention for only a split second, dictated the look of billboards. The most successful combined art and message and conformed to historian Hamilton King's dictum that a poster should "seize a moment, exploit a situation with one daring sweep [of line and color] . . . all that can be told of a tale in the passing of an instant. It is dramatic and imaginative, yet it is saliently sincere."

Reeling from the Great Depression, American industry began its uphill drive to repair the damage during the 1930s. The twenty-four-sheet billboard became a symbol of this recovery. Aesthetics improved as some designers became more involved with the creative process. Advertisers accepted the seductive powers of modernistic imagery to sell their wares. And rather than a blight, billboards heralded the new industrial age, fostered a new consumerism, and symbolized a brighter future.

In 1933 Charles Chaplin wrote about the comic strip in society: "In a troubled world such as is the one in which we live, comic strips have become a powerful force to divert the public: to such a degree, in fact, that newspaper circulation depends largely upon their popularity. A comic artist is, therefore, lost if he does not reflect the public mind and appeal to the masses." At the same time cultural critic Gilbert Seldes wrote: "The comic strip is the most despised art form, yet with the exception of the movies it is also the most popular."

The comics offered diversions from daily life. They offered new heroes and antiheroes, spoke new languages and dialects, and fueled the imagination in ways unequaled by any other mass form. "The readership of the comics is one of the amazing phenomena of our contemporary society . . . ," wrote advertising analyst Harvey Zorbaugh. "Readership surveys indicate that every week more than sixty million adult men and women pore over the Sunday comic supplement." Everyone identified with comic characters—kids dressed like Buster Brown and parents named their babies Snookums after the character in *The Newlyweds*. Comic characters were like real people. In the late 1920s and 1930s, as comics became less comical and more dramatic (e.g., *Mary Worth*), they also hit hard and hit home on the basic themes of human nature.

The comic strip has always been a democratic form. Its word/ image construction invites easy access and is, therefore, an ideal vehicle for promoting ideas. Not surprisingly, during the 1930s—and lasting well into the 1950s—the comic strip was used to sell products as diverse as vegetable shortening, laundry detergent, acne medicine, breakfast cereal, light bulbs, toothpaste, towels, and automobiles. A few of the ads were penned by the masters themselves, but most were produced by anonymous copyists or acolytes working in advertising bullpens and art-service studios. The quality ranged from primitive comics to highly polished renderings to panels of photographs with speech balloons. Although the majority of the texts were written by hack copywriters, some were entertaining. Who can forget the famous Charles Atlas body-building ads where a weakling is humiliated, loses the girl, eats sand, and ultimately takes the Atlas course and gets revenge?

No one knows who conceived the first comic strip ad, but the comic strip was ignored by advertisers for almost three decades. Only after the pollster George Gallup released a report in 1930, at the height of the Great Depression, that ninety percent of all Americans read the comics and comic pages, did advertisers begin to use the form. In 1935 M. C. Gaines, manager of the color printing department of the McClure Newspaper Syndicate, wrote in *PM* magazine: "As a result of [the] discovery that the comics enjoy the widest appeal of all newspaper features, it is estimated that close to $1 billion worth of space has been filled with advertising of the comic strip type. . . . Color comic advertising has proven so profitable that, in the opinion of one of the country's foremost research authorities, there is a possibility that newspapers will be forced to print comics in color several times a week."

Evidence of the appeal of comic strip advertising was significant. In 1932, six months after initiating a comics advertising campaign to boost failing sales of its Grape Nuts cereal, General Foods announced an unprecedented surge in profits. Soon afterward, J. Walter Thompson's advertising agents requested comic strip ads for all their accounts, regardless of the appropriateness. The 1930s became known in advertising circles as "the balloon talk period." In a contemporary advertising trade journal a columnist wrote: "Psychologically the use of the comic technique is sound . . . Pictures [are] one of the best attention getting devices. . . . Simple human interest material, based on basic wants, holds interest and the brevity with which the story must be told [says] the reader is not asked to concentrate too long to get the story." Moreover, wrote Roland Marchand in *Advertising the American Dream: Making Way for Modernity 1920–40* (University of California Press, 1985), comic strip formats, like radio commercials, gave print advertisements a time dimension. Viewers also identified with the true story melodramas and real people testimonials so common in strips. No wonder advertisers hopped on the soap opera bandwagon when the *living comic strip* premiered in the mid-1930s.

To introduce the section on comic strip advertising in the *Fourteenth Annual of Advertising Art* (1935) the editor wrote that this new form "has been the complete overthrow of the government of advertising by conventional rule. With the aplomb of Ignatz Mouse tossing a brick at Krazy Kat, continuity and comic strips have impudently tossed aside advertising tradition, become legitimate and frequently astonishingly effective expressions. . . ."

Despite mass appeal and financial success, critics railed against comics, and serious advertising men deplored the comics' frivolity, childish escape, and otherwise degraded standards. Certain advertisers believed that the comic strip craze marked the nadir of an honorable profession, a catering to mindlessness. Despite advancements in advertising media, the Great Depression ultimately caused advertisers to try any scheme to sell their wares. "The cumulative effect of a decade of radio had crushed the vision of advertising as a broad educational force that would lift consumers to higher aesthetic tastes and intellectual pursuits," wrote Roland Marchard.

The critics could not, however, squelch the comics frenzy and were forced into the realization that the American people were not interested in high-brow advertising techniques. The consumer wanted a message that could be quickly and easily understood. The comic strip may have erred on the side of puerility, but until the mid-1950s, when television stole its thunder, comic strip ads were a mainstay of American advertising.

Alex Steinweiss created the first
record albums with original cover
art in the late 1930s. What seems
commonplace today was
revolutionary back then, when
heavy shellac seventy-eight rpm
records were packaged in
unadorned cardboard covers with
craft paper sleeves bound inside.
The title of the album was usually
embossed on the cover's front and
spine, and on rare occasions an
album might include a
reproduction of a famous
painting. Steinweiss's art was both
original and stylish, conforming

to contemporary French and German poster fashions where symbolic forms
and metaphors expressed the message. Rather than a portrait of the
recording artist, Steinweiss believed, and the management of Columbia
Records concurred, that provocative graphic symbols would stimulate the
audience's interest in the music. According to a 1939 article in *Newsweek*,
sales of the first illustrated album cover rose over 800 percent.

"I tried to get into the subject," Steinweiss explained in an
interview, "either through the music or the life and times of the
artist/composer. For example, for a Bartok piano concerto I took the
elements of the piano—the hammers, keys, strings—and composed them in
a contemporary setting. Since Bartok is Hungarian, I also put in the
suggestion of a peasant figure." For the album *La Conga* Steinweiss painted
an enlarged pair of hands playing on a stylized conga drum. For Gershwin's
original recording of *Rhapsody in Blue* he placed a piano on a dark blue field
illuminated only by the yellow glow of a lone street lamp. The moody scene
captured both the music and the city.

Steinweiss's designs maximized the limited image space. All the
characteristics of a large poster were brought to the forefront: strong central
image, eye-catching typography or lettering, and contrasting colors. At the
time the illustrated album cover was first introduced, record stores, which

were often sections near the record players in appliance stores, comprised shelf upon shelf of dreary album spines facing outward (they were called *tombstones* in the trade). Steinweiss's albums not only brightened up the surroundings, but the imagery also provided focal points for the consumer. Merchants began to display albums as objects of art, and listeners related the music to this art. Steinweiss inspired other record companies to use evocative covers, but until after World War II his were definitely the most distinctive.

For its formal strength and emotional force the most memorable was his cover for *Songs of Free Men* by Paul Robeson—a slave's chained hand holding a knife resonated as a symbol of freedom and heroism. Other European-inspired, though decidedly original, designs included his constructivist *Eddy Duchin* album and the cubist *Le Sacre du Printemps*. In addition to stylistic sampling, Steinweiss used classical typefaces, though he often complemented (or contrasted) them with a contemporary novelty face. For the cover for *La Bohème* he used an ornamental circus letter because it spoke to the frivolous nature of the opera. By the 1950s, with the advent of Swiss modernism, which proffered economical design, and the increased use of photography, Steinweiss's illustrative work looked dated. But for a moment in design history his invention pushed packaging conventions into an entirely new design genre.

A standing ovation at the Fillmore East, New York's premier music hall during the late 1960s, was reserved for rock-and-roll royalty. The Fillmore hosted the best bands of the age, and Fillmore audiences were jaded, demanding, and sometimes rude in the bargain. On one occasion, early in their career, the members of the band Sly and the Family Stone were shouted off stage because the audience could not wait a second longer for the evening's headliner, Jimi Hendrix, who received one of the longest and loudest ovations ever. That is, with the exception of the time in fall 1968 when Janis Joplin announced to the assembled fans that the cover for *Cheap Thrills*, the recent Big Brother and the Holding Company album, was illustrated by underground cartoonist R. Crumb. The audience went wild as a slide of the image filled the huge screen behind her.

Back then, Crumb (b. 1943) was as popular as any rock star. His cartoon inventions, Fritz the Cat, Mr. Natural, Honeybunch Kominsky, the Keep on Truckin' chorus line, and scores of raucous and ribald comix published in underground newspapers such as the *Bee, East Village Other*, and *Gothic Blimp Works* had earned him hero status throughout youth culture. He was in the vanguard of artists who forever busted the timidity and mediocrity that had been enforced since the mid-1950s by the industry's self-censoring organ, the Comics Code Authority. Through a combination of zany raunch and artful acerbity wed to unequaled pen-and-ink draftsmanship, Crumb's drawings of big-hipped hippie chicks, bug-eyed nerdy guys, and weird average-American white folk engaged in extraordinary (if unspeakable) acts pounded at the propriety and sanctity of an aged establishment. No wonder the union of Joplin and Crumb (who were born in the same year) was greeted with ecstatic delight when it was made public. There is no telling how many records were sold from that night's debut, but, musically, it was Big Brother's best album and graphically it was the most memorable cover art of the generation.

The *Cheap Thrills* cover was an ersatz comic strip with panels radiating from a central circle. Like illustrated liner notes, each panel contained a cartoon reference to either Joplin, Big Brother, or a song on the album. For the cut "I Need a Man to Love," Crumb has a zaftig Janis (his signature female archetype) almost bursting out of her tight clothes, fetchingly strewn on a bed. For "Ball and Chain," Joplin's classic tour de force, the same character drags along a leg iron attached to a ball and chain, as if in an endless search for the right man. For "Summertime," Joplin's masterful cover of the old standard, Crumb uses a dubious caricature of a black woman, a throwback to vintage racist mammy cartoon images from the nineteenth century, holding a wailing baby with cartoon tears radiating around its head. Separately, each panel is a slapstick gag in the comic tradition; together they form a curiously hypnotic, multi-image narrative that in retrospect visually reflects the San Francisco music scene of the day.

Aside from Crumb's bawdy humor, what made this album cover such an icon was its good timing. Produced at a moment when cultural innovations were introduced at a fast and furious pace, this was the pinnacle of 1960s exuberance and invention, just prior to its neutering and commodification by marketers and entrepreneurs. Which is not to say that marketers and entrepreneurs were not already maneuvering in the wings— they were. But even the consumer outlets—FM radio, the record industry, head shops, and so on—seemed not to be constrained by market or conventions and were willing to take risks that went beyond "most advanced yet acceptable." For an all-too-brief moment, youth-hippie-alternative culture was in a state of grace when everything seemed new and unfettered. Music and art were rebellious, expressive, and instinctive. Formulas, clichés, and stereotypes had yet to exert a viselike grip on creativity. Crumb's cover for *Cheap Thrills* was not just a calculating effort to win market share; it was the marriage of two artists and two art forms that truly spoke to the gut of the same audience without pretense or conceit. Joplin's music was raw emotion; Crumb's art was pure wit.

Nevertheless, *Cheap Thrills* was a product of a well-established music industry. In the wake of the mid-1960s British pop invasion, the American music establishment responded to the popular groundswell toward psychedelic and folk rock emanating from San Francisco by quickly signing as many top local bands as possible (Jefferson Airplane, Grateful Dead, Country Joe and the Fish, and more). It churned out albums (instead of 45s, the standard music medium of the preceding generation), and with albums came a need for eye-catching cover art that telegraphed the eccentricity of the new rock. In competition with the visionary psychedelic posters that advertised San Francisco's music palaces, simple photographs of band members were no longer sufficiently engaging to attract record buyers by the late 1960s. With the art-based collage on the Beatles' *Revolution* in 1966 and the elaborate fantasy photograph on *Sgt. Pepper's Lonely Hearts Club Band* in 1967, concept album art became a viable alternative to studio photography. Record company art director/designers were unleashed to test the limits of conceptual presentation.

The veteran Bob Cato (1923–1999) was among the more conceptually astute. During ten years as an art director and, subsequently, as the vice president of creative services for CBS/Columbia Records, working with such decidedly contrasting musicians as Leonard Bernstein, the Band, Glenn Gould, and Johnny Mathis, Cato developed or directed the creation of some of the most memorable record-album covers of the 1960s. As a student of and assistant to the legendary art director and designer Alexey Brodovitch, Cato cut his art directorial teeth on the fashion magazine *Harper's Bazaar,* where Brodovitch had transformed editorial and fashion design with his innovative mixture of white space, elegant typography, photography, and modernist art. The former *New York Times* advertising columnist Randall Rothenberg says that these "were characteristics that would also define Cato's own work during the next several decades."

Many of Cato's album covers featured his own photography, but for others he enlisted some of the era's most influential painters, designers, and photographers, among them Andy Warhol, Robert Rauschenberg, Francesco Scavullo, and Irving Penn. But Cato did more than just conceive and execute album covers. "He was also intimately involved in the conception and even the naming of the recordings themselves," says Rothenberg. One of these was *Cheap Thrills*.

As was customary at CBS, Joplin came to see him about the design of her record. Originally, Cato wanted to shoot the group in a fabricated "hippie pad," but Big Brother balked at the pretentious set. Instead, both Janis and Cato agreed that Crumb's artwork was a perfect way to give the album a look sufficiently raw to match the music. Crumb worked without interference. Joplin wanted a title that was synonymous with her life and the epoch in which she lived, insisting that the album be called "Sex, Dope, and Cheap Thrills." Given her soaring popularity, CBS records executives were tempted to give in. Nevertheless, "the title didn't seem quite right to me," Cato wrote years later in an unpublished memoir. "It said too much, gave away too much. Besides, even in the 1960s, the recording business was still a business, and there was only so much you could get away with."

Cato, who was no novice when it came to taming celebrity egos, calmly suggested to Joplin that the words "sex" and "dope" on the cover would limit the record's radio airplay, recommending that she use only the last two words of this phrase for the title. Joplin demurred. "Well, I've always settled for cheap thrills, anyway," she said. With Crumb's comic splash panel at the top, *Cheap Thrills* the record went on to become one of the biggest-selling rock albums of all time.

In 1833 the first book jacket was used by
Longmans & Co., a British publisher, to
protect books from the corrosive effects of
dust and light. The heavy paper wrapped
around the cloth binding was meant to be
discarded after purchase. Such was the
ignominious beginning of what in the 1920s
and 1930s became a unique artist's medium.
For its first fifty years the dust jacket was a
plain paper wrapper usually with a window
cut out to reveal the title and author's name.
The binding of the average trade book
(which included the spine and front and
back covers) was occasionally stamped or
embossed with a modest filigree or vignette
for decoration. In the late 1890s decoration
was introduced with more regularity. The
designs of Aubrey Beardsley, in England,
and Will Bradley, in America, were

reproduced on book covers as a kind of miniature poster. Soon, in order to
increase advertising and eye appeal, publishers also printed on the paper
jacket, and by the turn of the century the dust jacket had become the
publishing industry's standard promotional tool.

Veteran book designers, however, considered the dust jacket an
unwanted appendage. In the classical tradition it was not an intrinsic part
of a book's design, which only included the cover, binding, and interior
pages. Many esteemed book designers did not design the jackets for their
books, but rather passed that dubious assignment on to a "specialist"—
usually a layout artist trained in the requisites of commerce. As late as the
1950s the jacket was viewed as the unwanted stepchild. "It could be argued
that the jacket is part of the book, [a jury of book critic/practitioners
including Herbert Bayer, Merle Armitage, and Sidney Jacobs] feels that
this is a temporary and fallacious point of view," wrote Marshall Lee in
Books for Our Times (Oxford University Press, 1951). "One need only
consider the absurdity of having one expensive cover designed that will
permanently conceal another! Either the jacket is a temporary protection

and sales device meant to be torn from the book the moment it is sold or it is an indispensable cover. If the latter were true, the logical procedure would be to dispense with the costly, unseen binding design. The jacket then becomes the binding, and the function of both binding and jacket will be the same."

Dust jackets were the low end of graphic design practice, tainted by their association to crass advertising departments. As mini billboards, they followed the principles of mass marketing applied to packaging. Dust jackets were ephemera and readers habitually discarded them before books were entombed on the bookshelf. Moreover, during the 1920s and 1930s, trade book jackets were illustrated by taking a key sentence or word and rendering it verbatim as a monumental vignette in either a sentimentally realistic or fashionably stylized (art deco) manner. The lettering was usually done by hand in the *au courant* novelty style of the time. The sole purpose of the jacket was to attract and hook a reader (similar to the movie posters of the era). The pictorial representation often had little to do with the book's essence. Even the classics sometimes acquired contemporary imagery and design motifs in order to eschew any hint of mustiness. It might have been false advertising, but the disparity between the author's intent and the artist's interpretation was accepted for marketing reasons. "This technique of allegory," wrote historian Stephen Greengard in *The Journal of Decorative and Propaganda Art* (No. 7, Winter 1988), "does not require the artist to read the book itself, merely to distill from its pages a high impact visual which may be apprehended at a single glance."

"It seems ironic," wrote Greengard, "so many great, important ideas, the products of the finest minds of humanity, [were] wrapped in pieces of whimsical, brilliantly colored paper." During the 1920s and 1930s, in addition to providing protection, promotion, and genre identification, the design of book jackets made a variety of fiction and nonfiction books appealing and accessible to broad audiences. The old saying "you can't tell a book by its cover," is usually true, but the cover piqued interest. In some cases the cover was the best part of the book.

Common wisdom holds that a poster must lure the eye from a distance of five city blocks (or a quarter of a mile) away and build to a visual crescendo at five feet. This means that a successful poster must not only function in its original size, but also, given the prescribed distance, at the size of a postage stamp.

Between the turn of the century and the late 1920s when the *Sachplakat,* or object poster (a German poster genre that employed minimal lettering and a simple image of a product), was at its peak, the most effective posters were those that could be printed both enlarged and reduced without sacrificing any essential visual information. Lucian Bernhard was the master of this form. His stark, colorful images for Priester Matches, Adler Typewriters, and Osram Lightbulbs were equally suited for mammoth or Lilliputian reproduction. Hollerbaum and Schmidt, Bernhard's selling agent and printer, realized the business potential inherent in this versatile medium and began printing small, adhesive-backed poster stamps as a service to their advertising customers.

Sure, the term *poster stamp* is a contradiction. But semantics aside, what began as a means to earn greater printing revenues became a popular and—like the poster itself— collectible method of increasing advertising exposure during an epoch when modern advertising was in its infancy. Poster stamps were affixed to all manner of things where posters would not fit. Ultimately the genre became a thriving international industry with thousands of original designs and miniaturized reprises produced annually.

A wide range of products and messages were advertised on these tiny perforated manifestoes. Insurance agencies, hotels, electric companies, banks, tobacco, food, clothing, and manufacturing companies were among the most prolific users. The aesthetic quality was surprisingly high because many stamps began as larger posters or point-of-purchase displays, and quite a few were designed by well-known artists. But there was another interesting quality: at this scale even the most clichéd image was curiously transformed into a striking miniature. Even trite ideas were made new in this form.

English, French, German, Austrian, and American stamps from between 1910 and 1930 are fragments of commercial history that chronicle as effectively as any official commemorative stamp the burgeoning of free trade and market capitalism. Stamps for light bulbs, lamps, and appliances, for instance, reveal the unrelenting push by industry for electrification of the private home. Stamps for automobiles prefigure the huge budgets later expended on major advertising campaigns.

However, owing to strict postal regulations that legislated what was allowed on mailing envelopes and the rise in high-visibility advertising outlets, by the late 1930s the production of commercial advertising stamps was virtually abandoned. In the postwar years junk mail replaced the advertising stamp as the favored means of invading the consumer's privacy and consciousness. Given the poor quality of these pesky missives, the Lilliputian poster stamps re-emerge from the attic of advertising history as infinitely more appealing.

General Dynamics was one of the wellsprings of design innovation. Formed in 1953 as the parent for a number of manufacturing firms that catered to the defense needs of the United States, General Dynamics' products included atomic-powered submarines, electric motors for ships, the B-58 supersonic jet bomber, and the commercial 880 jet transport. It also sponsored research in electronics, astronautics, aerodynamics, hydrodynamics, and nuclear physics. In the mid 1950s nuclear energy was thought to herald the new age, and General Dynamics' president, John Jay Hopkins, believed that his company should be positioned in the public's mind as a purveyor of peace. General Dynamics would benefit all mankind through its scientific research, and communicating this message was one of the president's primary goals.

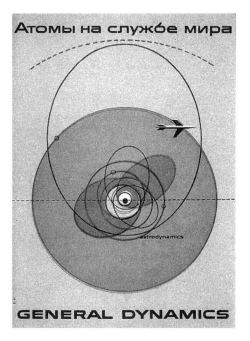

Hopkins understood that a skilled graphic designer could successfully forge and promote General Dynamics' image, and so hired Erik Nitsche (1908–1998), a Swiss who had freelanced in the United States since the 1930s, away from the ad agency that originally had the General Dynamics account. Working from his own studio in New York, Nitsche had been responsible for some early ads and promotional materials that wed abstract imagery to functional typography, which gave General Dynamics its progressive image. Hopkins gave Nitsche complete freedom to build a total graphic identity from scratch. He served as art director between 1955 and 1960 and his identity program—which included posters, advertisements, and annual reports—was a unique mix of modernism and individualism.

In the spring of 1955 Nitsche was given the first major assignment to design an exhibit that would have far-reaching implications for the company. General Dynamics had agreed to attend the International

Conference on the Peaceful Uses of Atomic Energy in Geneva, Switzerland, in August of that year. Hopkins wanted a display that would stand apart from the other mammoth technology firms, including General Electric, Union Carbide, and Westinghouse. As builders of the *Nautilus*, the first atomic submarine, and with contracts to produce the first atomic-powered airplane, General Dynamics had the perfect showpieces. Yet they had nothing to show. The *Nautilus* design was so top secret that Nitsche was only given a vague description of its ultimate design. In the absence of an actual product he had to devise a symbol. Pursuing the idea of "Atoms for Peace" he used graphics to convey the message.

Framing the exhibit, the initial corporate clarion was a series of six multilingual posters with either abstract or symbolic images—in English, Russian, German, French, Hindi, and Japanese—designed specifically for those nations where atomic energy was being used for peaceful purposes. Strongly influenced by Paul Klee since childhood, Nitsche turned to geometric forms and intersecting color planes to symbolize this new energy source. But the principle icon for the most memorable poster was not like Klee at all, but rather a painting of a huge nautilus shell from which shot out a sleek submarine. The *Nautilus*, named after Jules Verne's fictional vessel in *Twenty Thousand Leagues Under the Sea*, was not presented as a missile of war, but as a missive of peace. On some of the posters a text from Isaiah read: "They shall beat swords into plowshares, and their spears into pruning hooks: nation shall not lift up sword against nation, neither shall they learn war anymore." Isaiah's testament was, of course, dramatic, yet ironic in light of the ship's prime mission as a defensive weapon (preserving the peace).

The poster campaign was well received and Nitsche was commissioned to produce what amounted to three different series of twenty-four images. Hopkins wanted to acquaint the public "with the spirit of discovery that motivates the corporation's diverse developments." And so Nitsche's work soon influenced General Dynamics' total corporate style, including the otherwise staid annual reports, which he turned into kinetic displays of visual imagery. Nitsche's crowning achievement, however, was the design of a mammoth book of corporate history entitled *Dynamic America*. With its tip-ins and foldouts, *Dynamic America* was an exhibition between boards, a fast-paced visual document of the nation's military and industrial history that intersected with the development of General Dynamics Company from its roots in 1880 as Electro Dynamic.

Nitsche's book design was a lesson in economy. He favored dynamic silhouettes and vignettes of historical artifacts, giving the book a didactic quality. Nitsche knew how to make historical engravings and paintings appear timeless. His typography was clean and crisp, a marriage of classical and modern approaches. A progenitor of information design, he virtually invented the modern time line, giving the reader textual and visual information in parallel strips. He further focused on key pieces of visual information through frequent scale changes and juxtapositions. The amazing thing about this book is that if the type were removed, it would reveal a perfect visual narrative.

Wolfschmidt

George Lois

George Lois (b. 1931), the agent provocateur of advertising's Creative Revolution of the 1960s, didn't force vodka down America's throat, but from 1960 to 1963 he put Wolfschmidt on everyone's lips. The breakthrough ad campaign, which he conceived and art directed, featured a Wolfschmidt bottle bantering with fruits and vegetables. It changed consumers' perceptions and raised the sales of a lackluster brand. Lois had served up the perfect mix of humor with a wit chaser.

Advertising was serious business back in the 1950s. Despite trailblazing ads by Paul Rand in the 1940s and Helmut Krone's VW campaign starting in the late 1950s, real wit was about as common in national ad campaigns as sophisticated typography (which was pretty scarce). Goofy cartoons and comic strips were routinely used, but the humor was usually corny or slapstick. In addition, the design of most ads was dreadful. Liquor advertising was even more dour than most, mainly because tried-and-true conventions were slavishly followed—such as showing a bottle and shot glass set against pictures of men drinking with business associates. By the early 1960s the ubiquitous cocktail party scene appeared and women were added, but they never held drinks.

Anyway, there is nothing inherently funny about liquor. In the 1950s consumers remained loyal to a particular brand either because of perceived prestige or because their cronies preferred it. In liquor advertising a vintage whiskey, its bottle labeled with the heraldic marks of a venerable distillery, had more appeal than some rotgut without heritage. And since it was inappropriate to show guzzlers in advertisements, the bottle became the emblem of consumer allegiance. Even when so-called image advertising did not offer enough of a competitive edge—when, for instance, flavor was emphasized in the copy instead—the bottle icon was always prominent.

The goal of all liquor advertising was to get the consumer to identify with the label and, therefore, order the brand by name.

Advertising conventions were ostensibly the same for vodka and the darker liquors, but there was one essential difference: vodka has very little taste. So the advertising challenge was how to distinguish one flavorless drink from another. The solution boiled down to concept, which was also the key distinction between conventional and Creative Revolution advertisements. The latter introduced the so-called Big Idea, which dispelled the notion that advertising was simply hucksterism. The new theory went that advertising was best when it was also entertaining. And one of the earliest campaigns to prove this hypothesis was created in the mid 1950s for Smirnoff vodka, which on the strength of its creative advertising owned seventy percent of the market for almost a decade, far surpassing Wolfschmidt's meager 8- to 10-percent share.

Smirnoff's clever catch-line "Leaves You Breathless" signaled that it was okay for noontime drinkers to guiltlessly imbibe. Smirnoff vodka, unlike scotch and gin, which caused tell-tale whiskey breath, was touted as tasteless and, therefore, undetectable. Sales soared on the strength of the claim alone, but to further get the message across, the advertising employed smartly elegant, conceptual photography by Irving Penn and Ben Somoroff, who photographed the campaign at different times. Each was typically shot against a white seamless backdrop, adding a modern aura, in which both celebrities and fantasy characters—including Marcel Marceau in one ad and a Minotaur in another—enticed the reader to stop, look, and read the minimal copy below. The requisite Smirnoff bottle was, however, reduced and placed unobtrusively next to the text as a mnemonic device.

Smirnoff's advertising went unsurpassed for many years. Despite the campaign's success, other leading distillers remained conservative in their own advertising. Joseph E. Seagram & Sons, Inc., one of America's foremost distilleries, was resigned to the fact that its own brand, Wolf-schmidt vodka, would forever trail behind. But in 1960 Samuel Bronfman, Seagrams' hard-nosed founder and chief executive, turned the failing brand over to his twenty-eight-year-old son, Edgar, as a test of his ability—or one might say, a rite of passage. The younger Bronfman was left on his own to sink or swim. But as fate would have it, he met George Lois, a twenty-eight-year-old former Doyle Dane and Bernbach art director who, confidently, had just opened his own agency, Papert Koenig Lois (Julian Koenig was the writer on the team that conceived the Volkswagen "Think Small" campaign) in the Seagrams building on Park Avenue in New York.

When Bronfman approached him, Lois (with Koenig) had just developed the Allerest brand name and print advertising campaign for

Pharmacraft Laboratories, which was partially owned by the Bronfman family, and was hungrily looking for a new project with which to launch his agency and reputation. "It hit me like a shot," Lois recalled, "Smirnoff said it had no taste, so I simply said Wolfschmidt did have taste. Smirnoff's was aimed at the lunch crowd, I aimed Wolfschmidt at the party crowd."

Lois boasted that in one day he devised the entire campaign. He paired a life-size Wolfschmidt bottle (to both satisfy and satirize conventional wisdom) with an assortment of fruits and vegetables—oranges, tomatoes, celery, etc.—in comic banter. The first ad, however, was a photograph of a bunch of indistinguishable shot glasses with a headline that asked which one was the Wolfschmidt? The answer was "the one with taste," of course. But the now famous second ad that really launched the campaign showed a bottle saying to a ripe tomato, "You're some tomato. . . . We could make a difference. . . ." in a kind of playboy cadence that might seem sexist today but by early 1960s standards was racy, erotic, and unheard of in national advertising. The ad premiered in *Life* magazine and subsequently in other key outlets. And just one week later a third ad was released with the bottle saying: "You sweet doll, I appreciate you. I've got taste. I'll bring out the real orange in you. I'll make you famous. Kiss me." And the orange responded: "Who was that tomato I saw you with last week?" This was the first time that an ad referred back to a previous ad, and it set the serial tone for all future ads. "It was an underground thing to do," continued Lois. "It couldn't be more direct, but it had real style."

The Wolfschmidt campaign was also what Lois called "a purist piece of design." It was not only minimalist layout and typography in the modern tradition, but also, and at the time more importantly, it was storyboarded entirely by Lois himself, which was unheard of in advertising circles. Before the Creative Revolution took hold in the mid-1950s most advertising—with the exception of Paul Rand's work at Weintraub Agency throughout 1940s—was devised by copywriters, who gave precise roughs to art directors, who then supervised the final sketches. Even in the early years of the Creative Revolution, when copywriters and art directors worked more or less together, ads were roughed out by art directors and then precisely painted or comped by bullpen sketch artists. Clients were used to seeing finished paintings. But in one fell swoop Lois changed all that by doing the entire presentation on his own, from sketches to comp. The brash young Lois also broke another taboo: he sold his ideas directly to the client without going through an account executive.

Yet history would be different if young Bronfman had showed his father the first couple of ads before they ran. Lois thinks that "old Sam" probably would have balked or killed them entirely. Luckily, the action in the stores was immediate. "They tickled people," he said. "They were talked about at parties." And since orders came rolling in, the elder Bronfman allowed the rest of the campaign to proceed, even though, according to Lois, "Massa Sam never laughed." In fact, Lois recalled when showing him an ad in the series headlined "Taste my screwdriver" he seemed stunned. "For California," Lois explained.

Decades before Absolut ruled vodka, Wolfschmidt absolutely owned the market. This was not only a testament to the power of smart advertising, it was one hundred percent proof that wit and humor could capture market share. Ultimately, even conservative distilleries began using humor in their ads. Lois notes that the first woman appeared in a primary role in a 1961 Ronrico Rum ad. It featured an eighty-one-year-old "Aunt Agatha," holding a glass of the liquor. "It was a very funny concept," he recalled, "but got the Daughters of the American Revolution up in arms."

The Wolfschmidt campaign continued for three years and included ten different print ads and a couple of posters. However, it abruptly ended, according to Lois, in a dispute when Edgar Bronfman acquired a handful more Seagram brands and did not award any of the new accounts to Papert Koenig Lois. Julian Koenig was furious and summarily pulled the agency off the Wolfschmidt account. It was the end of that relationship, but Lois left behind a remarkable legacy that set the standard, not only for a genre of liquor advertising practiced today, but for helping to inaugurate a period in advertising history when wit and humor were the state of the art.

NYNEX

Chiat/Day/Mojo

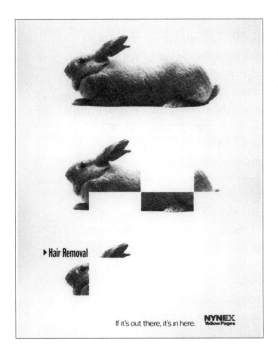

▸ Hair Removal

If it's out there, it's in here.   **NYNEX**
Yellow Pages

The average infantry soldier's life expectancy is twelve seconds on a battlefield. New York City's streets might not be as dangerous as a battlefield, but the average life of an advertising poster is certainly comparable. Bills illegally posted on construction scaffolding are routinely defaced within hours. Postings on legal hoardings fare only slightly better; few remain unscathed until the end of their official display periods. This limited life expectancy demands that advertisers often think like military strategists; they must hold as many key positions as possible, accept massive casualties, and reinforce when needed. For a campaign to succeed it must totally capture the hearts, minds, and discretionary income of consumers.

Street posters continue to be the first wave in advertising campaigns for such industries as entertainment, clothing, and consumables. An intensive saturation campaign can be extremely effective in piquing the interest of an often jaded urban public. But what has made the war for consumers and against the vandals and the citigoths a bit easier to win are the protected bus shelters with illuminated display capabilities that have been on New York's streets for nearly two decades. This kind of shelter was developed in Paris decades ago, but until its introduction to New York in the late 1970s, street advertising was limited to large exposed billboards and illegal hoardings. Today more than three thousand shelters throughout New York provide a relatively secure space for more than six thousand posters. And six thousand illuminated posters have had a decisive impact not only on the public's consciousness, but also on advertising designers, as well.

Bus shelters have given certain advertising agencies the impetus to counter mediocre mass-market poster concepts and therefore alter standards. During the past several years shelters have also contributed to a resurgence in the time honored "tease-and-reveal" posters—an image that runs without words for two weeks and then with words for another two, or more. The most innovative example from this renaissance has been NYNEX's 1995 series for the New York Yellow Pages Business Directory, created by Chiat/Day/Mojo and based on various riddle/puns of arcane Yellow Page entries.

The fulcrum of this year-long campaign was a series of quirky photographs, such as one of a blue rabbit and another of Barbie and Ken wearing nurse and doctor outfits, originally posted without text (not even the NYNEX logo), then replaced by another poster with the same image and also a caption and the slogan, "If it's out there, it's in here: NYNEX." The caption was a painfully forced pun. For example, the blue hare illustrated "Hair Coloring" and the nurse Barbie and doctor Ken illustrated "Plastic Surgeons."

The degree to which the pun strained was actually the mark of its success. The initial posting of the first billboard displayed a huge blue rabbit in repose; the second posting showed rectangular portions of the same rabbit missing; and the final posting showed all but a small portion of the rabbit's head and ears with the title "Hair Removal." The print campaign, which also appeared as television commercials directed by Godley and Creme, ran in bimonthly cycles with six different concepts presented throughout the year, offering the public a titillating game of wits.

NYNEX's campaign, which echoed the Big Idea advertising concepts of the 1960s, was built on a simple premise: when smartly applied, even dumb humor has incalculable appeal, and the more esoteric the better. Although the sport of deducing the riddle could easily have backfired by overwhelming the message itself, the year-long barrage of ubiquitous posters and commercials gave the NYNEX Yellow Pages total recognition among consumers.

The graphic design in this series was transparent. Like masterful serial ads that came before it—Levy's Jewish Rye Bread and Volkswagen—the NYNEX campaign was photographed and filmed for TV against a white seamless backdrop. The idea was the only focal point. The single line of sans-serif typography echoed a heading in the Yellow Pages and was effectively balanced with the NYNEX logo. The campaign totally dominated the New York streetscape, but its handlers knew when to stop. As delightful and provocative as it was, it ceased before it became trite.

Ades, Dawn. *Photomontage.* London: Thames and Hudson, 1986.

Aldersey-Williams, Hugh. *New American Design.* New York: Rizzoli, 1988.

Barron, Stephanie, and Maurice Tuchman, eds. *The Avant-Garde in Russia 1910–1930.* Cambridge and London: MIT Press, 1980.

Beirut, Michael, William Drenttel, Steven Heller, and DK Holland, eds. *Looking Closer: Critical Writings on Graphic Design.* New York: Allworth Press, 1994.

Beirut, Michael, William Drenttel, Steven Heller, and DK Holland, eds. *Looking Closer 2: Critical Writings on Graphic Design.* New York: Allworth Press, 1997.

Berger, John. *Ways of Seeing.* New York: Vintage International, 1985.

Blackwell, Lewis. *20th Century Type.* New York: Rizzoli, 1992.

Blackwell, Lewis, and David Carson. *The End of Print.* San Francisco: Chronicle Books, 1995.

Blauvelt, Andrew. "Desperately Seeking David." *Emigre,* #38. 1996.

Broos, Kees, and Paul Hefting. *Dutch Graphic Design: A Century.* Cambridge: The MIT Press, 1993.

Bruinsma, Max. "Studio Dumbar: Enigma Variations." *EYE,* Vol. 5, No. 19. 1995.

Burdick, Anne. "Decoding the Monster." *Emigre,* #23. 1992.

Carter, Rob. *American Typography Today.* New York: Van Nostrand Reinhold, 1989.

Celant, Germano, Mildred Constantine, David Revere McFadden, Joseph Rykwert. *Design: Vignelli.* New York: Rizzoli, 1990.

Chermayeff, Ivan. "Designing in Tongues: What's so Universal about the Visual Language?" *AIGA Journal of Graphic Design,* Vol. 12, No. 2. 1994.

Chwast, Seymour, Steven Heller, eds. *The Left-Handed Designer.* New York: Harry N. Abrams, 1985.

———. *Cranbrook Design: The New Discourse.* New York: Rizzoli, 1990.

Cullen, Moira. "Tibor Kalman." *EYE,* Vol. 5, No. 20. 1996.

Dooley, Michael. "Defending Joe Camel, Sort Of." *Print,* L:IV. 1999.

Farrelly, Liz. "Rick Valicenti: One from the Heart." *EYE,* Vol. 2, No. 6. 1992.

Freeman, Judi. *The Dada & Surrealist Word-Image.* Cambridge and London: MIT Press, 1989.

Friedman, Dan. *Dan Friedman: Radical Modernism.* New Haven and London: Yale University Press, 1994.

Friedman, Mildred, ed. *Graphic Design in America: A Visual Language History.* Minneapolis and New York: Walker Art Center and Harry N. Abrams, 1989.

Glaser, Milton. *Milton Glaser Graphic Design.* Woodstock New York: Overlook Press, 1973.

Glauber, Barbara, ed. *Lift and Separate: Graphic Design and the Vernacular*. New York: Herb Lubalin Study Center of Design and Typography, 1993.

Gottschall, Edward M. *Typographic Communications Today*. Cambridge, Massachusetts, London, England: MIT Press, 1989.

Greiman, April. *Design Quarterly*, #133. Cambridge, Mass. and London, England: MIT Press for Walker Art Center, 1986.

Greiman, April. *Hybrid Imagery*. New York: Watson-Guptill, 1990.

Greiman, April. "Information Texture." *Octavo, 86.1*. 1986.

Heller, Steven, and Anne Fink. *Covers & Jackets*. Glen Cove, New York: PBC International Inc., 1993.

Heller, Steven, and Julie Lasky. *Borrowed Design: The Use and Abuse of Historical Form*. New York: Van Nostrand Reinhold, 1993.

Heller, Steven, and Karen Pomeroy. *Designing with Illustration*. New York: Van Nostrand Reinhold, 1990.

Heller, Steven. *Innovators of American Illustration*. New York: Van Nostrand Reinhold, 1986.

Heller, Steven. "Alex Steinweiss: For the Record." *Print,* XLVI:II. New York: 1992.

Heller, Steven. "Dr. Leslie's Type Clinic." *EYE*, Vol 4, No. 15. 1994.

Heller, Steven, and Barbara Kruger. "Smashing the Myths." *AIGA Journal of Graphic Design*, Vol. 9, No. 1. 1991.

Heller, Steven. "Alvin Lustig: Born Modern." *EYE*, Vol. 3, No. 10. 1993.

Heller, Steven. "Big Ideas that Build the American Art Director." *EYE*, Vol. 6, No. 22. 1996.

Heller, Steven. "Oz Cooper: Telling and Selling." *EYE*, Vol. 2, No. 7. 1992.

Heller, Steven. "Sutnar." *EYE*, Vol. 4, No. 13. 1994.

Heller, Steven. "Mapbacks: High End of a Low Art." *Print,* XLVIII:III. New York: 1994.

Heller, Steven. "Street Theater" *Print,* L:III. New York. 1996.

Heller, Steven. "Commercial Modern: American Design Style 1925–1933." *Print* XLIX:V. New York. 1995.

Heller, Steven. "Life: Magazine of the Century." *Print* XLVII:III. New York. 1994.

Heller, Steven and Gail Anderson. *American Typeplay*. New York: PBC International, Inc., 1994.

Heller, Steven and Seymour Chwast. *Graphic Style: From Victorian to Postmodern*. New York: Harry N. Abrams, Inc., 1988.

Henrion, FHK. *Top Graphic Design*. Zurich: ABC Verlag, 1983.

Hollis, Richard. *Graphic Design: A Concise History*. London: Thames and Hudson, 1994.

Homans, Katy. "BJ. Robert Brownjohn: The Ultimate Conceptualist Reassessed." *EYE*, Vol. 1, No. 4. 1991.

Jacobs, Karrie. "Barbara Kruger." *EYE*, Vol. 2, No. 5. 1991.

Julier, Guy. *The Thames and Hudson Encyclopaedia of 20th Century Design and Designers*. London: Thames and Hudson, 1993.

Kinross, Robin. *Modern Typography: An Essage in Critical History*. London: Hyphen Press, 1992.

Kruger, Barbara. *Remote Control*. Cambridge and London: MIT Press, 1993.

Kruger, Barbara, and Kate Linker. *Love for Sale: The Words and Pictures of Barbara Kruger*. New York: Harry N. Abrams, 1990.

Labuz, Ronald. *Contemporary Graphic Design*. New York: Van Nostrand Reinhold, 1991.

Lears, Jackson. *Fables of Abundance*. New York: Basic Books, 1994.

Livingston, Alan and Isabella. *Dictionary of Graphic Design and Designers*. London: Thames and Hudson, 1992.

Lupton, Ellen. *Mixing Messages*. New York: Princeton Architectural Press, 1996.

Lupton, Ellen. "The Academy of Deconstructed Design." *EYE*, Vol. 1, No. 3. 1991.

Lupton, Ellen, and J. Abbott Miller. "Deconstruction and Graphic Design: History Meets Theory." *Visible Language, 28.4.* 1994.

Margolin, Victor, ed. *Design Discourse*. Chicago and London: University of Chicago Press, 1989.

———. "Massimo Vignelli vs. Ed Benguiat." *Print,* XLV:V. 1991.

McCoy, Katherine. "American Graphic Design Expression." *Design Quarterly,* #148. 1990.

McCoy, Katherine. "The Evolution of American Typography." *Design Quarterly, #148.* Walker Art Center and MIT. 1990.

Meggs, Phil. *A History of Graphic Design (Second Edition)*. New York: Van Nostrand Reinhold, 1992.

Meggs, Philip B. *Type and Image*. New York: Van Nostrand Reinhold, 1989.

Miller, Abbott J. "Quentin Fiore: Massaging the Message." *EYE*, Vol. 2, No. 8. 1993.

Nöth, Winifred. *Handbook of Semiotics*. Bloomington and Indianapolis: Indiana University Press, 1990.

Pachnicke, Peter, and Klaus Honnef, eds. *John Heartfield*. New York: Harry N. Abrams, Inc., 1992.

Poynor, Rick and Edward Booth Clibborn. *Typography Now: The Next Wave*. Cincinnati, Ohio: F & W Publications, 1992.

Poynor, Rick. *The Graphic Edge*. London: Booth-Clibborn Editons, 1993.

Poynor, Rick. "Pierre Bernard." *EYE*, Vol. 1, No. 3. 1991.

Poynor, Rick. "Jon Barnbrook." *EYE*, Vol. 4, No. 15. 1994.

Poynor, Rick. "American Gothic." *EYE* Vol. 2, No. 2. 1992.

Poynor, Rick. "Remove Specific and Convert to Ambiguities." *EYE*, Vol. 5, No. 20. 1996.

Poynor, Rick. "David Carson Revealed." *I.D.*, Vol. 42, No. 6. 1995.

Poynor, Rick. "Katherine McCoy." *EYE*, Vol 4, No. 16. 1995.

Poynor, Rick. "Neville Brody Faces the Future." *I.D.*, Vol. 41. 1992.

Poynor, Rick. "Neville Brody." *EYE*, Vol. 2, No. 6. 1992.

Rand, Paul. *Paul Rand: A Designer's Art.* New Haven and London: Yale University Press, 1985.

Rea, Peter. "Dan Friedman." *EYE*, Vol. 4, No. 14. 1994.

Remington, R. Roger and Barbara J. Hodik. *Nine Pioneers in American Graphic Design.* Cambridge and London: MIT Press, 1989.

Rock, Michael. "Fuse: Beyond Typography." *EYE*, Vol. 4, No. 15. 1994.

Schwemer-Scheddin, Yvonne. "Interview with Wolfgang Weingart." *EYE*, Vol. 1, No. 4. 1991. London.

Scotford, Martha. "Cipe Pineles: The Tenth Pioneer." *EYE*, Vol. 5, No. 18. 1995.

Scott, Douglass. "Bradbury Thompson, Designer and Teacher." *Print*, L:III. 1996.

Shapiro, Ellen. "No More War." *Print*, L:IV. 1996.

Smith, Terry. *Making the Modern: Industry, Art, and Design in America.* Chicago: University of Chicago Press, 1993.

Snyder, Gertrude and Alan Peckolick. *Herb Lubalin: Art Director, Graphic Designer and Typographer.* New York: American Showcase Inc., 1985.

Spencer, Herbert, ed. *The Liberated Page.* San Francisco: Bedford Press, 1987.

Stermer, Dugald. "Louise Fili." *Communication Arts,* September/October 1986.

Tufte, Edward R. *Envisioning Information.* Connecticut: Graphics Press, 1990.

Varnedoe, Kirk and Adam Gopnik. *High and Low: Modern Art Popular Culture.* New York: The Museum of Modern Art, 1990.

Thompson, Bradbury. *Bradbury Thompson: The Art of Graphic Design.* New Haven and London: Yale University Press, 1988.

Thrift, Julia. "Rudy Vanderlans." *EYE*, Vol 2, No. 7. 1992.

Vanderlans, Rudy. "Second Wind." *Emigre*, #24. 1992.

Vanderlans, Rudy. "A Telephone Conversation between Rudy Vanderlans and David Carson." *Emigre,* #27. 1993.

VanderLans, Rudy and Zuzana Licko with Mary E. Gray. *Emigre: Graphic Design into the Digital Realm.* New York: Van Nostrand Reinhold, 1993.

Weingart, Wolfgang. "How Can One Make Swiss Typography? Theoretical and practical typographic results from the teaching period 1968–1973 at the School of Design, Basel." *Octavo, 87.4. An International Journal of Typography.* London: 1987.

Weingart, Wolfgang. "Graphic Design in Switzerland." *Emigre*, #14. 1990.

Whitford, Frank, ed. *The Bauhaus: Masters & Students by Themselves.* Woodstock, New York: Overlook Press, 1993.

Wozencroft, Jon. *The Graphic Language of Neville Brody.* New York: Rizzoli, 1988.

Wye, Deborah. *Thinking Print.* New York: The Museum of Modern Art, 1996.